Mathematics of BUSINESS APPLICATIONS

K.R. MacLaughlin   M.E. MacLaughlin

Copp Clark Pitman Ltd.
Toronto

ISBN 0–7730 – 4333–0

Cover design/Riitta A. Malm
Typesetting/Q Composition Inc.
Printing/John Deyell Company

ACKNOWLEDGEMENTS
To Brooke Barker, Success Angus Business
College, in appreciation for a comprehensive
review of this text.
To Gord Moran and Joanne Lukashal, Ontario
Business College, in appreciation for their work
with the text.

Canadian Cataloguing in Publication Data

MacLaughlin, K. R. (Kenneth Ralph)
  Mathematics for business applications

ISBN 0-7730-4333-0

1. Business mathematics. I. MacLaughlin, M. E.
(Margaret Elizabeth). II. Title.

HF5691.M33 1984   513'.93   C84-099739-6

Printed and bound in Canada

INTRODUCTION

This text provides students with explanations, examples, and exercises that will lead to an understanding of and skill in performing calculations necessary in the world of business. The material covered will serve as a background course for many business subjects as well as presenting the student with the mathematical knowledge essential for consumer and personal use.

Unit 1 gives an opportunity to sharpen skills in the basic arithmetic operations while Unit 2 provides a comprehensive review of measurements. Units 3 and 4 cover the basic business mathematics skills necessary for entrance into the business community and for dealing with that community in every day affairs. The student is then introduced to more specific business applications and to the mathematics of finance in Units 5 and 6.

Throughout this text, every effort has been made to present clear examples explaining the calculations involved in each topic and leading the student to the most accurate method of performing the exercises which follow. Students who study the examples carefully should find little difficulty in working through the exercises.

In the major portion of this text, a sufficient number of exercises have been included to provide material for students who require an in depth study of the mathematics of business as well as those who need only a basic overview of business arithmetic.

The authors suggest that instructors allow students to use hand-held or office calculators as early as possible after completing the unit on fundamental arithmetic operations. Calculators are a basic tool of business and the algebraic logic built into their performance should become very familiar to anyone entering the business world.

TABLE OF CONTENTS

UNIT
1

Fundamental Operations

INTRODUCTION

Chapters 1, 2, 3, and 4 are intended to be worked *without* the use of a calculator. Basic skills of addition, subtraction, multiplication, and division are reviewed and some short methods of calculation are demonstrated in this unit.

Since pocket calculators are cheap and easy to use, we need to be careful not to forget our basic skills in fundamental arithmetic operations. Frequently it is faster to total a short column of figures or to calculate small multiplication or division problems mentally rather than obtaining a calculator and going through the process of entering the figures on its keyboard.

A calculator may be very accurate, but the operator can, and frequently does, make errors in entering digits. Learn to trust your own skills; errors such as incorrect entries and reversing digits when using a calculator waste time and money. Learn when it is easier and faster to make the calculation yourself rather than using an electronic calculator.

CHAPTER 1
ADDITION

1·1 WARM UP ON BASICS

EXERCISE 1

Total.

1.	2 3	3 3	2 5	2 6	4 4	2 4	4 3	5 2	6 3
2.	3 5	2 7	8 2	3 8	5 5	2 9	7 4	6 4	3 7
3.	6 7	7 8	6 6	5 7	6 8	8 7	6 5	3 9	7 5
4.	7 7	6 9	5 9	8 4	9 8	9 7	8 5	6 7	9 4

5.
$$\begin{array}{c}6\\ \underline{6}\end{array}\quad \begin{array}{c}8\\ \underline{9}\end{array}\quad \begin{array}{c}9\\ \underline{9}\end{array}\quad \begin{array}{c}7\\ \underline{4}\end{array}\quad \begin{array}{c}8\\ \underline{6}\end{array}\quad \begin{array}{c}9\\ \underline{4}\end{array}\quad \begin{array}{c}5\\ \underline{8}\end{array}\quad \begin{array}{c}9\\ \underline{6}\end{array}\quad \begin{array}{c}8\\ \underline{8}\end{array}$$

6.
$$\begin{array}{c}6\\ \underline{4}\end{array}\quad \begin{array}{c}5\\ \underline{4}\end{array}\quad \begin{array}{c}7\\ \underline{2}\end{array}\quad \begin{array}{c}9\\ \underline{3}\end{array}\quad \begin{array}{c}6\\ \underline{5}\end{array}\quad \begin{array}{c}6\\ \underline{8}\end{array}\quad \begin{array}{c}7\\ \underline{9}\end{array}\quad \begin{array}{c}9\\ \underline{8}\end{array}\quad \begin{array}{c}8\\ \underline{5}\end{array}$$

7.
$$\begin{array}{c}3\\ \underline{7}\end{array}\quad \begin{array}{c}5\\ \underline{8}\end{array}\quad \begin{array}{c}4\\ \underline{2}\end{array}\quad \begin{array}{c}6\\ \underline{0}\end{array}\quad \begin{array}{c}9\\ \underline{6}\end{array}\quad \begin{array}{c}8\\ \underline{4}\end{array}\quad \begin{array}{c}8\\ \underline{3}\end{array}\quad \begin{array}{c}8\\ \underline{7}\end{array}\quad \begin{array}{c}8\\ \underline{5}\end{array}$$

8.
$$\begin{array}{c}9\\ \underline{2}\end{array}\quad \begin{array}{c}6\\ \underline{6}\end{array}\quad \begin{array}{c}7\\ \underline{3}\end{array}\quad \begin{array}{c}9\\ \underline{5}\end{array}\quad \begin{array}{c}4\\ \underline{8}\end{array}\quad \begin{array}{c}9\\ \underline{9}\end{array}\quad \begin{array}{c}5\\ \underline{8}\end{array}\quad \begin{array}{c}6\\ \underline{4}\end{array}\quad \begin{array}{c}9\\ \underline{7}\end{array}$$

EXERCISE 2

Total.

1.
$$\begin{array}{c}16\\ \underline{3}\end{array}\quad \begin{array}{c}27\\ \underline{5}\end{array}\quad \begin{array}{c}38\\ \underline{4}\end{array}\quad \begin{array}{c}42\\ \underline{9}\end{array}\quad \begin{array}{c}37\\ \underline{6}\end{array}\quad \begin{array}{c}39\\ \underline{2}\end{array}\quad \begin{array}{c}49\\ \underline{9}\end{array}\quad \begin{array}{c}63\\ \underline{7}\end{array}\quad \begin{array}{c}75\\ \underline{6}\end{array}$$

2.
$$\begin{array}{c}42\\ \underline{5}\end{array}\quad \begin{array}{c}48\\ \underline{6}\end{array}\quad \begin{array}{c}36\\ \underline{7}\end{array}\quad \begin{array}{c}63\\ \underline{8}\end{array}\quad \begin{array}{c}19\\ \underline{4}\end{array}\quad \begin{array}{c}39\\ \underline{5}\end{array}\quad \begin{array}{c}44\\ 8\end{array}\quad \begin{array}{c}28\\ \underline{7}\end{array}\quad \begin{array}{c}45\\ \underline{8}\end{array}$$

3.
$$\begin{array}{c}64\\ \underline{9}\end{array}\quad \begin{array}{c}73\\ \underline{8}\end{array}\quad \begin{array}{c}48\\ \underline{9}\end{array}\quad \begin{array}{c}45\\ \underline{8}\end{array}\quad \begin{array}{c}63\\ \underline{9}\end{array}\quad \begin{array}{c}57\\ \underline{7}\end{array}\quad \begin{array}{c}46\\ \underline{8}\end{array}\quad \begin{array}{c}37\\ \underline{5}\end{array}\quad \begin{array}{c}65\\ \underline{9}\end{array}$$

4.
$$\begin{array}{c}38\\ \underline{8}\end{array}\quad \begin{array}{c}67\\ \underline{9}\end{array}\quad \begin{array}{c}49\\ \underline{6}\end{array}\quad \begin{array}{c}36\\ \underline{6}\end{array}\quad \begin{array}{c}34\\ \underline{7}\end{array}\quad \begin{array}{c}65\\ \underline{6}\end{array}\quad \begin{array}{c}27\\ \underline{8}\end{array}\quad \begin{array}{c}56\\ \underline{9}\end{array}\quad \begin{array}{c}46\\ \underline{6}\end{array}$$

5.
$$\begin{array}{c}36\\ \underline{7}\end{array}\quad \begin{array}{c}47\\ \underline{9}\end{array}\quad \begin{array}{c}34\\ \underline{7}\end{array}\quad \begin{array}{c}32\\ \underline{9}\end{array}\quad \begin{array}{c}49\\ \underline{3}\end{array}\quad \begin{array}{c}36\\ \underline{7}\end{array}\quad \begin{array}{c}55\\ \underline{6}\end{array}\quad \begin{array}{c}66\\ \underline{8}\end{array}\quad \begin{array}{c}34\\ \underline{9}\end{array}$$

6.
$$\begin{array}{c}79\\ \underline{9}\end{array}\quad \begin{array}{c}38\\ \underline{4}\end{array}\quad \begin{array}{c}38\\ \underline{8}\end{array}\quad \begin{array}{c}59\\ \underline{9}\end{array}\quad \begin{array}{c}67\\ \underline{6}\end{array}\quad \begin{array}{c}56\\ \underline{9}\end{array}\quad \begin{array}{c}35\\ \underline{8}\end{array}\quad \begin{array}{c}77\\ \underline{9}\end{array}\quad \begin{array}{c}47\\ \underline{7}\end{array}$$

7.
$$\begin{array}{c}29\\ \underline{3}\end{array}\quad \begin{array}{c}26\\ \underline{7}\end{array}\quad \begin{array}{c}35\\ \underline{6}\end{array}\quad \begin{array}{c}77\\ \underline{8}\end{array}\quad \begin{array}{c}45\\ \underline{7}\end{array}\quad \begin{array}{c}36\\ \underline{8}\end{array}\quad \begin{array}{c}34\\ \underline{9}\end{array}\quad \begin{array}{c}39\\ \underline{9}\end{array}\quad \begin{array}{c}43\\ \underline{9}\end{array}$$

8.
$$\begin{array}{c}37\\ \underline{7}\end{array}\quad \begin{array}{c}88\\ \underline{9}\end{array}\quad \begin{array}{c}78\\ \underline{8}\end{array}\quad \begin{array}{c}35\\ \underline{8}\end{array}\quad \begin{array}{c}46\\ \underline{9}\end{array}\quad \begin{array}{c}59\\ \underline{5}\end{array}\quad \begin{array}{c}38\\ \underline{4}\end{array}\quad \begin{array}{c}67\\ \underline{6}\end{array}\quad \begin{array}{c}36\\ \underline{8}\end{array}$$

EXERCISE 3

Total.

1.
| 32 | 43 | 44 | 42 | 33 | 82 | 84 | 82 | 73 |
| 83 | 93 | 85 | 67 | 94 | 76 | 34 | 84 | 96 |

2.
| 63 | 34 | 22 | 88 | 74 | 27 | 63 | 55 | 32 |
| 85 | 96 | 87 | 42 | 37 | 83 | 58 | 65 | 89 |

3.
| 49 | 36 | 45 | 77 | 36 | 85 | 56 | 44 | 99 |
| 93 | 87 | 56 | 88 | 76 | 77 | 68 | 89 | 10 |

4.
| 77 | 48 | 38 | 77 | 85 | 76 | 45 | 78 | 77 |
| 87 | 69 | 78 | 59 | 98 | 89 | 69 | 74 | 46 |

EXERCISE 4

Total horizontally.

1. 16 + 7 = ____, 22 + 3 = ____, 32 + 3 = ____, 25 + 4 = ____
2. 33 + 4 = ____, 62 + 6 = ____, 34 + 4 = ____, 32 + 4 = ____
3. 33 + 5 = ____, 64 + 6 = ____, 22 + 7 = ____, 38 + 2 = ____
4. 27 + 3 = ____, 33 + 8 = ____, 45 + 5 = ____, 32 + 9 = ____
5. 26 + 6 = ____, 25 + 6 = ____, 29 + 3 = ____, 36 + 7 = ____
6. 34 + 9 = ____, 49 + 9 = ____, 26 + 8 = ____, 46 + 6 = ____
7. 37 + 7 = ____, 78 + 9 = ____, 58 + 8 = ____, 67 + 9 = ____
8. 46 + 9 = ____, 45 + 9 = ____, 38 + 4 = ____, 67 + 6 = ____
9. 12 + 17 = ____, 18 + 12 = ____, 17 + 13 = ____, 14 + 17 = ____
10. 15 + 15 = ____, 12 + 19 = ____, 13 + 18 = ____, 14 + 16 = ____
11. 22 + 13 = ____, 63 + 13 = ____, 32 + 15 = ____, 33 + 16 = ____
12. 64 + 14 = ____, 42 + 16 = ____, 33 + 14 = ____, 24 + 15 = ____
13. 33 + 15 = ____, 24 + 16 = ____, 32 + 17 = ____, 48 + 12 = ____
14. 27 + 13 = ____, 33 + 18 = ____, 45 + 15 = ____, 22 + 19 = ____
15. 29 + 13 = ____, 26 + 17 = ____, 35 + 16 = ____, 47 + 18 = ____
16. 25 + 17 = ____, 36 + 18 = ____, 34 + 19 = ____, 49 + 19 = ____
17. 37 + 17 = ____, 28 + 19 = ____, 38 + 18 = ____, 27 + 19 = ____
18. 66 + 19 = ____, 45 + 19 = ____, 38 + 14 = ____, 67 + 16 = ____

19. $32 + 43 =$ ____, $43 + 36 =$ ____, $23 + 43 =$ ____, $62 + 34 =$ ____

20. $54 + 44 =$ ____, $22 + 45 =$ ____, $32 + 36 =$ ____, $43 + 54 =$ ____

21. $33 + 55 =$ ____, $34 + 46 =$ ____, $42 + 17 =$ ____, $48 + 32 =$ ____

22. $45 + 25 =$ ____, $63 + 28 =$ ____, $47 + 43 =$ ____, $34 + 27 =$ ____

23. $39 + 43 =$ ____, $46 + 27 =$ ____, $25 + 36 =$ ____, $47 + 28 =$ ____

24. $35 + 47 =$ ____, $36 + 48 =$ ____, $44 + 39 =$ ____, $29 + 39 =$ ____

1·2 TOTALLING BY TENS

EXAMPLE 1   Total, selecting the groups of digits that add to 10.

```
7
5
6
3
4
```

SOLUTION

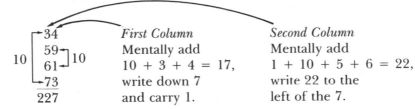

Mentally add: $10 + 10 + 5 = 25$

EXAMPLE 2   Develop the same skill with two column addition. Total.

```
34
59
61
73
```

SOLUTION

	First Column	*Second Column*
	Mentally add	Mentally add
	$10 + 3 + 4 = 17$,	$1 + 10 + 5 + 6 = 22$,
	write down 7	write 22 to the
	and carry 1.	left of the 7.

```
  ┌─34
  │ 59─┐
10│ 61─┤10
  └─73
   227
```

EXERCISE

Total, using the method of Example 1.

1.	**2.**	**3.**	**4.**	**5.**
8	3	5	8	7
8	2	4	1	3
4	7	5	3	1
3	8	5	2	4
7	2	6	9	6

Total, using the method of Example 2.

6.	**7.**	**8.**	**9.**	**10.**
83	79	84	74	16
58	28	13	72	21
22	31	22	36	43
92	42	64	49	44
78	67	66	61	66

1·3 TOTALLING LARGER AMOUNTS

When you are adding columns of figures you should always check your work. This is done by adding *up* the column first and then starting at the top of the column and adding *down* the column. You have proved that your work is correct if both totals are the same.

EXAMPLE

```
2 2 8 6
  3 6 9
  7 1 2
  6 4 8
  5 5 7
2 2 8 6
```

EXERCISE 1

Total.

1.	**2.**	**3.**	**4.**	**5.**
50	80	123	120	808
55	88	321	320	798
60	90	456	578	663
66	99	654	579	870
70	85	789	520	870
77	95	987	630	368

6.	**7.**	**8.**	**9.**	**10.**
223	990	643	9 987	1 235
391	808	259	6 306	6 731
768	651	387	7 891	8 473
430	364	908	3 924	9 832
651	892	921	5 763	8 575
796	963	670		

11.	**12.**	**13.**	**14.**	**15.**
6 617	3 130	22 343	86 362	21 239
3 595	7 609	62 982	55 955	91 643
4 069	3 975	81 034	43 633	72 042
3 966	2 425	95 575	69 039	80 003
7 063	6 383			

EXERCISE 2

1. Marilyn Lee kept a list of her family's expenses for a month.

Public Utilities (gas, water)	$ 53
Heat	140
Telephone	21
Food	300
Clothing	120
Car (gas)	65
Miscellaneous	75

Calculate the total expenses.

_____

2. Calculate the weekly sales for each department.

Date	Department Sporting Goods	Hardware	Stationery	Clothing
September 10	$1 056	$1 365	$ 863	$2 761
September 11	1 872	1 972	942	2 896
September 12	1 369	1 545	909	2 275
September 13	1 754	2 212	1 076	2 867
September 14	1 963	2 567	1 212	3 125
September 15	2 549	2 739	1 373	3 578
Weekly Totals				

3. Pro Wholesale Sporting Goods made a list of bicycles sold during the year. Calculate the total number of each type of bicycle sold.

Month	10-Speed Racing	5-Speed Racing	Regular	3-Speed Touring	5-Speed Touring
January	72	45	51	7	3
February	176	83	91	15	11
March	357	174	172	117	89
April	592	292	203	182	116
May	369	168	191	203	211
June	353	154	178	231	242
July	291	133	157	192	202
August	154	79	82	87	156
September	103	54	63	81	98
October	105	52	60	73	71
November	68	27	31	16	5
December	212	109	89	156	173
Total					

4. Calculate the total area and the total population.

South America		
Country	**Area (km²)**	**Population**
Argentina	2 778 300	20 959 100
Bolivia	1 098 800	3 416 000
Brazil	8 513 800	66 302 300
Chile	741 800	7 551 000
Colombia	1 138 300	14 131 700
Ecuador	273 800	4 298 400
Paraguay	406 600	1 728 300
Peru	1 285 200	10 857 000
Uruguay	187 000	2 800 000
Venezuela	911 900	6 609 000
Total		

5. Here is a deposit slip for a commercial account. Follow the instructions.

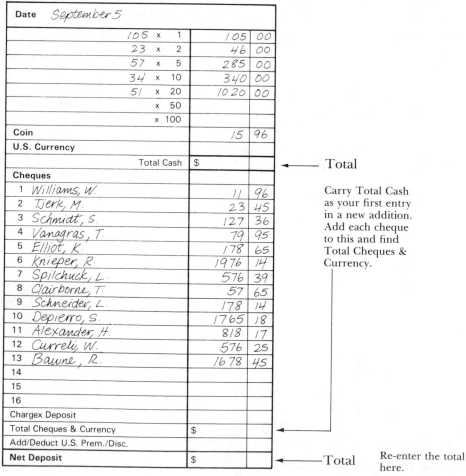

Date	September 5			
	105 x	1	105	00
	23 x	2	46	00
	57 x	5	285	00
	34 x	10	340	00
	51 x	20	1020	00
	x	50		
	x	100		
Coin			15	96
U.S. Currency				
	Total Cash	$		
Cheques				
1 Williams, W.			11	96
2 Tjerk, M.			23	45
3 Schmidt, S.			127	36
4 Vanagras, T.			79	95
5 Elliot, K.			178	65
6 Knieper, R.			1976	14
7 Spilchuck, L.			576	39
8 Clairborne, T.			57	65
9 Schneider, L.			178	14
10 Depierro, S.			1765	18
11 Alexander, H.			818	17
12 Curreli, W.			576	25
13 Bawne, R.			1678	45
14				
15				
16				
Chargex Deposit				
Total Cheques & Currency		$		
Add/Deduct U.S. Prem./Disc.				
Net Deposit		$		

←——— Total

Carry Total Cash as your first entry in a new addition. Add each cheque to this and find Total Cheques & Currency.

←——— Total   Re-enter the total here.

8 ADDITION

1·4 DECIMAL QUANTITIES IN ADDITION

In business problems you will be required to add columns of figures expressed in dollars and cents. You may also have to add quantities that relate to sizes, dimensions, and mass. These quantities may contain decimal parts that require more skills in addition.

DECIMAL NUMBERS

What is meant by $5.25? We recognize immediately that this means 5 dollars and 25 cents. There are 100 cents in a dollar, so we can also think of $5.25 as meaning 5 dollars plus 25 parts of a dollar. Decimals are parts of one unit.

In considering $5.25, we are thinking about the unit as a dollar. We have 5 complete units of one dollar each plus 25 parts (cents) out of a possible 100 parts (100 cents = 1 dollar).

If you poured equal amounts of a litre of milk into 10 small glasses, each glass would contain 1 part out of the 10 parts into which the litre was divided.

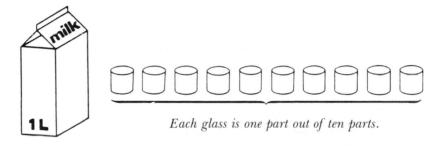

Each glass is one part out of ten parts.

You can divide the number line in a similar manner.

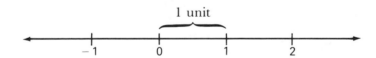

Divide the distance between zero and one into 10 parts.

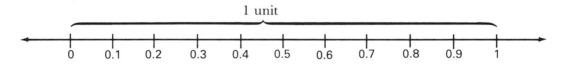

As you measure from 0 to 0.1, you have measured 1 part out of the 10 parts from 0 to 1.
As you measure from 0 to 0.2, you have measured 2 parts out of the 10 parts from 0 to 1.
As you measure from 0 to 0.5, you have measured 5 parts out of the 10 parts from 0 to 1.

Here are some examples:
0.1 means 1 part out of 10 parts into which the unit has been divided.
0.2 means 2 parts out of 10 parts into which the unit has been divided.
0.5 means 5 parts out of 10 parts into which the unit has been divided.

You can continue dividing a unit into smaller parts. For example, divide the distance between 0 and 1 on the number line into 100 parts. Each part is 1 part out of the 100 parts into which the unit has been divided.

Here are some examples:
0.01 means 1 part out of 100 parts into which the unit has been divided.

$1   100 cents   1¢   1 cent = $0.01

0.05 means 5 parts out of the 100 parts into which the unit has been divided.

1¢   1¢   1¢   1¢   1¢   5 cents = $0.05

5¢

DECIMAL PLACE VALUES

Each box in this diagram represents the position of a digit in a decimal quantity and its value.

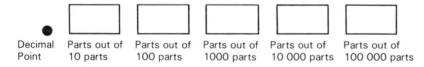

Decimal   Parts out of   Parts out of   Parts out of   Parts out of   Parts out of
Point   10 parts   100 parts   1000 parts   10 000 parts   100 000 parts

Here are some examples:
0.06 means 6 parts out of 100 parts.
0.007 means 7 parts out of 1000 parts.
1.369 means: 1 unit + 3 parts out of 10 parts + 6 parts out of 100 parts +
             9 parts out of 1000 parts.

EXAMPLE Total the following amounts expressed in dollars and cents.

SOLUTION ADD the columns from right to left.

$25.75
  3.33
  4.00
 12.19
 21.44
  5.95
$72.66

EXERCISE 1

Total.

	1.	2.	3.	4.	5.
	$ 2.95	$ 7.26	$ 8.46	$ 1.25	$ 2.49
	5.74	3.91	6.63	2.31	3.33
	6.93	8.50	7.00	9.98	7.89
	3.46	9.99	8.49	7.56	6.56
	8.04	4.00	6.53	8.86	6.89
	3.99	6.55	7.87	1.49	7.69

	6.	7.	8.	9.	10.
	$ 5.48	$ 1.49	$ 2.99	$ 3.65	$ 2.21
	3.98	3.36	8.49	7.21	3.05
	7.65	2.29	6.20	5.00	7.96
	1.04	1.09	3.41	7.40	8.34
	9.89	3.40	9.09	3.85	4.45
	1.43	5.51	5.70	6.60	5.65

	11.	12.	13.	14.	15.
	$ 18.64	$ 21.45	$ 89.95	$ 11.95	$ 17.00
	25.95	87.63	21.34	16.45	16.36
	83.60	91.99	18.88	23.41	21.71
	90.91	84.56	25.45	56.65	36.95
	22.45	62.40	25.95	41.18	18.00
	71.49	65.67	13.95	29.05	32.64

	16.	17.	18.	19.	20.
	$ 45.80	$ 86.87	$ 22.35	$ 21.75	$ 76.43
	29.95	20.00	67.67	89.64	59.95
	36.60	36.53	35.00	29.95	21.35
	41.45	47.97	60.06	21.00	27.35
	62.63	86.86	71.24	88.08	83.34
	75.95	91.94	19.89	76.41	19.29

	21.	22.	23.	24.	25.
	$ 125.36	$ 24.00	$ 889.98	$ 18.89	$ 8.33
	2.95	895.06	226.36	204.04	1.44
	14.05	91.21	8.49	339.63	221.95
	23.89	3.49	19.69	5.95	396.96
	248.61	6.63	134.56	18.71	395.69
	1.14	117.65	545.00	5.45	23.45
	395.95	89.94	449.49	13.95	79.97
	14.85	149.00	81.03	724.40	400.00

26.	27.	28.	29.	30.
$ 175.06	$ 2 197.63	$ 21.24	$ 1 056.63	$ 2 971.04
18.91	449.95	7.95	2 761.14	303.81
49.65	5 075.00	846.51	8 976.41	3 765.45
1 076.21	6 187.97	80.09	202.63	999.49
75.57	756.64	1 814.24	1 967.04	595.00
8.00	500.00	675.00	689.18	7 865.45
845.65	50.00	2 020.00	2 707.16	7 107.73
2 996.47	1 768.18	594.36	3 659.81	897.47
6.87	14.55	8.09	549.89	228.28
9.95	7.97	89.91	4 718.80	8 757.49

Always arrange numbers containing a decimal quantity so that the decimal point in each number is lined up vertically with the decimal point in the number above it.

EXAMPLE   Total 1.234, 21.25, 3.3, 119.0074, 1.57, and 0.365.

SOLUTION   Arrange the numbers vertically and total.

```
    1.234
   21.25
    3.3
  119.007 4
    1.57
    0.365
  146.726 4
```

EXERCISE 2

Arrange the numbers in each question vertically and total.

1. 59.5, 1.25, 295.5, 31.33, 60.4, 29.47 _____

2. 1.2, 59.6, 30.01, 8.45, 46.44, 7.2 _____

3. 123.34, 21.1, 0.5, 4.55, 11.75, 6.76 _____

4. 1.445, 12.3, 495.56, 0.61, 84.78, 0.774 _____

5. 8.9, 0.16, 39.95, 0.426, 29.997, 81.2 _____

6. 61.5, 889.7, 1.35, 20.063, 0.29, 1.147 _____

7. 3347.239, 21.76, 519.7, 30.05, 0.5176, 2195.6 _____

8. 8.748 12, 0.000 36, 1.001, 21.01, 3.140 07 _____

9. 21 342.6, 2579.732, 777.12, 6876.9, 22.312 _____

10. 3.042 15, 0.0314, 22.876 66, 1.121, 23.679 57 _____

11. Total the following invoice.

Bell Lumber
Tara, Ontario

To: Mr. James Coroni   **Date:** 19— 09. 07
71 Maple Street, Owen Sound, Ont.   N4K 4V1

3	Pkg. door closers	2.19
9	Wood Knobs	4.23
1	Liquid Solder	0.49
9	Pkg. amerock hinges	13.05
8	Pieces wood trim	7.60
	Ontario Sales Tax	1.93
	Total	

◄ Add on the sales tax.

12. Find the weekly total for each item of cafeteria sales.

Day	Soup	Sandwiches	Dinner Plate	Dessert	Milk
Monday	$20.20	$35.70	$68.30	$36.17	$42.10
Tuesday	18.80	40.35	59.35	40.95	38.89
Wednesday	21.40	32.15	62.75	38.39	45.16
Thursday	16.60	29.56	58.30	42.27	39.27
Friday	22.60	25.85	71.45	41.86	48.28
Weekly Total	$	$	$	$	$

13. Find the total length of running metres for each type of hall carpet.

Regular	Hard-Twist	Shag
10.30 m	11.15 m	5.75 m
8.90 m	3.80 m	8.30 m
4.25 m	6.60 m	9.10 m
11.60 m	7.75 m	13.40 m
21.35 m	8.90 m	12.25 m
2.75 m	15.70 m	9.70 m
18.60 m	6.10 m	10.30 m
9.15 m	11.25 m	18.60 m
4.90 m	3.80 m	10.70 m
13.70 m	4.70 m	5.80 m
5.20 m	15.40 m	11.60 m

14. Lot frontages along Maple Avenue from Dunlop Street to Ross Street are resurveyed. Find the total length of the street.

Lot	Frontage (in metres)
#1	18.29
#2	36.58
#3	18.30
#4	18.25
#5	36.51
#6	18.31
#7	18.27
#8	36.59
#9	36.60
#10	37.02
Total	

15. Find the total amount of oil delivered.

Address		Oil Delivered (in litres)
18	First Street East	254.6
256	Second Avenue East	512.3
379	Fourth Avenue East	774.7
541	Third Street East	273.6
21	Second Street West	354.1
356	Second Avenue West	296.4
371	Third Street A West	621.6
981	Fourth Avenue West	436.7
761	Fifth Street West	376.5
Total		

For the following questions, list the numbers neatly in columns and total.

16. John ordered the following stamps from a stamp catalogue: a 6¢ Alexandria, Virginia listed at $0.89; a 10¢ Commemorative listed at $0.89; an 8¢ Yellowstone National Park listed at $0.86; an 11¢ Olympic Skiing airmail listed at $1.15; and a 30¢ Robert E. Lee listed at $1.25. What was the total cost of the stamps ordered? _____

17. Wendy spent the following amounts at the school cafeteria for lunches: Monday, $1.45; Tuesday, $1.82; Wednesday, $1.37; Thursday, $2.15; and Friday, $1.37. How much did she spend for the week? _____

18. At the camp canteen Peter spent the following amounts: candy, $2.75; T-shirt, $10.98; tennis cap, $3.99; chewing gum, $1.05; fruit, $2.50. What was the total expenditure?

_____

19. Cheryl went to a sale of remnants at a fabric store. She bought 0.85 m of nylon sheer for $4.25, 1.2 m of denim for $5.39, 0.5 m of gingham for $2.50, and 1.75 m of cotton for $8.47.
  a) How many metres of material did Cheryl buy? _____
  b) What was the total cost? _____

20. Homerite Construction purchased the following vinyl flooring for homes under construction: 20 m² for $395.50; 15 m² for $179.95; 17 m² for $287.75; 25 m² for $525; 22 m² for $437.50.
  a) What was the total cost of the flooring? _____
  b) How many square metres of flooring did Homerite purchase? _____

1·5 CROSS-CHECKING

EXAMPLE   Complete the following example of crosstotalling.

				Total
56	68	79	33	
21	83	46	57	
19	34	51	70	
50	18	11	39	
Total				

SOLUTION   To complete this example:
- Add *down* each column and enter the total at the bottom of the column.
- Add *across* each row and enter the total at the end of each row.
- Add the column totals; this is the *grand total* of the columns.
- Add the row totals; this is the *grand total* of the rows.
- The two grand totals should be the same. This fact verifies that all totals obtained are correct.

				Total
56	68	79	33	236
21	83	46	57	207
19	34	51	70	174
50	18	11	39	118
Total 146	203	187	199	735

EXERCISE

1. Total and verify.

					Total
265	898	643	11 264	12 863	
6 124	5 124	863	3 165	1 435	
10 165	1 002	2 346	7 292	15 165	
5 103	4 641	4 630	6 435	18 120	
6 775	5 172	6 927	9 124	19 620	
Total					

2. Total and verify.

					Total
47.03	4.75	33.067	25.641	0.64	
6.010	16.013	0.64	1.10	0.05	
7.355	0.667	0.891	2.641	29.642	
10.23	24.01	29.063	3.643	0.892	
0.005	0.641	0.77	0.007	0.641	
Total					

3. Complete the following Sales Summary by totalling individual columns and rows. Verify your work by adding the column totals and row totals. These answers should be the same.

Dept.	Monday	Tuesday	Wednesday	Thursday	Friday	Saturday	Total
A	$1 624.81	$1 732.04	$2 641.42	$1 641.11	$2 345.67	$3 415.66	$
B	225.63	881.55	763.22	645.23	516.52	421.62	
C	3 911.10	5 432.64	6 233.10	7 161.58	6 211.13	5 641.76	
D	4 633.11	3 476.22	5 621.11	6 810.00	4 633.15	3 421.10	
E	1 223.05	2 643.12	3 520.10	4 613.44	3 421.76	5 261.83	
F	864.77	764.02	921.24	861.10	795.14	645.10	
G	6 334.11	5 213.43	7 264.10	8 172.33	9 642.13	6 512.43	
H	265.33	165.41	324.51	614.77	522.76	621.63	
I	955.19	866.76	761.23	922.10	734.61	865.12	
J	624.88	762.11	811.36	943.55	864.00	927.10	
Total	$	$	$	$	$	$	$

4. Total individual columns and rows in the following Production Analysis Report. Then check your work by adding the column totals and row totals. These answers should be the same.

Plant	Monday	Tuesday	Wednesday	Thursday	Friday	Total
	Sound Manufacturing Production Analysis for the Week Ending June 30, 19____					
No. 1	362 107	463 124	365 123	521 164	702 834	
No. 2	97 103	86 521	72 513	62 142	72 165	
No. 3	287 184	342 841	446 125	527 127	421 625	
No. 4	427 355	512 643	341 621	231 622	541 243	
No. 5	35 766	42 128	52 153	34 665	26 785	
Total						

5. Add and verify the following Road Construction Report.

Kent County Road Construction Report for 1983-1986					
District	**1983**	**1984**	**1985**	**1986**	**Total**
Sussex	$67 123.44	$72 643.55	$86 165.20	$92 103.75	
Norton	23 126.55	24 163.22	25 126.55	26 521.10	
Hampton	10 164.23	12 642.24	13 123.67	14 163.06	
Seagrave	11 124.55	924.76	864.50	723.52	
Alma	4 162.42	5 126.55	6 134.10	8 164.81	
Albert	1 267.42	2 641.76	3 142.05	4 633.00	
Total					

6. Arrange the following production control figures in rows and columns. Total the hours that each machine was in use for the week and the number of hours that all the machines were in use each day.

Machine #706: Monday, 1.5 h; Tuesday, 12.75 h; Wednesday, 9.33 h; Thursday, 15.25 h; Friday, 11.5 h; Saturday, 6.25 h
Machine #707: Monday, 8.67 h; Tuesday, 3.25 h; Wednesday, 14.75 h; Thursday, 11.5 h; Friday, 18.67 h; Saturday, 13.75 h
Machine #709: Monday, 15.5 h; Tuesday, 13.5 h; Wednesday, 11.67 h; Thursday, 12.75 h; Friday, 16.5 h; Saturday, 3.75 h
Machine #710: Monday, 5.67 h; Tuesday, 11.5 h; Wednesday, 13.75 h; Thursday, 15.33 h; Friday, 2.5 h; Saturday, 0 h

1·6 REVIEW

EXERCISE

Total.

	1.	2.	3.	4.	5.
	29	36	75	98	31
	72	42	28	19	14
	45	19	41	88	45
	50	78	93	62	15
	68	90	55	45	76
	31	25	13	41	89

	6.	7.	8.	9.	10.
	343	118	889	417	213
	189	403	963	369	763
	761	555	415	500	811
	432	876	505	225	909
	516	250	747	408	545
	411	199	319	679	681

11.	1 569	12.	3 868	13.	2 125	14.	5 454
	4 378		4 057		8 749		1 875
	1 909		6 681		3 376		2 367
	7 635		9 423		5 780		8 114
	5 476		8 107		1 199		5 496
	3 431		6 987		8 329		3 489

15.	1 009	16.	1.75	17.	27.96	18.	139.63
	3 175		3.49		33.39		786.40
	2 525		5.61		15.45		309.89
	6 073		2.25		88.89		212.15
	8 629		3.96		67.62		416.69
	7 832		4.50		54.49		878.91

19.	1 227.53	20.	21 673.45	21.	1.732	22.	3.7
	309.19		7 865.25		0.3		10.05
	2 355.61		433.67		12.68		5.61
	29.99		8 761.41		8.975		0.075
	542.18		30 686.59		37.5		360.79
	3 678.24		4 263.76		0.71		12.089

23.	21.7636	24.	3.565 14	25.	69.002	26.	437 800.109
	0.012		0.127 89		1 428.8		3 322.08
	37.10		31.899		339 769.54		960.008
	516.7		2.351		359.45		22 341.11
	4.05		2.351		77 561.23		35.1

Complete the following cross totals.

27.

							Total
5.96	4.36	3.78	7.48	1.50	3.56	
3.48	2.59	1.44	3.12	3.66	1.98	
2.79	6.47	1.44	2.45	9.19	7.47	
8.88	3.05	2.69	5.05	4.08	2.79	
6.56	4.55	8.08	6.70	2.22	1.47	
4.39	7.98	6.40	9.90	8.39	8.39	
Total						

28.

				Total
179.89	817.15	676.15	519.48	
39.97	136.09	415.12	22.77	
625.05	225.37	809.27	386.79	
569.88	178.38	345.56	356.19	
Total				

29.

					Total
1.763	6.36	0.56	1.055	5.05	
0.12	6.351	3.767	3.1	0.178	
5.879	8.082	2.126	0.012	0.099	
3.05	0.159	0.89	7.62	4.22	
Total					

30. The scores for the Hillcrest Bowling Team were as follows: Metcalfe–first game 153, second 161, third 184; Oroni–first game 185, second 191, third 186; Johannsen–first game 164, second 177, third 195; Braun-first game 187, second 181, third 192. Calculate the team total for each game.

_____ _____ _____

31. The Community Orchestra had a fund raising drive. Canvassers were divided into groups A, B, C, D, and E. Donations were reported each week. Make headings and a chart for the following summary of donations. Calculate the total donations for each group and the grand total of all donations by cross-checking.

Week ending Oct. 3: Group A $756.65, Group B $597.63, Group C $305.85, Group D $986.30, Group E $287.50
Week ending Oct. 10: Group A $774.50, Group B $610.25, Group C $590.45, Group D $1050.50, Group E $833.25
Week ending Oct. 17: Group A $835.40, Group B $715.50, Group C $817.45, Group D $365.25, Group E $425.00
Week ending Oct. 24: Group A $915.40, Group B $840.50, Group C $415.85, Group D $115.00, Group E $975.75

32. Total each employee's sales.

Employees' Sales Listing Sheet											

Date .... Sheet No. ....

Employee No.	(1)		(2)		(3)		(4)		(5)		(6)	
	$ 8	46	$ 6	01	$ 2	09	$ 5	11	$ 6	12	$ 1	99
	7	35	3	60	1	19	0	59	0	39	3	27
	3	28	0	79	4	45	1	59	1	11	2	25
	5	48	0	69	2	36	3	20	2	15	4	11
	6	79	2	21	1	50	1	76	4	16	1	66
	1	28	7	76	0	75	0	80	1	79	0	79
	3	11	3	01	3	20	1	11	0	66	0	29
	2	69	5	65	1	95	1	75	0	25	5	00
	1	55	3	49	2	40	1	60	3	14	0	36
	5	21	0	79	5	00	2	15	2	00	1	99
	7	07	1	29	1	10	4	20	6	50	1	99
	5	57	3	07	0	86	3	00	0	79	4	15
	3	09	4	59	7	95	0	75	0	89	2	10
	7	61	4	47	1	45	0	89	2	50	3	79
	0	56	3	61	3	10	1	14	2	25	0	60
	1	06	7	95	1	15	1	44	3	10	1	79
	2	29	1	25	4	12	2	12	1	15	2	00
	5	29	3	06	0	37	3	10	4	10	4	69
	3	39	0	69	2	11	5	06	1	44	3	50
	6	17	0	69	1	15	2	22	3	03	0	25
	1	44	1	21	4	10	3	15	0	89	2	10
Total	$		$		$		$		$		$	

CHAPTER 2

SUBTRACTION

2·1 WARM UP ON BASICS

EXERCISE 1

Subtract.

1.	5 3	6 3	9 5	7 5	7 4	8 6	8 4	6 4	9 6
2.	5 2	9 4	7 3	8 4	6 2	9 3	8 2	7 2	6 3
3.	8 5	10 6	9 7	10 2	11 7	10 3	11 8	10 5	11 9
4.	8 3	9 2	11 4	11 3	11 2	10 5	10 7	10 8	10 4
5.	12 3	13 7	11 6	15 8	12 6	12 7	14 8	13 9	18 9
6.	12 9	11 5	12 6	14 6	18 9	13 4	12 5	15 7	13 5
7.	14 9	17 9	16 8	13 8	15 9	14 9	12 4	16 9	13 6
8.	17 8	14 7	16 7	13 5	14 5	13 7	12 8	16 8	15 6

SUBTRACTION BY "BORROWING"

EXAMPLE   Subtract 28 from 62 and check the answer.

SOLUTION $\begin{array}{r} 5\ 12 \\ \not6\ \not2 \\ 2\ 8 \\ \hline 3\ 4\ (+28\ =\ 62) \\ \text{Check} \end{array}$ $\left\{\begin{array}{l} \text{Eight cannot be subtracted from 2.} \\ \text{"Borrow" 10 from 60 to give 12 in} \\ \text{the first column.} \end{array}\right.$

EXERCISE 2

Subtract and check by addition.

1.	25	36	19	37	47	38	28	36	29
	13	23	15	25	14	26	14	24	16

2.	25	39	47	38	26	39	28	37	26
	12	14	23	14	12	23	12	12	13

3.	38	40	29	20	31	30	41	30	41
	25	16	17	12	17	13	18	15	19

4.	47	34	46	53	44	23	32	46	45
	18	17	27	25	15	17	18	18	16

5.	43	53	41	55	52	32	54	34	58
	23	27	16	38	16	27	38	29	29

6.	54	57	46	53	65	44	42	46	53
	27	29	18	28	38	29	14	39	26

2·2 NEGATIVE BALANCES

Sometimes the number to be subtracted is larger than the number from which it is subtracted. When this happens, the result is a *negative balance*.

EXAMPLE   The sales for the month of February at Larry's Garden Centre are $2500. The total operating costs for the same period are $3000. Calculate the profit or loss.

SOLUTION   The profit or loss is the difference between the sales and the operating costs.

$$\begin{aligned} \text{Sales} &= \$2500 \\ \text{Operating costs} &= \underline{\hphantom{0}3000} \\ \text{Profit or loss} &= \$\hphantom{0}500 \end{aligned}$$

The difference is a loss because the operating costs were greater than the sales.

A loss can be shown as:
- $500 −, a minus sign after the negative balance; or
- ($500), the negative balance enclosed in brackets; or
- $500 Cr., the negative balance shown as a credit balance.

EXERCISE 1

Calculate the balance in each of the following using a minus sign, a bracket, or the symbol "Cr." to indicate a negative balance where necessary. Check your work.

1.	$ 57 − 69	**2.**	$ 37 − 76	**3.**	$ 73 − 91	**4.**	$ 65 − 85	**5.**	$ 89 − 103

6.	$ 86 239 − 98 112	**7.**	$ 6 543 − 19 968	**8.**	$ 125 699 − 829 344	**9.**	$ 14 293 − 96 234

EXERCISE 2

Complete the following Inventory Cards by finding the daily balances. First take the balance, then add the figure in the 'In' column and subtract the figure in the 'Out' column.

1.

Date	In	Out	Balance
Oct. 7			1 578
Oct. 9		321	
Oct. 10	415	197	
Oct. 11		279	
Oct. 12		346	
Oct. 13	555	157	
Oct. 16		329	
Oct. 17		152	
Oct. 18	375	127	
Oct. 19		105	
Oct. 20	450	256	

2.

Date	In	Out	Balance
Oct. 7			1 576
Oct. 9	345	547	
Oct. 10		448	
Oct. 11	575	215	
Oct. 12		317	
Oct. 13	285	178	
Oct. 16	445	379	
Oct. 17		513	
Oct. 18	625	210	
Oct. 19		343	
Oct. 20	700	376	

3.

Date	In	Out	Balance
Oct. 7			2 047
Oct. 9		1 347	
Oct. 10	1 500	865	
Oct. 11		1 242	
Oct. 12	3 000	357	
Oct. 13		1 451	
Oct. 16		853	
Oct. 17	2 750	907	
Oct. 18		1 564	
Oct. 19	2 250	1 008	
Oct. 20		1 576	

4.

Date	In	Out	Balance
Oct. 7			20 354
Oct. 9	7 350	2 850	
Oct. 10		3 765	
Oct. 11	5 470	5 455	
Oct. 12		8 764	
Oct. 13	10 250	5 860	
Oct. 16	5 755	4 975	
Oct. 17		6 127	
Oct. 18	6 750	6 342	
Oct. 19		5 930	
Oct. 20	6 000	7 560	

Calculate the number of kilograms of freight delivered by each shipper. Verify your totals. (Net Mass = Gross Mass − Mass of Truck)

5.

Continental Products Windsor, Ontario			October 15, 19___
Shipped by	**Gross Mass**	**Mass of Truck**	**Net Mass**
Bonhomme, J.	1 578 kg	905 kg	
Conach, K.L.	1 963 kg	1 256 kg	
Hanson, B.	1 256 kg	875 kg	
Lasker, A.L.	2 027 kg	1 389 kg	
Lestac, M.	2 315 kg	1 612 kg	
Paulsen, R.	1 985 kg	1 027 kg	
Quirck, S.	2 579 kg	1 879 kg	
Wright, R.S.	2 066 kg	1 517 kg	
Total			

6.

MILLER'S FLOUR CO. Winnipeg, Manitoba			October 21, 19___
Shipped By	**Mass**	**Mass of Truck**	**Net Mass**
Boni, M.	1 896 kg	970 kg	
Delaney, D.	2 357 kg	1 236 kg	
Doman, A.	1 563 kg	1 167 kg	
Detham, E.	2 173 kg	1 334 kg	
Fournier, S.	1 887 kg	897 kg	
Greve, T.	1 965 kg	1 276 kg	
Marani, K.	2 598 kg	1 319 kg	
Ozadsuk, T.	1 587 kg	995 kg	
Rek, V.	2 469 kg	1 538 kg	
Total			

Calculate the unpaid balance for each contract. (The unpaid balance is obtained by subtracting the trade-in allowance from the list price and adding the carrying charges.)

7.

HOPPS MOTOR SALES October 9, 19___				
Sales Contract Memorandum				
Contract	**List Price New Car**	**Trade-In Allowance**	**Plus Carrying Charges**	**Unpaid Balance**
B-307	$3 995	$1 367	$207	
B-308	4 150	2 550	236	
B-309	3 889	1 898	549	
B-310	4 576	895	475	
B-311	4 237	2 786	368	

8.

HOPPS MOTOR SALES				October 10, 19___
Sales Contract Memorandum				
Contract	List Price New Car	Trade-In Allowance	Plus Carrying Charges	Unpaid Balance
B-312	$3 889	$ 901	$456	
B-313	5 045	2 760	307	
B-314	4 389	1 680	412	
B-315	4 237	2 055	329	
B-316	5 568	2 986	417	

2·3 DECIMAL QUANTITIES IN SUBTRACTION

As with addition of decimal quantities, always be sure to arrange numbers containing a decimal quantity so that the decimal point is lined up vertically with the decimal point in the number above it.

EXAMPLE   Subtract 27.635 from 109.46. Check the answer.

SOLUTION   Arrange the numbers vertically.

$$109.46$$
$$\underline{27.635}$$

Place a zero in the third place after the decimal in the number 109.46 before subtracting.

$$109.460$$
$$\underline{27.635}$$
$$81.825 \ (+27.635 = 109.460)$$
$$\text{Check}$$

EXERCISE 1

Arrange the numbers in each question vertically and subtract. Check by addition.

1. 28.52 from 131.68 _____

2. 65.63 from 115.07 _____

3. 86.25 from 113.74 _____

4. 24.00 from 95.87 _____

5. 281.52 from 888.82 _____

6. 20.063 from 61.55 _____

7. 29.764 from 119.5 _____

8. 3.042 15 from 22.876 _____

9. 327.112 from 6910.3 _____

10. 1965.5 from 2579.732 _____

EXERCISE 2

Check the following invoices. Make corrections by drawing a straight line through the incorrect amount and writing the correct amount beside it.

1.

Lamps Unlimited

Pine Tree Plaza   No. 1887   681-8201

Sold to: *Janice Tonelli* .... Phone: ....

Address: ....

Sold By	Date	Chargex or MasterCharge	On Acct.	Balance	Date Order
JD	*July 20*				

B/O	Qty.	Description		Price	Amount
	1	12 × 13 × 13 shade			$ 17.20
	2	717 shades		$ 6.00	12.00
	1	707 shade			5.61
					34.80
				Less	8.90
					24.90
				Tax	1.81
				Total	27.71

2.

Chapins Wallpaper Paints				976 Hall Street Victoria, B.C. V8S 2P3	

6319 Fairview Way, Duncan, B.C. V9L 3Y6

Terms		C.O.D.		Taken ☐		Deliver ☐		Clerk	

Quant.	Items	Description	Price	Amount
2	1 L	Latex 118-1		$ 5.70
2	1 L	Undercoat 118-1		6.38
1	4 L	Gem 118-1		9.95
				22.03
			Less	4.40
				18.63
			Tax	1.23
				19.86

Returns must be made within 30 days accompanied by this invoice.
2% per month charge on overdue accounts.

Customer's Copy

Calculate the daily balances in each bank statement. Subtract the withdrawals and add the deposits.

3.

Date	Withdrawals		Deposits		Balance	
Oct 1					609	29
7	23	50				
10			764	28		
12	125	90				
23			264	95		
27			869	22		
30	642	08				

4.

Date	Withdrawals		Deposits		Balance	
Dec 1					964	20
3	86	40				
5	125	95				
6	239	60				
13			866	42		
20	12	60				
27	64	26				

Subtract the cheques and add the deposits to find the daily balances for each bank statement.

5.

savings and loan bank
28 Second Avenue E., Owen Sound, Ont.

Mr. W. J. Snow
18 Alpha Street
Owen Sound, Ontario

Account No. 6852

Cheques		Deposits	Date	Balance
			Apr. 1	$ 2 865.82
125.80	12.45		Apr. 3	_____
		925.80	Apr. 5	_____
406.92	1.80 SC		Apr. 11	_____
89.50 CC		868.50	Apr. 12	_____
68.20	40.30 LN		Apr. 17	_____
9.50	0.70 SC		Apr. 20	_____
50.45		1 265.95	Apr. 23	_____
180.20		188.38	Apr. 25	_____
68.25	1.38		Apr. 27	_____
		718.50	Apr. 29	_____

Explanation of Symbols

CC — Certified Cheque   SC — Service Charge   IN — Interest   LN — Payment on Loan   EC — Error Corrected

6.

savings and loan bank
28 Second Avenue E., Owen Sound, Ont.

Miss Judy Warrilow
825 Fourth Avenue West
Owen Sound, Ontario

Account No. 5557

Cheques		Deposits	Date	Balance
265.80 CC	89.50	650.40	May 1	$9 769.50
		125.80	May 3	_____
86.50	2.50 SC	8.60 IN	May 9	_____
12.80	186.90		May 16	_____
		1 652.50	May 19	_____
428.90			May 22	_____
685.20	6.80 SC		May 25	_____
925.88			May 28	_____
86.50	86.50		May 29	_____
1.25	50.90		May 31	_____

Explanation of Symbols

CC — Certified Cheque   SC — Service Charge   IN — Interest   LN — Payment on Loan   EC — Error Corrected

Total and verify the following sales reports. (Net Sales = Gross Sales − Sales Returns)

7.

397 West Street
Windsor, Ontario N8S 2C3

Store No. 12   Oct. 19, 19___

Dept.	Gross Sales	Sales Returns	Net Sales
201	$ 314.84	$ 86.30	
202	1 730.17	217.40	
203	563.31	21.97	
204	2 237.18	311.87	
205	1 139.39	287.65	
206	1 386.95	325.75	
Total			

8.

international

20 Huron Road
Edmonton, Alberta T5A 1B5

Store No. 5   Oct. 20/___

Dept.	Gross Sales	Sales Returns	Net Sales
001	$ 5 205.22	$ 751.03	
002	705.07	61.54	
003	1 150.71	127.39	
004	3 376.17	379.07	
005	452.33	32.87	
006	944.00	53.29	
007	1 686.60	150.70	
008	1 009.07	38.85	
009	1 380.66	99.12	
010	2 815.95	278.16	
011	761.44	57.79	
012	1 852.65	240.04	
013	907.40	23.78	
Total			

9. An oil tank holds 45 kL of oil. Oil delivery trucks holding 3600 L, 3500 L, 3000 L, and 3800 L were filled from the full tank. How many kilolitres of oil were left in the tank? (1 kL = 1000 L) _____

10. An empty bin in Harris Hardware was filled with 25 kg of nails. During the day purchases of 500 g, 550 g, 250 g, 1.5 kg, and 2 kg of nails were made. How many kilograms were left in the bin at the end of the day? _____

11. On January 31, my gas meter read 424.5 m³. The gas company calculates the number of cubic metres of gas used each month by subtracting last month's meter reading from this month's meter reading. My gas meter readings were:
Feb. 28: 459.7 m³; Mar. 31: 485.3 m³; Apr. 30: 511.2 m³; May 31: 529.3 m³

   a) How much gas did I use each month? _____ _____ _____ _____

   b) What is the total volume of gas used from January 31 to May 31? _____

2·4 CALCULATING BALANCES

When it is necessary to subtract the sum of several amounts from a given amount, total the amounts to be subtracted and then subtract this total from the given amount.

EXAMPLE   The gross wages in a payroll are $516 and deductions are $6.18, $27.45, and $89.55. Calculate the net pay.

SOLUTION   Total.   Subtract.
             $ 6.18 $516.00
                27.45   123.18
                89.55 $392.82
             $123.18

The net pay is $392.82.

EXERCISE 1

Calculate each balance.

1.

Withdrawals	Balance
	$519.83
$ 26.34	
151.72	
89.95	_____

2.

Withdrawals	Balance
	$ 921.80
$ 80.34	
125.45	
256.11	_____

3.

Withdrawals	Balance
	$1 678.50
$ 125.88	
765.21	
112.11	_____

4.

Withdrawals	Balance
	$2 564.88
$ 180.60	
35.65	
1 184.55	_____

Complete the following payroll sheets.
- Work horizontally. Subtract the deductions from the gross wages to calculate each employee's take home pay.
- Work vertically. Add to calculate the total of each column.
- To check your work, subtract the deductions totals from the gross wages total. The results should equal the total take home pay.

5.

Employee	Gross Wages	Deductions				Take Home Pay
		Income Tax	Unemp. Ins.	Pension	Hosp.	
Schmidt, W.	$320.00	$35.70	$5.29	$4.55	$4.55	
Waugh, H.	352.00	44.75	5.78	5.11	4.00	
Potter, A.	485.00	46.05	8.00	7.53	8.00	
McLean, S.	420.00	30.40	6.93	6.36	8.00	
Korch, B.	530.50	59.40	8.74	8.34	8.00	
Taylor, B.	440.75	35.60	7.27	6.73	4.00	
Zeller, C.	410.50	27.80	6.77	6.19	4.00	
Totals						

6.

Employee	Gross Wages	Deductions				Take Home Pay
		Income Tax	Unemp. Ins.	Pension	Hosp.	
Abrens, W.	$350.75	$ 8.65	$ 5.79	$ 5.12	$20.00	
Chalmers, R.	415.50	23.10	6.86	6.28	25.00	
Diebel, G.	420.85	15.40	6.95	6.38	25.00	
Frank, S.	400.25	10.55	6.60	6.00	12.00	
Helwig, H.	500.30	46.25	8.26	7.81	17.00	
Hill, L.	504.80	51.30	8.33	7.39	20.00	
Klein, C.	540.50	46.00	8.95	8.56	17.00	
Monk, D.	585.20	56.60	9.65	9.33	25.00	
Rusk, J.	780.85	129.05	12.89	12.86	17.00	
Ward, R.	331.50	33.70	5.47	0.77	20.00	
Witter, J.	998.75	282.00	7.15	17.42	25.00	
Totals						

EXERCISE 2

Calculate the balance due after each transaction on the following ledger cards. Add the charge or subtract the credit to find the new balance due.

1.

Hammond Equipment
Edmonton, Alberta

Name: D. Legassic .... No. 7635

Date	Charge	Credit	Balance Due
10-9			742.65
06-9	87.52		
08-9		150.75	
11-9	307.67		
15-9	37.46		
16-9		425.35	
18-9	29.79		
20-9	47.56		
22-9		340.36	
24-9	56.66		
26-9	137.47		
27-9		250.00	

2.

harrison & brown company
Ottawa, Ontario

Name: John Mah .... No. 9821

Date	Charge	Credit	Balance Due
10 10			875.00
02 10	37.65		
04 10		253.37	
08 10	48.95		
10 10	137.67		
12 10	97.35		
15 10	276.30		
18 10		342.50	
19 10	32.90		
20 10		125.00	
22 10	227.50		
24 10	59.64		
26 10	314.50		
27 10		224.60	

Complete the following reports.
- Work horizontally to calculate the gross profit and the net profit for each store.
  Gross Profit = Sales − Cost of Sales
  Net Profit = Gross Profit − Expenses
- Work vertically. Total the columns headed *Sales, Cost of Sales, Gross Profit, Expenses,* and *Net Profit.*
- Work horizontally to verify the total gross profit and the total net profit.

3.

Wallace Sales

For the month of June, 19___

Branch	Sales	Cost of Sales	Gross Profit	Expenses	Net Profit
Halifax	$15 864.25	$11 769.11	$	$1 260.13	$
Sussex	7 233.86	4 602.73		983.65	
Quebec	18 605.33	12 744.85		1 523.10	
North Bay	27 884.10	19 825.76		5 411.63	
Brandon	30 649.26	25 421.95		2 642.89	
Yorkton	9 860.42	6 100.23		1 721.44	
Red Deer	10 265.11	7 321.42		1 984.20	
Vernon	29 420.33	24 641.35		2 891.48	
Total	$	$	$	$	$

4.

X'MAS CARDS LIMITED

For the month of July, 19___

Outlet	Sales	Cost of Sales	Gross Profit	Expenses	Net Profit
Nelson	$ 35 641.25	$ 30 433.76	$	$ 3 745.76	$
Kitimat	12 864.77	8 441.65		2 989.10	
Banff	26 235.23	21 624.11		3 600.25	
Regina	47 210.80	36 861.23		9 235.27	
Morden	10 867.44	6 251.35		2 914.60	
Dryden	13 675.89	10 641.35		2 130.28	
Owen Sound	95 216.43	84 100.29		8 652.33	
Oshawa	106 642.91	95 621.43		10 821.60	
St. Jean	14 235.16	10 265.69		2 641.10	
Moncton	125 896.25	113 644.23		10 692.25	
Total	$	$	$	$	$

5.

Superior Novelties Ltd.

For the month of October, 19____

Branch	Sales	Cost of Sales	Gross Profit	Expenses	Net Profit
Borden	$ 9 621.38	$ 6 523.47	$	$ 2 650.28	$
Hampton	13 826.40	11 628.55		1 925.45	
Chatham	39 263.25	32 891.00		5 264.73	
Truro	48 640.23	43 642.23		3 629.35	
Sydney	89 865.23	78 194.28		10 841.10	
Kentville	12 235.75	9 184.39		2 186.76	
St. George	7 644.10	5 640.25		1 624.17	
Midland	14 792.86	10 840.23		3 689.25	
Guelph	129 643.10	125 236.76		4 236.90	
Vernon	144 827.50	129 860.02		12 680.27	
Total	$	$	$	$	$

6. Complete the following report.
- Calculate the gross sales by adding the daily sales in each department.
- Subtract the return sales from the gross sales to determine the net sales.

WARLOW'S DEPARTMENT STORE

Sales Report for Week Ended ___October 31, 19—___

Dept.	Daily Sales						Gross Sales	Return Sales	Net Sales
	Mon.	Tues.	Wed.	Thurs.	Fri.	Sat.			
A	$2130.61	$2576.90	$1723.68	$2963.93	$4693.16	$6093.62	$	$ 980.70	$
B	3765.23	4001.21	1921.63	5620.32	6872.35	7200.82		1609.50	
C	4365.11	5017.33	2110.95	5729.15	6092.33	7365.91		2103.71	
D	8162.44	9021.36	3102.01	7235.33	8671.22	9635.45		2521.11	
E	865.10	923.66	321.45	965.43	907.34	998.78		282.04	

7. Calculate each marina's gross sales and net sales, then calculate the total net sales.

GRAND LAKE MARINAS, LTD

Sales Report for the Period Ended August 31, 19____

Marina Number	Monthly Sales				Gross Sales	Return Sales	Net Sales
	May	June	July	August			
1	$43 165.77	$55 863.10	$60 921.61	$10 821.03		$5 101.25	
2	52 633.63	65 281.46	75 029.34	23 164.78		6 782.76	
3	12 890.42	14 126.89	19 628.70	9 264.05		1 624.33	
4	107 243.75	270 135.64	395 112.60	90 113.64		25 863.03	
5	8 621.32	10 113.44	15 129.38	5 134.90		1 117.20	
6	43 129.76	48 634.17	60 921.44	32 064.27		5 542.67	
						Total Net Sales	

8. Complete and balance the following semi-annual cafeteria report. Subtract the total monthly expenses from the total monthly receipts to find the profit.

Albert County College

Cafeteria Receipts and Expenses for the period ended June 25, 19____

Month	Receipts Week Ending Friday					Total Monthly Receipts	Total Monthly Expenses	Profit
	1st Week	2nd Week	3rd Week	4th Week	5th Week			
Jan.		$4 296.11	$4 376.25	$4 291.11	$3 520.90		$11 539.41	
Feb.	$5 291.83	4 876.10	5 110.77	6 176.21	—		15 018.24	
March	4 876.21	3 964.17	4 325.91	4 921.60	—		10 621.70	
April	5 011.65	6 235.66	4 965.22	—	2 651.20		11 671.30	
May	4 352.72	4 911.85	5 621.63	3 629.16	—		12 511.28	
June	4 905.26	5 094.11	4 870.10	2 116.95	—		10 721.75	
Totals								

9. **(i)** Complete and balance the following semi-annual cafeteria report. Subtract the total monthly expenses from the total monthly receipts to find the profit.

(ii) On June 25, the cafeteria spent $950.50 on a cold buffet appliance. How much money was left from the total profit? _____

						South Bay College		
			Cafeteria Receipts and Expenses for the period ended June 25, 19___					
	Receipts Week Ending Friday					**Total Monthly Receipts**	**Total Monthly Expenses**	**Profit**
Month	**1st Week**	**2nd Week**	**3rd Week**	**4th Week**	**5th Week**			
Jan.		$6 741.76	$7 263.21	$6 940.76	$3 871.10		$12 411.27	
Feb.	$8 421.71	5 926.75	7 276.91	8 016.43	—		19 620.72	
March	7 852.50	6 910.80	5 605.76	6 680.73	—		18 275.86	
April	7 259.73	7 875.43	6 071.85	—	4 920.85		18 162.11	
May	5 626.83	5 593.34	5 921.65	4 716.63	—		14 523.76	
June	6 129.11	6 326.79	5 637.80	3 092.36	—		14 930.10	
Totals								

10. Jack's Marina had a balance of $397.30 on July 3. Sales for the week ending July 9 were $1540.91 while expenses were $981.89. For the week ending July 16, sales were $1769.47 and expenses were $1079.56. Calculate the balance on July 9, then total to find the balance on July 16. _____ , _____

11. Helen Szaki had a bank balance of $597.63 on September 30. During October she wrote the following cheques: October 5, $19.38; October 12, $136.47; October 14, $89.95; October 18, $57.45; October 21, $34.94; October 25, $8.79. Helen deposited $255.50 on October 15 and $235.55 on October 31. Calculate Helen's balance on October 15 and her balance on October 31, in each case after she made her deposit.

_____ , _____

12. At the start of the business day, Sugar and Spice Candy Shoppe had the following money in the cash register: $75 in bills, $10.50 in 50-cent coins, $15.75 in quarters, $44.70 in dimes, $22.30 in nickels, and $2.72 in pennies. At the end of the day there was: $249 in bills, $28.50 in 50-cent coins, $37.25 in quarters, $32.30 in dimes, $18.40 in nickels, and $1.53 in pennies.

a) Calculate the total amount of money in the cash register at the end of the day.

_____

b) From this total, subtract the amount in the cash register at the beginning of the day to calculate the total sales for the day. _____

EXERCISE

Subtract.

1.	1 923	2.	28.35	3.	125.64	4.	655.11	5.	1 643.02
	645		11.73		96.15		86.93		964.78

6.	8 634.76	7.	435.016	8.	65.026 3	9.	836.102 9	10.	89 623.01
	96.01		8.321		1.962 8		521.63		7 829.36

Fill in the daily balances in the ledger accounts. State whether the balance is Debit or Credit.

NOTE   The two kinds of account balances are **Debit balance** and **Credit balance**. A Debit balance (Dr.) is obtained when the total of the Debit items is greater than the total of the Credit items. A Credit balance (Cr.) is obtained when the total of the Credit items is greater than the total of the Debit items.

11.

Account No. 265

Date	Debit	Credit	Balance
May 1	Brought forward		976.44 Dr.
3	872.44		———— ——
8		137.45	———— ——
12	128.50		———— ——
15	65.78	485.65	———— ——

12.

Account No. 468

Date	Debit	Credit	Balance
October 2	Brought forward		1 265.62 Dr.
5	925.88		———— ——
10		685.50	———— ——
15	685.40	925.88	———— ——
20	125.90	86.20	———— ——
25	1 682.40		———— ——
29		325.40	———— ——

13.

Account No. 865			
Date	**Debit**	**Credit**	**Balance**
January 3	Brought forward		925.58 Dr.
8	1 268.50		_____ ____
9	868.90		_____ ____
12		1 268.50	_____ ____
15	650.20	280.90	_____ ____
21	12.80		_____ ____

14. Complete the following report.
- Calculate the gross sales by totalling the daily sales in each department.
- Subtract the return sales from the gross sales to determine the net sales.

PAQUETTE'S DEPARTMENT STORE
Sales Report for the Week Ended November 30, 19____

Dept.	Daily Sales						Gross Sales	Return Sales	Net Sales
	Mon.	Tues.	Wed.	Thurs.	Fri.	Sat.			
A	$3 425.12	$4 361.75	$2 635.01	$5 621.35	$6 092.44	$7 631.24		$1 680.33	
B	5 791.83	6 020.23	3 762.58	7 886.55	8 920.48	9 126.56		2 352.16	
C	8 621.01	9 252.45	4 110.32	7 912.44	8 625.10	9 851.23		2 760.77	
D	922.86	725.02	301.66	625.70	896.63	921.63		252.25	
E	680.11	692.32	460.91	782.44	926.62	998.01		300.45	
F	232.60	321.96	192.20	325.76	498.75	521.65		114.70	

Calculate the balances for each date on the following perpetual inventory cards. Add the items in the *In* column to the balance and subtract those in the *Out* column.

15.

Perpetual Inventory

Item: Mosaic Tileboard

Measurement: 38 mm x 89 mm

Date		In	Out	On Hand
December	3			1 653
	8		927	
	9	828	28	
	10		186	
	18	386	37	
	20		128	
	22		24	
	27	1 230	248	
	31		98	

16.

Perpetual Inventory

Item: Mosaic Tileboard

Measurement: 89 mm x 178 mm

Date		In	Out	On Hand
October	2			2 375
	5	892	125	
	12		68	
	15	795		
	19		165	
	21		283	
	28		28	
	30	745	268	
	31	950	383	

17. (i) Complete and balance the following semi-annual cafeteria report. Subtract the total monthly expenses from the total monthly receipts to find the profit.

(ii) On June 30, the cafeteria committee spent $4450 to build bleachers. How much money was left from the total profit after this expenditure? _____

	\multicolumn{5}{l	}{Receipts Week Ending Friday}	Total Monthly Receipts	Total Monthly Expenses	Profit
Month	1st Week	2nd Week	3rd Week	4th Week	5th Week			
Jan.	—	$4 291.65	$5 682.05	$6 091.20	$3 689.11		$17 360.11	
Feb.	$5 623.77	6 280.43	7 129.42	8 623.65	—		24 143.66	
March	7 621.43	6 891.03	5 269.57	6 143.21	—		23 320.19	
April	7 313.83	7 283.61	7 042.10	—	5 621.33		24 243.07	
May	6 125.78	6 893.44	6 725.23	5 129.64	—		17 651.34	
June	5 210.66	4 163.20	2 641.75	1 063.70	—		11 629.33	
Totals								

Elgin College

Cafeteria Receipts and Expenses for the period ended June 16, 19____

18. Bakker's Lumber purchased 1000 m of 50 mm by 100 mm lumber. These amounts were sold to customers: 18 m, 33 m, 9 m, 72 m, 51 m, 27 m, 105 m, and 36 m. How many metres of lumber were left? _____

19. King's Road Groceteria bought 500 kg of butter. During the week these amounts were sold: Monday, 35.5 kg; Tuesday, 82.5 kg; Wednesday, 40.75 kg; Thursday, 91.25 kg; Friday, 102.5 kg; Saturday, 125.75 kg. How many kilograms of butter were left at the end of the week? _____

20. K. Conrad has a charge account at a department store. At the end of September he owed $89.76. During October he bought goods for the following amounts and charged them to his account: $8.98, $3.79, $11.63, and $25.36. He paid the store $75 on October 14. What did he owe at the end of October? _____

CHAPTER 3

MULTIPLICATION

3·1 WARM UP ON BASICS

EXERCISE 1

Multiply.

1. $2 \times 2 =$ ___, $2 \times 7 =$ ___, $2 \times 5 =$ ___, $2 \times 4 =$ ___

2. $2 \times 8 =$ ___, $2 \times 3 =$ ___, $2 \times 6 =$ ___, $2 \times 9 =$ ___

3. $3 \times 6 =$ ___, $3 \times 5 =$ ___, $3 \times 4 =$ ___, $3 \times 9 =$ ___

4. $3 \times 7 =$ ___, $3 \times 8 =$ ___, $3 \times 3 =$ ___, $3 \times 10 =$ ___

5. $4 \times 5 =$ ___, $4 \times 7 =$ ___, $4 \times 4 =$ ___, $4 \times 8 =$ ___

6. $4 \times 6 =$ ___, $4 \times 9 =$ ___, $4 \times 10 =$ ___, $4 \times 11 =$ ___

7. $5 \times 7 =$ ___, $5 \times 8 =$ ___, $5 \times 5 =$ ___, $5 \times 6 =$ ___

8. $5 \times 9 =$ ___, $5 \times 11 =$ ___, $5 \times 10 =$ ___, $5 \times 12 =$ ___

9. $6 \times 8 =$ ___, $6 \times 9 =$ ___, $6 \times 6 =$ ___, $6 \times 7 =$ ___

10. $6 \times 12 =$ ___, $6 \times 11 =$ ___, $6 \times 10 =$ ___, $6 \times 3 =$ ___

11. $7 \times 7 =$ ___, $7 \times 8 =$ ___, $7 \times 9 =$ ___, $7 \times 6 =$ ___

12. $7 \times 5 =$ ___, $7 \times 10 =$ ___, $7 \times 11 =$ ___, $7 \times 12 =$ ___

13. $8 \times 8 =$ ___, $8 \times 9 =$ ___, $8 \times 4 =$ ___, $8 \times 7 =$ ___

14. $8 \times 3 =$ ___, $8 \times 10 =$ ___, $8 \times 11 =$ ___, $8 \times 12 =$ ___

15. $9 \times 9 =$ ___, $9 \times 7 =$ ___, $9 \times 3 =$ ___, $9 \times 6 =$ ___

16. $9 \times 4 =$ ___, $9 \times 10 =$ ___, $9 \times 11 =$ ___, $9 \times 12 =$ ___

EXERCISE 2

Multiply.

1. 64	**2.** 72	**3.** 49	**4.** 47	**5.** 86
$\underline{\times\ 3}$	$\underline{\times\ 4}$	$\underline{\times\ 6}$	$\underline{\times\ 8}$	$\underline{\times\ 7}$

6. 81	**7.** 37	**8.** 73	**9.** 59	**10.** 92
$\underline{\times\ 5}$	$\underline{\times\ 7}$	$\underline{\times\ 8}$	$\underline{\times\ 3}$	$\underline{\times\ 5}$

11. 86	**12.** 73	**13.** 95	**14.** 97	**15.** 98
6	8	7	8	9

MULTIPLICATION BY POWERS OF TEN
EXAMPLES
$512 \times 10 = 5120$

Take the zero of the 10 and add it to the right of 512 to give a product of 5120.

$512 \times 100 = 51\,200$

Take the *two* zeros of the 100 and add them to the right of 512 to give a product of 51 200.

$512 \times 1000 = 512\,000$

Take the *three* zeros of the 1000 and add them to the right of 512 to give a product of 512 000.

MULTIPLICATION BY MULTIPLES OF TEN
EXAMPLE
Multiply 3 by 5 to obtain 15.

$300 \times 50 = 15\,000$

Add the *two* zeros of 300 to the *one* zero of 50 to obtain *three* zeros.
Add these to the end of 15 to obtain 15 000.

EXERCISE 3

Calculate the products.

1. $311 \times 100 =$ _____
2. $47 \times 1000 =$ _____
3. $25 \times 10\,000 =$ _____

4. $250 \times 10 =$ _____
5. $500 \times 1000 =$ _____
6. $20 \times 70 =$ _____

7. $600 \times 30 =$ _____
8. $2000 \times 200 =$ _____
9. $80 \times 900 =$ _____

ESTIMATING PRODUCTS
EXAMPLE 1 Estimate the product of 21 and 89.

SOLUTION 21 lies between 20 and 30; it is closer to 20. This is called rounding off
89 lies between 80 and 90; it is closer to 90. to the nearest 10.
$20 \times 90 = 1800$

The estimated product of 21 and 89 is 1800.

EXAMPLE 2 How many digits will there be in the product of 527 and 392?

SOLUTION 527 lies between 500 and 600; it is closer to 500. ⎫ This is called rounding off
392 lies between 300 and 400; it is closer to 400. ⎭ to the nearest 100.
$500 \times 400 = 200\ 000$

There will be 6 digits in the product.

EXAMPLE 3 How many digits will there be in the product of 28 and 3297?

SOLUTION 28 lies between 20 and 30; it is closer to 30.
3297 lies between 3200 and 3300; it is closer to 3300.
$30 \times 3300 = 99\ 000$

There will be 5 digits in the product.

NOTE The estimating products examples shown above use a method called *rounding off*. You will use this method later in other work.

Rule

When estimating products, round off to give numbers easily multiplied in your head.

EXERCISE 4

Estimate the product and the number of digits in each.

1. 63×97 _____, ____

2. 122×398 _____, ____

3. 79×9 _____, ____

4. 32×867 _____, ____

5. 89×223 _____, ____

6. $19 \times 67\ 180$ _____, ____

7. 113×6230 _____, ____

8. 8976×2398 _____, ____

9. 460×1103 _____, ____

10. 42×2003 _____, ____

3·2 LONG MULTIPLICATION

EXAMPLE Multiply 2874 by 358.

SOLUTION

$$
\begin{array}{r}
2874 \\
358 \\
\hline
22992 \\
14370 \\
8622 \\
\hline
1028892
\end{array}
$$

22992 ⟶ 2874×8
14370 ⟶ 2874×5
8622 ⟶ 2874×3
Total ⟶ 1028892

EXERCISE 1

Calculate each product, using long multiplication.

1. $45 \times 32 =$ _____

2. $79 \times 48 =$ _____

3. $58 \times 59 =$ _____

4. $87 \times 24 =$ _____

5. $64 \times 58 =$ _____

6. $981 \times 34 =$ _____

7. $546 \times 23 =$ _____

8. $889 \times 85 =$ _____

9. $765 \times 42 =$ _____

10. $667 \times 37 =$ _____

11. $118 \times 143 =$ _____

12. $555 \times 177 =$ _____

13. $332 \times 320 =$ _____

14. $512 \times 398 =$ _____

15. $865 \times 617 =$ _____

16. $1872 \times 124 =$ _____

17. $2751 \times 240 =$ _____

18. $3019 \times 495 =$ _____

EXERCISE 2

1. Calculate the total length of each item. Multiply the number of pieces by the length in metres.

fashion textile limited
Receiving Ticket

Item: Cotton

October 21, 19--

Item No.	No. of pieces	No. of metres per piece	Total length in metres
183-A	109	29	
196-C	65	37	
207-A	123	31	
156-D	101	52	
247-E	105	42	
315-A	37	39	
212-D	117	47	
111-A	43	48	
302-C	62	55	
106-E	116	38	

2. Calculate the total mass of each shipment. Multiply the mass per case by the number of cases for each shipment.

Legassuc
Shipping
Company

Shipping Record   Date: October 19, 19--

Shipment No.	No. of Cases	Mass (in kg) per Case	Total Mass (in kg)
501	83	175	
502	68	224	
503	165	89	
504	285	43	
505	96	149	
506	429	31	
507	117	103	
508	513	27	

3. For each machine, multiply the number of hours in production by the parts produced per hour to obtain the total parts produced. The total parts produced per period is obtained by totalling the amounts in the final column.

WORTMANN MANUFACTURING COMPANY LIMITED

Production Record   Period: Oct. 1 to Nov. 1

Machine	Hours in Production	Parts Produced Per Hour	Total Parts Produced
#12	272	1 373	
#14	357	987	
#16	403	1 076	
#20	297	936	
#24	426	1 132	
#28	398	1 262	
Total Parts Produced For Period:			

4. Judy drives a car that averages 9 kilometres per litre of gas. If the gas tank of her car holds 65 L of gas, how far can Judy travel on a full tank? _____

5. Bob can package 36 parcels in one hour. How many parcels can he package in a week of 45 working hours? _____

6. On a map, 1 cm represents 45 km. How many kilometres apart are two cities if they are 32 cm apart on the map? _____

7. If an airplane can average 1160 km/h, how far can it fly in 13 h? _____

8. On a long trip, Jim can travel an average of 75 km/h. He kept a record of how many hours he travelled each day: day 1, 6 h; day 2, 7 h; day 3, 9 h; day 4, 5 h; day 5, 8 h. How far did Jim travel? _____

3·3 DECIMAL QUANTITIES IN MULTIPLICATION

EXAMPLE   Multiply 1.67 by 2.3.

SOLUTION
$$
\begin{array}{r}
1.67 \\
2.3 \\
\hline
501 \\
334 \\
\hline
3841
\end{array}
$$

$501 \longrightarrow 167 \times 3$

$334 \longrightarrow 167 \times 2$

- Count the total number of places after the decimal in the two numbers.
  2.3 (1 place)
  1.67 (2 places)
  Total: 3 places
- Place the decimal point 3 places to the left of the last digit in the product: 3.841
- The product: 3.841

EXERCISE 1 _____

Calculate each product.

1. $124 \times 1.25 = $ _____

2. $367 \times 0.75 = $ _____

3. $25.7 \times 3.5 = $ _____

4. $33.9 \times 5.25 = $ _____

5. $124.7 \times 1.09 = $ _____

6. $32.33 \times 2.8 = $ _____

7. $51.14 \times 6.26 = $ _____

8. $25.79 \times 0.36 = $ _____

9. $279.87 \times 0.72 = $ _____

10. $138 \times 1.125 = $ _____

11. $256.3 \times 0.354 = $ _____

12. $429.7 \times 1.076 = $ _____

13. $1286.3 \times 2.114 = $ _____

14. $335.12 \times 1.397 = $ _____

15. $12.33 \times 2.056 =$ _____

16. $25.67 \times 32.509 =$ _____

17. $136.59 \times 17.818 =$ _____

18. $27.636 \times 4.077 =$ _____

19. $14.939 \times 2.763 =$ _____

20. $223.125 \times 26.617 =$ _____

ROUNDING OFF DECIMALS

In most practical multiplication problems involving numbers containing decimal quantities, only an indicated number of decimal places is required in the product. Your answer should then contain only the required number of places after the decimal. Any digits after these should be dropped. This is called *rounding off* the answer.

EXAMPLE   Multiply 3.25 by 1.125. Round off the product correct to two places after the decimal.

SOLUTION $3.25 \times 1.125 = 3.656\ 25$ Multiply using the method of the previous example.

$\qquad\qquad\qquad\ = 3.66$ Round off to two places after the decimal.

Rule

- If the first digit after the number of decimal places asked for is 4 or smaller, drop this digit and all digits following.
- If the first digit after the number of decimal places asked for is 5 or larger, drop this digit and all digits following, but add 1 to the last digit retained.

EXERCISE 2 _____

Multiply. Round off the products correct to two places after the decimal.

1. $32.7 \times 2.27 =$ _____

2. $15.6 \times 7.14 =$ _____

3. $5.73 \times 6.7 =$ _____

4. $20.39 \times 4.66 =$ _____

5. $3.27 \times 1.732 =$ _____

6. $5.61 \times 2.333 =$ _____

7. $21.76 \times 17.87 =$ _____

8. $36.98 \times 22.73 =$ _____

9. $7.667 \times 5.954 =$ _____

10. $8.015 \times 3.703 =$ _____

Multiply. Round off the products correct to three places after the decimal.

11. $12.15 \times 3.25 =$ _____

12. $27.99 \times 8.76 =$ _____

13. $32.68 \times 5.96 =$ _____

14. $51.09 \times 0.32 =$ _____

15. $123.7 \times 0.595 =$ _____

16. $22.76 \times 1.498 =$ _____

17. $5.043 \times 1.992 =$ _____

18. $0.367 \times 0.115 =$ _____

19. $1.732 \times 0.999 =$ _____

20. $2.004 \times 5.1 =$ _____

MULTIPLICATION BY POWERS OF 10
EXAMPLES

$67.894 \times 10 = 678.94$

There is *one* zero in the multiplier.
Move the decimal point *one* place to the right.

$3.562\ 91 \times 100 = 356.291$

There are *two* zeros in the multiplier.
Move the decimal point *two* places to the right.

$0.962\ 115 \times 1000 = 962.115$

There are *three* zeros in the multiplier.
Move the decimal point *three* places to the right.

Rule

When you multiply by 10, 100, 1000, etc., count the number of zeros in the multiplier and move the decimal point that number of places to the *right* in the number that is being multiplied. When you have done this you have obtained the product.

MULTIPLICATION BY MULTIPLES OF 10
EXAMPLE

$519.642 \times 300 = 155\ 892.6$

Move the decimal
point *two* places
to the right to
obtain 51 964.2. ⟶ Multiply 51 964.2 by 3.

EXERCISE 3

Calculate the products.

1. $27.995 \times 10 =$ _____

2. $27.995 \times 100 =$ _____

3. $27.995 \times 1000 =$ _____

4. $1.768\ 956 \times 1\ 000\ 000 =$ _____

5. $36.748 \times 20 =$ _____

6. $36.748 \times 2000 =$ _____

7. $1.665 \times 30 =$ _____

8. $21.19 \times 400 =$ _____

9. $18.765 \times 5000 =$ _____

10. $9.874 \times 60 =$ _____

MULTIPLICATION BY 0.1, 0.01, 0.001, ETC.
EXAMPLES
$31.72 \times 0.1 = 3.172$

The first digit in the multiplier occurs in the *first* place after the decimal point. Move the decimal point *one* place to the *left*.

$563.119 \times 0.01 = 5.631\ 19$

The first digit in the multiplier occurs in the *second* place after the decimal point. Move the decimal point *two* places to the *left*.

$92\ 376.55 \times 0.001 = 92.376\ 55$

The first digit in the multiplier occurs in the *third* place after the decimal point. Move the decimal point *three* places to the *left*.

Rule

When you multiply by 0.1, 0.01, 0.001, etc., determine in which place after the decimal point the first digit of the multiplier occurs. Move the decimal point that number of places to the *left* in the number that is being multiplied. When you have done this you have obtained the product.

MULTIPLICATION BY MULTIPLES OF 0.1, 0.01, 0.001, ETC.
EXAMPLE
$133.617 \times 0.04 = 5.344\ 68$

Move the decimal point *two* places to the *left* to obtain 1.336 17. ⟶ Multiply 1.336 17 by 4.

EXERCISE 4

Calculate the products.

1. $536.78 \times 0.01 =$ _____

2. $536.78 \times 0.1 =$ _____

3. $7895.1 \times 0.001 =$ _____

4. $55.3 \times 0.1 =$ _____

5. $44\ 563.26 \times 0.0001 =$ _____

6. $27.6 \times 0.2 =$ _____

7. $375 \times 0.02 =$ _____

8. $23\ 450.1 \times 0.04 =$ _____

9. $317.25 \times 0.005 =$ _____

10. $3475 \times 0.06 =$ _____

EXERCISE 5

Extend the following summaries. Multiply each quantity ordered by the list price per unit to obtain the total cost.

1.

**Williams
Department
Store**

Summary of Merchandise Ordered

Dept.: _Silverware_   Date: _Nov. 7, 19—_

Stock No.	Quantity Ordered	List Price Per Unit	Total Cost
G816S	12	$23.25	$
G819S	8	24.96	
G823S	16	24.56	
G827S	9	39.96	
G832S	15	7.96	
G835S	21	9.49	
G837S	17	18.46	
G841S	24	13.45	

When calculating cost or price, always round off to the nearest cent.

2.

**Williams
Department
Store**

Summary of Merchandise Ordered

Dept.: _Glassware_   Date: _Nov. 7, 19—_

Stock No.	Quantity Ordered	List Price Per Unit	Total Cost
G915R	8	$ 18.46	$
G920R	15	11.40	
G923R	7	23.76	
G927R	18	12.46	
G929R	22	8.99	
G931R	26	8.50	
G932R	12	16.96	
G936R	25	9.00	

3.

**Williams
Department
Store**

Summary of Merchandise Ordered

Dept.: *Bar Accessories*   Date: *Nov. 7, 19—*

Stock No.	Quantity Ordered	List Price Per Unit	Total Cost
H 291 Q	15	$ 7.97	$
H 292 Q	25	4.86	
H 293 Q	35	2.96	
H 294 Q	36	3.40	
H 295 Q	24	5.45	
H 296 Q	12	14.48	
H 297 Q	5	13.49	
H 298 Q	10	10.98	

Extend and total the following inventory cards.
- Multiply the number of square metres by the price per square metre to find the total price.
- Total the columns showing the number of square metres and the total price to find the total number of square metres in the inventory and the total value of the inventory.

4.

FURNITURE • **Jack's** • RUGS

Inventory   SALES OUTLET   Date: Nov. 10, 19--

No. of Square Metres	Description	Price per Square Metre	Total Price
13.5	C72-No. 1 nylon pile red	$7.99	$
18.7	C72-No. 1 nylon pile off-white	7.99	
20.5	C72-No. 2 nylon pile brown	8.99	
22.5	C72-No. 2 nylon pile avocado	8.99	
15.6	C72-No. 8 nylon triple tone	7.19	
Totals			$

5.

FURNITURE • JaCKs • RUGS

| Inventory | | SALES OUTLET | Date: Nov. 10, 19--. |

No. of Square Metres	Description	Price per Square Metre	Total Price
12.8	C73-M01 nylon shag, gold	$18.95	$
15.6	C73-M02 nylon shag, burnt orange	17.95	
9.5	C73-M05 nylon shag, pumpkin	18.50	
16.2	C73-M07 nylon shag, beige/white	17.69	
20.5	C73-M08 nylon shag, rust	19.95	
Totals			$

6.

FURNITURE • JaCKs • RUGS

| Inventory | | SALES OUTLET | Date: Nov. 10, 19--. |

No. of Square Metres	Description	Price per Square Metre	Total Price
12.5	W72-P03 vinyl flooring	$3.69	$
15.5	W72-P12 vinyl flooring	3.98	
18.5	W72-P17 vinyl flooring	4.19	
20.5	W72-P21 vinyl flooring	4.39	
25.5	W72-P25 vinyl flooring	4.69	
Totals			$

Complete the following reports to find the total value of the stock withdrawn.
- Total to find the number of units of each item withdrawn during the week.
- Multiply the total units withdrawn by the unit price to find the cost of stock withdrawn. Round off your answers to the nearest cent (correct to two places after the decimal).
- Total the *Cost of Stock Withdrawn* column to calculate the total cost of stock withdrawn.

7.

KLAGES
MANUFACTURING CO. LTD.
Chatham, N.B.
Stock Depletion Report
Week Ending November 10, 19--

Item No.	No. of Units Withdrawn						Total Units Withdrawn	Unit Price	Cost of Stock Withdrawn
	Mon.	Tues.	Wed.	Thurs.	Fri.	Sat.			
161-B	12.5		5.25	10.125		6.25		$0.755	
211-C	165	20.5	67.75	52.5	174			0.385	
232-A	20.75	57		32.25		18.125		0.155	
305-B	51.5	30.375	76		22.75	55.5		0.315	
319-A	8.25	10.5	9.75	11.125	6.25	8.5		0.925	
325-C	132	150	75.75	25.5	50.125	1.75		0.025	
					Total Cost of Stock Withdrawn				

8.

KLAGES
MANUFACTURING CO. LTD.
Chatham, N.B.
Stock Depletion Report
Week Ending November 17, 19--

Item No.	No. of Units Withdrawn						Total Units Withdrawn	Unit Price	Cost of Stock Withdrawn
	Mon.	Tues.	Wed.	Thurs.	Fri.	Sat.			
161B	16.75	8.125	11.5	15		9.25		$0.755	
211C		36.75	72.5	80.125	82.5	91.5		0.385	
232A	25.125	30.75	37.5	29.25	30.375	35.5		0.155	
305B	49.5	50.25	56.125		45.25	52.5		0.315	
319A	10.125	9.5		8.175	11.25	12.375		0.925	
325C	156	172.5	89.75		105.375	115		0.025	
					Total Cost of Stock Withdrawn				

9.

	KLAGES								

MANUFACTURING CO. LTD.

Chatham, N.B.

Stock Depletion Report

Week Ending November 24, 19--

Item No.	No. of Units Withdrawn						Total Units Withdrawn	Unit Price	Cost of Stock Withdrawn
	Mon.	Tues.	Wed.	Thurs.	Fri.	Sat.			
161B	15.125	9.75	11.25	10.5	8.75			$0.755	
211C		75.375	81.25	85.5	76.75	71.125		0.385	
232A	30.375	31	29.5	29.5	32.125	25.75		0.155	
305B	52.75	60.5		59.5	55.375	50.5		0.315	
319A	11.5		9.75	12.125	10.75	10.395		0.925	
325C	132.5	101.75		152.25	95.625	161		0.025	
					Total Cost of Stock Withdrawn				

10. A sporting goods store bought 18 pairs of hockey skates for $51.50 a pair and sold them for $71.95 a pair. Calculate the profit. _____

11. Jason stopped at a service station and filled the tank of his car with gasoline. It took 41.5 L of gasoline to fill the tank. If gasoline is priced at 49.5¢/L, how much did Jason have to pay? _____

12. J. Jackson, a building contractor, was declared bankrupt. His creditors are paid 52.3¢ on the dollar. If Jackson owed you $1219.76, how much would you receive?

_____

EXERCISE 6

Calculate the total price for each item on the following shipping orders.
(Total Price = No. of Pieces × Length per Piece × Price per Metre)

1.

BUILDING SUPPLIES LTD.
ROCKVILLE, ONTARIO
Sold to: Ms. Jan Kalte

Date Ordered	Salesman	Terms Net 30 Days	Invoice and Shipping Date:		
No. of Pieces	**Length per Piece**	**Description**		**Price per Metre**	**Total Price**
26	2.4 m	38 mm × 89 mm spruce		$0.36	
89	3.0 m	38 mm × 89 mm spruce		0.36	
263	2.4 m	38 mm × 140 mm spruce		0.69	
58	4.8 m	38 mm × 184 mm spruce		1.05	
179	4.8 m	38 mm × 235 mm spruce		1.38	

Shipper's Copy

2.

BUILDING SUPPLIES LTD.
ROCKVILLE, ONTARIO
Sold to: Mr. John Rupp

Date Ordered	Salesman	Terms Net 30 Days	Invoice and Shipping Date:		
No. of Pieces	**Length per Piece**	**Description**		**Price per Metre**	**Total Price**
35	2.4 m	38 mm × 89 mm spruce		$0.36	
76	3.0 m	38 mm × 89 mm spruce		0.36	
293	2.4 m	38 mm × 140 mm spruce		0.69	
127	3.0 m	38 mm × 140 mm spruce		0.69	
64	4.8 m	38 mm × 184 mm spruce		1.05	
151	4.8 m	38 mm × 235 mm spruce		1,38	

Shipper's Copy

For the following statements of pay:
- Calculate the regular earnings by multiplying regular hours × hour rate.
- Calculate the overtime earnings by multiplying overtime hours × hour rate × 1.5.
  (Employees are usually paid *time and one half* for overtime work.)
- Calculate the gross earnings by totalling the regular earnings and the overtime earnings.

3.

| Total Hours | | Hour Rate | Earnings | | Gross Earnings |
Regular	Overtime		Regular	Overtime	
40	7	6.95			

4.

| Total Hours | | Hour Rate | Earnings | | Gross Earnings |
Regular	Overtime		Regular	Overtime	
40	3	4.87			

5.

| Total Hours | | Hour Rate | Earnings | | Gross Earnings |
Regular	Overtime		Regular	Overtime	
40	8	7.29			

6.

| Total Hours | | Hour Rate | Earnings | | Gross Earnings |
Regular	Overtime		Regular	Overtime	
40	5	6.27			

7.

| Total Hours | | Hour Rate | Earnings | | Gross Earnings |
Regular	Overtime		Regular	Overtime	
40	6	5.38			

8.

| Total Hours | | Hour Rate | Earnings | | Gross Earnings |
Regular	Overtime		Regular	Overtime	
40	4	4.57			

For the following payrolls:
- Calculate the total hours worked.
- Multiply the total hours by the hourly rate to obtain the gross pay.

9.

Employee	Hours					Total Hours	Hourly Rate	Gross Pay
	Mon.	Tues.	Wed.	Thurs.	Fri.			
M. Ard	8	7.5	8	7.5	8		5.25	
G. Botz	7	8.5	8.5	7	8		4.25	
K. Doucette	8	6	8.75	8.75	8		5.35	
S. Gould	8	7.5	7.5	7.5	8		4.25	
A. Hill	7.5	8	8	8	8		5.75	
R. Eder	7.5	7.5	7.5	7.5	8		4.75	
C. McGregor	8	8	6	8	8		5.25	
B. Moyse	7	8.5	6	8.5	8		4.85	
J. Potci	8	8.5	7	8.5	8		5.50	
R. Simon	7	8.5	8.5	8	8		4.25	

10.

Employee	Hours					Total Hours	Hourly Rate	Gross Pay
	Mon.	Tues.	Wed.	Thurs.	Fri.			
M. Ard	8	8	8	8	7		5.25	
G. Botz	7	7.5	7.5	7.5	8		4.25	
K. Doucette	7.5	8.5	7	8	8		5.35	
S. Gould	8	7	8	8	8		4.25	
A. Hill	8	8	4	8	8		5.75	
R. Eder	8	6	8	6.5	8		4.75	
C. McGregor	7.5	7.5	7	7	8		5.25	
B. Moyse	8	8	4.5	8	8		4.85	
J. Potci	8	8	8	7	5.5		5.50	
R. Simon	7.5	7.5	7.5	7.5	8		4.25	

For the following payrolls:
- Calculate the total number of parts produced by each employee.
- Multiply the total parts by the piece rate to obtain the gross pay.
- Total the *Gross Pay* column to obtain the total gross pay.

11.

Payroll Record

Week Ending Nov. 18/--

SELDON MANUFACTURING COMPANY

Employee	No. Parts Daily					Total Parts	Piece Rate	Gross Pay
	Mon.	Tues.	Wed.	Thurs.	Fri.			
Bleich, John	128	132	125	131	136		$0.24	
Catto, Henry	63	65	67	63	67		0.49	
Gibbons, Carol	251	237	256	253	255		0.11	
Hahn, Jim	31	31	39	35	36		1.09	
Louks, Hal	256	259	261	267	269		0.125	
Plourde, Jean	35	39	41	39	39		1.11	
Skine, Tim	133	127	131	126	125		0.235	
Tesck, John	61	60	59	61	62		0.455	
							Total Pay	

12.

Payroll Record

Week Ending Nov. 25/--

SELDON MANUFACTURING COMPANY

Employee	No. Parts Daily					Total Parts	Piece Rate	Gross Pay
	Mon.	Tues.	Wed.	Thurs.	Fri.			
Bleich, John	132	133	131	132	135		$0.245	
Catto, Henry	63	66	63	65	65		0.49	
Gibbons, Carol	253	251	249	253	255		0.115	
Hahn, Jim	32	35	35	39	40		1.095	
Louks, Hal	257	259	260	269	269		0.125	
Plourde, Jean	35	40	41	40	40		1.11	
Skine, Tim	130	129	130	125	125		0.235	
Tesck, John	62	63	65	62	65		0.47	
							Total Pay	

Extend and total the following invoices.
- Multiply the quantity (number of units) by the price (price per unit) to obtain the amount.
- Total the amount column to obtain the total cost.

13.

TOGS	Children's clothing Country Mall Victoria, B.C.			Notre Numero Our Number		5955

Vendu à
Sold to .... Date ....

Adresse
Address...

.... via ....

Comm du Client Customer's Order	: Vendeur : Salesman	*Jd* : Conditions : Terms	*Cash* :FAB :FOB		
Qty.	**Description**		**Price**		**Amount**
2	Jeans size 10		$ 10	95	
2	Cords size 10		11	95	
3	Shirts size 10		5	95	
6 pr.	Boy's Socks		1	29	
			Total		

14.

	Baker Meats Wholesale—Retail Paris, Ontario		Notre Numero Our Number 45954		

Date *Nov. 3/—*

Mr. John A. Schmidt, 1010 Tenth St. E., Owen Sound, Ont. N4K 1T6

Qty.	**Description**		**Price**		**Amount**
1.5 kg	rib roast		$ 4	06	
0.75 kg	sausage		2	14	
2.5 kg	ham		4	79	
0.5 kg	bacon		4	29	
0.5 kg	stewing beef		1	89	
0.75 kg	ground chuck		2	39	
			Total	$	

15.

nursery gardens
R.R. #4 Brockville, Ontario

Name...

Address...

.........................Date.........

Qty.	Description	Price	
3	Boston Ivy	$ 2.59	
5	Pkg. Veg. Seeds	0.52	
0.25 kg	Corn Seed	8.36	
0.25 kg	Carrot Seed	16.49	
9	Boxed Veg. Plants	0.69	
		Total	

16.

JAMES DELICATESSEN

Name...

Address...

.........................Date.........

Qty.	Description	Price	Amount
0.25 kg	Sliced Chicken Lf.	$ 3.19	
0.25 kg	Pastrami, sliced	3.49	
0.5 kg	Potato salad	1.09	
0.5 kg	Bean salad	1.19	
1	Black Forest Cake	4.75	
3	Bottles Pop	0.49	
		Total	

17.

groceries ⋅ HUBBARD'S CUPBOARD ⋅ meat ⋅ 392 7681

Name...... Smith ....   Date...... November 15 ...19......

Address..... 392 First Street .....

Qty.	Description	Price	Amount
3	Cans Soup, per can	$ 0.25	
2	Cans Tomatoes, per can	0.35	
3	Cans Mixed Vegs., per can	0.34	
4	Cans Mushrooms, per can	0.59	
6	Cans Spaghetti, per can	0.61	
3 kg	Flour, per kilogram	0.38	
		Total	

18.

```
           ✦ groceries ✦  HUBBARD'S  ✦ meat ✦ 392 7681
                            CUPBOARD

Name.... Kastner ................  Date...... November 15 .19 ....
Address.... 18 Alpha Street
```

Qty.	Description	Price	Amount
7	Cans Salmon, per can	$ 1.17	
2.5 kg	Round Steak, per kilogram	2.27	
1.5 kg	Butter, per kilogram	2.46	
3 btls.	Ketchup, per bottle	1.07	
2 pkgs.	Cereal, per package	0.89	
1.6 kg	Peaches, per kilogram	1.13	
		Total	

3·4 REVIEW

EXERCISE

Multiply.

1. $13 \times 17 =$ _____

2. $47 \times 43 =$ _____

3. $62 \times 68 =$ _____

4. $52 \times 45 =$ _____

5. $38 \times 53 =$ _____

6. $203 \times 98 =$ _____

7. $92 \times 96 =$ _____

8. $102 \times 105 =$ _____

Calculate the products. Do not round off.

9. $237 \times 85 =$ _____

10. $487 \times 185 =$ _____

11. $1764 \times 356 =$ _____

12. $89.7 \times 5.5 =$ _____

13. $15.6 \times 12.73 =$ _____

14. $32.4 \times 8.97 =$ _____

15. $123.67 \times 3.35 =$ _____

16. $285.61 \times 11.78 =$ _____

Multiply. Round off each product correct to three places after the decimal.

17. $19.65 \times 8.35 =$ _____

18. $12.17 \times 9.91 =$ _____

19. $8.48 \times 1.366 =$ _____

20. $3.72 \times 0.765 =$ _____

21. $29.14 \times 0.098 =$ _____

22. $1.686 \times 2.754 =$ _____

23. $8.471 \times 0.132 =$ _____

24. $15.6 \times 1.1732 =$ _____

25. $9.37 \times 0.9999 =$ _____

26. $0.54 \times 0.5616 =$ _____

Complete the following orders.

27.

Delivery Order

WAREHOUSE & COLD STORAGE COMPANY
Halifax Nova Scotia

No. Packages	Description		Mass
24	Dinner Ham	@ 3 kg/package	
32	Smoked Ham	@ 5 kg/package	
56	Smoked Cod	@ 12 kg/package	
42	Cod Fillets	@ 23 kg/package	
33	Haddock Fillets	@ 25 kg/package	
27	Boston Blue Fish	@ 22 kg/package	
35	Lamb Legs	@ 18 kg/package	
21	Beef Liver	@ 15 kg/package	
38	Chicken Legs	@ 11 kg/package	
51	Chicken Wings	@ 17 kg/package	
		Total Mass	

Received the Above in Good Order by: .... *Art Giordi* ....

28.

```
≈≈≈≈≈≈≈≈≈≈≈≈≈≈≈≈≈≈≈≈≈≈≈≈≈≈≈≈≈≈≈≈≈
```
ROSS & COMPANY LIMITED
```
≈≈≈≈≈≈≈≈≈≈≈≈≈≈≈≈≈≈≈≈≈≈≈≈≈≈≈≈≈≈≈≈≈
```

Box 612, St. John

New Brunswick E2K 1X3

Sold to: R. McArthur 115 — 6th St. E.

Date of Order	Order No.	Terms:Net 15 Days 2% per Month on Overdue Accounts		Invoice No.	
No. Ordered	**Description**			**Price**	**Amount**
4	Prs. Knee High Hose			$ 0.63/pr	
6	Prs. Mens' Socks			1.19/pr	
5.5 m	Double Knit Fabric			3.89/m	
1	Blanket			11.66	
2	Pouches ink crayons			1.33	
2	Fluorescent desk lamps			12.97	
5	Packages of exercise books			0.88	
3.25 m	Broadcloth Fabric			1.03/m	
			Sub Total		
			Prov. Tax		$ 6.04
			Pay This Amount ☞		

For the following cost sheets
- Subtract the ending balance from the beginning balance to obtain the quantity used.
- Multiply the quantity used by the item price to obtain the cost of items used.
- Calculate the cost of each job by totalling the *Cost of Items Used* column.

29.

WM WOODBRIDGE MANUFACTURING LTD.

Cost of Material Used for Jobs __37, 38__

Job No.	Item Stock No.	Beginning Balance	Ending Balance	Quantity Used	Item Price	Cost of Items Used
	26A	1 532	1 386		$ 1.37	$
	37C	876	459		0.27	
37	56B	1 869	1 135		0.13	
	24C	376	354		2.10	
	33A	1 245	984		0.58	
					Cost of Job 37	$
	37A	763	729		2.38	
	21B	1 998	1 427		0.35	
38	52C	854	713		1.09	
	29A	1 267	985		0.30	
	49C	546	384		0.92	
					Cost of Job 38	$

30.

WM WOODBRIDGE MANUFACTURING LTD.

Cost of Material Used for Jobs _39, 40_

Job No.	Item Stock No.	Beginning Balance	Ending Balance	Quantity Used	Item Price	Cost of Items Used
39	36 B	917	836		1.73	
	18 A	1 311	972		0.34	
	27 B	818	514		0.42	
	31 A	1 721	1 294		0.09	
	32 C	475	418		2.52	
				Cost of Job 39		$
40	44 C	1 876	1 516		1.18	
	39 A	397	318		2.23	
	17 C	1 235	876		0.14	
	21 A	643	371		0.47	
	45 B	1 811	1 231		0.07	
				Cost of Job 40		$

31. Complete the following payroll record.
- Calculate the total number of parts produced by each employee.
- Multiply the total parts by the piece rate to obtain the gross pay.
- Total the *Gross Pay* column to obtain the total gross pay.

Payroll Record

Wk. Ending 12/9/--

SELDON MANUFACTURING COMPANY

Employee	No. Parts Daily					Total Parts	Piece Rate	Gross Pay
	Mon.	Tues.	Wed.	Thurs.	Fri.			
Bleich, John	127	133	126	130	137		$0.245	
Catto, Henry	64	65	62	64	64		0.49	
Gibbons, Carol	255	253	248	254	256		0.115	
Hahn, Jim	34	36	36	40	41		1.095	
Louks, Hal	260	261	258	263	265		0.125	
Plourde, Jean	36	42	42	41	41		1.115	
Skine, Tim	131	130	126	126	130		0.235	
Tesck, John	65	65	64	65	56		0.475	
						Total Pay		

CHAPTER 4

DIVISION

4·1 WARM UP ON BASICS

EXERCISE 1

Divide.

1. $6 \div 2 =$ ___, $12 \div 3 =$ ___, $21 \div 3 =$ ___, $18 \div 2 =$ ___

2. $16 \div 8 =$ ___, $15 \div 3 =$ ___, $20 \div 4 =$ ___, $24 \div 4 =$ ___

3. $40 \div 5 =$ ___, $35 \div 5 =$ ___, $30 \div 6 =$ ___, $42 \div 6 =$ ___

4. $40 \div 8 =$ ___, $35 \div 7 =$ ___, $28 \div 7 =$ ___, $56 \div 8 =$ ___

5. $63 \div 9 =$ ___, $72 \div 8 =$ ___, $54 \div 9 =$ ___, $81 \div 9 =$ ___

6. $144 \div 12 =$ ___, $96 \div 8 =$ ___, $60 \div 12 =$ ___, $108 \div 12 =$ ___

EXERCISE 2

Divide by short division.

1. $\dfrac{2632}{2} =$ _____

2. $\dfrac{3702}{3} =$ _____

3. $\dfrac{6416}{4} =$ _____

4. $\dfrac{1895}{5} =$ _____

5. $\dfrac{3414}{6} =$ _____

6. $\dfrac{6216}{7} =$ _____

7. $\dfrac{2776}{8} =$ _____

8. $\dfrac{6372}{9} =$ _____

9. $\dfrac{3784}{11} =$ _____

4·2 DIVISION OF WHOLE NUMBERS

EXAMPLE   Divide 1288 by 28.

SOLUTION

$$
\begin{array}{r}
46 \\
28\overline{)1288} \\
112 \\
\hline
168 \\
168 \\
\hline
000
\end{array}
$$

$112 \longrightarrow 28 \times 4$

$168 \longrightarrow 28 \times 6$

$$1288 \div 28 = 46$$

EXERCISE 1

Calculate the quotients.

1. $180 \div 15 =$ _____
2. $900 \div 36 =$ _____
3. $2553 \div 69 =$ _____
4. $3784 \div 44 =$ _____
5. $7398 \div 137 =$ _____

6. $20\,046 \div 78 =$ _____
7. $78\,408 \div 132 =$ _____
8. $345\,345 \div 805 =$ _____
9. $786\,016 \div 1276 =$ _____
10. $4\,584\,712 \div 7864 =$ _____

DIVISION WITH DECIMALS IN THE QUOTIENT

EXAMPLE   Divide 2367 by 39. Obtain the quotient correct to two places after the decimal.

SOLUTION   Step 1 $39\overline{)2367.000}$

Step 2
$$
\begin{array}{r}
60.692 \\
39\overline{)2367.000}
\end{array}
$$

$\underline{234} \longrightarrow 39 \times 6$

270 39 is larger than 27, bring down 0.

$\underline{234} \longrightarrow 39 \times 6$

360

$\underline{351} \longrightarrow 39 \times 9$

90

$\underline{78} \longrightarrow 39 \times 2$

$2367 \div 39 = 60.69$

EXERCISE 2

Calculate the quotients correct to two places after the decimal.

1. $5678 \div 40 =$ _____
2. $379 \div 41 =$ _____
3. $18\,672 \div 984 =$ _____
4. $17\,651 \div 556 =$ _____

5. $456\,897 \div 112 =$ _____
6. $23\,496 \div 231 =$ _____
7. $47\,324 \div 347 =$ _____
8. $593\,241 \div 213 =$ _____

4·3 DIVISION OF DECIMAL QUANTITIES

EXAMPLE   Divide 36.978 by 2.2. Obtain the quotient correct to two places after the decimal.

SOLUTION   Step 1 $2.2\overline{)36.978}$ Move the decimal point in the divisor to the *end* of the divisor. Count the number of places it was moved.

Step 2 $22\overline{)369.78}$ Move the decimal point in the dividend the *same* number of places to the right. Place a decimal point above this point in the space left for the quotient.

Step 3
$$
\begin{array}{r}
16.808 \\
22\overline{)369.780} \\
\underline{22} \\
149 \\
\underline{132} \\
177 \\
\underline{176} \\
180 \\
\underline{176} \\
\end{array}
$$
Using long division, calculate the quotient until three places after the decimal have been obtained.

Round off the quotient correct to two places after the decimal.
36.978 ÷ 2.2 = 16.81

EXERCISE 1 _____

Calculate the quotients correct to two places after the decimal.

1. 4678 ÷ 50 = _____

2. 18 672 ÷ 984 = _____

3. 5.395 ÷ 7.64 = _____

4. 1.976 ÷ 13.33 = _____

5. 48.19 ÷ 18.67 = _____

6. 89.81 ÷ 27.2 = _____

7. 6.75 ÷ 10.18 = _____

8. 4.707 ÷ 0.166 = _____

9. 0.5892 ÷ 0.37 = _____

10. 2.3656 ÷ 9.41 = _____

Calculate the quotients correct to three places after the decimal.

11. 379 ÷ 41 = _____

12. 17 651 ÷ 556 = _____

13. 23.5 ÷ 17.18 = _____

14. 123.6 ÷ 5.964 = _____

15. 15.9 ÷ 0.98 = _____

16. 36.14 ÷ 0.517 = _____

17. 5.113 ÷ 10.9 = _____

18. 90.37 ÷ 148 = _____

19. 0.598 ÷ 0.164 = _____

20. 1.3723 ÷ 2.11 = _____

DIVISION BY POWERS OF 10
EXAMPLES

$319.2 \div 10 = 31.92$

There is *one* zero in the divisor.
Move the decimal point *one* place to the *left*.

$319.2 \div 100 = 3.192$

There are *two* zeros in the divisor.
Move the decimal point *two* places to the *left*.

$319.2 \div 1000 = 0.3192$

There are *three* zeros in the divisor.
Move the decimal point *three* places to the *left*.

Rule

When you divide by 10, 100, 1000, etc., count the number of zeros in the divisor and move the decimal point that number of places to the *left* in the dividend. When you have done this, you have obtained the quotient.

DIVISION BY MULTIPLES OF 10
EXAMPLE

$3172.6 \div 200 = 15.863$

Move the decimal
point *two* places
to the left to
obtain 31.726. ⟶ Divide 31.726 by 2.

EXERCISE 2

Calculate the quotients.

1. $213.7 \div 10 =$ _____

2. $213.7 \div 100 =$ _____

3. $213.7 \div 1000 =$ _____

4. $48.6 \div 20 =$ _____

5. $48.6 \div 200 =$ _____

6. $4676.5 \div 500 =$ _____

7. $5.65 \div 500 =$ _____

8. $372.6 \div 60 =$ _____

9. $101.5 \div 700 =$ _____

10. $2943 \div 900 =$ _____

DIVISION BY 0.1, 0.01, 0.001, ETC.

EXAMPLES

$5.3162 \div 0.1 = 53.162$

The first digit in the divisor occurs in the *first* place after the decimal point. Move the decimal point *one* place to the right.

$5.3162 \div 0.01 = 531.62$

The first digit in the divisor occurs in the *second* place after the decimal point. Move the decimal point *two* places to the right.

$5.3162 \div 0.001 = 5316.2$

The first digit in the divisor occurs in the *third* place after the decimal point. Move the decimal point *three* places to the right.

Rule

When you divide by 0.1, 0.01, 0.001, etc., determine in which place after the decimal point the first digit of the divisor occurs. Move the decimal point that number of places to the *right* in the dividend. When you have done this, you have obtained the quotient.

DIVISION BY MULTIPLES OF 0.1, 0.01, 0.001, ETC.

EXAMPLE

$2.048 \div 0.04 = 51.2$

Move the decimal point *two* places to the *right* to obtain 204.8. ⟶ Divide 204.8 by 4.

EXERCISE 3

Calculate the quotients.

1. $1.732 \div 0.1 =$ _____

2. $1.732 \div 0.01 =$ _____

3. $1.732 \div 0.001 =$ _____

4. $52.36 \div 0.1 =$ _____

5. $0.7654 \div 0.001 =$ _____

6. $5.3376 \div 0.01 =$ _____

7. $2.482 \div 0.02 =$ _____

8. $2.388 \div 0.04 =$ _____

9. $3.75 \div 0.05 =$ _____

10. $3.75 \div 0.005 =$ _____

4·4 APPLICATIONS

EXERCISE

For each report:
- Divide the total cost by the number of units to obtain the cost per unit.
- When obtaining a quotient to be expressed in dollars and cents, calculate the quotient correct to three places after the decimal.
- Round off the quotient correct to two places after the decimal (that is, to the nearest cent).

1.

Shopper's Market   Retail Cost Report   December 31, 19--

Unit Code	No. of Units	Total Cost	Cost per Unit
64A	241	$636.40	$
64B	337	899.43	
65A	117	349.73	
66A	179	478.68	
66B	365	997.66	
66C	223	548.58	
67A	207	675.45	
67B	412	846.56	

2.

Shopper's Market   Retail Cost Report   February 28, 19--

Unit Code	No. of Units	Total Cost	Cost per Unit
54A	575	$1 369.80	$
54B	409	1 086.56	
55A	487	1 265.65	
55B	598	1 764.44	
55C	387	1 123.33	
56A	451	1 426.72	
57B	678	2 025.37	
57C	354	988.63	

For each Production Report:
- Divide the total units produced by the number of hours that the machine is in operation to obtain the average hourly production.
- In these reports, the average hourly production of units is calculated correct to *one* place after the decimal. Calculate to at least *two* places after the decimal. Round off your answer correct to *one* place after the decimal.

3.

Roche
Manufacturing Company Limited
Production Report for Week Ending November 30, 19--

Machine No.	Total Units Produced	No. of Hours Machine in Operation	Average Hourly Production
21	7376	62.5	
34	5879	59.25	
37	8073	67.75	
45	4168	60.5	
46	9917	17.75	
51	7167	65.25	
55	8819	66.75	
57	5534	60.25	

4.

Roche
Manufacturing Company Limited
Production Report for Week Ending December 31, 19--

Machine No.	Total Units Produced	No. of Hours Machine in Operation	Average Hourly Production
21	8124	64.25	
34	5796	58.5	
37	7973	66.75	
45	5636	61.5	
46	9008	70.25	
51	7354	65.5	
55	8065	65.5	
57	6163	61.75	

5.

Roche

Manufacturing Company Limited

Production Report for Week Ending January 31, 19--

Machine No.	Total Units Produced	No. of Hours Machine in Operation	Average Hourly Production
21	8336	65.75	
34	6061	50.25	
37	8115	68.5	
45	4921	59.75	
46	9813	95.25	
51	8381	66.5	
55	9197	70.5	
57	8313	71.25	

4·5 REVIEW

EXERCISE

Divide the following correct to two places after the decimal. A reminder — to obtain the answer correct to two places after the decimal, calculate the answer to the third place after the decimal, and round off.

1. $147.892 \div 26.01 =$ _____

2. $24.163 \div 8.65 =$ _____

3. $73 \div 42.01 =$ _____

4. $127.352 \div 65.01 =$ _____

5. $9.621 \div 4.35 =$ _____

6. $621.013 \div 126.222 =$ _____

Divide the following correct to three places after the decimal. A reminder — calculate the answer to the fourth place after the decimal and round off.

7. $26.321 \div 7.65 =$ _____

8. $126.29 \div 13.63 =$ _____

9. $621.041 \div 123.601 =$ _____

10. $11\ 126.4 \div 16\ 121.3 =$ _____

11. $98\ 169.2 \div 13\ 129.3 =$ _____

12. $126\ 110.3 \div 14\ 165.2 =$ _____

Calculate the unit cost of production in the following reports.

• Divide the total cost by the number of units.

13.

Unit Cost Report June 30, 19-- Wallace Manufacturing			
Model No.	No. of Units	Total Cost	Cost per Unit
J 125	860	$1 625.30	$
J 650	920	2 529.30	
J 720	786	2 250.55	
J 755	225	1 621.21	
J 960	163	925.77	
J 985	982	3 610.21	

14.

Unit Cost Report July 31, 19-- Wallace Manufacturing			
Model No.	No. of Units	Total Cost	Cost per Unit
L 125	12 693	$14 261.50	$
L 263	9 128	10 126.77	
L 311	14 632	15 611.10	
L 420	18 920	22 683.52	
L 426	6 231	8 123.77	
L 498	9 236	12 160.50	

15. Calculate each labour cost per unit.

Roche

Manufacturing Company Limited

Cost Control Report   For Month Ending November 30, 19--

Employee	Weekly Unit Production				Total Production	Gross Wages	Labour Cost per Unit (to nearest cent)
	Week #1	Week #2	Week #3	Week #4			
Anthes, R.	39	47	41	45		$795.64	
Choi, S.	123	121	119	124		811.14	
Holtz, A.	211	211	212	210		922.72	
Letang, C.	27	29	25	31		838.18	
Sethu, T.	81	87	80	84		667.44	

UNIT
2

Measurements

CHAPTER 5

LINEAR MEASURE AND PERIMETER

5·1 CANADIAN METRIC SYSTEM AND LINEAR MEASURE

Canada's metric system is based on an international system of units of measurement – the International System of units of scientific measurement (the **SI system**). This system gives base units and standards for these units that are the same world wide.

One of these base units is the unit of length – the **metre**. Originally the scientists who chose and set the standards for these units intended that they be used in multiples of a thousand and in sub-multiples of thousandths. For example:

Base Unit – metre (m)

Multiples	Sub-multiples
1 *kilo*metre = 1 000 metres	1 metre = 1 000 *milli*metres
1 *mega*metre = 1 000 000 metres	1 metre = 1 000 000 *micro*metres
1 *giga*metre = 1 000 000 000 metres	1 metre = 1 000 000 000 *nano*metres

As each country adopted the SI system of units, however, it adopted other units from the old metric system which originated in France as units which could be used along with the SI base units. In Canada, for example, the Canadian Standards Commission allows the centimetre (0.01 m) to be used in consumer goods. Different types of industry are helping set the standards for SI use within their industries as well.

UNITS OF LENGTH

The base unit of length is the metre (m).
Other units of length are listed below.

Unit	Abbre-viation	Relation to the metre	Unit	Abbre-viation	Relation to the metre
millimetre	mm	1 m = 1000 mm 1 mm = 0.001 m	decametre	dam	1 dam = 10 m 1 m = 0.1 dam
centimetre	cm	1 m = 100 cm 1 cm = 0.01 m	hectometre	hm	1 hm = 100 m 1 m = 0.01 hm
decimetre	dm	1 m = 10 dm 1 dm = 0.1 m	kilometre	km	1 km = 1000 m 1 m = 0.001 km

NOTE The preferred units in the International System are: metre, kilometre, and millimetre.

Here is a chart of some useful relations between units of length.

Unit	Relation between units	Unit	Relation between units
metre	1 m = 1000 mm 1 m = 100 cm 1 m = 10 dm 1 m = 0.1 dam 1 m = 0.01 hm 1 m = 0.001 km	centimetre	1 cm = 0.01 m 1 cm = 0.1 dm 1 cm = 10 mm
		millimetre	1 mm = 0.1 cm 1 mm = 0.01 dm 1 mm = 0.001 m
		kilometre	1 km = 1000 m

EXAMPLE 1 Convert 3 m to: **a)** centimetres, **b)** millimetres.

SOLUTION
a) 1 m = 100 cm
∴ 3 m = 3 × 100 cm
3 m = 300 cm

b) 1 m = 1000 mm
∴ 3 m = 3 × 1000 mm
3 m = 3000 mm

EXAMPLE 2 Convert 5000 mm to: **a)** metres, **b)** centimetres.

SOLUTION
a) 1 mm = 0.001 m
∴ 5000 mm = 5000 × 0.001 m
5000 mm = 5 m

b) 1 mm = 0.1 cm
∴ 5000 mm = 0.1 × 5000 cm
5000 mm = 500 cm

EXAMPLE 3 Convert 2.5 cm to: **a)** metres, **b)** millimetres.

SOLUTION
a) 1 cm = 0.01 m
∴ 2.5 cm = 2.5 × 0.01 m
2.5 cm = 0.025 m

b) 1 cm = 10 mm
∴ 2.5 cm = 2.5 × 10 mm
2.5 cm = 25 mm

EXERCISE • SET 1

Convert each length.

	Length in	centimetres	millimetres	kilometres
1.	3.75 m			
2.	10.2 m			
3.	520 m			
4.	0.65 m			
5.	21.7 m			

	Length in	metres	millimetres	kilometres
6.	300 cm			
7.	52 cm			
8.	55.5 cm			
9.	8.2 cm			
10.	2560 cm			

EXERCISE • SET 2

1. Convert 687 m to:

   a) millimetres, _____   **b)** centimetres, _____   **c)** kilometres. _____

2. Convert 32.5 km to:

   a) metres, _____   **b)** centimetres, _____   **c)** decimetres. _____

3. Convert 3479 cm to:

   a) metres, _____   **b)** decimetres, _____   **c)** kilometres. _____

4. Convert 5860 mm to:

   a) centimetres, _____   **b)** kilometres, _____   **c)** decimetres. _____

5. Convert 762 dm to:

   a) metres, _____   **b)** centimetres, _____   **c)** kilometres. _____

EXERCISE • SET 3

1. Total the following lengths in millimetres and convert to metres.

   a) 1350 mm, 1500 mm, 150 mm, 450 mm _____, _____

   b) 965 mm, 712 mm, 406 mm, 202 mm _____, _____

2. Total the following lengths in metres and convert to millimetres.

   a) 0.50 m, 1.25 m, 0.67 m _____, _____

   b) 0.712 m, 1.220 m, 1.372 m _____, _____

3. John Weenik ordered 27 two by fours each 231 cm long. How much did the order cost if the lumber is $0.67 per metre? _____

4. A bolt of cloth contains 2000 linear centimetres of material.
   a) If the cost to the retailer is $2.89 per metre, how much does the complete bolt cost? _____

   b) If the retailer sells the material at $4.99 per metre, what profit does she make if she sells the complete bolt? _____

5. Mary Thiel wants to put new carpeting on her stairway. If she needs 20 running feet of stair carpet, how much will she have to pay to purchase the style she likes if the price is $11.95 a running metre? (1 inch = 2.54 cm) _____

5·2 PERIMETER OF A RECTANGLE

A **rectangle** has opposite sides equal and parallel, with all angles 90°, (all angles are right angles).

Formula

$$P = 2(l + w)$$

Where: P is the perimeter.
l is the length.
w is the width.

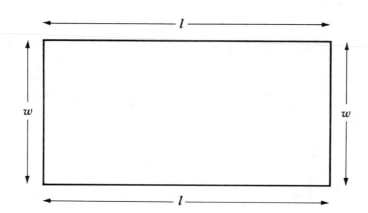

EXAMPLE 1   Calculate the perimeter of a rectangle with length 756 mm and width 379 mm.

SOLUTION $P = ?$ $P = 2(l + w)$
$l = 756$ mm $= 2(756 + 379)$
$w = 379$ mm $= 2(1135)$
                    $= 2270$

The perimeter of the rectangle is 2270 mm.

EXAMPLE 2 Calculate the perimeter of a rectangle with length 3.17 m and width 2.69 m.

SOLUTION

$P = ?$
$l = 3.17$ m
$w = 2.69$ m

$P = 2(l + w)$
$\quad = 2(3.17 + 2.69)$
$\quad = 2(5.86)$
$\quad = 11.72$

The perimeter of the rectangle is 11.72 m.

NOTE Always complete the operations in the brackets first.

EXERCISE • SET 1

Given the following dimensions, calculate the perimeter of each rectangle in the smaller unit of the given dimensions.

	Length	Width	Perimeter
1.	251 mm	195 mm	
2.	347 mm	221 mm	
3.	10.6 cm	7.9 cm	
4.	15.8 cm	11.7 cm	
5.	521 mm	23.6 cm	
6.	79.3 cm	532 mm	
7.	1.3 m	89 cm	
8.	159 cm	1.28 m	

EXERCISE • SET 2

1. How many metres of fencing are required to fence a yard 17 m long by 13 m wide?

_____

2. How many metres of baseboard are needed for a room 7 m long by 5 m wide?

_____

3. How many metres of ceiling moulding are needed for a room 850 cm long by 675 cm wide? _____

4. The outside dimensions of a tool shed are 4.20 m by 2.75 m. What is the perimeter:

a) in metres? _____   **b)** in millimetres? _____

5. The inside dimensions of a room are 5250 mm by 6780 mm. What is the perimeter:

a) in millimetres? _____   **b)** in metres? _____

1. Jill is planning to put weather stripping around her front door which is 2.4 m high by 1 m wide.

  a) How much weather stripping does she need? _____

  b) How much will it cost at $0.52 per metre? _____

2. A window is 1.35 m high by 0.67 m wide. How much will it cost to frame the window with moulding which costs $1.97 per metre? _____

3. A picture to be framed is 26 cm high by 54.5 cm wide. How much will it cost for picture moulding which is priced at $15.95 per metre? _____

4. Karen is planning to put moulding around the top of a chest which is 960 mm long by 475 mm wide. How much will it cost for mahogany moulding which is priced at $1.85 per metre? _____

5. Carl rode his bicycle around a block which is 400 m long by 250 m wide. How many times would he have to ride around the block to travel 13 km? _____

5·3 PERIMETER OF A SQUARE

A **square** is a rectangle with all sides equal, opposite sides parallel and all angles right angles.

Formula

$$P = 4s$$

Where: P is the perimeter.
s is the length of each side of the square.

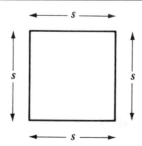

EXAMPLE 1 Calculate the perimeter of a square with each side 378 mm.

SOLUTION $P = ?$
$s = 378$ mm

$P = 4s$
$= 4 \times 378$
$= 1512$

The perimeter of the square is 1512 mm.

EXAMPLE 2   Calculate the perimeter of a square with each side 2.78 m.

SOLUTION $P = ?$ $P = 4s$
               $s = 2.78$ $= 4 \times 2.78$
                              $= 11.12$

The perimeter is 11.12 m.

EXERCISE • SET 1

Given the following dimensions, calculate the perimeter of each square.

	Side	Perimeter
1.	137 mm	
2.	275 mm	
3.	22.4 cm	
4.	31.8 cm	
5.	5.68 dm	
6.	7.29 dm	
7.	2.35 m	
8.	5.69 m	

EXERCISE • SET 2

1. a) What length of steel mesh fencing is needed to enclose a swimming pool area, 17 m by 17 m? _____

    b) How much would the fencing cost at $6.19 a running metre? _____

2. A square table top is 96 cm to a side. What is the perimeter of the table top in metres? _____

3. A room is a square 5500 mm to a side. How much would it cost to install moulding around the ceiling if the moulding costs $2.75 a running metre? _____

4. A square window is 125 cm to a side. How much would it cost to install weather stripping priced at $0.59 per metre? _____

EXERCISE • SET 3

1. Henry Georgas prepares a large box, in the shape of a cube 1.2 m to each side, for shipping. He fastens 3 steel straps around it. Allowing an extra 10 cm for fastening each strap, what total length of strapping does Henry need? _____

2. A square bedroom 3200 mm to a side has a square rug on the floor. It leaves a border between it and the wall of 530 mm on all sides. Calculate the perimeter of the rug.

_____

3. A square plot of grass in a park has a gravel path 130 cm wide around it. If the grass plot is 4.5 m to a side, what is the perimeter of the outer edge of the gravel path?

_____

4. What is the difference between the perimeter of a rectangle 800 mm long by 200 mm wide and the perimeter of a square 400 mm to a side? _____

5·4 CIRCUMFERENCE OF A CIRCLE

> **Formula**
>
> $$C = 2\pi r$$
>
> Where: C is the circumference.
> π is a constant approximately equal to 3.14.
> r is the radius of the circle.

NOTE π is a number discovered by ancient builders. They found that the ratio of the circumference of a circle to its diameter was always close to $\frac{22}{7}$. Modern measuring instruments give a much more accurate value for this ratio; but when it is converted to a decimal number, there is no end to the number of places after the decimal which can be calculated. Its value is rounded off to the accuracy necessary in different technological situations. When it is used here, we will consider that its value is 3.14.

If you are using a calculator which has a key marked π, do *not* use this key. The internal accuracy of the value for π will be different in different makes of calculator and you will find that answers obtained are not the same as given here.

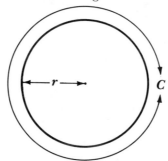

EXAMPLE 1 Calculate the circumference of a circle with radius 63 mm.

SOLUTION $C = ?$ $C = 2\pi r$
        $r = 63$ mm $= 2 \times 3.14 \times 63$
                  $= 395.64$

The circumference of the circle is 395.64 mm.

EXAMPLE 2 Calculate the circumference of a circle with radius 5.7 cm correct to two places after the decimal.

SOLUTION

$C = ?$

$r = 5.7$ cm

$C = 2\pi r$

$= 2 \times 3.14 \times 5.7$

$= 35.796$

The circumference of the circle is 35.80 cm

EXERCISE • SET 1

Calculate the circumference of each circle.

	Radius	Circumference
1.	72 mm	
2.	3.5 cm	
3.	1.6 m	
4.	2.63 m	
5.	0.57 m	
6.	0.39 m	

EXERCISE • SET 2

EXAMPLE 3 Calculate the radius of a circle whose circumference is 51 cm correct to two places after the decimal.

SOLUTION The formula $C = 2\pi r$ can be arranged to give this formula: $r = \dfrac{C}{2\pi}$

$r = ?$

$C = 51$ cm

$r = \dfrac{C}{2\pi}$

$= \dfrac{51}{2 \times 3.14}$

$= 8.121$

The radius of the circle is 8.12 cm.

Calculate the radius of each circle correct to one place after the decimal.

	Circumference	Radius
1.	66 cm	
2.	31 cm	
3.	378 mm	
4.	569 mm	
5.	9 m	
6.	15 m	

1. If the radius of a circular table is 67 cm, what is its circumference correct to two places after the decimal? _____

2. If the circumference of a tree trunk is 1.75 m, what is its radius correct to two places after the decimal? _____

3. If the radius of each wheel of a bicycle is 33 cm,
   a) how far does the bicycle travel when the wheels revolve once? _____

   b) how many times do the wheels revolve if the bicycle is ridden 1 km? _____

   Calculate each answer correct to two places after the decimal.

4. Calculate the length of weather stripping needed to go around the edge of the window correct to the nearest centimetre. _____

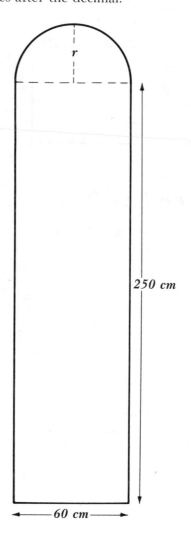

r

250 cm

60 cm

5·5 REVIEW

EXERCISE • SET 1

1. Calculate the perimeter of a rectangle with length 25 mm and width 19 mm:

   a) in millimetres, _____

   b) in centimetres. _____

2. Calculate the perimeter of a rectangle with length 105 cm and width 92 cm:

   a) in centimetres, _____

   b) in metres. _____

3. Calculate the perimeter of a rectangular field with length 100.6 m and width 56.4 m:

   a) in metres, _____   b) in decimetres, _____   c) in kilometres. _____

4. Calculate the perimeter of a square with each side 35 mm:

   a) in millimetres, _____

   b) in centimetres. _____

5. Calculate the perimeter of a square with each side 47 cm:

   a) in centimetres, _____

   b) in decimetres. _____

6. Calculate the perimeter of a square field with each side 90 m:

   a) in metres, _____

   b) in decimetres. _____

7. Calculate the circumference of a circle with radius 32 mm correct to the nearest millimetre. _____

8. Calculate the circumference of a circle with radius 5.2 cm correct to three places after the decimal. _____

9. Calculate the circumference of a circle with radius 2.9 m correct to three places after the decimal. _____

EXERCISE • SET 2

1. How many metres of baseboard are needed for a room 7.6 m long by 6.3 m wide?

   _____

2. a) What length of steel mesh fencing is necessary to enclose a yard 16.7 m by 33.4 m?

   _____

   b) What would the fencing cost at $6.19 a running metre? _____

3. A square field is 36 m to a side. What will it cost to fence it if fencing expenses are $4.75 a metre? _____

4. A room in the shape of a square 4300 mm to a side, is to have baseboard installed at $0.95 per metre. What is the cost of the installation? _____

5. A circular window has a radius of 3.25 m. What is its circumference to the nearest centimetre?

_____

6. If the circumference of a circular table is 11 600 cm, what is its radius correct to two places after the decimal? _____

EXERCISE • SET 3 _____

1. A picture to be framed is 30 cm high by 62.5 cm wide. How much will it cost to frame it with moulding priced at $12.95 per metre? _____

2. How much will it cost to put pine moulding around the top of a chest which is 85 cm long by 45.5 cm wide if the moulding costs $1.19 per metre? _____

3. A living room is square in shape with each side 450 cm long. A square rug almost covers the floor leaving a border which is 350 mm wide on all sides. Calculate the perimeter of the rug in metres. _____

4. What is the difference in metres between the perimeter of a rectangle 80 cm long by 20 cm wide and the perimeter of a square 60 cm to a side? _____

5. The circumference of a circular rug is 12.567 m. What is its radius in millimetres correct to two places after the decimal? _____

6. Calculate the circumference of the following figure in metres. _____

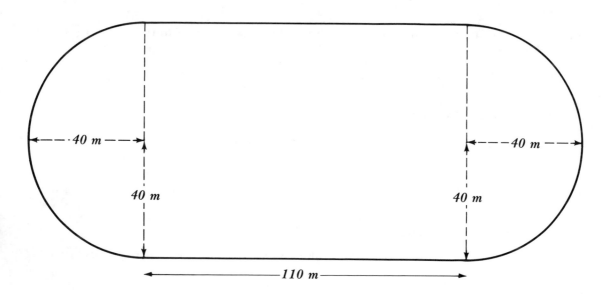

CHAPTER 6

AREA

6·1 AREA OF A RECTANGLE

Formula

$$A = l \times w$$

Where: A is the area.
       l is the length.
       w is the width.

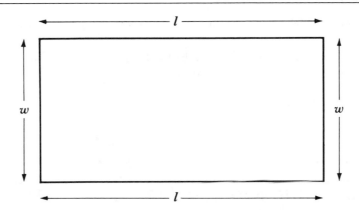

EXAMPLE 1   Calculate the area of a rectangle with length 3 m and width 2.5 m.

SOLUTION $A = ?$ $A = l \times w$
               $l = 3$ m $= 3 \times 2.5$
               $w = 2.5$ m $= 7.5$

               The area is 7.5 m².

NOTE   m² means square metres.

EXAMPLE 2   Calculate the area of a rectangle with length 282 mm and width 216 mm.

SOLUTION $A = ?$ $A = l \times w$
               $l = 282$ $= 282 \times 216$
               $w = 216$ $= 60\ 912$

               The area is 60 912 mm².

NOTE   mm² means square millimetres.

NOTE   The area of the rectangle in Example 2 is 60 912 mm². This is a very large number to express a relatively small area (about the size of a sheet of letter size paper). A number this large should be changed to the next larger unit, in this case, into square centimetres.

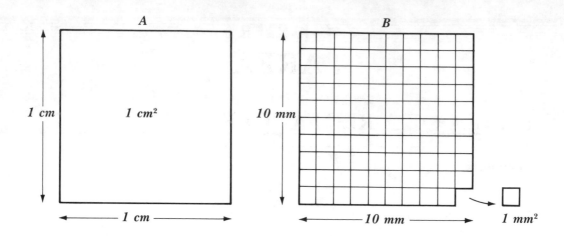

NOTE cm² means square centimetres.

In diagram A, one square centimetre of area is magnified. Each side of the square is 1 cm in length.

Since 1 cm = 10 mm, each side of area A is also 10 mm in length as shown in diagram B. One square centimetre of area contains 10 mm × 10 mm.

$1 \text{ cm}^2 = 100 \text{ mm}^2$

Our answer in Example 3 can be changed.

$$60\ 912 \text{ mm}^2 = 60\ 912 \div 100 \text{ cm}^2$$
$$= 609.12 \text{ cm}^2$$

Here is a chart of some useful relations between units of area.

Unit	Relation between units	Unit	Relation between units
square metre	1 m² = 100 dm² = 10² dm² 1 m² = 10 000 cm² = 10⁴ cm² 1 m² = 1 000 000 mm² = 10⁶ mm²	square centimetre	1 cm² = 100 mm² 1 cm² = 0.01 dm² 1 cm² = 0.0001 m²
		square decimetre	1 dm² = 0.01 m² 1 dm² = 100 cm² 1 dm² = 10 000 mm²
hectare (ha) (used for land measurement)	1 ha = 10 000 m² 1 ha = 0.01 km²		
square kilometre	1 km² = 1 000 000 m² = 10⁶ m² 1 km² = 100 ha	square millimetre	1 mm² = 0.01 cm² 1 mm² = 0.0001 dm²

EXERCISE • SET 1

Given the following dimensions, calculate the area of each rectangle.

	Length	Width	Area
1.	52 mm	30 mm	
2.	315 mm	211 mm	
3.	26 cm	51 cm	
4.	225 cm	615 cm	
5.	3.5 m	8.6 m	
6.	2.1 m	3.5 m	
7.	1.2 km	1.7 km	
8.	53 dm	237 dm	
9.	1250 m	2371 m	
10.	3275 cm	2978 cm	

EXERCISE • SET 2

1. In Question 1 of Exercise • Set 1, convert the answer to square centimetres. _____

2. In Question 2 of Exercise • Set 1, convert the answer to square centimetres. _____

3. In Question 4 of Exercise • Set 1, convert the answer to square decimetres. _____

4. In Question 4 of Exercise • Set 1, convert the answer to square metres. _____

5. In Question 7 of Exercise • Set 1, convert the answer to hectares. _____

6. In Question 8 of Exercise • Set 1, convert the answer to square centimetres. _____

7. In Question 9 of Exercise • Set 1, convert the answer to square kilometres. _____

8. In Question 10 of Exercise • Set 1, convert the answer to square metres. _____

EXERCISE • SET 3

1. a) How many square metres of carpet would be required to carpet a room 7 m long by 5 m wide wall-to-wall? _____

  b) How much would the carpeting cost at $18.95 per square metre? _____

2. Ray's Cleaners shampoo rugs for $4.25 per square metre. What will it cost to have a rug 3.5 m by 5.5 m shampooed? _____

3. Sod costs $4.98 per square metre. What will it cost to have a lawn sodded if the lawn is 18.3 m wide by 10.5 m deep? _____

4. A porch floor is 2.1 m long by 4.25 m wide. How many litres of paint will be required to give it 2 coats of paint if a litre of outside floor enamel paint will cover approximately 18 m²? _____

5. a) A ceiling is 8 m by 4.5 m and a litre of interior paint will cover approximately 20 m². How many litres of paint are required to paint the ceiling with 2 coats of paint?

_____

    b) If the interior paint is priced at $6.25 a litre, what will it cost to paint the ceiling?

_____

6. A township concession is 2 km by 2 km. Calculate the number of farms of 40 ha each into which the concession can be divided. _____

6·2 AREA OF A SQUARE

> **Formula**
>
> $$A = s^2$$
>
> Where: A is the area.
> s is the length of a side.

NOTE In the formula $A = s^2$, s^2 means $s \times s$.

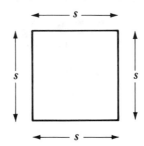

EXAMPLE Calculate the area of a square with each side 5.6 cm.

SOLUTION

$$A = ?$$
$$s = 5.6 \text{ cm}$$

$$A = s^2$$
$$= 5.6 \times 5.6$$
$$= 31.36$$

The area of the square is 31.36 cm².

EXERCISE • SET 1

Given the following dimensions, calculate the area of each square.

	Side	Area
1.	5.8 cm	
2.	27.3 cm	
3.	1.9 m	
4.	122.7 m	
5.	25 mm	
6.	309 mm	
7.	2.3 km	
8.	0.5 km	
9.	3.2 dm	
10.	51.6 dm	

EXERCISE • SET 2

1. In Question 2 of Exercise • Set 1, convert your answer to square decimetres. _____

2. In Question 4 of Exercise • Set 1, convert your answer to hectares and round off correct to two places after the decimal. _____

3. In Question 6 of Exercise • Set 1, convert your answer to square centimetres. _____

4. In Question 8 of Exercise • Set 1, convert your answer to hectares. _____

5. In Question 10 of Exercise • Set 1, convert your answer to square metres and round off correct to two places after the decimal. _____

EXERCISE • SET 3

1. What is the area of a square 6.5 m to a side, in square decimetres? _____

2. What will it cost to paint a square attic floor which is 12.8 m to a side if a litre of floor enamel will cover 20 m² and costs $4.98 per litre? _____

3. A-One Cleaners clean drapes for $0.79 per square metre. What would it cost to have a pair of drapes cleaned if each drape measures 2.13 m long by 2.13 m wide? _____

4. Regal Cleaners clean rugs for $2.97 per square metre. What would it cost to have a square rug 525 cm to a side cleaned? _____

6·3 AREA OF A CIRCLE

> **Formula**
>
> $$A = \pi r^2$$
>
> Where: A is the area.
>
> π is a constant approximately equal to 3.14.
>
> r is the radius of the circle.

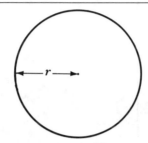

EXAMPLE   Calculate the area of the circle that has a radius of 2.37 cm and round off the answer correct to two places after the decimal.

SOLUTION $A = ?$

$r = 2.37$ cm

$A = \pi r^2$

$= 3.14 \times 2.37 \times 2.37$

$= 17.637\ 066$

The area of the circle is 17.64 cm².

EXERCISE • SET 1

Calculate the area of each circle correct to two places after the decimal.

	Radius	Area
1.	22 mm	
2.	35 mm	
3.	3.7 cm	
4.	5.31 cm	
5.	3.79 dm	
6.	1.56 dm	
7.	0.37 dm	
8.	2.1 m	
9.	3.15 m	
10.	0.75 m	

EXERCISE • SET 2

1. In Question 2 of Exercise • Set 1, convert your answer to square centimetres. _____

2. In Question 3 of Exercise • Set 1, convert your answer to square millimetres. _____

3. In Question 4 of Exercise • Set 1, convert your answer to square decimetres. _____

4. In Question 5 of Exercise • Set 1, convert your answer to square metres. _____

5. In Question 7 of Exercise • Set 1, convert your answer to square centimetres. _____

6. In Question 10 of Exercise • Set 1, convert your answer to square decimetres. _____

EXERCISE • SET 3

1. Toby's Cleaning Co. cleans rugs for $3.95 per square metre. How much will it cost to have a circular rug with radius 135 cm cleaned? _____

2. A room 5.5 m long by 3.4 m wide has a circular rug with a radius of 155 cm. How much floor space is not covered by the rug? Give your answer in square metres, correct to two places after the decimal. _____

3. A circular garden with radius 10.7 m has a circular grass path around it which is 75 cm wide. Find the total area of the grass path. Give the answer in square centimetres. _____

6·4 SURFACE AREA OF A CYLINDER

Formula

$$S = 2\pi r^2 + 2\pi rh$$

Where: S is the surface area of the cylinder.

r is the radius of the base.

h is the height.

$\pi = 3.14$

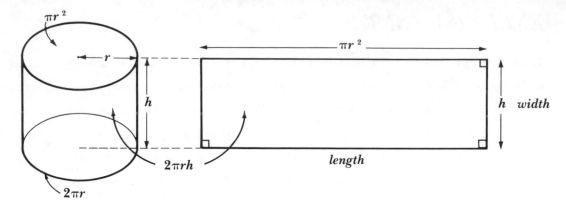

The curved surface can be opened out to form a rectangle.
The length of the rectangle is equal to the circumference of the base of the cylinder.
The width of the rectangle is equal to the height of the cylinder.

EXAMPLE   Calculate the surface area of a frozen orange juice can which has the radius of the base equal to 3.6 cm and the height 12 cm. Give your answer correct to two places after the decimal.

SOLUTION $S = ?$

$r = 3.6$ cm

$h = 12$ cm

$S = 2\pi r^2 + 2\pi rh$
$= 2 \times 3.14 \times (3.6)^2 + 2 \times 3.14 \times 3.6 \times 12$
$= 81.3888 + 271.296$
$= 352.6848$

The surface area of the can is 352.68 cm².

EXERCISE • SET 1

Calculate the surface area of each cylinder.

	Radius of Base	Height	Surface Area
1.	5.2 cm	16 cm	
2.	52 mm	160 mm	
3.	2.7 m	3 m	
4.	120 cm	200 cm	
5.	0.36 m	1.2 m	

EXERCISE • SET 2

1. Convert your answer for Question 1 in Exercise • Set 1 to square millimetres. _____

2. Convert your answer for Question 2 in Exercise • Set 1 to square centimetres. _____

3. Convert your answer for Question 4 in Exercise • Set 1 to square metres. _____

4. Convert your answer for Question 5 in Exercise • Set 1 to square centimetres. _____

EXERCISE • SET 3

1. Calculate the surface area of a cylindrical oil tank with radius 0.5 m and height 1.5 m.

   _____

2. a) Calculate the surface area of a can of ketchup supplied to restaurants if the radius of the base is 11 cm and the height is 50 cm. _____

   b) If the label cost $0.075 per square metre to produce, how much was the cost of the label? NOTE   The label covers only the curved surface. _____

3. If the surface area of the oil tank in Question 1 costs $0.000 25 per square centimetre to rust proof, what would be the cost of rust proofing the tank? _____

4. A cylindrical water tank with the radius of the base 28 m and the height 56 m is to have its surface painted. If painting costs $0.000 25 per square decimetre, what is the cost of painting the water tank? _____

6·5 REVIEW

EXERCISE • SET 1

Calculate the area of each rectangle.

	Length	Width	Area
1.	63 mm	21 mm	
2.	32 cm	43 cm	
3.	1.5 m	2.7 m	
4.	2 km	3.2 km	
5.	8 dm	12 dm	

Calculate the area of each square.

	Side	Area
6.	213 mm	
7.	15.5 cm	
8.	2.7 m	
9.	1.6 km	
10.	9.7 dm	

Calculate the area of each circle.

	Radius	Area
11.	38 mm	
12.	29.3 cm	
13.	2.63 m	
14.	1.4 km	
15.	3.27 dm	

Calculate the surface area of each cylinder.

	Radius of Base	Height	Surface Area
16.	32 cm	41 cm	
17.	180 mm	200 mm	
18.	1.7 m	0.2 m	
19.	19 cm	21 cm	
20.	0.375 m	0.8 m	

EXERCISE • SET 2

1. Convert your answers to Questions 1, 6, 11, and 17 in Exercise • Set 1 to square centimetres.

_____ , _____ , _____ , _____

2. Convert your answers to Questions 2, 7, 9, and 16 in Exercise • Set 1 to square metres.

_____ , _____ , _____ , _____

3. Convert your answers to Questions 4, 10, 15, and 19 in Exercise • Set 1 to square metres.

_____ , _____ , _____ , _____

4. Convert your answers to Questions 5, 10, and 15 in Exercise • Set 1 to square centimetres.

_____ , _____ , _____

EXERCISE • SET 3

1. a) How much carpeting is needed to carpet a room 8.5 m long by 6.25 m wide?

_____

   b) How much will it cost if the carpeting is $20.75 per square metre? _____

2. How much will it cost to put 3 coats of white paint on a black wall, 5025 mm long by 2140 mm high if a litre of paint will cover 20 m² and costs $5.95 per litre? _____

3. Taylor's Cleaners dye drapes for $2.17 per square metre. What will it cost to have 3 pairs of drapes dyed if each drape is 2.27 m long by 2.27 m wide? _____

4. A square plot of grass has a walk around it 2.7 m wide. If the plot of grass is 18.1 m to a side, what is the area of the walk? _____

5. A room 6.1 m long by 3.2 m wide has a circular rug on the floor with a radius of 1600 mm. How much floor space is not covered by the rug? Give the answer in square metres. _____

6. Calculate the area of the figure in square metres. _____

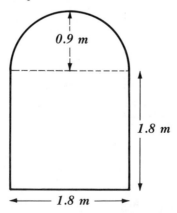

CHAPTER 7
VOLUME, CAPACITY, AND MASS

7·1 VOLUME OF A RECTANGULAR SOLID

> **Formula**
>
> $$V = l \times w \times h$$
>
> Where: V is the volume.
> l is the length.
> w is the width.
> h is the height.

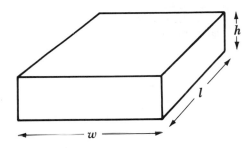

EXAMPLE 1 Calculate the volume of a rectangular solid with length 3.5 cm, width 2.7 cm, and height 1.8 cm correct to two places after the decimal.

SOLUTION $V = ?$ | $V = l \times w \times h$
$l = 3.5$ cm | $= 3.5 \times 2.7 \times 1.8$
$w = 2.7$ cm | $= 17.01$
$h = 1.8$ cm |

The volume is 17.01 cm³.

NOTE   cm³ means cubic centimetres.

EXAMPLE 2 Calculate the volume of a rectangular box 110 mm long, 98 mm wide, and 72 mm high.

SOLUTION $V = ?$ | $V = l \times w \times h$
$l = 110$ mm | $= 110 \times 98 \times 72$
$w = 98$ mm | $= 776\ 160$
$h = 72$ mm |

The volume is 776 160 mm³.

NOTE   mm³ means cubic millimetres.

NOTE The volume of the box in Example 2 is 776 160 mm³. This is a very large number to express a relatively small volume. When we reach a number of this size it should be converted to the next larger unit, in this case cubic centimetres. If one cubic centimetre is magnified:

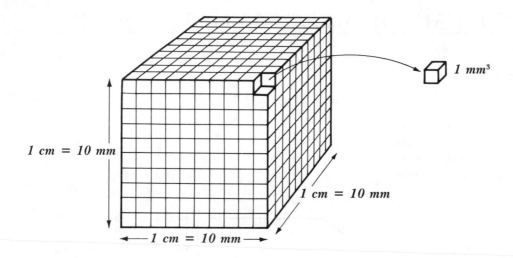

$$1 \text{ cm}^3 = 10 \text{ mm} \times 10 \text{ mm} \times 10 \text{ mm}$$
$$= 10 \times 10 \times 10 \text{ mm}^3$$
$$1 \text{ cm}^3 = 1000 \text{ mm}^3$$

$$\therefore 1 \text{ mm}^3 = 1 \text{ cm}^3 \div 1000$$
$$1 \text{ mm}^3 = 0.001 \text{ cm}^3$$

The answer to Example 2 can be converted.
$$776\ 160 \text{ mm}^3 = 776\ 160 \times 0.001 \text{ cm}^3$$
$$= 776.16 \text{ cm}^3$$

Here is a chart of some useful relations between units of volume.

Unit	Relation between units
cubic metre	$1 \text{ m}^3 = 1000 \text{ dm}^3$ $1 \text{ m}^3 = 1\ 000\ 000 \text{ cm}^3$
cubic decimetre	$1 \text{ dm}^3 = 1000 \text{ cm}^3$ $1 \text{ dm}^3 = 1\ 000\ 000 \text{ mm}^3$
cubic centimetre	$1 \text{ cm}^3 = 1000 \text{ mm}^3$ $1 \text{ cm}^3 = 0.001 \text{ dm}^3$ $1 \text{ cm}^3 = 0.000\ 001 \text{ m}^3$
cubic millimetre	$1 \text{ mm}^3 = 0.001 \text{ cm}^3$

EXERCISE • SET 1

Given the following dimensions, calculate the volume of each rectangular solid.

	Length	Width	Height	Volume
1.	3.2 cm	2.5 cm	1.5 cm	
2.	5.7 cm	3.1 cm	2.6 cm	
3.	55 cm	38 cm	22 cm	
4.	72 cm	53 cm	45 cm	
5.	52 mm	36 mm	24 mm	
6.	115 mm	91 mm	66 mm	
7.	300 mm	256 mm	197 mm	
8.	2.7 dm	1.3 dm	0.9 dm	
9.	12.6 dm	11.5 dm	9.8 dm	
10.	27.9 dm	25.5 dm	20.7 dm	

EXERCISE • SET 2

In the questions in Exercise • Set 1:

1. Convert your answer for Question 3 to cubic decimetres. _____

2. Convert your answer for Question 4 to cubic decimetres. _____

3. Convert your answer for Question 6 to cubic centimetres. _____

4. Convert your answer for Question 7 to cubic centimetres. _____

5. Convert your answer for Question 8 to cubic centimetres. _____

6. Convert your answer for Question 10 to cubic metres. _____

EXERCISE • SET 3

1. How many cubic metres of top soil are required to fill a flower box 2 m long by 500 mm wide to a depth of 600 mm? _____

2. How many cubic metres of sand are required to fill a sand box 3 m square to a depth of 20 cm? _____

3. A packing carton is 30 cm wide by 30 cm long by 23 cm high. How many cereal boxes 150 mm long by 50 mm wide by 230 mm high will it hold? _____

4. A room has dimensions of 5000 mm by 3000 mm by 2400 mm. If an air conditioner recirculates the air at the rate of 2 m³ per minute, how long will it take to recirculate all the air in the room? _____

7·2 VOLUME OF A CUBE

> **Formula**
>
> $$V = s^3$$
>
> Where: V is the volume of the cube.
> s is the length of each side.

NOTE s^3 means $s \times s \times s$.

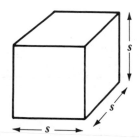

EXAMPLE Calculate the volume of a cube with each side 2.7 cm.

SOLUTION $V = ?$ $V = s^3$
$s = 2.7$ cm $= 2.7 \times 2.7 \times 2.7$
               $= 19.683$

The volume of the cube is 19.683 cm³.

EXERCISE • SET 1

Given the following dimensions, calculate the volume of each cube.

	Side	Volume
1.	3.2 cm	
2.	29 cm	
3.	56 cm	
4.	43 mm	
5.	91 mm	
6.	105 mm	
7.	2.2 dm	
8.	13.25 dm	
9.	1.6 dm	
10.	1.2 m	

EXERCISE • SET 2

In the questions in Exercise • Set 1:

1. Convert your answer for Question 2 to cubic decimetres. _____

2. Convert your answer for Question 3 to cubic decimetres. _____

3. Convert your answer for Question 5 to cubic centimetres. _____

4. Convert your answer for Question 6 to cubic centimetres. _____

5. Convert your answer for Question 8 to cubic metres. _____

6. Convert your answer for Question 9 to cubic centimetres. _____

EXERCISE • SET 3

1. A metal box, in the shape of a cube 150 mm to a side, is filled with sand to make a doorstop. How many cubic centimetres of sand are needed to fill the box? _____

2. A cubical packing case is 30 cm to a side. How many cubical boxes 50 mm to a side can be packed in the case? _____

3. Each side of a cube is 10 cm in length. If each side of the cube were doubled, by how many times is the volume increased? _____

4. A wooden box, in the shape of a cube 300 cm to a side, is to be sunk into a garden. How many cubic metres of earth must be removed? _____

7·3 VOLUME OF A CYLINDER

Formula

$$V = \pi r^2 h$$

Where: V is the volume of the cylinder.
π is a constant approximately equal to 3.14.
r is the radius of the base of the cylinder.
h is the height of the cylinder.

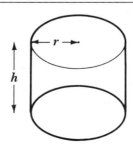

EXAMPLE   Calculate the volume of a cylinder which has a circular base with radius 3.2 cm and a height of 8 cm correct to two places after the decimal.

SOLUTION $V = ?$
                  $r = 3.2$ cm
                  $h = 8$ cm

$V = \pi r^2 h$
    $= 3.14 \times 3.2 \times 3.2 \times 8$
    $= 257.2288$

The volume of the cylinder is 257.23 cm³.

EXERCISE • SET 1

Calculate the volume of each cylinder.

	Radius of Base	Height	Volume
1.	2.5 cm	6 cm	
2.	4.6 cm	11 cm	
3.	3.1 dm	5 dm	
4.	1.7 dm	4.5 dm	
5.	1.3 m	2.2 m	
6.	0.7 m	3.35 m	
7.	13 cm	10 cm	
8.	15 cm	8 cm	
9.	20 dm	9 dm	
10.	14 dm	7.5 dm	

EXERCISE • SET 2

In the questions in Exercise • Set 1:

1. Convert your answer for Question 6 to cubic centimetres. _____

2. Convert your answer for Question 8 to cubic decimetres. _____

3. Convert your answer for Question 9 to cubic metres. _____

4. Convert your answer for Question 10 to cubic centimetres. _____

EXERCISE • SET 3

1. A cylindrical fruit juice can has a radius of 5.5 cm and a height of 18 cm. How many cubic decimetres of juice does it hold? _____

2. A cylindrical water tank has a radius of 1.5 m and a height of 3 m. How many cubic decimetres of water does it hold? _____

3. A cylindrical oil can has a radius of 5.1 cm and a height of 13 cm. If a cubic decimetre of oil costs $2.17, what is the cost of the oil in the can? _____

7·4 CAPACITY

CAPACITY IN LITRES

$1 \text{ dm}^3 = 1 \text{ L}$

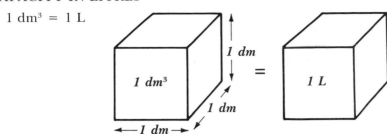

To measure milk, ice cream, soft drinks, etc., the capacity of a volume of **one cubic decimetre** is named **one litre**.

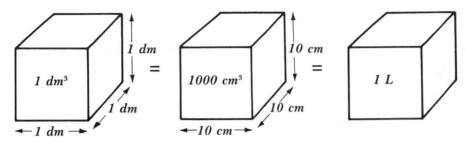

Since 1 dm = 10 cm
and $1 \text{ dm}^3 = 1000 \text{ cm}^3$
a volume of 1000 cm^3 has a capacity of 1 L.

CAPACITY IN MILLILITRES

A litre can be divided into 1000 smaller parts called **millilitres** (mL).

$1 \text{ L} = 1000 \text{ mL}$

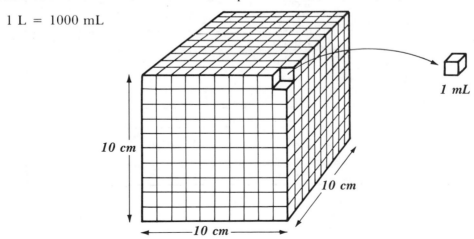

Since 1 L = 1000 mL
but $1 \text{ dm}^3 = 1000 \text{ cm}^3$
a volume of 1 cm^3 has a capacity of 1 mL.

CAPACITY IN KILOLITRES

Similarly

Since 1 kL = 1000 L
and 1 m³ = 1000 dm³
a volume of 1 m³ has a capacity of 1 kL.

EXAMPLE 1   What is the capacity of a bottle whose volume is 2.3 dm³?

SOLUTION   If a volume of 1 dm³ has a capacity of 1 L
then a volume of 2.3 dm³ has a capacity of 2.3 L.

EXAMPLE 2   What is the capacity of a plastic cube 9.5 cm to a side?

SOLUTION   The volume of the cube is:
$$V = (9.5 \text{ cm})^3$$
$$= 857.375 \text{ cm}^3$$
The capacity of the plastic cube is 857.375 mL.

EXAMPLE 3   What is the capacity of a rectangular water tank 3 m by 2 m by 0.5 m?

SOLUTION   The volume of the tank is:
$$V = 3 \text{ m} \times 2 \text{ m} \times 0.5 \text{ m}$$
$$= 3.0 \text{ m}^3$$
The capacity of the tank is 3.0 kL.

EXERCISE • SET 1

Calculate the volume and the capacity of each rectangular container.

	Length	Width	Height	Volume	Capacity
1.	5 cm	3 cm	2 cm		
2.	3.2 cm	2.7 cm	1.5 cm		
3.	3.1 dm	3 dm	2.5 dm		
4.	2.8 dm	0.9 dm	0.5 dm		
5.	5 m	4 m	3.2 m		
6.	3.7 m	2 m	0.6 m		
7.	28 cm	28 cm	28 cm		
8.	32 dm	30 dm	27 dm		
9.	0.03 dm	0.02 dm	0.01 dm		
10.	250 mm	200 mm	125 mm		

EXERCISE • SET 2

In the questions concerning capacity in Exercise • Set 1:

1. Convert your answer for Question 2 to litres. _____

2. Convert your answer for Question 4 to millilitres. _____

3. Convert your answer for Question 6 to litres. _____

4. Convert your answer for Question 9 to millilitres. _____

EXERCISE • SET 3

1. A rectangular storage tank has dimensions of 3 m by 7 m by 2.5 m. How many litres of water will it hold? _____

2. A cylindrical gasoline tank has a radius of 0.5 m and a height of 2.35 m. How many litres of gasoline will it hold? _____

3. A leaking faucet drips 12.75 L of water every hour. How long will it take to fill a cylindrical container with radius 13.5 cm and height 45 cm? _____

4. When an object is immersed in water in a graduated cylinder with a radius of 2 cm, the level of the water in the cylinder rises from 100 cm to 230 cm. What volume of water is displaced? _____

7·5 MASS

The base unit of mass is the **kilogram** (kg).
If you filled a plastic container of capacity 1 L with water, the water would have a mass of almost exactly 1 kg.
1 L of water has a mass of 1 kg.

Since 1 L = 1000 mL and 1 kg = 1000 g
Then, 1000 mL of water has a mass of 1000 g.
Then, 1 mL of water has a mass of 1 g.

Another unit of mass is the **metric tonne** (t).

   1 t = 1000 kg

And another unit of mass is the **milligram** (mg).

   1 g = 1000 mg

Here is a chart of some useful relations between units of mass.

Unit	Relation between units
kilogram	1 kg = 1000 g 1 kg = 0.001 t 1 kg = 10^6 mg
gram	1 g = 1000 mg 1 g = 0.001 kg
milligram	1 mg = 0.001 g

EXAMPLE 1   What is the mass of 13.5 L of water?

SOLUTION   1 L of water has a mass of 1 kg.
Therefore 13.5 L of water have a mass of 13.5 kg.

EXAMPLE 2   **a)** What is the volume of a rectangular plastic box 3.6 cm by 3.2 cm by 1.9 cm?
b) What is its capacity?
c) If the box were filled with water, what would be the mass of the water?

SOLUTION   **a)** V = 3.6 × 3.2 × 1.9
        = 21.888
        The volume is 21.888 cm³.
   b) Therefore the capacity is 21.888 mL.
   c) The mass of the water is 21.888 g.

EXERCISE • SET 1

Given the following dimensions, calculate the volume, the capacity, and the mass of water required to fill each container.

	Container	Dimensions	Volume	Capacity	Mass of Water
1.	metal box	2.3 cm by 1.8 cm by 2.1 cm			
2.	plastic cube	side 3.25 dm			
3.	plastic box	25 cm by 22 cm by 25 cm			
4.	cylindrical can	radius 50 mm, height 75 mm			
5.	metal cube	side 1.3 m			
6.	cylindrical vat	radius 1.5 m, height 1.2 m			
7.	wooden box	2 m by 1.5 m by 0.2 m			
8.	plastic cube	side 80 mm			

	Container	Dimensions	Volume	Capacity	Mass of Water
9.	cylindrical plastic cup	radius 3.5 cm, height 6.5 cm			
10.	cylindrical plastic cup	radius 4.5 cm, height 7.9 cm			
11.	cylindrical waste basket	radius 16 cm, height 36 cm			
12.	cylindrical coffee mug	radius 37 mm, height 90 mm			
13.	cylindrical kettle	radius 9.25 cm height 11.5 cm			
14.	cylindrical plant pot	radius 0.15 m, height 0.28 m			

EXERCISE • SET 2

In the questions in Exercise • Set 1:

1. Convert your answer for mass in Question 2 to grams. _____

2. Convert your answer for mass in Question 3 to grams. _____

3. Convert your answer for mass in Question 4 to milligrams. _____

4. Convert your answer for mass in Question 5 to tonnes. _____

EXERCISE • SET 3

1. If a millilitre of ice cream has exactly the same mass as a millilitre of water, what mass of ice cream can be packed in an ice cube tray 24 cm long by 10 cm wide by 35 mm deep? _____

2. The food storage compartment of a refrigerator is 0.64 m long by 0.48 m wide by 1 m high. If 1 L of food has the same mass as 1 L of water, how many kilograms of food would it hold? _____

3. The frozen food storage compartment of a refrigerator is 0.64 m long by 0.48 m deep by 0.34 m high. If a litre of frozen food has the same mass as a litre of water, how many kilograms of frozen food can be stored in the compartment? _____

4. A can of motor oil has a radius of 5 cm and a height of 12.6 cm. If 1 mL of motor oil has the same mass as 1 mL of water, what is the mass of the oil in the can? _____

7·6 REVIEW

EXERCISE • SET 1

Calculate the volume of:

1. a rectangular solid with length 31 mm, width 27 mm, and height 8 mm. _____

2. a rectangular solid with length 29 cm, width 22 cm, and height 15.5 cm. _____

3. a rectangular solid with length 4.2 m, width 3.3 m, and height 2.1 m. _____

4. a cube with each side 135 mm. _____

5. a cube with each side 56.2 cm. _____

6. a cylinder with radius 42 mm and height 115 mm. _____

7. a cylinder with radius 51 cm and height 127 cm. _____

Calculate the capacity of each container and determine the mass of water required to fill it. Determine each answer correct to two places after the decimal where necessary.

8. a plastic box 8.3 cm by 6.5 cm by 5.7 cm _____, _____

9. a metal box 2.1 dm by 3.1 dm by 1.5 dm _____, _____

10. a cement tank 31 m long by 31 m wide by 3.5 m deep _____, _____

11. a cylindrical can with radius 4.2 cm and height 7.5 cm _____, _____

12. a cylindrical jug with radius 7.3 cm and height 26 cm _____, _____

13. a cylindrical water tower with radius 7.5 m and height 15 m _____, _____

EXERCISE • SET 2

In the questions in Exercise • Set 1:

1. Convert your answer for Question 1 to cubic centimetres. _____

2. Convert your answer for Question 2 to cubic decimetres. _____

3. Convert your answer for Question 3 to cubic decimetres. _____

4. Convert your answer for Question 4 to cubic centimetres. _____

5. Convert your answer for Question 5 to cubic metres. _____

6. Convert your answer for Question 6 to cubic decimetres. _____

7. Convert your answer for Question 7 to cubic metres. _____

8. Convert your answer for mass in Question 8 to kilograms. _____

9. Convert your answer for mass in Question 9 to tonnes. _____

10. Convert your answer for mass in Question 10 to kilograms. _____

11. Convert your answer for mass in Question 11 to kilograms. _____

12. Convert your answer for mass in Question 12 to kilograms. _____

EXERCISE • SET 3 _____

1. A rectangular cement gasoline tank is 2.1 m by 3.5 m by 96.4 cm. If a cubic metre of gasoline weighs the same as a cubic metre of water, what is the mass of the gasoline in the tank when it is full? _____

2. A cubical plastic food container with each side 11 cm is filled with juice. If 1 mL of juice has the same mass as 1 mL of water, what is the mass in grams of the juice? _____

3. The interior of a rectangular freezer is 1.5 m by 0.7 m by 1 m. How many kilograms of food can be stored in it if 1 L of food has the same mass as 1 L of water? _____

4. A cylindrical can of fruit juice has a radius of 5.25 cm and a height of 18 cm. If the mass of 1 L of juice is the same as the mass of 1 L of water, what is the mass of the juice in the can? _____

UNIT

3

Fundamental

Business

Calculations

CHAPTER 8

RATIO AND PROPORTION

8·1 RATIO

When you make lemonade from a can of frozen lemonade concentrate, you mix one can of concentrate with three cans of water.

Lemonade = one can of concentrate to three cans of water
          = 1 part concentrate to 3 parts water
          = 1 part to 3 parts

The ratio of concentrate to water is 1 to 3 or 1:3 or $\frac{1}{3}$. **Ratio** means a comparison of two numbers.

EXAMPLE 1   A sugar syrup is made by mixing 3 cups of sugar with 5 cups of water. What is the ratio of sugar to water?

SOLUTION   The ratio is 3 parts sugar to 5 parts water.

The ratio of sugar to water is 3 to 5 or 3:5 or $\frac{3}{5}$.

NOTE   The form $\frac{3}{5}$ is preferred in most mathematical work.

EXAMPLE 2   A cement mixture contains 1 part cement and 3 parts sand. What is the ratio of sand to cement?

SOLUTION   The ratio of sand to cement is 3 to 1 or 3:1 or $\frac{3}{1}$.

EXAMPLE 3   What is the ratio of 500 mm to 73 cm?

SOLUTION   The comparison must be made in the same units.
500 mm = 50 cm

The ratio is 50 to 73 or 50:73 or $\frac{50}{73}$.

EXAMPLE 4   What is the ratio of 500 mL to 1 L?

SOLUTION   1 L = 1000 mL

The ratio is 500 to 1000 or 500:1000 or $\frac{500}{1000}$.

This ratio is not left in the form of $\frac{500}{1000}$. It is simplified, or reduced.

Step 1:	Step 2:	Steps 1 and 2 combined:

$$\frac{500}{1000} = \frac{5 \times 100}{10 \times 100} \qquad \frac{5}{10} = \frac{1 \times 5}{2 \times 5} \qquad \frac{500}{1000} = \frac{500 \times 1}{500 \times 2}$$

$$= \frac{5}{10} \times \frac{100}{100} \qquad = \frac{1}{2} \times \frac{5}{5} \qquad = \frac{1}{2}$$

$$= \frac{5}{10} \times 1 \qquad = \frac{1}{2} \times 1$$

$$= \frac{5}{10} \qquad = \frac{1}{2}$$

The ratio of 500 mL to 1 L is 1:2 or $\frac{1}{2}$.

In the ratio of 1:2, the terms 1 and 2 cannot be reduced any further. The ratio 1:2 has been reduced to its **lowest terms**.

EXERCISE • SET 1

Find the following ratios. If a ratio can be reduced, reduce it to its lowest terms.

1. $13 to $25 _____

2. 5 cm to 7 cm _____

3. 3 L to 8 L _____

4. 133 mm to 172 mm _____

5. 1 cm to 30 mm _____

6. 2 L to 3000 mL _____

7. 5 cm to 30 mm _____

8. 2 kg to 5000 g _____

9. 3 kg to 8000 g _____

10. 3 L to 1000 mL _____

11. 12 cm to 15 cm _____

12. 3 L to 12 L _____

13. 15 mm to 25 mm _____

14. 3 cm to 150 mm _____

15. 6 L to 300 mL _____

16. 300 g to 6 kg _____

17. 15 kg to 2500 g _____

18. 9 mm to 1.5 cm _____

19. 1.5 kg to 900 g _____

20. 3.5 kL to 2500 L _____

8·2 PROPORTION

When two ratios are equal they form a **proportion**.

Since the ratio $\frac{15}{25}$ can be reduced to the ratio $\frac{3}{5}$, the ratio of 15:25 can be compared with the ratio 3:5 as follows:

15:25 = 3:5 (Read: 15 is to 25 as 3 is to 5.)

$\frac{15}{25} = \frac{3}{5}$ (Read: 15 over 25 equals 3 over 5 or 15 over 25 is proportional to 3 over 5.)

Either statement is called a proportion.

EXAMPLE 1   The sales tax on a sweater priced at \$35.00 is \$2.45; the sales tax on a sweater priced at \$45.00 is \$3.15. Find the ratio of sales tax to price for each sweater and express the two ratios as a proportion.

SOLUTION   For the first sweater

$$\frac{\text{Sales Tax}}{\text{Price}} = \frac{2.45}{35.00}$$

For the second sweater

$$\frac{\text{Sales Tax}}{\text{Price}} = \frac{3.15}{45.00}$$

The proportion is $\dfrac{2.45}{35.00} = \dfrac{3.15}{45.00}$.

EXAMPLE 2   Find the number that fits in the square (the unknown number in the proportion). $\dfrac{\square}{16} = \dfrac{30}{48}$

SOLUTION   We can reduce $\dfrac{30}{48}$ to $\dfrac{10}{16}$.

Therefore, $\dfrac{\square}{16} = \dfrac{10}{16}$

and $\square = 10$

The required number is 10.

EXAMPLE 3   Find the unknown number in this proportion. $\dfrac{\square}{15} = \dfrac{36}{10}$

SOLUTION   This is a more difficult problem than Example 2. A mathematical operation called **cross-multiplication** is used to solve this example.
Multiply both sides of the proportion by 15.

$$15 \times \frac{\square}{15} = 15 \times \frac{36}{10}$$

$$\overset{1}{\cancel{15}} \times \frac{\square}{\underset{1}{\cancel{15}}} = \overset{3}{\cancel{15}} \times \frac{\overset{18}{\cancel{36}}}{\underset{1}{\cancel{10}}}$$

$$\square = 54$$

The unknown number is 54.

Or use this method.

$$\frac{\square}{15} = \frac{36}{10}$$

THINK   the 15 moves up across the equal sign to be multiplied by 36.

$$\frac{\square}{15} \diagup \frac{36}{10}$$

$$\square = \frac{15 \times 36}{10}$$

$$\square = 54$$

NOTE   Always perform the division operation last.

EXAMPLE 4 Find the unknown number in this proportion. $\frac{2}{3} = \frac{\square}{24}$

SOLUTION $\frac{2}{3} = \frac{\square}{24}$

Cross-multiply by 24.

THINK the 24 moves up across the equal sign to be multiplied by 2.

$$\frac{2}{3} \diagdown \frac{\square}{24}$$

$$\frac{2 \times 24}{3} = \square$$

$$16 = \square$$

The unknown number is 16.

EXAMPLE 5 Find the unknown number in this proportion. $\frac{5}{9} = \frac{35}{\square}$

SOLUTION Cross multiply the 9 and the $\square$.

THINK the 9 moves up across the equal sign to be multiplied by 35 and the $\square$ moves up across the equal sign to be multiplied by 5.

$$\frac{5}{9} \diagdown \frac{35}{\square}$$

$$5 \times \square = 9 \times 35$$

Divide each side by 5.

$$\square = \frac{9 \times 35}{5}$$

$$\square = 63$$

The unknown number is 63.

EXAMPLE 6 Find the unknown number in this proportion. $\frac{12}{\square} = \frac{3}{16}$

SOLUTION Cross-multiply the $\square$ and the 16.

$$\frac{12}{\square} \diagup \frac{3}{16}$$

$$12 \times 16 = \square \times 3$$

Divide each side by 3.

$$\frac{12 \times 16}{3} = \square$$

$$64 = \square$$

The unknown number is 64.

Find the unknown number in each proportion.

1. $\frac{\square}{3} = \frac{35}{15}$, $\square =$ _____

2. $\frac{\square}{18} = \frac{2}{3}$, $\square =$ _____

3. $\frac{\square}{7} = \frac{9}{21}$, $\square =$ _____

4. $\frac{\square}{64} = \frac{3}{4}$, $\square =$ _____

5. $\frac{\square}{6} = \frac{15}{18}$, $\square =$ _____

6. $\frac{2}{3} = \frac{\square}{15}$, $\square =$ _____

7. $\frac{16}{18} = \frac{\square}{27}$, $\square =$ _____

8. $\frac{1}{3} = \frac{\square}{48}$, $\square =$ _____

9. $\frac{2}{9} = \frac{\square}{63}$, $\square =$ _____

10. $\frac{9}{21} = \frac{\square}{14}$, $\square =$ _____

11. $\frac{2}{5} = \frac{8}{\square}$, $\square =$ _____

12. $\frac{3}{7} = \frac{12}{\square}$, $\square =$ _____

13. $\frac{6}{18} = \frac{2}{\square}$, $\square =$ _____

14. $\frac{15}{9} = \frac{5}{\square}$, $\square =$ _____

15. $\frac{4}{7} = \frac{16}{\square}$, $\square =$ _____

16. $\frac{3}{\square} = \frac{18}{24}$, $\square =$ _____

17. $\frac{16}{\square} = \frac{4}{3}$, $\square =$ _____

18. $\frac{25}{\square} = \frac{5}{2}$, $\square =$ _____

19. $\frac{7}{\square} = \frac{21}{27}$, $\square =$ _____

20. $\frac{8}{\square} = \frac{64}{72}$, $\square =$ _____

21. $\frac{5}{18} = \frac{\square}{90}$, $\square =$ _____

22. $\frac{\square}{56} = \frac{2}{7}$, $\square =$ _____

23. $\frac{\square}{6} = \frac{10}{12}$, $\square =$ _____

24. $\frac{24}{\square} = \frac{36}{21}$, $\square =$ _____

EXERCISE • SET 2

EXAMPLE 7   The scale on a diagram of a box is 1:20. If I measure 2.3 cm on the diagram, what length would this represent on the box?

SOLUTION   If the scale is 1:20, then

$$\frac{\text{length on diagram}}{\text{length on box}} = \frac{1}{20}$$

$$\frac{2.3 \text{ cm}}{\text{length on box}} = \frac{1}{20}$$

Cross-multiply.
$20 \times 2.3 \text{ cm} = 1 \times \text{length on box}$
$\phantom{20 \times 2.3 \text{ cm}} 46 \text{ cm} = \text{length on box}$
The length on the box is 46 cm.

For each question, set up a proportion and solve it.

1. A cake recipe uses 375 mL of flour and 200 mL of sugar.

    a) What is the ratio of sugar to flour? _____

    b) If the recipe is to be increased and 300 mL of sugar are used, how much flour should be used? _____

2. Cement is mixed in the ratio of 1 part cement to 3 parts sand.

    a) If you have 2.5 kg of cement, how much sand do you need? _____

    b) What is the mass of the mixture? _____

3. Dry cells sell at 4 for $2.59. What is the cost of one dry cell to the nearest cent?

    _____

4. Raspberries are selling at 2 boxes for $1.89. How much will 8 boxes cost? _____

5. Plastic water pipe sells at $2.49 per 3 m length. How much will 10 m cost (to the nearest cent)? _____

6. Copper wire cable with ground for electrical wiring costs $8.40 for a 30 m coil. What will 85 m cost (to the nearest cent)? _____

7. Cat food is on sale at 4 cans for $1.68. What will 50 cans cost? _____

8. I can buy a 400 g box of breakfast cereal for $1.49 and a 600 g box of the same cereal for $2.13. Which is the better buy? (HINT: Set up proportions to find what 100 g of each box costs in cents.) _____

9. The Olde Fashioned Ice Cream Parlor is having a sale: 2 L cartons are on sale for $2.39 and 0.25 L cartons are on sale for $0.31. Which has the cheaper unit price?

    _____

10. If the 0.25 L cartons in Question 9 had been priced at 2 for $0.55, which size carton would have the cheaper unit price? _____

EXERCISE • SET 3 _____

1. The monthly income statement for the Blue Water Electric Company shows this month's total sales as $9000; total expenses, $5000; and net income, $4000. Find:

    a) the ratio of net income to sales, _____

    b) the ratio of total expenses to sales. _____

    Reduce each ratio to its lowest terms.

2. The scale on this segment of a road map is 1:880 000.

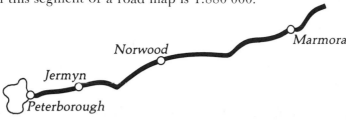

a) If I measure the distance on the map from the outskirts of Peterborough to Jermyn to be 1.5 cm, what is the distance in kilometres from the outskirts of Peterborough to Jermyn? _____

b) I measure the distance on the map from the outskirts of Peterborough to Marmora to be 8.0 cm. What is the distance in kilometres from the outskirts of Peterborough to Marmora? _____

c) What is the distance in kilometres from Jermyn to Marmora? _____

3. The monthly income statement for Caccio's Drugs shows this month's sales to be $10 000; total expenses, $5800; salaries, $2100; and net income, $4200. Find the ratios of:

a) net income to sales, _____

b) salaries to net income, _____

c) total expenses to sales, _____

d) total expenses to net income. _____

Reduce each ratio to its lowest terms.

4. A photograph which is 79 mm in length and 57 mm in width is to be enlarged. In the enlargement the width will be 85.5 mm. What will be the length of the enlargement?

_____

8·3 USING RATIO AND PROPORTION

EXAMPLE 1 The sales for departments A, B, and C in a department store are in the ratio of 2:3:4 respectively. If total sales for the three departments were $108 000 in October, what were the sales for each department?

SOLUTION   The $108 000 represents 2 equal parts for department A, 3 equal parts for department B, and 4 equal parts for department C.
Total parts = 2 + 3 + 4 = 9 parts
9 parts = $108 000
1 part = $108 000 ÷ 9 = $12 000

Therefore:
Sales for department A = 2 × $12 000 = $24 000
Sales for department B = 3 × $12 000 = $36 000
Sales for department C = 4 × $12 000 = $48 000

NOTE To check the answer, the departmental sales of $24 000, $36 000, and $48 000 should total $108 000.

EXAMPLE 2 Three friends Barbara, Jack, and Rick opened a restaurant and contributed $2500, $3000, and $4500 respectively to the venture. How should they share profits of $150 000 for the first year of business?

SOLUTION The friends' contributions are in the ratio of:

$$2500 : 3000 : 4500 = 25 : 30 : 45$$
$$= 5 : 6 : 9$$
$$\text{Total parts} = 5 + 6 + 9 = 20$$
$$1 \text{ part} = \$150\ 000 \div 20$$
$$= \$7500$$

Barbara's share is: 5 × $7500 = $37 500
Jack's share is: 6 × $7500 = $45 000
Rick's share is: 9 × $7500 = $67 500
Does the answer check?

EXERCISE • SET 1

1. The sales for the grocery department and the meat department of a supermarket are in the ratio of 3:5. If total sales for the two departments were $24 000 in November, what were the sales for each department? _____, _____

2. Rent expense is allotted to each department of a department store according to the number of square metres of floor space used by each department. If the floor space used by the jewellery, the men's wear, and accessories departments is in the ratio of 2:5:7, how would a total rent expense of $4200 for the three departments be allotted?

   _____, _____, _____

3. Mary, Harry, and Bob paid for a lottery ticket in the ratio of 2:1:2. If they won the $50 000 prize, how should they share their winnings? _____, _____,

   _____

4. Ricco, Smith, and Van den Deen bought a race horse and paid for it in the ratio of 3:2:4. How should they share winnings of $180 000? _____, _____,

   _____

5. Woodforth and Heinecke invested $10 000 and $20 000 respectively in an electronics repair business. How should they share profits of $21 000? _____, _____

6. The rent expense in a department store is based on the area of floor space used by each department. Some departments are: hardware, 70 m²; housewares, 80 m²; and garden equipment, 50 m². How should a total rent of $800 be allocated? _____ ,

_____ , _____

7. Three friends James, Alice, and Karen pool some savings to invest in the stock market. James contributes $200; Alice, $300; and Karen, $500. After six months, they have made a profit of $600 by buying and selling stock. How should the friends share this profit? _____ , _____ , _____

8. Brontman and Rickle formed a partnership. Brontman contributed $15 000 in capital, and Rickle $20 000 in capital. How should they share $70 000 in profits? _____ ,

_____

EXERCISE • SET 2

1. Due to the amount of their original investments in a partnership, Kibble and Behron agreed to divide the profits and losses in the ratio of 3:5 respectively. How should they divide

a) a profit of $32 000, _____ , _____

b) a loss of $20 000? _____ , _____

2. Irvine and Kohl formed a partnership and agreed to share any profit in the ratio of their original investments. If Irvine invested $8000 and Kohl $14 000, how should they share a profit of $11 000? _____ , _____

3. Kestler, Clark, and LeFevre formed a partnership to purchase an apartment building. They agreed to share the profits in the ratio of their original investments. If Kestler invested $70 000; Clark, $90 000; and LeFevre, $120 000; how should they share a profit of $56 000? _____ , _____ , _____

4. Hutchison, Legassuc, and Sneider formed a partnership in a real estate business and agreed to share the profits and losses according to the amount that each of them invested. Hutchison invested $10 000; Legassuc, $12 000; and Sneider, $8000. How should they share a loss of $3000? _____ , _____ , _____

5. Three doctors formed a partnership and built their own clinic. LeClerk contributed $20 000; Jordaines, $30 000; and McIntosh, $40 000. How should they share a bill for property taxes of $919.80? _____ , _____ , _____

6. Shannon, Ressler, and Ziegler have $50 000, $60 000, and $70 000 invested in a partnership which, out of the year's profits, pays them each $1500 a month and divides the remaining profit between them in proportion to their investments. How much does each partner receive, including salary, out of this year's profit of $70 000?

_____ , _____ , _____

1. Mary Seigel and Joan Kahn invested $8000 and $10 000 respectively in a food store and restaurant. They agreed to share the profits in the ratio of their original investments. One year later, Joan was forced to withdraw $2000 of her original investment from the partnership.

   a) In what ratio should Mary and Joan share a $2500 profit for the second year?

   _____

   b) How much of that profit should each receive? _____ , _____

2. Ruth Lesko and Peter Malette invested $15 000 and $10 000 respectively in a retail outlet and agreed to share profits in the ratio of their investments. One year later, Peter found it necessary to withdraw $5000 of his investment from the business. How should Peter and Ruth share a profit of $18 000 for the second year of business?

   _____ , _____

3. Hirst and Liddle formed a partnership with Hirst investing $20 000 and Liddle, $25 000. They agreed to share the profits in the ratio of their investments. Six months later Liddle had to withdraw $15 000 of his investment. How should the partners share a profit of $7500 for the first year of business? Complete the solution.

   SOLUTION
   Split the year into 2 six-month periods.

   Average, Hirst $= \dfrac{20\ 000 + 20\ 000}{2} =$ _____

   Average, Liddle $= \dfrac{25\ 000 + 10\ 000}{2} =$ _____

   Ratio of averages: $\dfrac{\text{Average, Hirst}}{\text{Average, Liddle}} =$ _____

   Total parts = _____ + _____ = _____

   Ratio, Hirst = _____

   Ratio, Liddle = _____

   Share of profit, Hirst = _____

   Share of profit, Liddle = _____

4. Visser and Schmidt formed a partnership with Visser investing $15 000 and Schmidt, $20 000 agreeing to share profits in the ratio of their investments. Six months later Visser had to withdraw $4000 of her investment. How should the partners share a profit of $29 700 for the first year of business? Complete the solution.

SOLUTION

Split the year into 2 six-month periods.

$$\text{Average, Visser} = \frac{\underline{\qquad} + \underline{\qquad}}{2} = \underline{\qquad}$$

$$\text{Average, Schmidt} = \frac{\underline{\qquad} + \underline{\qquad}}{2} = \underline{\qquad}$$

Ratio of averages = _____

Total parts = _____

Ratio, Visser = _____

Ratio, Schmidt = _____

Share of profit, Visser = _____

Share of profit, Schmidt = _____

5. Kawaga and McDonald formed a partnership investing $20 000 each and agreeing to share profits in the ratio of their average investment for the year. Three months later McDonald withdrew $5000 of his investment and at the end of six months he put an investment of $7500 back into the business. At the end of nine months, Kawaga put a further investment of $10 000 into the business. How should the partners share a profit of $34 000 for the year? Complete the solution.

SOLUTION

Split the year into 4 three-month periods.

$$\text{Average, Kawaga} = \frac{20\ 000 + 20\ 000 + 20\ 000 + 30\ 000}{4} = \underline{\qquad}$$

$$\text{Average, McDonald} = \frac{20\ 000 + 15\ 000 + 22\ 500 + 22\ 500}{4} = \underline{\qquad}$$

Ratio of averages = _____

Number of parts = _____

Ratio, Kawaga = _____

Ratio, McDonald = _____

Share of profit, Kawaga = _____

Share of profit, McDonald = _____

6. Meyer and Ing formed a partnership investing $15 000 each and agreeing to share profits in the ratio of their average investment for the year. Three months later, Meyer withdrew $5000 of her investment and, at the end of nine months, she reinvested $5000 in the business. Ing invested a further $5000 at the end of three months, $5000 more at the end of six months, and $5000 more at the end of nine months. How should the partners share a profit of $28 000 for the year? Complete the solution.

SOLUTION
Split the year into 4 three-month periods.

$$\text{Average, Meyer} = \frac{\quad + \quad + \quad + \quad}{4} = \underline{\hspace{2cm}}$$

$$\text{Average, Ing} = \frac{\quad + \quad + \quad + \quad}{4} = \underline{\hspace{2cm}}$$

Ratio of averages = \underline{\hspace{2cm}}

Number of parts = \underline{\hspace{2cm}}

Ratio, Meyer = \underline{\hspace{2cm}}

Ratio, Ing = \underline{\hspace{2cm}}

Share of profit, Meyer = \underline{\hspace{2cm}}

Share of profit, Ing = \underline{\hspace{2cm}}

7. Wismer, Racine, and Jobe formed a partnership. From the annual profit Wismer and Racine each receive $300 salary a week and Jobe receives $500 a week. The partners agree to share the remaining profit in proportion to their investments. Wismer invested $30 000; Racine, $40 000; and Jobe, $20 000. How much in wages and profits did each partner receive (salary and profit) out of a year's profits of $75 000?

\underline{\hspace{3cm}}, \underline{\hspace{3cm}}, \underline{\hspace{3cm}}

8·4 REVIEW

EXERCISE • SET 1

Express the ratios as fractions reduced to their lowest terms.

1. 16:36 = \underline{\hspace{2cm}}

2. 15:25 = \underline{\hspace{2cm}}

3. 21:56 = \underline{\hspace{2cm}}

4. 27:81 = \underline{\hspace{2cm}}

What is the ratio of:

5. 8 h to 3 d? = \underline{\hspace{2cm}}

6. 50 d to 1 a? = \underline{\hspace{2cm}}

7. 2 weeks to 1.5 a? = \underline{\hspace{2cm}}

8. 50 cm to 3 m? = \underline{\hspace{2cm}}

9. 5 mm to 4 cm? = \underline{\hspace{2cm}}

10. 35 mL to 1 L? = \underline{\hspace{2cm}}

Find the unknown term in each proportion correct to one place after the decimal if necessary.

11. $\dfrac{\square}{7} = \dfrac{24}{28}$, $\square = $ _____

12. $\dfrac{\square}{28} = \dfrac{30}{35}$, $\square = $ _____

13. $\dfrac{5}{6} = \dfrac{\square}{72}$, $\square = $ _____

14. $\dfrac{14}{6} = \dfrac{\square}{27}$, $\square = $ _____

15. $\dfrac{2}{11} = \dfrac{6}{\square}$, $\square = $ _____

16. $\dfrac{63}{15} = \dfrac{21}{\square}$, $\square = $ _____

17. $\dfrac{5}{\square} = \dfrac{25}{35}$, $\square = $ _____

18. $\dfrac{26}{\square} = \dfrac{39}{15}$, $\square = $ _____

19. $\dfrac{\square}{84} = \dfrac{24}{63}$, $\square = $ _____

20. $\dfrac{5}{\square} = \dfrac{3}{2}$, $\square = $ _____

21. The sales for the stationery, the book, and the cosmetic departments are predicted to be in the ratio of 1:4:5. If total sales predicted for the three departments are $50 000, what should the amount of sales for each department be? _____, _____, _____

22. Koegler, Smith, and Hahn formed a partnership. Koegler invested $10 000; Smith, $5000; and Hahn, $15 000. How should they share a profit of $45 000 at the end of the first year? _____, _____, _____

EXERCISE • SET 2

1. Your earnings from a part-time job were $110 and you spent $61.60 on a tape recorder. What is the ratio of the cost of the recorder to your earnings? _____

2. As accountant for a small firm you calculate that total sales for each month of the year are: January, $1200; February, $1100; March, $800; April, $900; May, $900; June, $1100; July, $1100; August, $1200; September, $1000; October, $900; November, $1000; December, $1600. Find the ratio of:

a) sales for March to sales for December, _____

b) sales for August to sales for December, _____

c) total sales for the first half of the year to total sales for the last half of the year, _____

d) sales for March to total sales for the year, _____

e) sales for December to total sales for the year. _____

3. Find the increase or decrease of November's figures over October's figures for each item in the Blue Water Electric Company's Income Statement. For each item's increase or decrease, find the ratio of the increase or decrease to the amount for October. Reduce each ratio to its lowest terms.

blue water electric	Comparative Income Statement For the Months Ended November 30, 19-- and October 31, 19--			
	Month Ended Nov. 30, 19--	**Month Ended Oct. 31, 19--**	**Increase or Decrease**	**Ratio**
	Amount	**Amount**	**Amount**	
Sales Revenue	$10 000	$9 000	_____	_____
Expenses:				
Salaries	5 000	4 500	_____	_____
Utilities	130	100	_____	_____
Telephone	30	20	_____	_____
Advertising	640	480	_____	_____
Total Expenses	5 800	5 100	_____	_____
Net Income	$ 4 200	$3 900	_____	_____

4. Western Manufacturing Company tries to maintain the ratio of total sales to production costs at 3:2. If total production of $1 325 000 is planned for the coming year, what amount should total sales be expected to reach? _____

5. Newton and Hunter form a partnership. Newton invests $15 000 and Hunter invests $20 000 in the partnership. Find the ratio (reduced to its lowest terms) of Newton's investment to Hunter's investment. _____

6. If the partnership in Question 5 earns $2800 profit, what should be each partner's share? _____ , _____

7. Department A has total sales of $14 000 and its total purchases amount to $10 000. If department B is to have the same ratio of total sales to total purchases as that for department A, what should its total sales be if its total purchases are $15 000?

_____

8. Jill Lee and George Ballard invest $6000 and $10 000 respectively, in a joint project. If the investment earns a total of $20 000 profit, what should be each partner's share?

_____ , _____

EXERCISE • SET 3

1. A child's chair is scaled to an adult's chair in the ratio of 1:3. If the seat of the adult's chair is 400 mm high, how high should the seat of the child's chair be, correct to the nearest millimetre? _____

2. The scale of a map is 1 cm to 5 km. If the distance from Winston to Pleasant Point measures 75 mm on the map, what is the actual distance in kilometres? _____

3. Koenig, Johnson, and Lebrun form a partnership to purchase a warehouse. They agree to share profits according to the ratio of their investments. If the partners invest $25 000, $35 000, and $40 000 respectively, how should they share profits of $180 000?

   _____, _____, _____

4. Mary Caruso and John Mah invested $70 000 and $80 000 respectively in a car rental agency and agreed to share the profits in the ratio of their investments. One year later, Mary invested another $20 000 in the business. How should they share a profit of $68 000 for the second year of business? _____, _____

5. Jackson and Stegehuis formed a partnership with Jackson investing $10 000 and Stegehuis, $15 000. Six months later Stegehuis invested $10 000 more in the partnership. How should the partners share a profit of $82 500 at the end of the first year of business if they agreed to share this profit in the ratio of their average investments? _____, _____

6. Levesque, Turner, and McNabb opened a business investing respectively $20 000, $20 000, and $40 000. Levesque managed the business and drew a salary of $2000 a month and Turner worked with her, drawing a salary of $1500 per month. McNabb remained a silent partner and drew no salary. Salaries were paid out of annual profits. The remainder of the profit was shared in the ratio of the partners' average investments. If McNabb withdrew $10 000 of his investment after the first six months, how much should each partner receive (salary and profit) out of the first year's profit of $60 000? _____, _____, _____

CHAPTER 9

PERCENTAGE

9·1 EXPRESSING PERCENT AS A DECIMAL QUANTITY

Percent means "per 100".

When we write 5%, we mean 5 parts out of 100 parts.

5% is the ratio $\frac{5}{100}$.

The decimal equivalent of $\frac{5}{100}$ is 0.05.

REMEMBER   To divide by 100, move the decimal point 2 places to the left.

EXAMPLE 1   Find the decimal equivalent of 25%.

SOLUTION $25\% = \frac{25}{100}$

$\qquad\qquad = 0.25$

EXAMPLE 2   Find the decimal equivalent of 145%.

SOLUTION $145\% = \frac{145}{100}$

$\qquad\qquad = 1.45$

EXAMPLE 3   Find the decimal equivalent of 0.5%.

SOLUTION $0.5\% = \frac{0.5}{100}$

$\qquad\qquad = 0.005$

EXERCISE • SET 1

Find the decimal equivalents of the following percents. Do not use your calculator.

1. 35% _____	**6.** 115% _____	**11.** 6.25% _____	**16.** 0.4% _____
2. 45% _____	**7.** 130% _____	**12.** 9.5% _____	**17.** 0.75% _____
3. 50% _____	**8.** 200% _____	**13.** 10.75% _____	**18.** 0.25% _____
4. 62% _____	**9.** 175% _____	**14.** 8.25% _____	**19.** 0.01% _____
5. 70% _____	**10.** 235% _____	**15.** 11.75% _____	**20.** 0.05% _____

EXAMPLE 4 Express 0.35 as a percent.

SOLUTION $0.35 = \dfrac{35}{100}$ or $0.35 = 0.35 \times 100\%$

$\qquad\qquad\quad = 35\%\qquad\qquad\quad = 35\%$

NOTE To change a decimal to a percent, move the decimal point 2 places to the right.

Express the following decimal quantities as percents. Do not use your calculator.

1. 0.75 _____	**6.** 1.25 _____	**11.** 0.355 _____	**16.** 0.005 _____
2. 0.25 _____	**7.** 1.50 _____	**12.** 0.045 _____	**17.** 0.0025 _____
3. 0.05 _____	**8.** 1.60 _____	**13.** 0.0925 _____	**18.** 0.0075 _____
4. 0.01 _____	**9.** 2.35 _____	**14.** 0.055 _____	**19.** 0.001 _____
5. 0.03 _____	**10.** 2.55 _____	**15.** 0.085 _____	**20.** 0.0001 _____

9·2 FINDING THE PERCENTAGE OF A NUMBER

EXAMPLE 1 Find 2% of 235.

SOLUTION Since 2% means 2 parts out of 100 parts, the question really asks: "How many parts out of 235 parts equals the ratio, 2 parts out of 100 parts?"

$$\frac{\square}{235} = \frac{2}{100}$$

$$\square = \frac{2}{100} \times 235$$

$$\square = 0.02 \times 235$$

$$\square = 4.70$$

QUICK SOLUTION

To find a percentage of a given number:
- Change the percent to a decimal.
- Multiply the given number by this decimal quantity.

EXAMPLE 2 Find 15% of 120.

SOLUTION 15% of $120 = 0.15 \times 120$

$\qquad\qquad\qquad\qquad\quad = 18.00$

EXERCISE • SET 1

Calculate each percentage correct to two places after the decimal where necessary.

1. 2% of 500 _____
2. 3% of 250 _____
3. 40% of 85 _____
4. 75% of 120 _____
5. 7% of 184 _____
6. 6% of 362 _____
7. 25% of 180 _____
8. 18% of 275 _____
9. 2% of 923 _____
10. 9% of 162 _____
11. 4% of 725 _____
12. 5% of 820 _____

13. 12% of 892 _____
14. 4% of 912 _____
15. 35% of 640 _____
16. 33% of 165 _____
17. 115% of 325 _____
18. 117% of 863 _____
19. 225% of 212 _____
20. 107% of 723 _____
21. 110% of 235 _____
22. 135% of 1260 _____
23. 175% of 4263 _____
24. 118% of 6295 _____

EXERCISE • SET 2

Calculate each percentage correct to three places after the decimal where necessary.

1. 5% of 75 _____
2. 0.5% of 262 _____
3. 0.05% of 682 _____
4. 0.07% of 154 _____
5. 3.5% of 295 _____
6. 0.35% of 728 _____
7. 1.5% of 960 _____

8. 3.5% of 75 _____
9. 14.5% of 123 _____
10. 6.6% of 1163 _____
11. 17.8% of 8642 _____
12. 33.3% of 285 _____
13. 66.6% of 8634 _____
14. 125.5% of 765 _____

EXERCISE • SET 3

Calculate each percentage correct to four places after the decimal where necessary.

1. 5% of 86.34 _____
2. 0.5% of 98.25 _____
3. 7% of 1.234 _____
4. 7.5% of 2.341 _____
5. 7.05% of 8.128 _____

6. 0.251% of 6.34 _____
7. 1.327% of 25.32 _____
8. 10.667% of 11.7 _____
9. 175.251% of 84.3 _____
10. 37.75% of 9.876 _____

9·3 CALCULATING DOLLARS AND CENTS

When taking a percentage of an amount expressed in dollars and cents, always give your answer correct to two places after the decimal.

EXAMPLE   Calculate 15.5% of $125.35.

SOLUTION   15.5% of 125.35 $= 0.155 \times 125.35$
$$= 19.429\,25$$
$$= 19.43$$

15.5% of $125.35 is $19.43.

EXERCISE • SET 1

Calculate each percentage correct to the nearest cent.

1. 3% of $18.75 _____

2. 4% of $125.66 _____

3. 5% of $629.10 _____

4. 0.5% of $86.94 _____

5. 0.05% of $882 _____

6. 0.66% of $862.90 _____

7. 6.67% of $925.36 _____

8. 66.66% of $726.50 _____

9. 0.125% of $986.75 _____

10. 12.5% of $92.50 _____

11. 18.34% of $87.43 _____

12. 33.3% of $263.44 _____

13. 125.5% of $625.40 _____

14. 5.5% of $1163.04 _____

15. 7.2% of $81 234.50 _____

16. 45.7% of $9342 _____

EXERCISE • SET 2

Calculate each percentage correct to the nearest cent.

1. 12.5% of $93 110.75 _____

2. 0.6% of $76 345.76 _____

3. 0.667% of $4321.33 _____

4. 0.55% of $325.64 _____

5. 3.333% of $864.72 _____

6. 194.43% of $923.04 _____

7. 255.55% of $92.30 _____

8. 1.125% of $78.55 _____

9. 0.004% of $1972.24 _____

10. 9.756% of $27.96 _____

EXERCISE • SET 3

1. Anna Duceau reads in the morning paper that she can expect her local property tax to increase by 10.8% this year. If her property tax was $863.57 last year, what can Anna expect to pay this year? _____

2. Jim Cotter looked at a winter jacket he liked in Grainger's Men's Wear. It was priced at $99.95 and he decided to return the next week and buy it. The next day the store advertised a sale; all winter clothing was reduced by 35%. What would Jim pay for the jacket if he bought it at the reduced price? _____

3. The Millers estimate that they spend $475 a month on food purchases. They are planning their budget for next year when food costs are expected to rise by 8.6%. How much should the Millers estimate that they will spend on food next year?

_____

4. I bought a bond worth $500. Attached to the bond are coupons, each valued at 2.25% of the bond's value. How much is the money value of each coupon? _____

5. A pair of skis were priced at $89.50. The store clerk sold them at 20% off the price.

a) What was the price after the 20% reduction? _____

b) The clerk made up the sales slip and added a provincial sales tax of 7%. What was the total amount of the purchase? _____

6. A manufacturer can produce an electric drill at a total cost of $27.20. The selling price is $6.80 more than the total cost to the manufacturer. A federal sales tax of 13% of the selling price is added to the selling price. What does a store purchasing the drills from the manufacturer pay for each drill? _____

7. Mary Evans sells on commission. She is paid a commission of 15% on the first $5000 of sales and 20% on any sales over $5000. In December, Mary's total sales were $8769.50. How much money did she receive in commissions? _____

8. Jack Bondi sells on commission. His commission on the first $4500 of sales is 18% and 15% on any sales over this figure. In January, Jack's total sales were $8759.60. How much money did he receive in commissions? _____

9. Marc Lepierre sells on commission. His commission on the first $2000 of sales is 12%, on the next $4000 of sales 15%, and 20% on all sales over $6000. Marc made sales of $11 592 in January and was given a bonus of 2% on his sales for having the best sales for that month. How much money did Marc receive? _____

10. Jeanne Dewar sells on commission. She receives 8% on all sales plus 12% on all sales over $6000. If Jeanne had total sales of $9817.50 for December, how much money did she receive from commissions? _____

9·4 CALCULATING WHAT PERCENT ONE NUMBER IS OF ANOTHER

EXAMPLE 1 On a given day, 5 pupils were absent from a class of 20 pupils. What percent of the class was absent?

SOLUTION Percent means per 100. The question to be answered is: "How many parts out of 100 parts equal 5 parts out of 20 parts?"

$$\frac{\square}{100} = \frac{5}{20}$$

$$\square = \frac{5}{20} \times 100$$

$$\square = 25$$

SHORT METHOD

$$\text{Percent absent} = \frac{5}{20} \times 100$$

$$= 25$$

The number of students absent is 25% of the class.

EXAMPLE 2 Gerry earned $145.75 for his first week at a summer job. He went to a sporting goods store and paid $30.98 for tennis shorts. What percent of his earnings did Gerry spend on the tennis shorts?

SOLUTION

$$\text{Percent spent} = \frac{30.98}{145.75} \times 100$$

$$= 21.255$$

The amount spent on tennis shorts was 21.26% of his earnings.

EXAMPLE 3 255 is what percent of 347 (correct to two places after the decimal)?

SOLUTION

$$\text{Percent} = \frac{255}{347} \times 100$$

$$= 73.487$$

255 is 73.49% of 347.

EXERCISE • SET 1

Calculate each percent correct to two places after the decimal if necessary.

1. What percent is 50 of 80? _____

2. What percent is 35 of 140? _____

3. 13 is what percent of 65? _____

4. 12 is what percent of 48? _____

5. What percent is 18 of 144? _____

6. What percent is 32 of 512? _____

7. 125 is what percent of 200? _____

8. 10 is what percent of 55? _____

9. What percent is 40 of 45? _____

10. What percent is 15 of 90? _____

11. 1.7 is what percent of 2.9? _____

12. 1.5 is what percent of 87.5? _____

13. What percent is 8.67 of 5.94? _____

14. What percent is 589 of 478? _____

15. 0.125 is what percent of 0.225? _____

16. 0.258 is what percent of 1.375? _____

17. What percent is 1516 of 2363? _____

18. What percent is 417 848 of 536 917? _____

19. 5163.7 is what percent of 8371.6? _____

20. 10 379.67 is what percent of 11 896.54? _____

EXERCISE • SET 2 _____

EXAMPLE 4   What percent is 50 cm of 2 m?

SOLUTION   The quantities must be expressed in the same units. Usually, it is easier to change units from larger measurements to smaller measurements.

$$2 \text{ m} = 2 \times 100 \text{ cm}$$
$$= 200 \text{ cm}$$
$$\text{Percent} = \frac{50}{200} \times 100$$
$$= 25$$

50 cm is 25% of 2 m.

Calculate, correct to two places after the decimal if necessary, what percent:

1. 50 cm is of 3 m. _____

2. 5 mm is of 4 cm. _____

3. 300 mm is of 1 m. _____

4. 350 m is of 1 km. _____

5. 446 m is of 2.5 km. _____

6. 5 h is of 7 h. _____

7. 20 min is of 2 h. _____

8. 15 s is of 3 min. _____

9. 3000 s is of 5 h. _____

10. 4 min is of 8 min 10 s. _____

11. 35 mL is of 1 L. _____

12. 750 mL is of 2 L. _____

13. 800 g is of 1 kg. _____

14. 257 g is of 3 kg. _____

15. 5700 mg is of 8 g. _____

16. 35 weeks is of 2 years. _____

EXERCISE • SET 3 _____

EXAMPLE 5   Calculate what percent $5.89 is of $6.45 correct to three places after the decimal.

SOLUTION   Percent $= \dfrac{5.89}{6.45} \times 100$

$$= 91.3178$$
$$= 91.318$$

$5.89 is 91.318% of $6.45.

Calculate, correct to three places after the decimal, what percent:

1. $5.00 is of $10.50. _____

2. 78¢ is of $2.00. _____

3. $10.95 is of $25.95. _____

4. $4.77 is of $5.97. _____

5. $125.25 is of $555.75. _____

6. $349.49 is of $399.98. _____

7. $1275.75 is of $3479.65. _____

8. $5676.82 is of $10 879.44. _____

9. $11 765.44 is of $8432.50. _____

In the following questions, calculate each answer correct to two places after the decimal where necessary.

10. Anne worked at a part-time summer job and earned $588. At the end of the summer she had $298 in the bank and had spent the rest of her wages.

a) What percent of her earnings did Anne save? _____

b) What percent did she spend? _____

11. A lakeshore lot was purchased for $4500. Three years later it was sold for $11 900.

a) Calculate what percent the selling price is of the purchase price. _____

b) If the real-estate agent's fee for selling the lot was $1190, what was the profit made on the lot? _____

c) Calculate what percent the profit is of the purchase price. _____

12. The property taxes on a house assessed at $20 000 are $1020 per year.

    a) What percent is the property tax to the assessment value? _____

    b) If the house could be sold at $45 000, what is the percent of property tax to sale value? _____

13. A family has an income of $32 500 a year. The family spends $5200 this year on food.

    a) What percent of income is spent on food? _____

    b) If food prices go up by 11.25% next year and income by 8%, what percent of income will be spent on food next year? _____

9·5 CALCULATING PERCENT INCREASE OR DECREASE

EXERCISE • SET 1

To find the percent increase or decrease for the following Sales Reports:
- Subtract last month's sales from this month's sales.
- If this difference is a positive amount, the amount is an increase. Indicate this by placing a plus sign after the amount.
- If the difference is a negative amount, the amount is a decrease. Indicate this by bracketing the amount.
- To calculate the percent increase or decrease:

$$\text{Percent Increase or Decrease} = \frac{\text{Increase or Decrease}}{\text{Last Month's Sales}} \times 100\%$$

- Round off each percent correct to two places after the decimal.
  If the percent obtained is a percent of increase, indicate this by placing a plus sign after the percent.
  If the percent obtained is a percent of decrease, indicate this by placing a minus sign after the percent or bracketing the percent.

NOTE In finding the percent increase or decrease, always put the increase or decrease over the sales from which the increase or decrease takes place. This is usually the sales figure bearing the earlier date.

Complete each Sales Report. In calculating percents, always round off correct to *two* places after the decimal unless a different degree of accuracy is indicated.

1.

Roche

Manufacturing Company Limited

Sales Report   Month Ending Jan. 31, 19--

Dept.	This Month's Sales	Last Month's Sales	Amount of Increase or Decrease	Percent Increase or Decrease
A	$1 819.25	$1 748.50		
B	2 154.66	2 036.49		
C	1 495.49	1 582.91		
D	2 056.63	1 879.54		
E	1 979.84	2 136.45		
F	2 139.78	2 057.38		
G	2 165.45	1 965.56		
H	2 225.37	2 107.14		

2.

Roche

Manufacturing Company Limited

Sales Report   Month Ending Feb. 28, 19--

Dept.	This Month's Sales	Last Month's Sales	Amount of Increase or Decrease	Percent Increase or Decrease
A	$1 748.50	$1 636.75		
B	2 036.49	1 854.22		
C	1 582.91	1 697.40		
D	1 879.54	1 975.37		
E	2 136.45	1 917.58		
F	2 057.38	1 998.43		
G	1 965.56	2 054.37		
H	2 107.14	2 008.17		

3.

Roche

Manufacturing Company Limited

Sales Report   Month Ending March 31, 19--

Dept.	Sales for March	Sales for February	Amount of Increase or Decrease	Percent of Increase or Decrease
A	$2 027.39	$1 819.25	$	
B	1 963.52	2 154.66		
C	1 689.94	1 495.49		
D	2 278.65	2 056.63		
E	1 753.44	1 979.84		
F	1 668.23	2 139.78		
G	2 397.41	2 165.45		
H	2 076.56	2 225.37		

4.

Roche

Manufacturing Company Limited

Sales Report for 19_7

Dept.	Sales for 19_7	Sales for 19_6	Amount of Increase or Decrease	Percent of Increase or Decrease
A	$24 289.47	$19 687.44	$	
B	23 562.24	20 566.38		
C	20 279.28	17 354.75		
D	26 343.80	20 987.47		
E	21 041.28	20 356.68		
F	20 018.76	19 548.31		
G	26 768.93	21 649.30		
H	24 918.75	18 569.43		

EXERCISE • SET 2

To find what percent each department's sales are of the total sales:
- Calculate the total sales.
- Calculate what percent each department's sales are of the total sales:

$$\text{Percent of Total Sales} = \frac{\text{Department Sales}}{\text{Total Sales}} \times 100\%$$

- Calculate each percent correct to two places after the decimal.

Complete each Sales Report.

1.

LARRY'S DISCOUNT STORE

Sales Report   Month of April 19--

Department	Sales	Percent of Total Sales
Jewellery	$12 389.27	
Notions	10 561.39	
Appliances	19 242.15	
Kitchenware	7 654.91	
Toys	10 879.57	
Hardware	23 987.56	
Furniture	15 365.87	
Sports	18 487.25	
Total Sales	$	

2.

LARRY'S DISCOUNT STORE

Sales Report   Month of March 19--

Department	Sales	Percent of Total Sales
Jewellery	$13 569.14	
Notions	8 651.99	
Appliances	21 636.45	
Kitchenware	8 835.56	
Toys	8 561.47	
Hardware	20 357.49	
Furniture	12 654.61	
Sports	13 597.47	
Total Sales	$	

EXERCISE • SET 3 _____

1. Complete the following Sales Report.
- Calculate the amount of change by subtracting the first half-year sales from the second half-year sales.
- Calculate the percent change by dividing the amount of change by the first half-year sales and converting this decimal to a percent.
- Round off the percent to two places after the decimal.
- Indicate percent increases with " + " signs and percent decreases with " − " signs.

Fortune Sales

Sales Report
For year, 19 —

District	First Half Year Sales	Second Half Year Sales	Amount of Change	Percent Change
A	$ 28 685.12	$ 32 654.30	$ _____	_____
B	109 855.40	90 865.88	_____	_____
C	35 488.92	45 644.30	_____	_____
D	200 309.90	235 654.30	_____	_____
E	47 633.20	50 800.55	_____	_____
F	346 755.26	406 634.04	_____	_____
G	68 866.50	76 500.50	_____	_____
H	508 730.80	606 540.90	_____	_____

2. Complete the following sales analysis by calculating the percent, correct to two places after the decimal, each department's sales are of the total sales.

Easton Sales

Sales Analysis For year 19 —

Department	Sales	Percent of Total Sales
Jewelry	$ 78 654.60	_____
Men's Clothing	24 865.80	_____
Children's Clothing	34 600.50	_____
Women's Clothing	144 654.00	_____
Dry Goods	12 350.43	_____
Sporting Goods	108 733.22	_____
Hardware	54 399.90	_____
Drugs	9 872.00	_____
Total	$ _____	_____

3. Complete the following expense analysis by calculating what percent each department's expense is of the total expense, correct to three places after the decimal.

Wallace Machine Company Expense Analysis for the month of January, 19 —		
Department	**Expense**	**Percent of Total Expense**
A	$11 278.50	———————
B	6 674.40	———————
C	88 654.40	———————
D	50 832.06	———————
E	9 855.20	———————
F	45 340.66	———————
Total	$	———————

9·6 FINDING A NUMBER WHEN A PERCENT AND PERCENTAGE ARE KNOWN

EXAMPLE   If 25% of a number is 70, what is the number?

SOLUTION   Percent means per 100. The question to be answered is: "70 parts out of how many parts equals 25 parts out of 100 parts?"

Method 1   or   **Method 2**

$$\frac{70}{\square} = \frac{25}{100} \qquad\qquad \frac{70}{\square} = \frac{25}{100}$$

$$70 \times 100 = \square \times 25 \qquad \frac{70}{\square} = 0.25$$

$$\frac{70 \times 100}{25} = \square \qquad\qquad 70 = 0.25 \times \square$$

$$280 = \square \qquad\qquad\qquad \frac{70}{0.25} = \square$$

$$280 = \square$$

The number is 280.

Method 2 demonstrates that a shortcut is possible:

Step 1: 25% = 0.25

Step 2: The required number $= \dfrac{70}{0.25}$

$$= 280$$

The required number is 280.

Check this solution on your calculator.

EXAMPLE 2   If 105 is 35% of a number, what is the number?

SOLUTION   The required number $= \dfrac{\text{Percentage}}{\text{Percent}}$

$$= \frac{105}{0.35}$$
$$= 300$$

The required number is 300.

EXAMPLE 3   If 2025 is 135% of a number, what is the number?

SOLUTION   The required number $= \dfrac{2025}{1.35}$

$$= 1500$$

The required number is 1500.

EXERCISE • SET 1

Using the method shown in Example 3, calculate each answer correct to two places after the decimal where necessary.

1. 5 is 20% of what number? _____

2. 8 is 40% of what number? _____

3. 15 is 30% of what number? _____

4. 175 is 35% of what number? _____

5. 160 is 30% of what number? _____

6. 22 is 110% of what number? _____

7. 250 is 125% of what number? _____

8. $5 is 50% of what amount? _____

9. $5.25 is 30% of what amount? _____

10. $10.50 is 25% of what amount? _____

11. $2.50 is 12.5% of what amount? _____

12. $2.90 is 72.5% of what amount? _____

13. $125.50 is 25.5% of what amount? _____

14. $189.97 is 87.5% of what amount? _____

15. $379.60 is 35.5% of what amount? _____

16. $1359.50 is 125% of what amount? _____

17. $576.30 is 66.7% of what amount? _____

18. $5.95 is 3.25% of what amount? _____

19. $7.87 is 21.25% of what amount? _____

20. $1.98 is 33.33% of what amount? _____

21. $3.57 is 1.75% of what amount? _____

22. $137.95 is 115.5% of what amount? _____

23. $389.99 is 135.5% of what amount? _____

24. $4.98 is 150.5% of what amount? _____

EXERCISE • SET 2

Calculate each sales person's sales in the following reports (correct to the nearest cent),

$$\text{Sales} = \frac{\text{Commission}}{\text{Rate of Commission}}$$

where the rate of commission is expressed as a decimal quantity.

1.

Sales Report Month Ending January 31, 19--			
Salesperson	**Rate of Commission**	**Commission**	**Sales**
Bartley, T.	17%	$ 567.15	$
Donati, J.	15%	495.29	
Laplace, J.	15.5%	607.33	
MacKay, E.	16.5%	527.38	
Pelletier, S.	17.5%	631.92	
Steinberg, T.	15.25%	501.48	

2.

Sales Report Month Ending February 28, 19--			
Salesperson	Rate of Commission	Commission	Sales
Bartley, T.	17.25%	$ 594.36	$
Donati, J.	15.25%	515.27	
Laplace, J.	15.75%	628.31	
MacKay, E.	16.75%	556.42	
Pelletier, S.	17.75%	654.93	
Steinberg, T.	15.5%	527.48	

3.

Sales Report Month Ending March 31, 19--			
Salesperson	Rate of Commission	Commission	Sales
Bartley, T.	17.25%	$ 612.43	$
Donati, J.	15.25%	530.19	
Laplace, J.	15.75%	641.27	
MacKay, E.	16.75%	570.36	
Pelletier, S.	17.75%	667.85	
Steinberg, T.	15.5%	542.67	

Complete the following Monthly Estimates.

NOTE   The given rate of profit must be earned in order to cover the operating costs.

• Calculate the total operating costs by adding rent, utilities, and salaries.

• Calculate the estimated minimum sales for each store. This minimum is equal to:

$$\frac{\text{Total Operating Costs}}{\text{Rate of Profit on Sales}}$$

where the rate of profit on sales is expressed as a decimal quantity.

4.

Lalonde Retailers Limited Moncton, N.B. Estimates for Month of December						
	Operating Costs			Total Operating Costs	Rate of Profit on Sales	Estimated Minimum Sales
Store	Rent	Utilities	Salaries			
#1	$560.00	$256.95	$1250.75		30%	
#2	495.00	247.37	1090.63		32.5%	
#3	525.00	311.21	1385.50		28.5%	
#4	565.00	307.51	1186.50		31.5%	
#5	457.00	290.50	1278.90		33.5%	

5.

Lalonde Retailers Limited
Moncton, N.B.
Estimates for Month of January

Store	Operating Costs			Total Operating Costs	Rate of Profit on Sales	Estimated Minimum Sales
	Rent	Utilities	Salaries			
#1	$560.00	$298.70	$1275.50		30%	
#2	495.00	285.55	1351.60		32.5%	
#3	535.00	340.75	1408.50		28.5%	
#4	565.00	336.80	1215.50		31.5%	
#5	495.00	305.95	1309.40		33.5%	

EXERCISE • SET 3

1. If five students are absent from a class and this represents 25% of the class, how many pupils are present? _____

2. Sales for December are usually 63% of July's sales at a drive-in restaurant. If sales for December are $8965.72, what are the expected sales for July? _____

3. The parts stocked in a car repair shop are not allowed to fall below 60% of total storage capacity. There are 36 hubcaps in the storage bin and this is the minimum of 60%.

   a) What is the total storage capacity? _____

   b) How many hubcaps must be ordered to reach capacity? _____

4. A hardware store must make a profit of 35% of sales to cover operating costs and salaries. If these average $3497.75 a month, what must average sales be per month?

   _____

5. A house is assessed at 82.5% of its resale value for calculating property taxes. If the assessment is $42 525, what is the resale value? _____

9·7 REVIEW

EXERCISE • SET 1

Calculate each percentage correct to the nearest cent.

1. 25% of $37.45 _____

2. 31.8% of $29.94 _____

3. 16.5% of $67.47 _____

4. 76.8% of $125.35 _____

5. 125.9% of $36.96 _____

6. 112.6% of $357.97 _____

7. 0.53% of $1356.40 _____

9. 255.7% of $1.98 _____

8. 1.8% of $974.64 _____

10. 0.36% of $32.98 _____

Calculate each percent correct to two places after the decimal where necessary.

11. What percent is 15 of 60? _____

12. 29 is what percent of 37? _____

13. What percent is 0.55 of 1.95? _____

14. What percent is 565 of 3549? _____

15. 27.625 is what percent of 15.45? _____

16. What percent is 60 cm of 2 m? _____

Calculate each answer correct to two places after the decimal or to the nearest cent.

17. 18 is 30% of what number? _____

18. 240 is 80% of what number? _____

19. 360 is 120% of what number? _____

20. $6 is 30% of what amount? _____

21. $7.50 is 12.5% of what amount? _____

22. $197.65 is 15.5% of what amount? _____

23. $2597.50 is 166.7% of what amount? _____

24. $8.97 is 5.25% of what amount? _____

25. $228.50 is 125.5% of what amount? _____

26. $6.83 is 175.25% of what amount? _____

27. ● Calculate the increase or decrease of November's figures over October's figures for each item.
   ● For each item's increase or decrease, calculate the percent of the increase or decrease to the amount for October, correct to two places after the decimal.

	Month Ended Nov. 30, 19--	Month Ended Oct. 31, 19--	Increase or Decrease	Percent Increase or Decrease
	Amount	Amount	Amount	
Sales Revenue	$10 000	$9 000	_____	_____
Expenses:				
Salaries	5 000	4 500	_____	_____
Utilities	130	100	_____	_____
Telephone	30	20	_____	_____
Advertising	640	480	_____	_____
Total Expenses	5 800	5 100	_____	_____
Net Income	$ 4 200	$3 900	_____	_____

EXERCISE • SET 2

Calculate each percent correct to two places after the decimal.

1. What percent is 350 mL of 2.5 L? _____

2. 625 g is what percent of 1.5 kg? _____

3. What percent is 39¢ of $3? _____

4. $5.95 is what percent of $6.75? _____

5. $2.95 is what percent of $2.48? _____

6. $125.75 is what percent of $397.63? _____

7. What percent is $995.47 of $763.54? _____

For the following Sales Commission Reports
- Calculate each sales person's net sales where:
    Net Sales = Total Sales − Sales Cancelled
- Calculate the commission earned where:
    Commission Earned = Net Sales × Commission Rate
    Commission rate is expressed as a decimal quantity.
- Total salary and commission earned to obtain total earnings.

8.

WARREN'S WHOLESALE

Sales Commission Report   For Week Ended January 31, 19--

Salesperson	Total Sales	Sales Cancelled	Net Sales	Comm. Rate	Comm. Earned	Salary	Total Earnings
Allen, R.	$4257.60	$105.16		1.5%		$80.00	
Boyne, K.	4493.81	239.94		1.25%		85.00	
Dans, L.	3876.25	57.50		1.75%		75.00	
Lacq, R.	4868.92	239.75		1.25%		84.50	
Probert, K.	4099.87	156.72		1.5%		79.50	
Vamplew, S.	3978.98	27.95		2.0%		57.25	

9.

King-O'Leary Inc.

Importers   China, Pottery, Earthenware

Sales Commission Report   Week Ending January 31, 19--

Salesperson	Total Sales	Sales Cancelled	Net Sales	Comm. Rate	Comm. Earned	Salary	Total Earnings
Baker, S.	$4963.30	$597.64		1.5%		$80.00	
Kennedy, R.	4376.40	156.30		1.25%		87.50	
Lavergne, M.	3859.22	29.37		1.75%		77.50	
Bondi, K.	4979.56	527.42		1.25%		84.50	
Blanc, K.	4157.54	72.14		1.5%		79.50	
Van Alst, S.	4039.57	201.57		2.0%		70.50	

Calculate each sales person's sales.

$$\text{Sales} = \frac{\text{Commission Earned}}{\text{Rate of Commission}}$$

Rate of Commission is expressed as a decimal quantity.

10.

Wholesale Hardware		
Sales Report		
Month Ending January 31, 19--		

Salesperson	Rate of Commission	Commission Earned	Sales
Bradley, K.	17%	$514.36	$
Dort, T.	15%	497.60	
LaVerne, S.	15.5%	615.27	
Martin, P.	16.25%	513.42	
Previer, S.	17.25%	585.17	
Moses, R.	16.75%	498.78	

11.

Wholesale Hardware Sales Report Week Ending February 7, 19--			
Salesperson	**Rate of Commission**	**Commission Earned**	**Sales**
Bradley, K.	17%	$518.27	$
Dort, T.	15.5%	501.32	
LaVerne, S.	15%	682.95	
Martin, P.	16.25%	527.87	
Previer, S.	17.5%	605.72	
Moses, R.	16.75%	501.86	

EXERCISE • SET 3

Complete the Sales Reports.
- Calculate the total sales.
- Calculate what percent each department's sales are of the total sales.

$$\text{Percent of Total Sales} = \frac{\text{Department Sales}}{\text{Total Sales}} \times 100\%$$

- Calculate each percent correct to two places after the decimal.

1.

Jim's Electronics Sales Report Month of January, 19--		
Department	**Sales**	**Percent of Total**
Radio	$ 4 596.72	
T.V.	10 375.47	
Stereo	20 863.45	
Small Appliances	8 372.60	
Large Appliances	12 597.80	
Record & Tape	7 956.85	
Total Sales	$	

2.

Jim's Electronics Sales Report Month of February, 19--		
Department	**Sales**	**Percent of Total Sales**
Radio	$ 3 976.54	
T.V.	9 857.43	
Stereo	18 375.68	
Small Appliances	6 597.14	
Large Appliances	11 365.04	
Record & Tape	6 075.92	
Total	$	

3. Sheri's Gift Shop purchased 100 handmade leather belts at $7.95 per belt. Sheri marked 35 belts for sale at $12.98, 20 belts for sale at $12.49, 25 belts at $11.57, and the rest for sale at $9.59.

a) How much profit will Sheri's Gift Shop make if all the belts are sold? _____

b) Calculate the profit as a percent of the total cost of the belts, correct to two places after the decimal. _____

4. Last year George Black earned $10 395. This year he earned $11 275.

a) What is the dollar increase in George's earnings? _____

b) By what percent did George's earnings increase, correct to two places after the decimal? _____

c) If he gets a 9.25% increase next year, what will George earn? _____

CHAPTER 10

SIMPLE INTEREST

10·1 CALCULATING SIMPLE INTEREST

Interest is the money paid for the use of borrowed money; it is also the money earned when capital is invested. If, however you wish to save money in a bank account, the bank will pay you interest on this money because the bank uses it to make investments which earn more money for the bank. The government of Canada borrows money from the people of Canada by offering government bonds for sale to the general public and businesses. The government pays interest to these investors to pay for the use of their money.

Interest is usually quoted as a given percent per annum.

Formula

$$I = Prt$$

Where: I is the simple interest, the charge for the use of the money borrowed or lent.

P is the principal, the sum of money borrowed or lent.

r is the rate, the percent of the principal at which interest is charged for the year. This rate is expressed as a decimal quantity when used in calculating interest.

t is the time, the length of the period for which the principal is borrowed or lent, expressed in years.

EXAMPLE 1 Calculate the simple intcrest on $850.00 borrowed for 3 years at 11% per annum. Per annum means per year.

SOLUTION

$I = ?$
$P = \$850.00$
$r = 11\%$
$\quad = 0.11$
$t = 3 \text{ a}$

$I = Prt$
$\quad = 850 \times 0.11 \times 3$
$\quad = 280.50$

The interest is $280.50.

EXAMPLE 2 Calculate the simple interest on $625.50 at 12% per annum for 5 months.

SOLUTION

$I = ?$
$P = \$625.50$
$r = 12\%$
$\quad = 0.12$
$t = 5 \text{ months}$
$\quad = \frac{5}{12} \text{ a}$

$I = Prt$
$\quad = 625.50 \times 0.12 \times \frac{5}{12}$
$\quad = 31.275$

The interest is $31.28.

NOTE The calculation $625.50 \times 0.12 \times \frac{5}{12}$ is calculated as $625.50 \times 0.12 \times 5 \div 12$.

The operation of division, unless by a quantity less than 1, should always be performed last.

EXAMPLE 3 Calculate the simple interest on $595.00 at 9% per annum for 219 days.

SOLUTION

$I = ?$
$P = \$595.00$
$r = 9\%$
$\quad = 0.09$
$t = 219$ d
$\quad = \frac{219}{365}$ a

$I = Prt$
$\quad = 595.00 \times 0.09 \times \frac{219}{365}$
$\quad = 32.130$

The interest is $32.13.

NOTE The calculation $595 \times 0.09 \times \frac{219}{365}$ is calculated as $595 \times 0.09 \times 219 \div 365$.

EXERCISE • SET 1

Calculate the simple interest.

	Principal	Rate per Annum	Time in Years	Simple Interest
1.	$ 750.00	11%	4	
2.	395.50	9%	6	
3.	1 246.50	12%	5	
4.	2 569.25	8%	4	
5.	58.46	10%	15	
6.	875.50	11.5%	2	
7.	1 765.70	9.5%	6	
8.	3 872.56	10.5%	7	
9.	125.79	11.8%	3	
10.	5 976.86	12.25%	4	

	Principal	Rate per Annum	Time in Months	Simple Interest
11.	$ 950.00	11%	5	
12.	1 936.00	9%	7	
13.	4 157.00	12%	11	
14.	827.00	13%	5	
15.	5 389.00	8%	1	
16.	786.50	11.5%	7	
17.	1 547.80	12.5%	5	
18.	3 957.61	10.5%	11	
19.	89.75	9.5%	11	
20.	6 878.95	8.75%	1	

	Principal	Rate per Annum	Time in Days	Simple Interest
21.	$ 375.00	11%	215	
22.	1 572.00	12%	174	
23.	1 435.00	8%	89	
24.	3 892.20	10%	192	
25.	1 987.70	9%	28	
26.	547.63	11%	305	
27.	6 495.27	9%	212	
28.	39.55	6%	30	
29.	137.49	13%	56	
30.	9 876.12	12%	90	

	Principal	Rate per Annum	Time	Simple Interest
31.	$10 362.00	11%	100 d	
32.	23 578.00	12.25%	3 a	
33.	45 000.00	13.75%	7 months	
34.	31 978.50	14%	5 a	
35.	9 980.75	15%	90 d	
36.	8 324.68	11.75%	4.5 a	
37.	15 050.50	10.25%	10 a	
38.	27 382.98	12.5%	30 d	
39.	19 866.75	13.25%	6 months	
40.	49 372.25	9.75%	180 d	

EXERCISE • SET 2

Calculate the simple interest.

	Principal	Rate per Annum	Time	Simple Interest
1.	$ 655.00	11%	2.5 a	
2.	1 387.25	12.5%	3.5 a	
3.	6 827.59	11.5%	3.25 a	
4.	9 859.60	12.25%	5.25 a	
5.	58.95	10.25%	2.25 a	
6.	357.98	9.5%	6.5 months	
7.	1 854.27	11.5%	7.5 months	
8.	2 485.45	12.25%	8.5 months	
9.	78.55	11.75%	11.5 months	
10.	5 864.45	10.25%	9.5 months	
11.	788.49	11.5%	135 d	
12.	1 458.61	10.5%	120 d	
13.	142.56	9.5%	250 d	
14.	2 357.92	11.25%	267 d	
15.	8 562.33	10.25%	30 d	

EXERCISE • SET 3

1. George Mulow purchased $4500 worth of 8% per annum government bonds. How much interest did he collect each year? _____

2. Jeanne Leblanc purchased $10 500 worth of 7.75% per annum government bonds. How much interest did she collect each year? _____

3. Giordi Fonti purchased savings certificates from an investment company. He bought $9500 worth of 9.75% per annum certificates. How much interest did Giordi receive at the end of one year? _____

4. June Eadie put $8000 into a special savings account. If she did not draw any of this money from the account, she was to receive interest at 6% per annum for the first year and interest at 8% per annum for the second year.

   a) How much interest did June receive at the end of the first year? _____

   b) If she took this interest from her account in cash and left her original deposit in the account, how much interest did she receive at the end of the second year?

   _____

5. Philip Curvella deposited $5450 in a special savings account that paid interest at the rate of 6.75% per annum for the first year and 8.25% per annum for the second year.

   a) How much interest did he receive at the end of the first year? _____

   b) If Philip drew this interest out of the account and left the original deposit in, how much interest did he receive at the end of the second year? _____

6. Jean MacKay deposited $525.50 in a savings account with chequing privileges and paying 3.25% per annum in interest. She did not write any cheques or make any withdrawals. The interest was calculated at the end of six months. How much interest did Jean receive? _____

7. George Leier borrowed $975.50 to be paid back, principal and interest, at 10.5% per annum in 90 days. How much did he pay back? _____

8. Marie Bretane borrowed $2500 on a short term loan from her bank at an interest rate of 7.5% per annum. If she paid it back in 35 days, how much did Marie have to pay, to repay both principal and interest? _____

9. A house is mortgaged for $23 000 at a rate of 11.5% per annum. The payments are to be made at the end of each year to include the interest for each year plus $1000 of the principal. What is the total payment on the mortgage at the end of the first year?

   _____

10. A house is mortgaged for $32 250 at a rate of 12.1% per annum. The payments are to be made at the end of every six months. They are to include the interest for the previous six months plus $750 of the principal. What is the total payment on the mortgage at the end of the first six months? _____

10·2 CALCULATING TIME BETWEEN GIVEN DATES

Interest payments are usually made over a time period calculated from a given date in the year to another date in the same year or a following year. Therefore, you must be able to calculate the number of days between two dates.

EXAMPLE 1 Find the number of days from November 10 to February 13 the next year.

SOLUTION From November 10 to November 30 (30 − 10) = 20 d left in November
                                                    = 31 d in December
                                                    = 31 d in January
             To February 13   = 13 d in February
                                                      95 d

The number of days from November 10 to February 13, the next year is 95.

REMEMBER Leave out the first date, count in the last date.
"30 days hath September; April, June, and November. All the rest have 31, save February . . ."

EXAMPLE 2   Find the number of days from 1985 10 15 to 1986 03 12.

SOLUTION   **REMEMBER**   1985   10   15
                                 Year   Month   Day

From 1985 10 15 to 1985 10 31 (31-15) =   16 d left in October
                                       =   30 d in November
                                       =   31 d in December
                                       =   31 d in January
                                       =   28 d in February
To 1986 03 12   =   12 d in March
                                          148 d

The number of days from 1985 10 15 to 1986 03 12 is 148.

NOTE   A year is a leap year if it is exactly divisible by 4. For example, 1988 is a leap year but 1990 is not.

1988 ÷ 4 = 497 exactly
1988 is a leap year.
An exception to this rule occurs at the beginning of a century. If a year's date ends in 00, it is a leap year only if it is exactly divisible by 400. Since 2000 is exactly divisible by 400, the year 2000 will be a leap year. The year 1900 was not a leap year.

EXERCISE • SET 1

Find the number of days between each pair of dates.

1. January 23, 1985 to March 7, 1985 _____

2. May 4, 1985 to October 12, 1985 _____

3. July 20, 1986 to November 5, 1986 _____

4. June 11, 1985 to December 18, 1985 _____

5. March 13, 1985 to December 9, 1985 _____

6. November 8, 1985 to February 4, 1986 _____

7. September 14, 1985 to January 4, 1986 _____

8. July 25, 1985 to March 11, 1986 _____

9. August 17, 1985 to June 28, 1986 _____

10. March 21, 1985 to May 8, 1986 _____

11. 1985 01 17 to 1985 03 05 _____

12. 1986 03 15 to 1986 10 18 _____

13. 1986 05 07 to 1986 12 23 _____

14. 1987 01 15 to 1987 09 15 _____

15. 1984 03 05 to 1986 05 17 _____

10·3 CALCULATING SIMPLE INTEREST BETWEEN DATES

EXAMPLE   Calculate the simple interest on $955.50 at 11.5% per annum from October 5, 1985 to December 12, 1985.

SOLUTION   Find the number of days.

From October 5, 1985 to October 31, 1985 $= 26$ d left in October
$= 30$ d in November

To December 12 $= \underline{12}$ d in December
68 d

Calculate the simple interest.

$$I = ?$$
$$P = \$955.50$$
$$r = 11.5\%$$
$$= 0.115$$
$$t = 68 \text{ d}$$
$$= \frac{68}{365} \text{ a}$$

$$I = Prt$$
$$= 955.50 \times 0.115 \times \frac{68}{365}$$
$$= 20.471$$
$$= 20.47$$

The interest is $20.47.

EXERCISE • SET 1

Find the number of days and calculate the simple interest.

	Principal	Rate per Annum	Time	Number of Days	Simple Interest
1.	$ 500.00	11%	Jan. 3, 1985 to Mar. 5, 1985		
2.	832.00	12%	Jan. 15, 1987 to July 15, 1987		
3.	1 724.50	10%	May 22, 1985 to Nov. 22, 1985		
4.	347.25	9.5%	Feb. 14, 1985 to Dec. 17, 1985		
5.	2 365.75	11.5%	1984 01 03 to 1984 02 06		
6.	5 489.65	12.5%	May 4, 1984 to July 7, 1984		
7.	827.63	11.25%	Apr. 10, 1985 to Sept. 13, 1985		
8.	1 357.54	12.75%	1984 11 08 to 1986 02 11		
9.	957.25	10.25%	Dec. 2, 1984 to Mar. 5, 1986		
10.	2 986.72	9.75%	Oct. 5, 1984 to Mar. 8, 1986		

EXERCISE • SET 2

Find the number of days and calculate the simple interest.

	Principal	Rate per Annum	Time	Number of Days	Simple Interest
1.	$ 922.38	10%	Jan. 2, 1985 to Apr. 2, 1985		
2.	868.25	9%	July 5, 1985 to Nov. 8, 1985		
3.	48.30	13%	Mar. 3, 1985 to Apr. 5, 1985		
4.	1 842.35	11%	Dec. 5, 1985 to Mar. 3, 1986		
5.	395.56	11.5%	Nov. 25, 1984 to Mar. 2, 1987		
6.	1 567.55	10.25%	1984 12 15 to 1989 01 05		
7.	2 387.45	11.75%	1984 12 12 to 1989 04 15		
8.	875.75	8.275%	1984 12 15 to 1985 02 18		
9.	938.85	10.375%	1984 12 05 to 1985 03 08		

EXERCISE • SET 3

1. Calculate the interest on $245 at 12% per annum from October 25 to December 18 of the same year. _____

2. A sum of $825.75 is lent for 226 d at a rate of 10.75% per annum. Calculate the interest and the total amount repaid. _____, _____

3. On January 2, 1987 John Anderson borrowed $2625.50 from Walter Summers at a rate of 10.25% per annum. He repays the loan on April 5, 1987. What does Walter receive in interest? _____

4. On August 31, 1985 Bob Harron borrowed $1550 to finance the purchase of a second-hand car. If the interest rate is 11.75% per annum, how much would Bob pay to settle his debt in full on February 9, 1986? _____

5. On July 5, 1986 Betty Walters borrowed $850 from her bank at 10.5% per annum. On September 8, she borrowed an additional $750.50 at the same rate. How much would Betty pay to settle her debt in full on March 21, 1987? _____

10·4 CALCULATING AMOUNT

When the term of a loan is complete, the borrower must pay back the original principal borrowed *plus* the interest due. This is called the **amount due**.

EXAMPLE   A loan of $167.95 at an interest rate of 12.25% per annum is to be paid back, principal and interest, in 93 days. How much is the total amount to be paid back?

SOLUTION   Step 1:

$I = Prt$

$$= 167.95 \times 0.1225 \times \frac{93}{365}$$

$$= 5.242$$

$$= 5.24$$

The interest is $5.24.

Step 2:
Amount to be repaid = Principal + Interest
$$= 167.95 + 5.24$$
$$= 173.19$$
The total amount to be paid back is $173.19.

EXERCISE • SET 1

Calculate the simple interest then the amount due.

	Principal	Rate per Annum	Time	Simple Interest	Amount
1.	$ 725.00	8%	5 a		
2.	12 596.00	11%	2 a		
3.	565.50	10.5%	0.5 a		
4.	1 845.75	11.5%	7 months		
5.	2 765.95	12.5%	1 month		
6.	1 385.25	12%	37 d		
7.	6 232.50	11%	105 d		
8.	3 768.80	10.5%	187 d		
9.	3 576.40	9.75%	209 d		
10.	860.50	11.25%	285 d		
11.	1 972.00	11%	Jan. 5, 1985 to Apr. 5, 1985		
12.	5 308.50	10.5%	July 3, 1985 to Nov. 11, 1985		
13.	92.42	15%	Mar. 10, 1984 to Apr. 30, 1984		
14.	592.70	11.5%	1986 12 05 to 1987 04 08		
15.	1 937.50	10.5%	1986 11 21 to 1987 06 24		

EXERCISE • SET 2

Calculate the simple interest then the amount due.

	Principal	Rate per Annum	Time	Simple Interest	Amount
1.	$ 625.00	10%	5 a		
2.	12 761.00	12%	2 a		
3.	765.50	9.5%	0.5 a		
4.	1 268.00	10.5%	4 months		
5.	846.25	9.75%	1 month		
6.	1 285.25	12%	23 d		
7.	6 123.30	9.5%	85 d		
8.	2 780.50	12.5%	230 d		
9.	2 761.50	10%	278 d		
10.	860.00	11%	187 d		
11.	6 123.18	11.5%	278 d		
12.	922.38	10%	Jan. 2, 1985 to Apr. 2, 1985		
13.	868.25	9%	July 5, 1986 to Nov. 8, 1986		
14.	48.30	13%	Mar. 3, 1986 to Apr. 5, 1986		
15.	1 842.35	11%	Dec. 5, 1986 to Mar. 3, 1987		

EXERCISE • SET 3

1. Gerry Durst forgot to pay his public utilities bill for $92.40. If the utility charges a 2% penalty for late payment, what amount did Gerry have to pay? _____

2. Mary Goetz lent George Reed $1000 for 30 days at 13.5% per annum. How much did George owe Mary at the end of the 30 days? _____

3. Joan Vandendam borrowed $975 at an interest rate of 12.25% per annum for 90 days. What did she owe at the end of the 90 days? _____

4. Elaine Achiu has an account at a department store that collects 2.25% per month on charges to the account. If Elaine owed $379.50 for one month, how much did she owe at the end of the month? _____

5. Harry Klowak purchased a computer for $1800. He paid $900 down and agreed to pay the remainder, principal and interest at 11.75% per annum, at the end of 1 month. What was the total amount that Harry paid for the computer? _____

10·5 CALCULATING PRINCIPAL

Sometimes you may be given the interest earned by a loan, the interest rate, and the time of the loan. From these, it is possible to calculate the principal of the loan.

> **Formula**
>
> $$P = \frac{I}{rt}$$
>
> Where : P is the principal.
> I is the simple interest.
> r is the annual rate of interest charged, expressed as a decimal quantity.
> t is the time in years.

EXAMPLE 1 What principal invested at 12% per annum will earn $155.25 interest in 3 years?

SOLUTION

$P = ?$
$I = \$155.25$
$r = 12\%$
$\quad = 0.12$
$t = 3$ a

$P = \dfrac{I}{rt}$

$\quad = \dfrac{155.25}{0.12 \times 3}$

$\quad = 431.25$

The principal invested is $431.25.

NOTE The expression, $\dfrac{155.25}{0.12 \times 3}$, may be interpreted algebraically as: 155.25 divided by 0.12 and the result of the division is divided by 3. That is: $155.25 \div 0.12 \div 3$.

EXAMPLE 2 Calculate the principal which invested at 9.5% per annum will earn $125.00 in 5 months.

SOLUTION

$P = ?$
$I = \$125.00$
$r = 9.5\%$
$\quad = 0.095$
$t = 5$ months
$\quad = \dfrac{5}{12}$ a

$P = \dfrac{I}{rt}$

$\quad = \dfrac{125.00}{0.095 \times \dfrac{5}{12}}$

(NOTE: Flip the fraction.)

$P = \dfrac{125.00 \times 12}{0.095 \times 5}$

$\quad = 3157.894$

$\quad = 3157.89$

The principal is $3157.89.

NOTE The expression, $\dfrac{125.00 \times 12}{0.095 \times 5}$, may be interpreted algebraically as: 125.00 is multiplied by 12 and the resulting product is divided by 0.095 and the resulting quotient is divided by 5. That is: $125.00 \times 12 \div 0.095 \div 5$.

EXAMPLE 3 What principal invested at 10.5% per annum will earn $325.50 in 263 days?

SOLUTION

$P = ?$
$I = \$325.50$
$r = 10.5\%$
$\quad = 0.105$
$t = 263$ d
$\quad = \dfrac{263}{365}$ a

$P = \dfrac{I}{rt}$

$\quad = \dfrac{325.50}{0.105 \times \dfrac{263}{365}}$

(NOTE: Flip the fraction.)

$P = \dfrac{325.50 \times 365}{0.105 \times 263}$

$\quad = 4302.281$

$\quad = 4302.28$

The principal is $4302.28.

NOTE For a business machine or calculator, $\dfrac{325.50 \times 365}{0.105 \times 263}$, is calculated as $325.50 \times 365 \div 0.105 \div 263$.

EXERCISE • SET 1

Using the method shown in Example 1, calculate the principal.

	Simple Interest	Rate per Annum	Time in Years	Principal
1.	$ 250.00	12%	5	
2.	108.00	9%	3	
3.	95.75	10%	2	
4.	87.47	11%	4	
5.	985.50	13%	7	
6.	325.00	11.5%	6	
7.	889.90	12.5%	2.5	
8.	1 765.70	10.5%	1.5	
9.	29.95	10.25%	1.25	
10.	165.75	11.25%	2.75	

NOTE Always divide by the smallest number first.

Calculate the principal using the methods shown in Examples 2 and 3.

	Simple Interest	Rate per Annum	Time	Principal
11.	$135.00	9%	5 months	
12.	85.50	12%	8 months	
13.	150.25	11%	7 months	
14.	25.75	10.5%	11 months	
15.	182.95	9.5%	10 months	
16.	250.00	8%	247 d	
17.	50.00	12%	124 d	
18.	75.80	11%	175 d	
19.	137.47	11.5%	80 d	
20.	126.25	10.5%	50 d	
21.	125.00	11.25%	93 d	
22.	89.95	10.25%	123 d	
23.	50.75	9.75%	from 1985 10 07 to 1986 02 10	
24.	8.95	12.2%	from Jan. 1, 1985 to Jan. 17, 1985	
25.	10.55	11.8%	from 1984 04 15 to 1984 06 18	

EXERCISE • SET 2

Calculate the principal.

	Principal	Rate per Annum	Time	Simple Interest
1.		8%	2 a	$ 28.60
2.		11%	2 a	68.52
3.		10.5%	3 a	186.26
4.		9%	0.5 a	56.85
5.		9.75%	3.5 a	5.60
6.		12%	1 month	27.57
7.		11%	2 months	91.35
8.		10%	5 months	12.35
9.		10.5%	9 months	128.50
10.		11.5%	1.5 months	173.20
11.		11%	163 d	92.20
12.		12%	173 d	168.43
13.		10%	from Jan. 2, 1987 to Mar. 3, 1987	8.33
14.		12%	from Dec. 5, 1986 to Apr. 2, 1987	23.51
15.		10.5%	from Mar. 3, 1986 to Apr. 30, 1986	8.35

EXERCISE • SET 3

1. How much money must be invested at 12.75% per annum to provide an annual income of $10 000? _____

2. How much money must be invested in investment certificates at 13.05% per annum to provide a monthly income of $500? _____

3. When Gord Dendino retired, his insurance agent told him that if he put the cash value of his life insurance into an annuity which paid 9.75% per annum, he would have an income of $370 per month. What was the cash value of Gord's life insurance policy?

_____

4. Jean Dalhous owns a house and rents it for $600 a month to a family who agree to pay all expenses. If money is worth 11.25%, what amount should she consider that she has invested in the house? _____

5. Jack's grandfather sold his business when Jack graduated from secondary school. The grandfather said that if Jack would attend college, he would put enough money in a trust account to provide Jack with an income of $250 per month. If the trust company pays interest at the rate of 11.5% per annum, how much must Jack's grandfather put in the account? _____

10·6 CALCULATING THE RATE

Sometimes you may be given the interest earned on a loan, the principal, and the period of the loan. From these, it is possible to calculate the annual rate of interest for the loan.

Formula

$$r = \frac{I}{Pt}$$

Where: r is the annual rate of interest expressed as a decimal quantity.
I is the simple interest.
P is the principal.
t is the time in years.

EXAMPLE 1   At what annual rate of interest will a principal of $525.50 earn interest of $125.72 in two years?

SOLUTION $r = ?$
$I = \$125.72$
$P = \$525.50$
$t = 2$ a

$$r = \frac{I}{Pt}$$
$$= \frac{125.72}{525.50 \times 2}$$
$$= 0.119\ 62$$
$$= 0.1196$$
$$= 11.96\%$$

The interest rate is 11.96%.

NOTE   Always calculate the rate at which interest is paid correct to two places after the decimal unless you are instructed otherwise.

EXAMPLE 2   A loan of $355.50 earned $25.75 in interest in seven months. Calculate the annual rate of interest.

SOLUTION $r = ?$
$I = \$25.75$
$P = \$355.50$
$t = 7$ months
$= \frac{7}{12}$ a

$$r = \frac{I}{Pt}$$
$$= \frac{25.75}{355.50 \times \frac{7}{12}}$$
(NOTE: Flip the fraction.)
$$r = \frac{25.75 \times 12}{355.50 \times 7}$$
$$= 0.124\ 17$$
$$= 0.1242$$
$$= 12.42\%$$

The rate of interest is 12.42%.

EXAMPLE 3   In 93 days, $625.50 earns $22.50 interest. Calculate the annual interest rate.

SOLUTION $r = ?$
$I = \$22.50$
$P = \$625.50$
$t = 93$ d
$= \frac{93}{365}$ a

$$r = \frac{I}{Pt}$$
$$= \frac{22.50}{625.50 \times \frac{93}{365}}$$
(NOTE: Flip the fraction.)
$$r = \frac{22.50 \times 365}{625.50 \times 93}$$
$$= 0.141\ 17$$
$$= 14.117\%$$
$$= 14.12\%$$

The interest rate is 14.12%.

Alternate Methods
You can move the decimal point first to change to percent and then round off (Example 3); or round off first, then change to a percent.

EXERCISE • SET 1

Calculate the rate of interest per annum correct to two places after the decimal where necessary.

	Principal	Simple Interest	Time	Rate per Annum
1.	$ 135.00	$ 29.70	2 a	
2.	175.00	105.00	5 a	
3.	295.50	88.05	3 a	
4.	1 565.50	82.18	0.5 a	
5.	976.30	168.41	1.5 a	
6.	95.00	4.99	7 months	
7.	185.00	16.65	5 months	
8.	376.50	37.96	11 months	
9.	88.95	5.63	8 months	
10.	115.38	1.11	1 month	
11.	225.00	3.61	65 d	
12.	179.50	5.03	93 d	
13.	137.86	4.56	127 d	
14.	235.50	9.05	Jan. 3, 1985 to May 5, 1985	
15.	127.80	9.06	1986 03 17 to 1986 10 15	

EXERCISE • SET 2

Calculate the rate of interest earned on each of the stock investments. This interest rate is generally called yield, or rate of income.

$$\text{Yield} = \frac{\text{Total Dividends Earned}}{\text{Amount of Investment} \times \text{Time Held (in years)}} \times 100\%$$

Round off each percent correct to two places after the decimal where necessary.

		Rate of Income on Investments			
		Portfolio of: J. Galadie Year Ending December 31, 19--			
	Holdings	Amount of Investment	Time Held	Total Dividends Earned	Yield
1.	Stock A	$1 500	1 a	$112.50	
2.	Stock B	2 000	1 a	160.00	
3.	Stock C	1 800	6 months	70.20	
4.	Stock D	3 250	6 months	112.13	
5.	Stock E	2 250	4 months	58.50	
6.	Stock F	1 925	3 months	43.79	

	Holdings	Amount of Investment	Time Held	Total Dividends Earned	Yield
	Rate of Income on Investments				
	Portfolio of: R. Connors Year Ending December 31, 19--				
7.	Stock #1	$5 600	1 a	$476.00	
8.	Stock #2	3 050	3 months	64.81	
9.	Stock #3	2 500	4 months	76.67	
10.	Stock #4	1 250	1 a	97.50	
11.	Stock #5	1 925	6 months	59.35	
12.	Stock #6	4 910	6 months	238.14	

EXERCISE • SET 3

Calculate all percents correct to two places after the decimal.

1. When John Price retired, the cash value of his life insurance was $21 954.60. He cancelled his life insurance and invested the money he received in bonds. The dividends from the bonds gave John a monthly income of $169.23. What annual rate of interest did the bonds pay? _____

2. George Friedman purchased $18 000 worth of stock. In the first year that he owned the stock he was paid $1350 in dividends. What annual rate of interest did the stocks pay?

3. Margot Cancilla received $12 000 from her uncle's estate. She invested it in bonds which paid her $555 in interest every six months. What annual rate of interest did the bonds pay? _____

4. Jean Smith bought a house for $36 575. She rents it to a family for $350 a month. If the tenants pay all the expenses on the house, what annual rate of interest is Jean receiving on her investment in the house? _____

5. Marie borrowed $600 from a loan company for one month. The amount owed at the end of the month was $611.50, covering principal and interest. What rate of interest per annum was Marie charged? _____

6. Jack was three months late making his last payment of $230 on his property taxes. He was charged $236.90, principal and interest. What annual rate of interest was Jack charged? _____

7. Jacques owns a duplex. He rents half the duplex and lives in the other half. The building cost $60 000 and the annual expenses are $1755.95. He charges $195.75 monthly rent for the rented part.

   a) What was the initial investment in the rented half of the building? _____

b) What is his net income from the rented half? _____

c) If the net income is considered to be interest on his investment, what annual interest rate does Jacques receive from his investment? _____

8. Elizabeth Rae owns an apartment building. The building is worth $120 000 and has four identical apartments. Elizabeth lives in one apartment and rents the other three for $255 each a month. Annual expenses are $3976.

   a) What was Elizabeth's initial investment in the rented part of the building?

   _____

   b) What is the net income from rentals? _____

   c) If the net income is considered to be interest on her investment, what annual rate of interest does Elizabeth receive from her investment? _____

9. When Dr. Dewar retired, she rented her clinic to two other doctors who each paid $525 per month rent. Heat and electricity for the building cost $1664 per year, taxes are $1573 per year and other expenses are $575.50 per year. If Dr. Dewar originally invested $126 350 in the building, what rate of interest is she receiving on her investment? _____

10·7 REVIEW

EXERCISE • SET 1 _____

Calculate the simple interest.

	Principal	Rate per Annum	Time	Simple Interest
1.	$ 125.36	11%	3 a	
2.	1 567.82	9.5%	5 a	
3.	311.27	11.5%	5 months	
4.	525.75	12.5%	7 months	
5.	1 595.85	11.5%	73 d	
6.	786.45	12.5%	185 d	
7.	1 287.95	9.5%	1989 01 15 to 1989 09 18	
8.	315.46	12.75%	Feb. 4, 1987 to Mar. 7, 1987	

Calculate the simple interest, then the amount.

	Principal	Rate per Annum	Time	Simple Interest	Amount
9.	$1 357.61	8%	7 a		
10.	589.95	11.5%	11 months		
11.	762.93	10.5%	235 d		
12.	1 548.76	10.75%	198 d		
13.	315.68	11.25%	92 d		
14.	835.95	12.25%	303 d		

Calculate the principal.

	Simple Interest	Rate per Annum	Time	Principal
15.	$ 85.57	12%	2 a	
16.	125.95	11.5%	1.5 a	
17.	36.45	12%	7 months	
18.	132.95	10.5%	11 months	
19.	21.75	9%	63 d	
20.	48.57	9.5%	84 d	
21.	137.85	11.5%	137 d	
22.	75.68	12.25%	213 d	

Calculate the interest rate per annum correct to two places after the decimal where necessary.

	Principal	Simple Interest	Time	Rate per Annum
23.	$3 131.00	$164.32	1 a	
24.	1 952.60	336.82	1.5 a	
25.	370.00	33.30	5 months	
26.	177.90	11.20	8 months	
27.	450.00	7.22	66 d	
28.	275.62	9.12	126 d	

EXERCISE • SET 2 _____

1. On October 3, 1985 George Elbon borrowed $1763.54 at a rate of 11.75% per annum. He repaid the loan on December 5, 1985. What amount did George repay?

_____

2. Jeanne holds a second mortgage of $15 000 on a house that she sold. She is to receive a monthly payment of $50 on the principal plus interest at a rate of 13.5% per annum on the unpaid balance. How much did Jeanne receive at the end of the first month?

_____

3. Marc owns a store in Loggieville which he rents to a merchant who uses the store for business purposes and lives in the apartment above the store. Marc charges $450 a month rent for the business section and $200 a month rent for the living quarters. The merchant pays all the expenses of the building. If current interest rates are 10.25% per annum, what value should Marc place on the building (what principal would yield interest equal to the rent)? _____

4. What principal must Walter Foreman invest to have an annual retirement income of $11 000, if he is able to make his investment at a rate of 12.75% per annum?

_____

5. Mary Conti purchased $5675 worth of stock. In the first year that she owned the stock, she received dividends of $464.75. Find the annual interest rate received on the stock correct to two places after the decimal. _____

Calculate the yield from each stock correct to two places after the decimal.

<table>
<tr><td colspan="6">Rate of Income on Investments</td></tr>
<tr><td colspan="3">Portfolio of: K. Marchant</td><td colspan="3">Year Ending March 31, 19--</td></tr>
<tr><td></td><td>Holdings</td><td>Amount of Investment</td><td>Time Held</td><td>Total Dividends Earned</td><td>Yield</td></tr>
<tr><td>6.</td><td>Stock A</td><td>$2 385</td><td>1 a</td><td>$189.30</td><td></td></tr>
<tr><td>7.</td><td>Stock B</td><td>4 210</td><td>6 months</td><td>175.50</td><td></td></tr>
<tr><td>8.</td><td>Stock C</td><td>3 935</td><td>6 months</td><td>180.20</td><td></td></tr>
<tr><td>9.</td><td>Stock D</td><td>5 863</td><td>4 months</td><td>131.50</td><td></td></tr>
<tr><td>10.</td><td>Stock E</td><td>3 362</td><td>3 months</td><td>71.30</td><td></td></tr>
<tr><td>11.</td><td>Stock F</td><td>3 597</td><td>3 months</td><td>76.80</td><td></td></tr>
</table>

EXERCISE • SET 3

1. George Esto purchased a house, making a down payment of $15 000 and assuming a mortgage of $40 000. The mortgage is to be paid back in payments of $1000 at the end of each year plus interest at the rate of 11.5% per annum on the unpaid balance.

    a) At the end of the first year, how much interest does George pay? _____

    b) If he had not bought the house and had invested the down payment at 12.25% per annum instead, how much money would he receive after one year? _____

2. A store is rented at $450 per month and the tenant pays all upkeep. Insurance costs the owner $260 per year, and commercial property taxes are $937 per year. The assessed value of the store is $47 560 and assessments in the locality are 75% of the resale value of property. What rate of interest per annum, correct to two places after the decimal, is the net store rental paying the owner? _____

3. Jean Verra is considering buying an apartment house which has three apartments. She has $17 000 invested at 12.75% per annum. Jean would use this as a down payment and assume a mortgage of $33 000. The mortgage would be repaid, principal and interest, at $308 per month. Jean would live in one apartment and rent the other two. One rents at $240 a month and the other at $215 a month. The insurance on the house is $186 a year and the taxes are $937 a year. The tenants pay for their own heat and utilities, but Jean would have to pay $35 a month for her utilities and $72.50 a month for 10 months each year for heat. She is renting an apartment at present for which she is paying $525 per month with heat and utilities included in the rent. If Jean buys the house, how much would she gain or lose in the first year after she purchases it?

    _____

CHAPTER 11

PRICING MERCHANDISE – MARKUP AND MARKDOWN

Merchants buy their merchandise from manufacturers or wholesale firms. The price at which the merchant buys the goods is called the wholesale price; the merchant usually calls this his **cost price**. The price at which the merchandise is sold is the retail price, and the merchant calls this his **selling price**.

The difference between the selling price and the cost price is the **gross profit**, which is also referred to simply as profit. From the gross profit of all sales, the retailer (or merchant) must pay salaries to employees, rent, utilities, other expenses, and of course her or his own salary.

When merchandise is received, it is unpacked, the shipping order is checked to make sure all items are in the shipment, and each individual item is priced. The selling price of each item is determined by the cost price to the retailer (obtained from the invoice sent to the retailer by the wholesaler or manufacturer) plus a **markup**, which is usually a percentage of the cost price. This markup is the gross profit, or profit, to the merchant.

Low-cost products that the merchant sells shortly after receiving them (groceries, clothing, variety goods, magazines) have relatively low percent markups. If the product is larger, more expensive or is not sold as rapidly (television sets, bicycles, furniture, large electrical appliances) its percent markup will be greater. Luxury items such as jewellery have very large percent markups.

11·1 CALCULATING MARKUP BASED ON COST PRICE

> *Formula*
>
> $$M = Cr$$
>
> Where: M is the markup.
> C is the cost price.
> r is the rate of markup, a percent expressed as a decimal quantity.

EXAMPLE 1   The cost price of a sweater is \$49.50. Marlene's Gift Shop has a regular rate of markup of 30% of the cost price. How much will the markup on the sweater be?

SOLUTION
$M = ?$
$C = \$49.50$
$r = 30\%$
$\quad = 0.30$

$M = Cr$
$\quad = 49.50 \times 0.30$
$\quad = 14.85$

The markup is \$14.85.

EXERCISE • SET 1

Calculate each markup. Round off your answers to the nearest cent.

	Cost Price	Rate of Markup	Markup
1.	$ 5.50	10%	$
2.	19.70	15%	
3.	39.85	25%	
4.	88.60	31%	
5.	15.25	13%	
6.	0.95	5%	
7.	105.79	35%	
8.	289.19	42%	
9.	512.50	50%	
10.	1 980.00	60%	

EXERCISE • SET 2

1. Bob's Supermarket has a standard rate of markup of 2% on canned goods, 5% on fresh produce, 20% on drugstore items, 30% on stationery, and 33% on paper products. From the following purchase order, calculate the unit cost and the markup on each unit.

Georgian Wholesale

To: Bob's Supermarket
       79 Eglinton Ave. East, Toronto, Ont. M4P 1G6

Date: Nov. 28/--
Order No.:   395

Quantity	Description	Unit	Extension	Unit Cost	Markup on Cost Price
20	Cases, 24 cans each, creamed corn	Can	$144.00		
10	Cases, 24 cans each, whole beets	Can	120.00		
50	Bags of potatoes	Bag	50.00		
10	Cases, 25 rolls each, paper towels	Roll	200.00		
50	Pkgs. envelopes	Pkg.	34.50		
75	Bags of oranges	Bag	61.50		
25	Cases, 20 cans each, fruit punch	Can	225.00		
		Total	$835.00		

1. Williams Heating Limited is to give an estimate for the installation of a heating system. The rate of markup is 20% on cost of all materials used. Calculate the markup on the given cost price of each item in the following list of materials: Item #1, 1 thermostat at $139.75; Item #2, 1 gas furnace at $515.95; Item #3, 152 m copper pipe at $0.97/m; Item #4, 20 elbows at $0.65 each; Item #5, 10 radiators at $157.00 each; Item #6, 10 radiator valves at $3.96 each. ———, ———, ———, ———, ———, ———

11·2 CALCULATING SELLING PRICE

When the markup is added to the cost price, the selling price is obtained.

Formula

$$S = C + M$$

Where: S is the selling price.
C is the cost price.
M is the markup.

EXAMPLE 1   The cost price of an electric clock is $12.97. H. Voss, a hardware dealer, has a rate of markup of 35% on all electrical goods. What is the markup on the clock? What is the selling price?

SOLUTION   Step 1:

$M = ?$	$M = Cr$
$C = \$12.97$	$= 12.97 \times 0.35$
$r = 35\%$	$= 4.539$
$= 0.35$	$= 4.54$

The markup is $4.54.

Step 2:

$S = ?$	$S = C + M$
$C = \$12.97$	$= 12.97 + 4.54$
$M = \$4.54$	$= 17.51$

The selling price is $17.51.

EXERCISE • SET 1

Calculate each markup and selling price using the method of Example 1.

	Cost Price	Rate of Markup	Markup	Selling Price
1.	$ 15.67	20%		
2.	20.99	25%		
3.	13.44	15%		
4.	295.60	42%		
5.	1.75	5%		
6.	3.89	5.5%		
7.	1 376.40	55%		
8.	10.95	11%		
9.	15.63	18%		
10.	1.99	7.5%		
11.	315.16	33.5%		
12.	89.97	28.5%		
13.	0.79	1.5%		
14.	129.33	30.5%		
15.	478.66	40.75%		

EXERCISE • SET 2

A combination formula may be used as a short method for finding the selling price.

> ### Formula
>
> $$S = C(1 + r)$$
>
> Where: S is the selling price.
> C is the cost price.
> r is the rate of markup expressed as a decimal quantity.

EXAMPLE 2   A service station manager receives tires costing $27.98 each and wants to put a rate of markup of 33% on the cost price. At what price should each tire be sold?

SOLUTION
$S = ?$
$C = \$27.98$
$r = 33\%$
$\quad = 0.33$

$S = C(1 + r)$
$\quad = 27.98 \, (1 + 0.33)$
$\quad = 27.98 \times 1.33$
$\quad = 37.213$
$\quad = 37.21$

The tires should be sold at $37.21 each.

Following the method given in Example 2, calculate each selling price.

	Cost Price	Rate of Markup	Selling Price
1.	$ 5.95	20%	
2.	123.50	30%	
3.	89.97	25%	
4.	15.45	22%	
5.	210.40	36%	
6.	54.45	27%	
7.	16.95	5%	
8.	21.50	18.5%	
9.	69.66	25.5%	
10.	133.49	33.3%	
11.	567.50	42.5%	
12.	1 964.70	55.5%	
13.	7.63	2.5%	
14.	8.98	2.25%	
15.	4.37	1.25%	

EXERCISE • SET 3

1. The Students' Council bought college sweaters for $21.50 each. A profit is needed so the Council decided to have a rate of markup of 25% of the cost price. At what price will the sweaters be sold to the students? _____

2. Blakney's Sports Store bought Pinto track shoes for $22.88. At what price should they be sold to have a rate of markup of 28% of the cost price? _____

3. Solomen's Hardware Store purchased all-purpose handsaws at $10.36 each. The selling price is to include a 32% markup on cost. What is the markup and the selling price of each saw? _____ , _____

4. Hanna Ingrum, a second year college student, wants to earn money during her vacation. She buys 100 birthstone rings for a total of $648. What is the markup and the selling price on each ring at a markup of 33% on cost price? _____ , _____

5. The Wolfe Lake Tennis Association is considering improving the surface of the courts. The Association decides to raise money to cover these improvements and buys Western aluminum rackets at $987.50 per dozen. At what price must each racket be sold to have a markup of 22% on the cost price? _____

6. Universal Hardware receives electric variable speed drills invoiced at $57.50 each. The rate of markup is 25% on the cost price. What is the selling price of each drill? _____

7. Ron's Appliance Shop receives five electric frying pans at a total invoice price of $175.

a) What is the shop's cost price for each frying pan? _____

b) If the shop puts a markup of 33% on cost on small appliances, what is the selling price of each frying pan? _____

8. Pro Sports received the invoice below. Pro Sports adds a 35% markup on cost on all goods sold. What is the selling price of each item on the invoice? _____,

_____ , _____

	A-1 WHOLESALE LTD.		
Sold to: Pro Sports Meaford, Ontario	**Via**: truck Date: Feb. 3, 19-- **Terms**: 2/10, n/30		
Quantity	**Description**	**Price**	**Extension**
1	#H-506, 7-piece golf set	$182.67	$182.67
1	#F-729, 11-piece golf set	235.50	235.50
3	#H-509, No. 1 iron men's right hand	56.25	168.75
			$586.92

11·3 CALCULATING RATE OF MARKUP AS A PERCENT OF COST PRICE

A retail business must compete with other businesses. Therefore it is necessary to price the goods sold at the same price as, or below, the price of competitors. Determining a selling price is not always just a matter of calculating markup from a fixed rate and adding it to the cost price. It is sometimes necessary to calculate the rate of markup obtained after a competitive price has been placed on the goods.

Formulas

$$M = S - C$$
$$r = \frac{M}{C} \times 100$$

Where: M is the markup.
S is the selling price.
C is the cost price.
r is the rate of markup expressed as a percent.

EXAMPLE   Dave's Electronics purchases a stereo component set for $245. A competitor sells an identical set for $299.95. Dave's Electronics decides to try selling the set at $294.00. What is the markup? What is the rate of markup on the cost price?

SOLUTION   Step 1:

$M = ?$
$S = \$294.00$
$C = \$245.00$

$$M = S - C$$
$$= 294.00 - 245.00$$
$$= 49.00$$

The markup is $49.00.

Step 2:

$r = ?$
$M = \$49.00$
$C = \$245.00$

$$r = \frac{M}{C} \times 100$$
$$= \frac{49.00}{245.00} \times 100$$
$$= 20$$

The rate of markup is 20%.

EXERCISE • SET 1

Calculate the rate of markup as a percent of the cost price. Round off your answers correct to two places after the decimal.

	Selling Price	Cost Price	Markup	Rate of Markup
1.	$ 5.50	$ 5.00		
2.	3.75	3.00		
3.	12.50	10.50		
4.	47.40	39.50		
5.	137.28	105.60		
6.	86.79	65.75		
7.	790.83	545.40		
8.	252.97	217.75		
9.	67.71	55.50		
10.	132.26	97.25		
11.	5.75	5.15		
12.	13.45	11.79		
13.	56.85	47.60		
14.	149.95	110.20		

EXERCISE • SET 2

NOTE   Always carry rates of markup correct to two places after the decimal unless otherwise instructed.

1. Marlene's Dress Shoppe is having a summer sale and reduces all its prices. A dress that cost the store $28.95 is now sold at $37.60. What is the rate of markup on the cost price? _____

2. A 36-cup automatic percolator is purchased by a hardware retailer from the wholesaler for $40.50. A chain store competitor is selling the same percolator for $49.95. If the hardware retailer sells the percolator for this price, what is the rate of markup on the cost price? _____

3. Snider's Leather Goods receives the invoice below. After checking competitive stores, Snider's decides to sell the luggage for the following prices:
   Tote bags at $22.50 each;
   3-Piece matched luggage sets at $105.95 per set;
   Flight bags at $11.88;
   Garment bags at $15.99.

   What is the rate of markup on the cost price for each unit? _____,

   _____, _____, _____

ACE MANUFACTURING			
Sold to: Snider's Leather Goods		**Date**: Feb. 16, 19--	
Saskatoon, Saskatchewan S7K 1R9		**Terms**: 3/10, 2/20, n/30	
Quantity	**Description**	**Unit Price**	**Extension**
5	Ladies' Tote Bags	$18.75	$ 93.75
8	Sets, 3-piece matching luggage, per set	85.50	684.00
10	Flight Bags	9.80	98.00
6	Executive Garment Bags	10.70	64.20
			$939.95

1. You are the bookkeeper for Blooms Men's Department Store. Blooms just had a Boxing Day sale when many articles were marked down. The manager has just brought you the following sheet and asked you to find the new rate of profit (markup) on the cost price of each article. You are to find each rate correct to two places after the decimal.

Item	Cost Price	Sale Price	Markup
men's ski jackets	$ 59.83	$ 75.00	_____
socks	1.95	2.49	_____
shirts	18.75	22.00	_____
sweaters	30.15	35.00	_____
hunting jackets	97.39	112.50	_____
hunting boots	58.89	73.75	_____
shoes	39.19	45.00	_____
briefs	1.92	2.22	_____
ski pants	55.49	75.89	_____
suits	150.63	175.99	_____
trousers	25.36	39.00	_____
sports jackets	110.98	135.00	_____

11·4 CALCULATING COST PRICE GIVEN SELLING PRICE

Formula

$$C = \frac{S}{1 + r}$$

Where: C is the cost price.

S is the selling price.

r is the rate of markup expressed as a decimal quantity.

EXAMPLE A retailer has an article for sale at $7.15. She needs to know the original cost, but does not have time to go back through the invoices. She knows, however, that she always places a markup of 30% on the cost price of all the goods that she sells in this price range. What was the cost price?

SOLUTION

$$C = ?$$
$$S = \$7.15$$
$$r = 30\%$$
$$= 0.30$$

$$C = \frac{S}{1 + r}$$
$$= \frac{7.15}{1 + 0.30}$$
$$= \frac{7.15}{1.30}$$
$$= 5.50$$

The cost price was $5.50.

EXERCISE • SET 1

Calculate the cost price of each item.

	Selling Price	Rate of Markup on the Cost Price	Cost Price
1.	$ 26.00	30%	
2.	105.00	40%	
3.	37.50	25%	
4.	750.00	50%	
5.	2.16	8%	
6.	35.95	15%	
7.	137.50	25%	
8.	99.99	18%	
9.	3.00	5%	
10.	437.40	45%	
11.	22.95	12.5%	
12.	8.76	7.5%	

EXERCISE • SET 2

Calculate the cost price of each item.

	Item	Selling Price	Rate of Markup on Cost Price	Cost Price
1.	Table Tennis Top 1.8 m × 0.9 m	$ 45.90	22%	
2.	Pool Table 1.8 m × 0.9 m	516.25	13%	
3.	Power-Jet Hockey Set	98.98	25%	
4.	Pool Cue, 1 m	11.60	28%	
5.	Pool Cue, 1.2 m	12.28	26%	
6.	Pool Cue, 1.3 m	15.69	25%	
7.	Standing Cue Rack	46.49	23%	
8.	Wall Cue Rack	30.55	22%	
9.	4-Player Table Tennis Set	25.86	15%	
10.	Pool Balls – Numbered Set	47.95	30%	
11.	Aluminum Tennis Racket	59.98	27%	
12.	Tennis Balls – White, tin of three	4.25	36.5%	
13.	Tennis Balls – Yellow, tin of three	4.98	35.2%	
14.	Squash Racket	38.60	28.5%	
15.	Tennis Bag – Vinyl	22.88	25.7%	

EXERCISE • SET 3

1. Modern Business Machines has Viscount Electronic Calculators, Model No. V729 in the showroom priced at $109.50. If Modern decided on a 15% markup on the cost price, what was paid for each machine? _____

2. Wallace Sales has listed in its sales catalogue Vandetti Non-Printer Electronic Calculator Model No. 70-21V at $98.95. There is a markup of 22% on cost price. What was the cost price? _____

3. Buyers Brands is having a sale of the following radios: Solid State Pocket Radio, No. SS 143, at $15.60; Solid State AM/FM Portable Radio, No. SS 275, at $18.90; and Solid State AM Portable Radio, No. SS 372, at $12.75. If Buyers has a markup of 21% on the cost price of all radios, what was the cost price of each radio being offered for sale? _____, _____, _____

4. Leblanc Sports has advertised the following motor cycles for sale: Tornado Motor Cycle 750, at $926.98; Tornado Motor Cycle 650, at $850.25; and a Tornado Motor Cycle 550, at $768.50. There is a markup of 28% on the cost price. What was the cost price of each motor cycle? _____, _____, _____

11·5 MARKUP CALCULATED ON SELLING PRICE

In many businesses the markup is taken as a percentage of the selling price. When this is done it is called the **gross margin of profit on sales**. This is generally abbreviated to **gross margin**, **margin of profit** or **margin**.

EXAMPLE 1   Calculate the cost price of a gas barbecue if the selling price is $149.99 and the gross margin is 37.5% of the selling price.

SOLUTION
$C = ?$
$S = \$149.99$
$m = 37.5\%$
$ = 0.375$

$C = S - M$
$ = 149.99 - (0.375 \times 149.99)$
$ = 149.99 - 56.25$
$ = 93.74$

The cost price is $93.74.

If a calculator is used to calculate cost price when selling price and rate of gross margin are known, the following formula reduces entries and re-entries into the calculator.

Formula

$$C = S(1 - m)$$

Where: C is the cost price.
$ S$ is the selling price.
$ m$ is the rate of gross margin of profit expressed as a decimal quantity.

EXAMPLE 2   Calculate the cost price of the gas barbecue in Example 1 using the above formula.

SOLUTION
$C = ?$
$S = \$149.99$
$m = 37.5\%$
$ = 0.375$

$C = S(1 - m)$
$ = 149.99 (1 - 0.375)$
$ = 149.99 \times 0.625$
$ = 93.74$

The cost price is $93.74.

EXERCISE • SET 1

Calculate each cost price.

	Selling Price	Gross Margin of Profit	Cost Price
1.	$ 99.95	32%	
2.	239.75	35%	
3.	595.50	50%	
4.	1 395.00	18%	
5.	2.98	28%	

EXERCISE • SET 2

Formula

$$S = \frac{C}{1 - m}$$

Where: S is the selling price.
$\quad\quad$ C is the cost price.
$\quad\quad$ m is the rate of gross margin of profit expressed as a decimal quantity.

EXAMPLE 3 . DeVeer's Automotive Parts Limited purchased all-purpose grease guns for $8.97 each. The expected profit is 30% of the selling price. What is the selling price?

SOLUTION
$S = ?$
$C = \$8.97$
$m = 30\%$
$\quad = 0.30$

$S = \dfrac{C}{1 - m}$

$\quad = \dfrac{8.97}{1 - 0.30}$

$\quad = \dfrac{8.97}{0.7}$

$\quad = 12.814$

$\quad = 12.81$

The selling price is $12.81.

Calculate each selling price.

	Cost Price	Margin of Profit on Selling Price	Selling Price
1.	$ 12.90	5%	
2.	68.25	15%	
3.	125.24	12%	
4.	86.28	25%	
5.	35.26	13%	
6.	627.64	29%	
7.	89.99	33%	
8.	125.63	38%	
9.	84.05	19%	
10.	96.33	37%	
11.	9.66	10.5%	
12.	189.25	18.3%	
13.	96.05	23.4%	
14.	8.91	36.4%	
15.	924.11	41.9%	

EXERCISE • SET 3

1. Warrilow's Hardware bought some copper pans at $30.66 each. At what price must they be sold to obtain a 35% margin of profit on the selling price? _____

2. The Sussex College Curling Club purchased curling brooms at $15.56 each. If the Club wants to make a 23% margin of profit, how much should the brooms be sold for in order to make this profit? _____

3. The Girls' Athletic Association of Hampton College decides to raise money to purchase school letters. A dinner is planned and the cost per serving is as follows: chicken, $0.68; vegetables, $0.42; salad, $0.15; beverage, $0.10; pie, $0.56. What should be charged per serving in order to obtain a 25% margin of profit on sales? _____,

_____, _____, _____, _____

4. Raquette's Hardware bought charcoal lighters at $859 per hundred. Should the lighters be sold at a) $8.95, b) $12.47, c) $12.45, or d) $12.65 each, in order to have a 31% margin of profit on sales? _____

11·6 CALCULATING EQUIVALENT RATES

It is sometimes necessary to compare the rate of markup based on cost with the rate of gross margin based on selling price. To make this comparison rate of markup is changed to rate of gross margin or rate of gross margin is changed to rate of markup. When these rates are compared, they are called equivalent rates.

$$r = \frac{m}{1 - m} \times 100$$

Where: r is the rate of markup based on the cost price, expressed as a percent.

m is the rate of gross margin based on the selling price, expressed as a decimal quantity.

EXAMPLE 1   The gross margin based on the selling price of a toaster is 30%. What is the equivalent rate, based on the cost price, correct to two places after the decimal?

SOLUTION $r = ?$

$m = 30\%$
$= 0.30$

$$r = \frac{m}{1 - m} \times 100$$

$$= \frac{0.30}{1 - 0.30} \times 100$$

$$= \frac{0.30}{0.70} \times 100$$

$$= 42.857$$

$$= 42.86$$

The equivalent rate is 42.86%.

Formula

$$m = \frac{r}{1 + r} \times 100$$

Where: m is the rate of gross margin based on the selling price, expressed as a percent.

r is the rate of markup based on the cost price, expressed as a decimal quantity.

EXAMPLE 2   The rate of markup on a waterbed is 60% of the cost price. What is the equivalent rate based on the selling price?

SOLUTION $m = ?$

$r = 60\%$
$= 0.60$

$$m = \frac{r}{1 + r} \times 100$$

$$= \frac{0.60}{1 + 0.60} \times 100$$

$$= \frac{0.60}{1.60} \times 100$$

$$= 37.50$$

The equivalent rate is 37.50%.

EXERCISE • SET 1

Calculate each equivalent rate as a percent correct to two places after the decimal.

	m	r
1.	50%	
2.	40%	
3.	20%	
4.	15%	
5.	10%	
6.	33%	

	m	r
7.		50%
8.		40%
9.		20%
10.		15%
11.		10%
12.		33%

EXERCISE • SET 2

Calculate each equivalent rate as a percent correct to two places after the decimal.

	m	r
1.	10.75%	
2.	31.5%	
3.	42.25%	
4.	39.5%	
5.	27.75%	
6.	18.25%	

	m	r
7.		10.75%
8.		31.5%
9.		42.25%
10.		39.5%
11.		27.75%
12.		18.25%

EXERCISE • SET 3

1. Charlie's Food Market is changing its markup base from cost price to selling price. Markup on cost on fresh fruit is 15%; on meats, 20%; on canned goods, 2%; and on dairy products, 10%. What should the equivalent rate of gross margin on selling price be for each product line? Express your answers correct to two places after the decimal. _____, _____, _____, _____

2. A buyer for Cecelia's Dress Shop is offered a line of clothing on which the wholesaler tells her that she can realize a 28% margin on selling price. The buyer's department marks up on cost. What will be the markup on cost correct to two places after the decimal? _____

3. Mainline Furniture Company is offered a line of furniture on which they can obtain a 55% markup on cost. Mainline usually marks up on selling price; what will be this markup correct to two places after the decimal? _____

4. Two manufacturers offer a buyer similar lines of goods at the same price. One manufacturer claims that his goods should bring a 22.5% margin on selling price, while the other manufacturer says that her goods should bring a 31.25% markup on cost. Which is the better offer? _____

5. A buyer for a hardware store is offered a line of dishes on which the salesman claims the store should be able to put a 45% markup on cost. If the store requires a 38.5% margin on selling price, should the buyer purchase the dishes? _____

11·7 CALCULATING MARKDOWN

When merchants find that items in their stores do not sell as quickly as expected or that they have too many seasonal products left over at the end of the season, the price of these articles is reduced to try to sell them. The selling price is marked down to a new selling price, or a **reduced price**. The rate of the reduction, or **markdown**, is usually taken as a percent of the selling price.

Formula

$$D = dS$$

Where: D is the markdown.
      d is the rate of markdown expressed as a decimal quantity.
      S is the selling price.

Formula

$$R = S - D$$

Where: R is the reduced price.
      S is the selling price.
      D is the markdown.

EXAMPLE 1 The fishing tackle prices at Eden's Marina are being reduced by a markdown of 30% of the selling price.
a) How much is the markdown for fishing lures which are priced at $2.95?
b) What is the reduced price?

SOLUTION **a)** $D = ?$ | $D = dS$
             $d = 30\%$ $= 0.30 \times 2.95$
               $= 0.30$ $= 0.89$
          $S = \$2.95$

The markdown is $0.89.

      b) $R = ?$ | $R = S - D$
             $S = \$2.95$ $= 2.95 - 0.89$
             $D = \$0.89$ $= 2.06$

The reduced price is $2.06.

EXERCISE • SET 1

Calculate each markdown and reduced price.

	Selling Price	Rate of Markdown	Markdown	Reduced Price
1.	$ 1.75	20%		
2.	25.95	40%		
3.	75.00	35%		
4.	125.50	25%		
5.	18.90	50%		
6.	20.95	25%		
7.	199.95	15%		
8.	8.75	33%		
9.	55.59	41%		
10.	137.50	27%		
11.	7.79	15.5%		
12.	18.44	33.3%		
13.	169.75	16.25%		
14.	11.27	7.5%		
15.	0.89	11.25%		

EXERCISE • SET 2

A combination formula may be used as a short method for finding the reduced price.

> **Formula**
>
> $$R = S(1 - d)$$
>
> Where: R is the reduced price.
> S is the selling price.
> d is the rate of markdown expressed as a decimal quantity.

EXAMPLE 2   In a store-wide sale, all items of stock are reduced in price by a markdown of 33% of the selling price. What is the reduced price of a ski jacket originally selling at $79.96?

SOLUTION $R = ?$
$S = \$79.96$
$d = 33\%$
$= 0.33$

$R = S(1 - d)$
$= 79.96 (1 - 0.33)$
$= 79.96 \times 0.67$
$= 53.573$
$= 53.57$

The reduced price is $53.57.

Following the method given in Example 2, calculate each reduced price.

	Selling Price	Markdown on Selling Price	Reduced Price
1.	$ 7.90	30%	
2.	120.50	40%	
3.	89.90	20%	
4.	13.40	25%	
5.	55.00	10%	
6.	8.95	18%	
7.	3.75	22%	
8.	15.85	33%	
9.	132.77	34%	
10.	57.55	5%	
11.	14.55	10.5%	
12.	179.99	15.5%	
13.	18.44	10.7%	
14.	312.14	25.75%	
15.	10.99	5.5%	

EXERCISE • SET 3

1. Pro Cycle Shop decides to reduce the selling price of all 10-speed bicycles by 20% of the selling price. A bicycle has an original selling price of $297.60.

   a) What will its reduced price be? _____

   b) If you buy it after prices are reduced, how much will you save? _____

2. At 9 p.m. on Friday, Bob's Supermarket has 5 flats of fresh strawberries selling at $1.49 a box. It is decided to mark down the selling price of the strawberries by 40% to try to sell them by 10 p.m.

   a) What is the reduced price of a box of strawberries? _____

   b) If there are 8 boxes to a flat and all the strawberries are sold Friday night, how much money did Bob's Supermarket lose by reducing the price of the strawberries? _____

3. The Christmas cards in Macrae's Department Store are marked down 50% after the holiday. If they were selling at the following prices before Christmas, what will be the reduced price of each box? Variety Box, $3.25; Snowflake Box, $3.75; Local Artists Box, $5.95; Wintertime Box, $4.75; Santa Design Box, $4.95 _____, _____,

   _____, _____, _____

11·8 REVIEW

EXERCISE • SET 1

Calculate each markup.

	Cost Price	Rate of Markup on Cost Price	Markup
1.	$ 5.75	20%	$
2.	397.00	33%	
3.	22.45	27%	
4.	3.95	15%	
5.	75.00	5%	
6.	44.95	10.5%	
7.	4.56	5.5%	
8.	84.37	1.5%	
9.	137.67	42.25%	
10.	279.39	35.75%	

Calculate each markup and selling price.

	Cost Price	Rate of Markup on Cost Price	Markup	Selling Price
11.	$ 50.00	20%	$	$
12.	127.50	30%		
13.	3.80	15%		
14.	28.00	26%		
15.	545.50	42%		
16.	8.95	15.5%		
17.	72.45	13.7%		
18.	2.97	4.5%		
19.	327.65	1.5%		
20.	66.36	7.75%		

Calculate each rate of markup on the cost price. Round off your answer correct to two places after the decimal where necessary.

	Selling Price	Cost Price	Rate of Markup on Cost Price
21.	$ 25.00	$ 20.00	
22.	36.00	30.00	
23.	155.00	125.00	
24.	575.00	500.00	
25.	1.50	1.25	
26.	36.95	32.00	
27.	58.60	41.20	
28.	295.45	173.56	
29.	134.99	98.87	
30.	5.76	5.25	

Calculate each selling price.

	Cost Price	Rate of Markup on Selling Price	Selling Price
31.	$ 19.20	20%	$
32.	26.25	25%	
33.	90.65	30%	
34.	4.83	16%	
35.	275.00	50%	
36.	15.45	21%	
37.	132.50	35%	
38.	486.37	45%	
39.	8.98	8%	
40.	3.24	1.5%	

Calculate each cost price.

	Selling Price	Rate of Markup on Cost Price	Cost Price
41.	$ 12.00	20%	$
42.	20.50	30%	
43.	2.76	15%	
44.	445.40	36%	
45.	108.50	24%	
46.	33.95	22%	
47.	5.99	17%	
48.	239.95	43%	
49.	46.75	28%	
50.	565.79	51%	

Calculate each reduced price.

	Selling Price	Rate of Markdown on Selling Price	Reduced Price
51.	$ 25.00	20%	$
52.	5.50	10%	
53.	135.40	35%	
54.	82.50	40%	
55.	536.60	25%	
56.	2.95	30%	
57.	16.79	15%	
58.	178.85	25%	
59.	11.99	5%	
60.	22.95	10.5%	

EXERCISE • SET 2 _____

Calculate each selling price.

	Cost Price	Rate of Markup on Cost Price	Selling Price
1.	$ 25.00	30%	$
2.	5.80	15%	
3.	3.90	10%	
4.	295.00	33%	
5.	81.50	42%	
6.	37.85	25%	
7.	89.27	32.5%	
8.	127.47	42.8%	
9.	59.96	8.9%	
10.	567.40	9.75%	

When calculating percents, give your answers correct to two places after the decimal.

11. Calculate the selling price of a pair of shoes if the cost price is $37.50 and the markup is 33.333% of the cost price. _____

12. Calculate the cost price of a humidifier if the selling price is $299.95 and the gross margin is 16.667% of the selling price. _____

13. Markup on cost price is 27.5%. What is the equivalent rate of markup on the selling price? _____

14. The markup on the selling price is 38.5%. What is the equivalent rate of markup on cost? _____

15. The cost price of a 5 L pail of paint is $15.95 and the selling price is $18.97.

    a) What is the markup? _____

    b) What is the rate of markup on cost? _____

16. The cost price of a side of beef is $2.28/kg. It is sold for an average of $2.68/kg.

    a) If there is no waste, what is the gross margin of profit? _____

    b) What is the rate of margin on the selling price? _____

17. The selling price of a pair of socks is $2.95 and the markup is 33.333% of the cost price. What is the cost price? _____

18. The cost price of an aluminum ladder is $35.50 and the gross margin of profit is 28% of the selling price. What is the selling price? _____

EXERCISE • SET 3

1. Bluelake Appliances paid the manufacturer $475.65 for a smooth-top stove. If markup is 25% of the cost price, what is the selling price of the stove? _____

2. Jerry's Furniture Store sells a reproduction of a Louis XV chair for $259.95. Margin of profit on the selling price is 33%. What was the cost price? _____

3. The cost of an earthenware dinner set is $80.25 and its selling price is $104.25.

   a) What is the markup? _____

   b) What is the rate of markup on the cost price, correct to two places after the decimal? _____

4. The cost price of a sabre saw is $17.85 and its selling price is $23.99.

   a) What is the margin of profit? _____

   b) What is the rate of margin of profit on the selling price, correct to two places after the decimal? _____

5. The selling price of a set of steak knives is $22.95. If the markup is 40% of the cost price, what is the cost price? _____

6. The cost price of a touring bike is $179.80. If the margin of profit is 23% of the selling price, what is the selling price? _____

7. A buyer is offered a line of purses on which the salesman tells her that she can realize a 32.5% markup on cost. What is the equivalent rate of markup on selling price, correct to two places after the decimal? _____

8. A store marks up its goods on cost price. It is offered a line of goods which would sell well if marked up 29% on the selling price. What rate of markup could it put on cost? _____

UNIT
4

Personal

Finance

CHAPTER 12

BANKING AND CREDIT

The Canadian chartered banks provide many services to individuals and to the business world. Originally intended to serve the function of keeping savings safer and acting as money lenders, banks are now the agency through which most businesses carry out money transactions. Little currency is exchanged in payments between businesses; cheques drawn on bank accounts serve as the medium of exchange.

Individuals use **chequing accounts** in paying their bills, **savings** and **investment accounts** as a means of saving money and planning for retirement income, and **bank loans** when they wish to finance purchases such as cars, furniture, and household appliances; or even to finance vacations.

This chapter deals mostly with the ways in which banks encourage savings and how they lend money to individuals and small businesses. Even though bank interest rates tend to be lower than those of other lending institutions, borrowers should be sure that the repayment terms are within the limits of what can be paid back easily from their income.

12·1 SAVING MONEY AND EARNING INTEREST

CHEQUING ACCOUNTS

Most workers are paid by cheque or by direct deposit into their accounts at a bank, trust company or credit union. Having some type of banking account is therefore, important. Cheques that you receive also can be cashed easily at one of these financial institutions if you have an account at the branch at which you cash the cheque. Most of these institutions offer banking accounts in which you can make deposits, from which you can make withdrawals, and on which you may write cheques to make payments.

Some of these **chequing accounts** allow you to write any number of cheques during a month at no cost. The service of accepting a cheque, withdrawing the money from your account, and arranging that this money is deposited in the account of the person to whom the cheque was written is free. No interest is paid on the money that remains in the account.

Chequing savings accounts are also available. On these accounts there is usually a service charge for cheques written on the account, but interest is paid on the minimum balance each half year at the rate of 3% to 4% per annum.

EXAMPLE 1 Mary Foster has a chequing savings account on which the minimum balance from October 31 to April 30 is $189.79. How much interest does she receive if interest is paid at the rate of 4% per annum? Assume that the year is not a leap year.

SOLUTION   Calculate the number of days.

Oct. 31 to Nov. 30	30 d
December	31 d
January	31 d
February	28 d
March	31 d
April	30 d
Total	181 d

NOTE   Don't count the first day; do count the last day.

Calculate the interest.

$$I = ?$$

$$P = \$189.79$$

$$r = 4\%$$
$$= 0.04$$
$$t = 181 \text{ d}$$
$$= \frac{181}{365} \text{ a}$$

$$I = Prt$$
$$= 189.79 \times 0.04 \times \frac{181}{365}$$
$$= 3.764\ 601\ 643$$
$$= 3.76$$

Mary receives $3.76 in interest.

EXAMPLE 2   George Atto has a chequing savings account on which the minimum balance from April 30 to October 31 is $291.85. How much interest does he receive if interest is paid at the rate of 3% per annum?

SOLUTION   Calculate the number of days.

April 30 to May 31	31 d
June	30 d
July	31 d
August	31 d
September	30 d
October	31 d
Total	184 d

Calculate the interest.

$$I = ?$$

$$P = \$291.85$$

$$r = 3\%$$
$$= 0.03$$
$$t = 184 \text{ d}$$
$$= \frac{184}{365} \text{ a}$$

$$I = Prt$$
$$= 291.85 \times 0.03 \times \frac{184}{365}$$
$$= 4.413\ 731\ 506$$
$$= 4.41$$

George receives $4.41 in interest.

EXERCISE • SET 1

Calculate the interest earned on the following chequing savings accounts.
*Consider that the year is *not* a leap year.

	Minimum Balance	Time	Interest Rate Per Annum	Interest Earned
1.	$ 256.38	April 30 to October 31	4%	
2.	256.38	April 30 to October 31	3%	
3.	1 727.95	October 31 to April 30*	4%	
4.	1 727.95	October 31 to April 30*	3%	
5.	5 250.00	April 30 to October 31	4%	
6.	5 250.00	April 30 to October 31	3%	

EARNING INTEREST ON SAVINGS

In recent years, financial institutions such as banks, trust companies, and credit unions have encouraged customers to save money in special accounts with them rather than investing savings in stocks and bonds to provide for future financial needs. These institutions offer many different plans which pay good interest rates on money intended purely as savings: premium (no chequing) savings accounts, savings or investment accounts; short and long term corporation notes; term deposits and investment certificates; Registered Retirement Savings Plans; and Registered Home Ownership Plans. Each institution competes with the others to offer the best interest profits on savings and therefore each set of savings plans is similar. The examples and questions will indicate the way in which many of these plans operate.

EXAMPLE 3 Richard Dubois has a premium savings account at a bank. His minimum balance over the period from April 30 to October 31 is $2000. The bank pays interest at the rate of 6.75% per annum. This interest is calculated on the number of days the money has been in the account. How much does Richard receive in interest for the above period?

SOLUTION Find the number of days.

April 30 to May 31	31 d
June	30 d
July	31 d
August	31 d
September	30 d
October	31 d
Total	184 d

Calculate the interest.

$$I = ?$$

$$P = \$2000$$

$$r = 6.75\%$$

$$\quad = 0.0675$$

$$t = 184 \text{ d}$$

$$\quad = \frac{184}{365} \text{ a}$$

$$I = Prt$$

$$\quad = 2000 \times 0.0675 \times \frac{184}{365}$$

$$\quad = 68.054\ 794\ 52$$

$$\quad = 68.05$$

Richard receives $68.05 in interest.

EXAMPLE 4   Joan McIntyre plans to save enough to take a year off work at the end of 6 years. She has $2000 to put into a savings plan. Joan can buy Savings Certificates at her bank which, if she holds them for 6 years, will pay simple interest at the rate of 10.43% per annum at the end of the 6 years. How much money does Joan receive at the end of the 6 years?

SOLUTION   Calculate the interest.

$$I = ?$$

$$P = \$2000$$

$$r = 10.43\%$$

$$\quad = 0.1043$$

$$t = 6 \text{ a}$$

$$I = Prt$$

$$\quad = 2000 \times 0.1043 \times 6$$

$$\quad = 1251.600\ 000$$

$$\quad = 1251.60$$

Calculate the amount.

$$A = ?$$

$$P = \$2000$$

$$I = \$1251.60$$

$$A = P + I$$

$$\quad = 2000 + 1251.60$$

$$\quad = 3251.60$$

Joan receives $3251.60.

EXAMPLE 5   Henry Aldii has $63 900 from the sale of his home. He plans to live in his cottage over the summer and purchase a new home in the fall. If Henry invests his money in a 90-d Term Deposit which pays 7.75% per annum, how much interest will he receive? (A 90-d Term Deposit means that the money must be left on deposit for no less than 90 days to receive the interest rate quoted. It can, however, be cashed in less than 90 days, if necessary, but interest will be paid at a lower rate.)

SOLUTION

$$I = ?$$

$$P = \$63\ 900$$

$$r = 7.75\%$$

$$\quad = 0.0775$$

$$t = 90 \text{ d}$$

$$\quad = \frac{90}{365} \text{ a}$$

$$I = Prt$$

$$\quad = 63\ 900 \times 0.0775 \times \frac{90}{365}$$

$$\quad = 1221.102\ 739$$

$$\quad = 1221.10$$

Henry receives an interest payment of $1221.10.

EXAMPLE 6 If Henry (in Example 5) could have kept his $63 900 in the bank for one complete year, he could have purchased a one-year Deposit Certificate on which interest is paid at the rate of 8.25% per annum. How much interest would he have received? (A Deposit Certificate can be cashed in less than one year but the interest will be paid at a reduced rate.)

SOLUTION

$I = ?$

$P = \$63\ 900$

$r = 8.25\%$

$\quad = 0.0825$

$t = 1\text{ a}$

$I = Prt$

$\quad = 63\ 900 \times 0.0825 \times 1$

$\quad = 5271.750\ 000$

$\quad = 5271.75$

Henry would have received an interest payment of $5271.75.

EXAMPLE 7 Henry (in Example 5) could have invested the money from his home in one-year Investment Certificates at a finance or trust company and received 8.5% interest per annum. But he would have no option to cash them at any time during the year. How much interest would Henry have received if he had decided to purchase these certificates for a year?

SOLUTION

$I = ?$

$P = \$63\ 900$

$r = 8.5\%$

$\quad = 0.085$

$t = 1\text{ a}$

$I = Prt$

$\quad = 63\ 900 \times 0.085 \times 1$

$\quad = 5431.500\ 000$

$\quad = 5431.50$

Henry would have received $5431.50 in interest.

EXAMPLE 8 Judy Goetz received $30 000 from the sale of a lot. She invested the money in non-cashable ten-year Investment Certificates. The interest is paid directly into her chequing account. Judy has the option of having this interest paid: a) annually at the rate of 10.5% per annum, or b) semi-annually at the rate of 10.25% per annum. How much interest would she lose annually if she chose to have interest payments made semi-annually?

SOLUTION A If she had chosen a) she would receive *one* payment of:

$I = ?$

$P = \$30\ 000$

$r = 10.5\%$

$\quad = 0.105$

$t = 1\text{ a}$

$I = Prt$

$\quad = 30\ 000 \times 0.105 \times 1$

$\quad = 3150.000\ 000$

$\quad = 3150.00$

Judy would receive $3150 in interest.

B If Judy chose b) she would receive *two* payments of:

$I = ?$

$P = \$30\ 000$

$r = 10.25\%$

$\quad = 0.1025$

$t = 0.5\text{ a}$

$I = Prt$

$\quad = 30\ 000 \times 0.1025 \times 0.5$

$\quad = 1537.500\ 000$

$\quad = 1537.50$

The total interest received for the year would be: $2 \times \$1537.50 = \$3075.00$

If Judy chose b) she would lose: $\$3150.00 - \$3075.00 = \$75.00$.

EXAMPLE 9 Harry Norstrom has a special savings account with his credit union. He arranged to have $100 withdrawn from his pay cheque at the end of each month and deposited in this savings account. A computer calculates the interest at a rate of 7% per annum at the end of each month and reports the simple interest accumulated at the end of each quarter. Harry had $500 in his savings account on August 31 and $100 was deposited, as instructed, at the end of September, the end of October, and the end of November. How much simple interest was paid to Harry on November 30?

SOLUTION

Date	Principal	Deposit	No. of Days	Simple Interest at 7%
September 30	$500	$100	30	$500 \times 0.07 \times \dfrac{30}{365} = \$ \ 2.88$
October 31	600	100	31	$600 \times 0.07 \times \dfrac{31}{365} = \quad 3.57$
November 30	700	100	30	$700 \times 0.07 \times \dfrac{30}{365} = \quad \underline{4.03}$
			Total Interest	$10.48

Harry was paid $10.48 in interest on November 30.

EXERCISE • SET 2

1. Al Veen has a chequing savings account in which the minimum balance from April 30 to October 31 was $578.63. If interest is paid at the rate of 3.5% per annum, how much interest does Al receive at the end of October? _____

2. Entries in Marion Vanderwal's chequing savings account from October 31 to April 30 are shown below. Calculate:

   a) the balance after each transaction, _____, _____, _____, _____,

   _____, _____, _____, _____, _____, _____

   b) the minimum balance for the period, _____

   c) the amount of interest that Marion receives at the end of April if the interest is calculated at 3.75% per annum on the minimum balance. (Assume that the year is not a leap year.) _____

   Entries: Oct. 31, balance, $789.30; Nov. 11, withdrawal, $105.15; Nov. 30, deposit, $300; Dec. 5, withdrawal, $158.60; Dec. 31, deposit, $150; Jan. 31, deposit, $200; Feb. 15, withdrawal, $55; Feb. 28, deposit, $250; March 31, deposit, $150; April 2, withdrawal, $976.36; April 30, deposit, $100

3. If Marion (in Question 2) had made the same deposits and withdrawals into a premium savings account paying interest on the minimum balance for the same period at the rate of 6.5% per annum, how much interest would she have received? _____

4. George Blais has a premium savings account in a trust company. During the period from April 30 to October 31, he had a minimum balance of $345.65. If the trust company pays interest at the rate of 7% per annum on the minimum balance for the period, how much interest does George receive? _____

5. Ann Martin received $1625 from the sale of some stock which her grandmother left to her. Ann purchased Investment Certificates with the money which pay 10.45% per annum in interest if she holds them for six years. How much money will she receive at the end of the six years? _____

6. Joan and Harry sold their cottage for $45 000. They plan to invest the money in other property, but want to take three or four months to find exactly what they want. Joan and Harry invest the money in a 90-d Term Deposit which pays interest at the rate of 7.5% per annum. How much interest will they receive? _____

7. John Hanshawe sold his farm for $95 000. He and his wife are renting an apartment in the city, so John invested the money in a one-year Deposit Certificate on which interest is paid at the rate of 8.5% per annum. How much interest does John receive at the end of the year? _____

8. John (in Question 7) could have invested the money from his farm in a trust company by purchasing one-year Investment Certificates and received interest at the rate of 8.75% per annum. How much interest would he have received if he had decided to purchase these certificates for a year? _____

9. Jane Priebe decided to become a realtor and sold her business in antiques for $75 000. She invested the money in non-cashable ten-year Investment Certificates from which interest is deposited directly into her chequing account. Jane can have this interest paid annually at the rate of 9.625% per annum or semi-annually at the rate of 9.375% per annum. How much interest would she gain if she chose to have interest payments made annually? _____

10. Joyce Rinehart has a special savings account with her credit union. On May 31 she has $750 in this account. Joyce arranges to have $150 withdrawn from her pay cheque and deposited to her savings account on June 30, July 31, and August 31. If a computer calculates simple interest at the rate of 6.875% per annum at the end of each month and reports the simple interest accumulated on August 31, how much total interest will be in Joyce's account? _____

EXERCISE • SET 3

1. John Baaker has a special savings account of $2000 which pays interest at 8.25% per annum. Interest is paid into the account at the end of every month and is added to the balance. Interest is then taken at the end of the next month on the new balance etc. If John's balance is $2000 at the beginning of June, find the balances on June 30, July 31, and August 31. _____ , _____ , _____

2. Vera Long has a daily interest savings account. The interest, at 8% per annum, is calculated by computer at the end of each day, and is added to her balance. This new balance is used as the principal on which interest is calculated the next day. If there was $5000 in Vera's account at the beginning of April, calculate the daily balances for the first ten days in April.

_____, _____, _____, _____, _____,

_____, _____, _____, _____, _____

3. Cathy Leblanc has a money management account which pays daily interest at the rate of 7.5% per annum on daily balances of $2000 or more and daily interest at the rate of 4% per annum on daily balances of under $2000. If Cathy had a balance of $5000 on June 1 and makes no transactions on the account until June 5 when she withdraws $3800 from the account, calculate Cathy's daily balances from June 1 to June 8.

_____, _____, _____, _____,

_____, _____, _____, _____

4. Karl Rosskopf has a U.S. dollar daily interest account in which he continually maintains savings of over $5000 for which he receives a bonus calculated on his total balance of 1.25% per annum deposited into the account at the end of each month. Daily interest is calculated at the rate of 6.5% per annum as well. If Karl had $6700 in the account on March 28 and makes no further transactions on the account, calculate his balances at the end of the day on March 28, March 29, March 30, March 31, and April 1. _____, _____, _____, _____, _____

12·2 BORROWING FROM A BANK

The chartered banks of Canada make it part of their business to lend money. Their interest rates are generally lower than those charged by loan companies or credit unions. Banks will grant loans to:
- borrowers known by the bank to have sufficient finances to repay the loan.
- borrowers who can present the bank with collateral security. The collateral may be bonds, stock, life insurance policies or mortgages which the bank holds until the loan is repaid. If for some reason the borrower is unable to repay the loan, the bank has the right to use the collateral as repayment of the loan.
- business firms who pledge their stock in trade as collateral.

There are two general types of bank loans: demand loans and personal instalment loans.

DEMAND LOANS

To make a demand loan, the borrower signs a demand note which the bank holds. The demand note bears no definite date of payment, but the bank expects the borrower to make reasonable payments at regular intervals (usually monthly).

Sample demand note.

An interest rate is quoted on the note; this interest on the unpaid balance of the loan is usually debited monthly to the borrower's account. The borrower may arrange to have monthly repayment instalments deducted from her or his bank account.

EXAMPLE On January 2, Gregory Jones borrowed $800 at 10% interest per annum on his demand note. Payments were made in the same year as follows: January 31, $200; February 28, $200; March 31, $400. How much interest was Gregory charged? Assume that the year was not a leap year.

SOLUTION

	Principal	Interest
Amount owing, January 2:	$800.00	
Interest charge from Jan. 2 to Jan. 31:		
$800 \times 0.1 \times \dfrac{29}{365}$		$ 6.36
Payment on loan, January 31:	200.00	
	$600.00	
Interest charge from Jan. 31 to Feb. 28:		
$600 \times 0.1 \times \dfrac{28}{365}$		4.60
Payment on loan, February 28:	200.00	
	$400.00	
Interest charge from Feb. 28 to Mar. 31:		
$400 \times 0.1 \times \dfrac{31}{365}$		3.40
Payment on loan, March 31:	400.00	
	$ 0.00	
Total interest charge		$14.36

EXERCISE • SET 1

Calculate the principal and interest at the time of each payment and the total interest paid for the following loans on a demand note.

1. A loan of $500 was borrowed on March 3, at 11% per annum.
Payments made the same year: $250 on March 31, $250 on April 30

	Principal	**Interest**
Amount owing, March 3:	$500	
Interest from March 3 to March 31:		
$500 $\times$ $\times$ =		_____
Payment, March 31:	_____	
	_____	
Interest from March 31 to April 30:		
$\times$ $\times$ =		_____
Payment, April 30:	_____	
	_____	
Total interest:		_____

2. A loan of $1000 was borrowed on July 5, at 12.25% per annum.
Payments made the same year: $300 on July 31, $300 on August 31, $400 on September 15

	Principal	**Interest**
Amount owing, July 5:	$1000	
Interest from July 5 to July 31:		
$\times$ $\times$ =		_____
Payment, July 31:	_____	
	_____	
Interest from July 31 to August 31:		
$\times$ $\times$ =		_____
Payment, August 31:	_____	
	_____	
Interest from August 31 to September 15:		
$\times$ $\times$ =		_____
Payment, September 15:	_____	
	_____	
Total interest:		_____

EXERCISE • SET 2

For the following loans on demand notes, calculate the total interest paid.

	Amount Borrowed	Date of Loan	Rate of Interest Charged per Annum	Payments (made the same year)	Total Interest Paid
1.	$1 500.00	May 2, 1985	10%	May 31, $500.00 June 30, $500.00 July 31, $500.00	
2.	700.00	July 1, 1985	10.5%	July 31, $200.00 Aug. 31, $200.00 Sept. 30, $200.00 Oct. 31, $100.00	
3.	250.00	Jan. 1, 1985	9.5%	Jan. 31, $50.00 Feb. 28, $50.00 Mar. 31, $50.00 Apr. 30, $50.00 May 31, $50.00	
4.	120.00	Feb. 1, 1985	11%	$20.00 plus interest at the end of each month starting Feb. 28, 1985 until loan paid	
5.	500.00	1985 09 01	10.5%	1985 09 30, $200.00 1985 10 31, $100.00 1985 11 30, $100.00 1985 12 31, $50.00 1986 01 31, $50.00	

EXERCISE • SET 3

Draw up and calculate, as in the example, a schedule of repayments of principal and interest for the following loans made on demand notes. Calculate, also, the total interest paid.

1. A loan of $300 was borrowed on January 5, 1985 at 9.5% per annum interest. Payments: January 31, 1985: $100; February 28, 1985: $100; March 31, 1985: $100
2. A loan of $525 was borrowed on April 15 at 10.25% per annum interest. Payments made in the same year: May 31, $125; June 30, $100; July 31, $100; August 31, $200
3. A loan of $1250 was borrowed on March 20 at an interest rate of 9.75% per annum. Payments made in the same year: April 30, $250; May 31, $200; June 30, $300; September 30, $500
4. A loan of $5000 was borrowed on July 1, 1985, at an interest rate of 10.25% per annum. Payments: September 30, 1985, $575; December 31, 1985, $1250; March 31, 1986, $1500; June 30, 1986, $1000; September 30, 1986, $675
5. A loan of $11 500 was borrowed on 1985 04 30 at an interest rate of 9.25% per annum. Payments were made as follows: 1985 06 30, $2000; 1985 08 31, $2000; 1985 10 31, $2000; 1985 12 31, $2500; 1986 02 28, $1500; 1986 04 30, $1500.

PERSONAL INSTALMENT LOANS

Money may be borrowed from the bank and repaid in equal monthly instalments. At the time of making a loan, the borrower is given the sum of money required and agrees to pay a certain sum every month until the loan plus interest is repaid. These payments can usually be made over a period of 6 to 60 months.

An advantage of this type of loan is that it carries life insurance. If the borrower dies before the loan is repaid, instalments still unpaid are paid by the insurance.

In general, the interest charged on this type of loan by the various Canadian chartered banks is almost the same. When computing interest on a personal loan, the bank considers all months as equal units of time.

EXAMPLE 1   Harry Simpson arranged a personal loan from his bank for $150. His instalment payments are $25.75 a month for six months. How much interest does he pay? The bank pays for the life insurance on the loan. (See statement on facing page.)

SOLUTION

$$\begin{aligned}
\text{Amount of loan} &= \$150 \\
\text{Total amount repaid} &= 6 \times \$25.75 \\
&= \$154.50 \\
\text{Interest} &= \$154.50 - \$150 \\
&= \$4.50
\end{aligned}$$

Harry pays interest of $4.50.

TRUE ANNUAL INTEREST RATE

In the previous example, Harry paid $4.50 in interest on a loan of $150 for a period of six months. The following formula gives a method of calculating the actual rate of interest per annum that is paid on an instalment loan.

Formula

$$r = \frac{2NI}{A(n + 1)}$$

Where: r is the true interest rate expressed as a decimal.
   N is the number of payments per year.
   I is the total interest paid on the loan.
   A is the amount of the loan.
   n is the total number of payments.

Form 3855 (1-78) 069228
Printed in Canada

Indirect and/or other advances

Card No.
Loan No. S3964
Account 304-129
Occupation Salesman
Name of Consumer
Loan Plan (if applicable)

Collateral security (Give brief details)

G/C, C.S.V., etc. $250.00
C/M Covering:— C.S.V. Royal life
                insurance policy

Classification per
Form 974

Number of   Six   @ $ 25.75   *
instalments   @ $

*Adjustment of interest when ADDED to first instalment
Dr G/L 484-380/ 484-381 $ _____   (see calculation of
Cr G/L 636-165 $ _____   Monthly Instalments)

_____ per month

L F 177 Can Rev Feb 1976   **Promissory Note—Firstbank Finance Plans**

Ref. No. S3964

Durham,   October 27,   19 __
(Branch)

        For value received, I promise to pay to the order of

the Durham branch

at the BANK OF MONTREAL here the sum of   One hundred fifty-four _____
                                                                    50 Dollars
                                                                   ———
                                                                   100
comprising   One hundred fifty _____
              XX   Dollars principal amount and   Four _____
             ———   5C   Dollars cost of
             100   ———
                                                     100
borrowing the said principal amount. The said sum is payable by me in instalments as follows
Twenty-five
75   Dollars on the   27th   day of   November   19 __ and   Twenty-
———   five
100
75   Dollars on the last   April
———   Dollars on the   27th   day of
100

day of each and every _____ month period thereafter until the 27th day of

19 __ on which date the balance of the said sum then unpaid shall be due and payable. In case
any said instalment is not paid on the day the same becomes due, the balance of the said sum
then unpaid shall forthwith become due and payable at the option of the holder of this note.

I will pay 10.8 % per annum on any overdue instalment or unpaid portion thereof from
its due date until payment thereof to the holder of this note.

The aforesaid cost of borrowing dollar amount expressed as a nominal annual percentage rate
is 10.3 %, subject to a fixed minimum charge of five dollars.

INSURED   Harry Simpson
                    Signature

                _____
                    Signature

The First Canadian Bank
Bank of Montreal Firstbank Finance Plans   S.C.S.

Name Harry Simpson   Payments Due   27th

Address Durham, Ontario   Tel.: Home   365-0011
                                                   Bus

Amortization Period

Payments		Loan, Other Charges		Date	Balance		Action Taken or Description of Charge	Charge	Paid
		154	50						
25	75			10/27	154	50			
25	75			11/27	128	75			
25	75			12/27	103				
25	75			1/27	77	25			
25	75			2/27	51	50			
25	75			3/27	25	75			
				4/27		ф			

Date	Action Taken or Description of Charge	Charge	Paid

NOTE: When loan repaid or refinanced record performance
       on original application form (507).

EXAMPLE 2   In Example 1, Harry paid $4.50 in interest to borrow $150 for six months. What true annual rate of interest did he pay? Give the answer correct to two places after the decimal.

SOLUTION $r = ?$
$N = 12$
$I = \$4.50$
$A = \$150$
$n = 6$ monthly payments

$$r = \frac{2NI}{A(n+1)}$$

$$= \frac{2 \times 12 \times 4.50}{150\,(6+1)}$$

$$= \frac{2 \times 12 \times 4.50}{150 \times 7}$$

$$= 0.102\,857\,142$$

$$= 10.285\,714\,2\%$$

$$= 10.29\%$$

Harry paid a true annual rate of interest of 10.29%.

EXERCISE • SET 1

Calculate the total amount repaid on each loan and the amount of money paid in interest charges.

	Amount of Loan	Number of Monthly Payments	Amount of Each Monthly Payment	Total Amount Repaid	Interest Charges
1.	$ 300.00	6	$ 51.50		
2.	1 000.00	12	88.33		
3.	2 000.00	12	176.67		
4.	2 000.00	18	121.11		
5.	2 000.00	24	93.33		
6.	2 000.00	30	76.67		
7.	2 000.00	36	65.56		
8.	3 000.00	36	98.33		
9.	3 500.00	36	114.72		
10.	4 000.00	36	131.11		

EXERCISE • SET 2

- Multiply the amount of each payment by the number of payments to obtain the total amount paid on the loan.
- Subtract the amount of the loan from the total amount paid on the loan to obtain the interest paid.
- Use the formula $r = \dfrac{2NI}{A(n + 1)}$ to obtain the true annual interest rate correct to two places after the decimal.

	Amount of Loan	Amount of Each Payment	How Paid	Total No. of Payments	Total Amount Paid on Loan	Total Interest Paid	True Annual Interest Rate
1.	$ 100	$ 8.83	monthly	12			
2.	350	21.19	monthly	18			
3.	2 000	65.56	monthly	36			
4.	855	39.85	monthly	24			
5.	3 500	133.58	monthly	30			
6.	5 000	164.16	monthly	36			
7.	2 500	243.88	quarterly	12			
8.	3 650	556.85	semi-annually	8			
9.	10 975	1 384.22	semi-annually	10			

EXERCISE • SET 3

Calculate all interest rates correct to two places after the decimal unless otherwise instructed.

1. Donna and James Jones borrow $1250 from the bank on a Personal Loan Plan. Their monthly payments are $57.53 for 24 months.

   a) How much interest do the Jones' pay? _____

   b) What is the true annual rate of interest on their loan? _____

2. Your mother is planning to have a new bathroom installed in your home. It will cost $1980. She finds that a Home Improvement Loan is the cheapest way of borrowing the money from the bank. If repayments of $53.92 must be made monthly for 3.5 years,

   a) what amount of interest will your mother pay, _____

   b) what is the true annual interest rate? _____

3. During his four years at university, a student borrows $1500 from his bank through the Canada Student Loans Plan. Six months after his graduation he arranges to repay the loan by making monthly payments of $46.37 for three years. If the loan is interest free until the time at which he arranges to make repayments,

   a) how much interest does he pay, _____

   b) what is the true annual interest rate? _____

12·3 BORROWING FROM A CREDIT UNION

Employees who work for the same employer or who belong to the same labour union often group together to form a **credit union**. Membership generally involves buying shares in the credit union. Also members may deposit regular savings with the credit union.

Members who wish to borrow money from the credit union may do so using their shares and savings in the credit union as collateral for the loan. When they wish to borrow more than their shares and savings will cover, their loans must be approved by a committee appointed by the credit union. Once the loan is made, regular monthly repayments are required, generally in the form of a stated amount per month plus interest on the unpaid balance. The interest charged by the credit unions is sometimes more than the bank interest on demand loans but less than the interest charged by finance companies.

NOTE Credit unions are non-profit organizations and at the end of a fiscal year distribute part of their earnings as rebates to their members on any loan interest. These rebates can lower the true annual interest rate by one to five per cent.

EXAMPLE 1 Gunter Stein borrows $300 from his credit union and agrees to make payments of $25 per month plus interest at the rate of 1% per month on the unpaid balance. Show Gunter's payments for 12 months and find the total interest paid.

SOLUTION The payments for 12 months are shown in the following table.

Month	Unpaid Balance at Beginning of Month	Interest (1% per Month on the Unpaid Balance)	Total Payment ($25 + Interest)	Unpaid Balance at End of Month
1	$300.00	$3.00	$28.00	$275.00
2	275.00	2.75	27.75	250.00
3	250.00	2.50	27.50	225.00
4	225.00	2.25	27.25	200.00
5	200.00	2.00	27.00	175.00
6	175.00	1.75	26.75	150.00
7	150.00	1.50	26.50	125.00
8	125.00	1.25	26.25	100.00
9	100.00	1.00	26.00	75.00
10	75.00	0.75	25.75	50.00
11	50.00	0.50	25.50	25.00
12	25.00	0.25	25.25	0.00

Total interest paid = Total of *Interest* column
$$= \$(3.00 + 2.75 + 2.50 + \ldots + 0.50 + 0.25)$$
$$= \$19.50$$

The total interest paid was $19.50.

EXAMPLE 2   Maureen Beyea borrows $300 from her credit union and agrees to make payments of $26.66 per month for 12 months. Find the total interest paid and the true annual rate of interest charged correct to two places after the decimal.

SOLUTION   Total amount repaid: $12 \times \$26.66 = \$319.92$
Loan   300.00
Total interest paid $ 19.92
To calculate the true annual interest rate:

$r = ?$
$N = 12$
$I = \$19.92$
$A = \$300$
$n = 12$

$$r = \frac{2NI}{A(n + 1)}$$
$$= \frac{2 \times 12 \times 19.92}{300 (12 + 1)}$$
$$= 0.122\ 584\ 615$$
$$= 12.258\ 461\ 5\%$$
$$= 12.26\%$$

The true annual interest rate paid is 12.26%.

EXERCISE • SET 1

Check the following statements of loan repayments. If you find an error, draw a line through the error and write the correct amount to the right of the error. If the error occurs before the last entry, it will be necessary to correct all following figures with calculations based on that amount. Interest is charged on each account at the rate of 1% per month.

1.

WESTERN CREDIT UNION

In account with James Loukes
15 George St., Lethbridge, Alberta T1J 3Y1

Account No. 276 351   **Loan No.** 22A 735

Date	Payment on Principal	Interest Payment	Balance
19-- 01 01			$600.00
19-- 01 31	$50.00	$6.00	550.00
19-- 02 28	50.00	5.05	500.00
19-- 03 31	50.00	5.00	450.00
19-- 04 30	50.00	4.50	400.00
19-- 05 31	50.00	4.00	346.00
19-- 06 30	50.00	3.46	296.00

2.

WESTERN CREDIT UNION

In account with Jean Telford
19 Mary St., Calgary, Alberta T2A 2V2

Account No. 391 542   **Loan No.** 22A 3197

Date	Payment on Principal	Interest Payment	Balance
19-- 03 01			$225.00
19-- 03 31	$25.00	$2.25	200.00
19-- 04 30	25.00	2.00	150.00
19-- 05 31	25.00	1.50	125.00
19-- 06 30	25.00	1.25	100.00
19-- 07 31	25.00	1.00	75.00
19-- 08 31	25.00	7.50	50.00

3.

WESTERN CREDIT UNION

In account with Frances Flagg
87 John St., North Bay, Ont. P1B 2G9

Account No. 476 357   **Loan No.** 22A 5937

Date	Payment on Principal	Interest Payment	Balance
19-- 04 01			$775.00
19-- 04 30	$75.00	$7.75	700.00
19-- 05 31	75.00	7.50	625.00
19-- 06 30	75.00	6.25	450.00
19-- 07 31		4.50	450.00
19-- 08 31	75.00	4.50	375.00
19-- 09 30	75.00	3.75	300.00

1. Catherine Bayliss borrows $600 for a credit union charter holiday. She agrees to repay her vacation loan in monthly payments of $50, plus interest on the unpaid balance at the rate of 1% per month. Make a schedule of Catherine's payments for 12 months and find the total interest paid.

Month	Unpaid Balance at Beginning of Month	Interest (1% per Month on the Unpaid Balance)	Total Payment	Unpaid Balance at End of Month
1	$	$	$	$
2				
3				
4				
5				
6				
7				
8				
9				
10				
11				
12				
Total Interest Paid				

2. Edward Lynam borrows $300 from his credit union and agrees to make monthly payments of $25, plus interest on the unpaid balance at the rate of 0.75% per month. Make a schedule of his payments for the 12 months. Find the total interest paid.
3. Byron Moldofsky borrows $400 from his credit union and agrees to make monthly payments of $50, plus interest on the unpaid balance at the rate of 1.25% per month, until the loan is repaid. Make a schedule of Byron's payments and find the total interest paid.
4. A credit union loan for $560 is repaid in 11 monthly payments of $46.67 plus interest on the unpaid balance at the rate of 1.5% per month, and one final payment of the balance of the principal, plus interest on the unpaid balance (at the same rate). Make a schedule of payments for the 12 months and find the total interest paid.
5. A credit union car loan for $1200 is repaid in quarterly payments of $75, plus interest on the unpaid balance at the rate of 2.25% per quarter. Make a schedule of payments for the first two years and find the total interest paid.

EXERCISE • SET 3 _____

1. A member borrows $225 from his credit union and agrees to make payments of $12.97 per month for 18 months. Find:

   a) the total interest paid, _____

   b) the true annual rate of interest charged correct to two places after the decimal.

   _____

2. If the loan in Question 1 had been paid back in 12 monthly payments of $19.97, find:

   a) the total interest paid, _____

   b) the true interest rate per annum correct to two places after the decimal. _____

3. The loan in Question 1 was repaid in 3 monthly payments of $76.50. Find:

   a) the total interest paid, _____

   b) the rate at which interest was charged per annum correct to two places after the decimal. _____

4. A credit union loan for $560 is repaid in 12 monthly payments of $49.19. Find the true interest rate per annum correct to two places after the decimal. _____

5. A credit union loan for $1200 is repaid in four years. The payments of $89.34 are made quarterly. What is the true annual rate of interest charged? Give your answer correct to two places after the decimal. _____

12·4 CREDIT ACCOUNTS AT RETAIL STORES

Large stores generally offer credit on purchases made within the store. The kind of credit offered depends on the size of the business, the sort of merchandise sold, and general business policy. There are three common methods of allowing credit to the purchaser.

REGULAR CHARGE ACCOUNT

Obtaining Credit

The customer is known to the merchant and is allowed to charge as much as he or she wants, but is expected to keep within the limit of what can be paid back at the end of each month.

Terms

No down payment is required at the time of purchase. A statement is sent out once a month and the *full* amount is due within 10 to 30 days after the billing date. After this due date, interest is charged. If payment is made promptly, the cost of the goods to the consumer is exactly the same as if cash had been paid at the time of purchase.

REVOLVING CREDIT OR BUDGET ACCOUNTS

Obtaining Credit

An account must be arranged through the credit department of the store. A limit is set on the total amount that the customer may borrow. The customer receives information as to the minimum monthly amount required for repayment. The interest or service charges on the unpaid balance will be added to the customer's account each month.

Terms

Most revolving credit accounts require no down payment on purchases. Customers may charge as many items to their accounts each month as they wish – up to a **credit limit** set by the store; the balance due at the end of each month cannot exceed this limit. The limit renews itself each time payments are made; once the account (or part of the account) is paid, more items can be charged.

The customer is required to make a minimum monthly payment on the account. The amount of this payment depends on the balance due from the previous month. **Carrying** or **service charges** are added to the balance due. These charges are calculated on the closing balance for the previous month. They may be listed on a chart given to the customer or may be a stated percentage of the unpaid balance. The payment is due at the time that the account is sent out or shortly after.

DEFERRED PAYMENT ACCOUNT

Obtaining Credit

The customer is expected to have opened a credit account through the store's credit department before making the purchase. Some stores require the customer to sign a conditional sales agreement upon opening this account. This type of credit is generally arranged for one large purchase only.

Terms

A down payment is usually required. The carrying or service charges are added to the amount due on the purchase. The amount due plus charges is divided by the number of months over which the payments are to be made, and the quotient is the amount of the monthly payment. The number of monthly payments is often limited to 36.

Credit Service Charge-Terms

A credit service charge of 1.75% per month (21.0% per annum), calculated on the unpaid balance, is added to the account each month.

Example Chart of a Revolving Credit or Budget Account Monthly Payments

Balance	Minimum Monthly Payments
Up to 55.00	5.00
55.01 to 75.00	6.00
75.01 to 100.00	7.00
100.01 to 125.00	8.00
125.01 to 165.00	9.00
165.01 to 195.00	10.00
195.01 to 225.00	11.00
225.01 to 245.00	12.00
245.01 to 260.00	13.00
260.01 to 275.00	14.00
275.01 to 295.00	15.00
295.01 to 315.00	16.00
315.01 to 340.00	17.00
340.01 to 360.00	18.00
360.01 to 375.00	19.00
375.01 to 400.00	20.00
Over 400.00	5%

EXAMPLE 1   Guy Morris purchased a dining room suite from a department store for $899.90. He paid $300 down and agreed to pay the remainder in 12 payments of $56.49 each. How much money did Guy pay in carrying charges?

SOLUTION

Purchase price	$899.90
Down payment	300.00
Balance owed	$599.90
Total amount repaid: 12 × $56.49	$677.88
Balance owed	599.90
Carrying charges	$ 77.98

Guy paid $77.98 in carrying charges.

EXERCISE • SET 1

Find the balance owed, the total amount repaid, and the carrying charges for each credit purchase.

	Amount of Purchase	Down Payment	Balance Owed	Number of Monthly Payments	Monthly Payments	Total Amount Repaid	Carrying Charges
1.	$ 357.45	$ 90.00		12	$25.19		
2.	599.79	150.00		12	41.98		
3.	1 296.76	400.00		12	83.70		
4.	149.89	50.00		12	9.16		
5.	415.75	125.00		12	27.14		
6.	576.47	125.00		18	29.60		
7.	1 176.99	10% of purchase price, to nearest cent		18	69.44		
8.	786.59	30% of purchase price, to nearest cent		20	33.13		

EXERCISE • SET 2

EXAMPLE 2   Ms. Jane Martin has a revolving credit account at a large department store. Minimum monthly payments and service charges are shown in the *Monthly Payment Chart* on page 215. Her account statement on January 31 shows the following items: Previous balance, $21.85; Purchases, $11.45; Payments, $5. Balance the account.

SOLUTION   January 31

Previous balance	$21.85
Plus service charges: 21.85 × 0.0175	0.38
	$22.23
Less payment	5.00
	$17.23
Plus purchases	11.45
Present balance	$28.68

The balance is $28.68.

EXAMPLE 3   Balance Ms. Martin's account at the end of each of the next four months if she makes the following purchases and payments.
February: Payments, $5; Purchases, $6.95
March: Payments, $25; Purchases, $8.78
April: Payments, $10; Purchases, $16.89
May: Payments, minimum payment on previous balance; Purchases, nil

SOLUTION   February 28

Previous balance	$28.68
Plus service charges	0.50
	$29.18
Less payment	5.00
	$24.18
Plus purchases	6.95
Present balance	$31.13

March 31

Previous balance	$31.13
Plus service charges	0.54
	31.67
Less payment	25.00
	$ 6.67
Plus purchases	8.78
Present balance	$15.45

April 30
Previous balance	$15.45
Plus service charges	0.27
	$15.72
Less payment	10.00
	$ 5.72
Plus purchases	16.89
Present balance	$22.61

May 31
Previous balance	$22.61
Plus service charges	0.40
	$23.01
Less payment (minimum on $22.61)	5.00
	$18.01
Plus purchases	0.00
Present balance	$18.01

For each monthly budget account
- Calculate the carrying charges at 1.75% per month.
- Add the carrying charges to the previous balance, deduct the payment, and add the purchase(s), to obtain the present balance.
- List the minimum monthly payment for each balance.

	Previous Balance	Carrying Charges	Payment	Purchases	Present Balance	Minimum Monthly Payment
1.	$ 51.75	$	$ 10.00		$	$
2.	139.72		9.00	$ 17.95		
3.	73.44		6.00	8.97, 5.64		
4.	209.25		25.00	23.95		
5.	331.61		100.00			
6.	536.36		30.00	29.85		
7.	389.95		20.00	102.50		
8.	279.60		20.00	195.37, 125.50		
9.	301.65		200.00	29.75, 245.35		
10.	476.36		150.00	225.95		

EXERCISE • SET 3

For these questions, use the terms on page 215 to calculate the service charges.

1. A monthly statement sent out on January 31 for a revolving credit or budget account shows the following items: Previous balance, $37.95, Purchases, $41.50; Payments, $25. Obtain the service charges and balance the account for the month. _____

2. Balance the revolving credit account from Question 1 for each of the next four months if the following purchases and payments were made.

   February: Purchases, $8.95; Payments, $15 _____

   March: Purchases, $18.88; Payments, $20 _____

   April: Purchases, $6.75; Payments, $10 _____

   May: Purchases, $11.44; Payments, $8 _____

3. A purchase amounting to $56.01 is charged to a revolving credit account. No further purchases are made and only the minimum payment is made each month.

   a) How many months does it take to reduce the balance to under $10? _____

   b) Find the total amount paid in service charges. _____

4. The purchase from Question 3 is charged to the same revolving credit account, but monthly payments of $10 are made until the balance is reduced to under $10.

   a) How many months does it take? _____

   b) Find the total amount paid in service charges. _____

12·5 REVIEW

EXERCISE • SET 1

Calculate the interest earned on each chequing savings account.

	Minimum Balance	Time	Interest Rate Per Annum	Interest Earned
1.	$ 763.43	April 30 to Oct. 31	3%	
2.	1 592.70	Oct. 31 to April 30 (not a leap year)	4%	

3. Calculate the principal and interest at the time of each payment and the total interest paid for a loan of $1500 borrowed on April 5, 1986 at 12.25% per annum. Payments: $500 on April 30, 1986; $500 on May 31, 1986; $500 on June 20, 1986

_____ , _____ , _____ , _____ , _____ , _____ , _____

Calculate the total amount repaid on each loan and the amount of money paid in interest.

	Amount of Loan	Number of Monthly Payments	Amount of Each Monthly Payment	Total Amount Repaid	Interest
4.	$5 000	12	$475.00		
5.	5 000	18	336.11		
6.	5 000	24	266.67		
7.	5 000	36	197.22		

8. Check the statement of loan repayments. Draw a line through any errors, and write the correct amount to the right of the error. Make any necessary adjustments to the following entries. Interest is charged at the rate of 1% per month.

S✚C SILVER CITY CREDIT UNION

In account with   J. Parks   20 Alpha St.
Swift Current, Sask. S9H 3A3

Account No: 196 530   Loan No: A-563-471

Date	Payment on Principal	Interest Payment	Balance
May 1			$575.00
May 31	75.00	5.75	500.00
June 30	50.00	5.00	450.00
July 31	25.00	4.50	420.50
Aug. 31	50.00	4.21	370.50
Sept. 30	75.00	3.71	295.50
Oct. 31	75.00	2.96	220.50
Nov. 30	75.00	2.21	145.50
Dec. 31		1.46	145.50
Jan. 31	50.00	1.46	995.50
Feb. 28	50.00	0.96	45.50
Mar. 31		0.46	45.50

Find the carrying charges for each credit purchase.

	Amount of Purchase	Down Payment	Balance Owed	Number of Monthly Payments	Monthly Payments	Total Amount Repaid	Carrying Charges
9.	$ 395	$ 90.00		12	$30.00		
10.	600	150.00		12	44.25		
11.	1 200	400.00		12	78.67		
12.	300	50.00		12	24.58		
13.	500	125.00		12	36.88		
14.	700	125.00		18	39.61		

EXERCISE • SET 2

1. Kay Hillyer has a premium savings account in a trust company. During the period from October 31 to April 30, she had a minimum balance of $5638.50. If the trust company pays interest at the rate of 7.25% per annum on the minimum balance for the period, how much interest does Kay receive (not a leap year)? _____

2. Henry Verra has a chequing savings account. The minimum balance from March 31 to October 31 is $3725.46. If interest is paid at the rate of 3.25% per annum,

   a) how much interest does Henry receive? _____

   b) If he had a premium savings account paying interest at the rate of 6.375% per annum over the same period with the same minimum balance, how much interest would Henry have received? _____

3. Jerry Vance invested $10 750 in a 60-d Term Deposit paying interest at the rate of 7.5% per annum. How much interest did he receive? _____

4. Kay Ringmann invested $45 000 in a 90-d Term Deposit at 8.5% per annum. What amount did she receive at the end of the 90 days? _____

5. Joyce Ingram sold a building lot for $22 500. She invested the money in ten-year Investment Certificates paying interest at the rate of 9.75% per annum.

   a) What interest payment does Joyce receive each year? _____

   b) Over the ten-year period, what total amount of interest does she receive?

   _____

6. Clare borrowed $750 from her bank on July 2, giving the bank Ontario Hydro Bonds as collateral. She signed a demand note for the amount borrowed at an interest rate of 9.75%. Clare authorized the bank to draw interest on the loan from her bank account on the last day of each month. She made the following payments in the same year: July 31, $50; August 31, $75; September 30, $50; October 31, $100.

a) After Clare's account was balanced on October 31, how much money did she still owe? _____

b) What total amount of interest had Clare paid? _____

For each instalment loan, calculate the total amount repaid, the total interest paid, and the true annual interest rate correct to two places after the decimal.

	Amount of Loan	Amount of Each Monthly Payment	Number of Monthly Payments	Total Amount Repaid	Total Interest	True Annual Interest Rate
7.	$ 300	$ 28.00	12			
8.	1 500	97.08	18			
9.	5 000	190.97	36			

For the following loans from a credit union, show each payment and calculate the interest paid each month until the loan is completely repaid, then calculate the total interest paid.

10. A loan of $1000.00 borrowed on June 1 is to be repaid by monthly payments of $200.00 plus interest at the rate of 1% per month on the unpaid balance.

_____ , _____ , _____ , _____ , _____ , _____

11. A loan of $300.00 borrowed on March 1 is to be repaid by payments of $50.00 a month plus interest at the rate of 1.5% per month on the unpaid balance.

_____ , _____ , _____ , _____ , _____ , _____

For each monthly budget account, calculate the carrying charges at the rate of 1.75% per month, add these to the previous balance, deduct the payment, and add any purchase(s) to obtain the present balance. Using the chart on page 215, list the minimum monthly payment for each present balance.

	Previous Balance	Carrying Charges	Payment	Purchases	Present Balance	Minimum Monthly Payment
12.	$ 76.98		$20.00			
13.	156.70		50.00	$21.95		
14.	265.40		75.00	7.68, 35.00		

EXERCISE • SET 3

1. Arthur Kazaris has a daily interest savings account. Interest, at 7.25% per annum, is calculated by computer at the end of each day and added to his balance. This new balance is used as the principal on which interest is calculated the next day. If there was $2500 in Arthur's account at the beginning of March and no transactions were made but accumulating interest, calculate the daily balance in the account for the first six days in March.

   _____ , _____ , _____ , _____ , _____ , _____

2. Joan borrowed $350 from her bank on June 20, giving the bank a $500 Canada Savings Bond as collateral. She signed a demand note carrying interest at 10.5% per annum for the amount borrowed. Joan authorized the bank to draw interest on the loan from her bank account on the last day of each month. She made the following payments: July 31, $50; August 31, $25; September 30, $25; October, no payment; November 30, $100.

   a) After Joan's account was balanced on November 30, how much money did she still owe? _____

   b) How much interest had she paid? _____

3. Gerry saw a stereo he wanted to buy for $599.95. He went to his bank and was able to arrange an instalment loan for $600. The loan manager arranged with Gerry to repay the loan in 24 monthly payments of $28 each.

   a) How much did Gerry actually pay for the stereo? _____

   b) What true annual rate of interest did he pay (correct to two places after the decimal)? _____

4. A member borrowed $500 from his credit union and agreed to make payments of $30.28 per month for 18 months. What true annual interest rate did he pay (correct to two places after the decimal)? _____

5. Margo Forrester purchased a chesterfield and chair for $797.99. She paid for them on an instalment plan of 18 monthly payments of $48.99.

   a) How much did Margo pay in interest? _____

   b) What was the true annual rate of interest paid (correct to two places after the decimal)? _____

CHAPTER 13

HOME OWNERSHIP

13·1 COSTS OF BUYING A HOUSE

At one time or another, every family desires to own its own home. As the population increases, serviced land in municipalities or close to urban centres becomes more expensive. The cost of home ownership is high and the family contemplating the purchase of a house should examine its financial situation much more closely than it does for any other purchase.

Some of the major financial factors to be considered are:

- The amount of extra income available *now* that could be put toward the cost of owning and maintaining a home. A family should not plan on future salary increases but buy only what it can afford now.
- The total fixed cost of owning the house: mortgage payments, taxes, insurance, utilities, and heat
- The additional essential costs of the purchase: lawyer's fees, moving expenses, and new appliances
- The added essential costs of maintenance: if the house is new, added costs might include storm and screen windows and doors, improvements to the driveway and sidewalks, tree planting, lawn mower and other garden implements, shrubs, grass seed, fertilizer, etc. Added costs such as these might not be large individually, but added together they can prove to be a serious drain on the family budget.
  If the house is not new, added costs might include any of the above costs plus a new roof, new plumbing, exterior painting, new heating system, repairs to the exterior of the house (damaged exterior walls, window frames, wood trim, etc.), repairs to the interior of the house (painting and wall papering, bathroom and kitchen fixtures, light fixtures, electrical outlets, basement repairs), etc.
- The additional car costs: if the wage earners have to drive to work when previously they did not, or if they must drive a further distance; if children must be driven to extra-curricular activities, clubs, etc.
- Is the house in a district where property values are constant or increasing so that there is no loss in capital investment?
- Is the house in a district where there will be pressure on the family to maintain a higher standard of living? This can become a problem even for the family with the firmest intentions to live the way they want rather than to compete with the neighbours.

EXAMPLE 1 John Dodd rents an apartment for himself and his family for $600 a month. The utilities (water and electricity) are paid by the owner. Mr. Dodd has saved $20 500 which is invested at 10.5% per annum. He wants to buy a house priced at $75 000 and cash his investment to make the down payment. He would assume a mortgage for $54 500 at 12.5%, on which the monthly payments are $625. Fixed costs of home ownership are estimated to be: utilities (water and electricity), $45 a month; taxes, $1007 per year; insurance, $175 per year; heating costs, $890 per year. How much more per month will it cost Mr. Dodd to own a house than to rent an apartment?

SOLUTION   The fixed costs of home ownership per month are

Mortgage payment	$625.00
Taxes: $1007 ÷ 12 =	83.92
Insurance: $175 ÷ 12 =	14.58
Heat: $890 ÷ 12 =	74.17
Utilities	45.00
Total fixed costs	$842.67

Interest loss:
Mr. Dodd loses his investment interest.

Loss per year: $20 500 × 0.105 = $2152.50
Loss per month: $2152.50 ÷ 12 = $179.38

The total fixed cost of ownership is $842.67 + $179.38 = $1022.05.
The increased cost per month is $1022.05 − $600.00 = $422.05.

It will cost Mr. Dodd $422.05 more per month.

EXAMPLE 2   When John Dodd makes his mortgage payment of $625 each month, part of this payment goes toward paying the interest he owes on the $54 500 he borrowed and the rest goes toward paying part of the borrowed $54 500 (the principal). Complete an amortization schedule showing payments of the principal for the first six payments.

SOLUTION   **Amortization Schedule**

Payment No.	(1) Unpaid Principal at First of Month	(2) Total Payment	(3) 12.5% Interest per month $(1) \times \dfrac{0.125}{12}$	(4) Payment on Principal (2) − (3)	(5) Unpaid Principal at End of Month (1) − (4)
1	$54 500.00	$625.00	$567.71	$57.29	$54 442.71
2	54 442.71	625.00	567.11	57.89	54 384.82
3	54 384.82	625.00	566.51	58.49	54 326.33
4	54 326.33	625.00	565.90	59.10	54 267.23
5	54 267.23	625.00	565.28	59.72	54 207.51
6	54 207.51	625.00	564.66	60.34	54 147.17

EXERCISE • SET 1

1. George Hahn purchases a house, making a down payment of $30 000 and assuming a mortgage for $32 500 on which the payments are $530 a month (principal and interest). The fixed costs of maintaining the house are estimated to be: taxes, $1200 per year; utilities, $60 per month; insurance, $104 semi-annually; and heating, $980 per year. Calculate the total fixed costs per month of owning the house if the down payment could have been invested at 9.75% per annum.

2. If George Hahn's mortgage carries interest at the rate of 12.75% per annum, amortize his mortgage for the first six months.

3. Betty LeGier purchases a house, making a down payment of $20 000 and assuming a mortgage of $52 000 on which payments are $650 per month (principal and interest). Fixed costs are: taxes, $950 per year; utilities, $160 every 2 months; insurance, $200 semi-annually; and heating, $1250 per year. If Betty could have invested the down payment at 10.75% per annum, calculate the fixed costs per month of owning the house.

---

4. If Betty's mortgage carries interest at the rate of 13.5% per annum, amortize her mortgage for the first 8 months.

EXERCISE • SET 2

In Examples 1 and 2, as Mr. Dodd makes his mortgage payment of $625 each month he is paying off some of the principal of $54 500 that he originally borrowed. As he does this, he also increases the amount of money that he has invested in the house, his **equity**.

EXAMPLE 3   Show the increase in Mr. Dodd's capital investment, his equity, for the first 6 months he owns the house.

SOLUTION   **Increase in Capital Investment**

Payment No.	(1) Equity at Beginning of Month	(2) Monthly Payment Toward Principal	(3) Equity at End of Month (1) + (2)
1	$20 500.00	$57.29	$20 557.29
2	20 557.29	57.89	20 615.18
3	20 615.18	58.49	20 673.67
4	20 673.67	59.10	20 732.77
5	20 732.77	59.72	20 792.49
6	20 792.49	60.34	20 852.83

1. In Question 2 of Exercise • Set 1, set up an increase in capital investment schedule for the first 6 months of George Hahn's mortgage.
2. In Question 4 of Exercise • Set 1, set up an increase in capital investment schedule for the first 8 months of Betty LeGier's mortgage.

EXERCISE • SET 3

A second method of making mortgage payments requires that payments be made on the principal at stated intervals (usually every year, six months or quarter of a year) *plus* interest on the unpaid balance.

EXAMPLE 4   Mr. Dodd (in Examples 1, 2, and 3) might have been given the option of paying his mortgage by making yearly payments of $1500 on the principal plus 12.5% interest on the unpaid balance. Make a schedule of repayments of the principal and interest and of the increase in equity for the first three years.

SOLUTION   **Amortization Schedule**

Year	(1) Unpaid Balance at Beginning of Year	(2) Payment on Principal	(3) Interest 12.5% of Unpaid Balance (1) × 0.125	(4) Total Payment (2) + (3)	(5) Unpaid Balance (1) − (2)	(6) Equity at End of Year (6) + (2)
0					$54 500	$20 500
1	$54 500	$1 500	$6 812.50	$8 312.50	53 000	22 000
2	53 000	1 500	6 625.00	8 125.00	51 500	23 500
3	51 500	1 500	6 437.50	7 937.50	50 000	25 000

1. In Question 2 of Exercise • Set 1, draw up an amortization table showing increase in equity for 3 years, as in Example 4, for George Hahn if he had taken up an option to pay off his mortgage in yearly payments of $1000 on the principal plus 12.75% per annum interest on the unpaid balance.
2. In Question 4 of Exercise • Set 1, draw up an amortization table showing increase in equity for 6 payments, as in Example 4, for Betty LeGier if she had chosen an option to pay her mortgage with a payment of $1000 on the principal every half year plus interest at the rate of 13.5% per annum on each half yearly unpaid balance.

13·2 REAL PROPERTY TAX

The average municipality raises money through property taxes and spends it on local services to residents. Although a municipality receives grants from higher levels of government, the burden of paying for the services provided (for example, education, police, fire protection, roads, street lights, garbage collection, etc.,) is borne by the property owners of the municipality.

All property in the municipality is **assessed** (valued) at a stipulated percent of its retail value. Each year the property owner pays a **property tax** which is a small percent of the assessed value of the property owned. This percent is called the **tax rate**.

> **Formula**
>
> **Property tax = Assessment × Rate**

The municipal governments have the sole right to levy real property taxes. The examples which follow show how tax rates are set and applied to individual properties.

EXAMPLE 1   A large municipality has a total property assessment of $375 000 000. The amount of its budget to be raised from property taxes is $22 500 000. What tax rate must the municipality set to collect the necessary amount?

SOLUTION   Property tax = Assessment × Rate

$$\text{Rate} = ?$$
$$\text{Property tax} = \$22\ 500\ 000$$
$$\text{Assessment} = \$375\ 000\ 000$$

$$\text{Rate} = \frac{\text{Property tax}}{\text{Assessment}}$$
$$= \frac{22\ 500\ 000}{375\ 000\ 000}$$
$$= 0.060\ 000\ 000$$
$$= 0.06$$

The rate is 0.0600 or 6 cents for every dollar of assessment.

Tax rates are usually expressed in **mills per dollar** where
1000 mills = $1.00
∴ 10 mills = 1¢
and 1 mill = 0.1¢
= $0.001
In Example 1 the tax rate is 0.060 000 000
= 0.060 000 000 × 1000 mills = 60.0 mills
The tax rate is 60.0 mills per dollar of assessment.

EXAMPLE 2   Will Bates, who lives in the municipality in Example 1, owns a house and lot assessed at $35 585. How much must he pay in property tax?

SOLUTION   Property tax = Assessment × Rate

$$\text{Assessment} = \$35\ 585$$
$$\text{Rate} = 60.0 \text{ mills per dollar}$$
$$\text{Property tax} = 35\ 585 \times 60.0 \text{ mills}$$
$$= 2\ 135\ 100 \text{ mills}$$
$$= 2\ 135\ 100 \times 0.001 \text{ dollars}$$
$$= \$2135.10$$

This value can be calculated directly.
$$\text{Property tax} = \$35\ 585 \times 0.0600$$
$$= \$2135.10$$

Will pays $2135.10 in property tax.

EXERCISE • SET 1

Find the tax rate in mills correct to one place after the decimal.

	Assessment	Property Tax	Rate (in mills)
1.	$75 600 000.00	$3 850 000.00	
2.	1 380 000.00	103 000.00	
3.	20 840.00	937.62	
4.	53 000 000.00	2 600 000.00	
5.	7 694 000.00	469 400.00	

Calculate the property tax to the nearest cent.

	Assessment	Rate (in mills)	Property Tax
6.	$15 563 400	63.0	
7.	27 469	63.5	
8.	55 641	82.0	
9.	25 904	39.5	
10.	13 760	54.5	
11.	25 400	34.5	
12.	17 805	53.5	
13.	18 695	33.3	

EXERCISE • SET 2

1. The town of Hope has a total assessment of $12 985 600 and it must collect $649 280 in property taxes. What tax rate must it set? Give your answer in mills correct to one place after the decimal. _____

2. Helen Smith owns a city lot assessed at $15 300. The current tax rate is 60 mills per dollar. What amount must Helen pay in property tax? _____

3. George Barnes has just received his property tax bill. He is asked to pay his taxes in three instalments: $300.14 on March 1; $192.36 on July 1; $192 on November 1.

   a) What is George's total property tax? _____

   b) If his property is assessed at $18 500, what tax rate in mills, correct to one place after the decimal, does George pay? _____

4. Priscilla and Reginald Rapport have three town lots assessed at $1300, $783, and $1576. If the tax rate is 63 mills per dollar, what is the Rapport's total tax bill? _____

EXERCISE • SET 3 _____

In some municipalities when permanent facilities are installed such as sewers, water mains, sidewalks, etc., they are paid for by the property owners. Usually the property owner is given the choice of paying for these **local improvements** in one lump sum or in equal payments added to the tax bill over a period of years. If he or she chooses to pay in instalments, interest is charged.

When property taxes are paid before the due date, a discount may be allowed. Similarly, a penalty may be charged on overdue taxes.

EXAMPLE 3   Arthur Wortmann owns a house and lot. The lot has a 40 m frontage. A sewer is installed in the street on which his property lies. Each property owner is charged $7.41/m of lot frontage for this local improvement. What does Mr. Wortmann pay?

SOLUTION
Cost = ?	Cost = Frontage × Rate
Frontage = 40 m	= 40 × 7.41
Rate = $7.41/m	= 296.40

Mr. Wortmann pays $296.40.

EXAMPLE 4   Eleanor Blakney owns property with 82 m of frontage. She is required to pay a local improvement tax for $5.37/m for new sidewalks. Ms. Blakney has the option of paying the total amount now or having $55.27 annually added to her tax bill for the next ten years. She chooses to make the instalment payments. How much interest does Eleanor pay?

SOLUTION   First calculate the instalment payment.

Cost = ?	Cost = Frontage × Rate
Frontage = 82 m	= 82 × 5.37
Rate = $5.37/m	= 440.34

The cost is $440.34.

Then calculate the interest charged on the deferred payment plan.
Cost, if paid now = $440.34
Total amount paid over 10 years is 10 × $55.27 = $552.70
Interest = Amount paid over 10 years − Cost now
         = 552.70 − 440.34
         = 112.36

Eleanor would pay $112.36 in interest.

EXAMPLE 5 A residential property of 33 m frontage is assessed as follows: lot, $26.10/m; buildings, $15 340. The property tax is 62 mills per dollar and a further tax of $10.41/m for local improvements is added. What is the amount of the tax bill?

SOLUTION Assessment on lot: $26.10 × 33 = $ 861.30
Assessment on buildings   15 340.00
Total assessment $16 201.30

To calculate the property tax:

Tax = ?   Tax = Rate × Assessment
Rate = 62 mills   = 0.062 × 16 201.30
     = $0.062   = 1004.48
The property tax is $1004.48.

To calculate the local improvement tax:

Tax   = ?   Tax = Frontage × Rate
Frontage = 33 m   = 33 × 10.41
Rate   = $10.41/m   = 343.53
The local improvement tax is $343.53.

Total tax bill = $1004.48 + $343.53
               = $1348.01
The tax bill is $1348.01.

EXAMPLE 6 George Harris receives his tax bill for $763.45 due on August 15. He pays the bill on March 15 and receives a discount of 0.5% for each full month that the tax bill is paid before due date. What amount does George pay?

SOLUTION Number of months early = 5
Discount rate = 5 × 0.5%
              = 0.025
Discount = 763.45 × 0.025
         = 19.086 25
         = $19.09
Amount paid = 763.45 − 19.09
            = $744.36

EXAMPLE 7 The next year George Harris's tax bill is $800.53, due on August 15. He is unable to pay his bill until October 10. George is charged 1% for each month or part of a month that the taxes are overdue. What amount does he pay?

SOLUTION Number of months overdue = 3
(August 15 to 30 is considered as one month, September as one month, and October as one month.)
Penalty rate = 3%
             = 0.03
Penalty = 800.53 × 0.03
        = 24.0159
        = $24.02
Amount paid = 800.53 + 24.02
            = $824.55

NOTE Remember how you used the short method to calculate selling price given cost price and rate of markup on page 173? Then you can perform the above calculation in one step.

$$800.53 \times 1.03 = 824.5459$$
$$= \$824.55$$

1. James Ross owns a property with a frontage of 21 m. A water main is installed along the street on which his property lies. James is charged a local improvement tax of $3.81/m of frontage. How much must he pay? _____

2. Catherine Davies owns property with a frontage of 45.5 m. She is charged a local improvement tax at the rate of $6.45/m for the installation of a sewer. Catherine has the option of paying the total amount now or of having $50.54 added to her tax bill for the next seven years. If she chooses to pay now, how much does she save in interest? _____

3. A residential property with a 24 m frontage is assessed at $22.50/m for the lot, and $8765 for the buildings. The local tax rate is 47 mills per dollar. In addition, a local improvement tax of $5.01/m of frontage is charged. What is the total tax bill?

_____

4. A property owner receives a tax bill for $379.63 due July 18. He pays it on April 10 and receives a discount of 0.25% per month for each full month that the tax bill is paid before the due date. What amount does the owner pay? _____

5. Elaine Sims receives a tax bill for $633.45 due July 1. She is unable to pay the bill until November 13. Elaine is charged 0.50% for the first month that the bill is overdue and 1% for each additional month or part of a month that it is late. How much must she pay? _____

6. Find the total tax bill for the following properties. Assume that the due date and the date paid are in the same tax year which, for example, might be from April 1, 1986 to March 31, 1987.

No.	Assessment Lot Frontage (metres)	Assessment ment per metre	Buildings	Total	Tax Rate per Dollar (in mills)	Local Improvement Tax	Due Date	Date Paid	Discount per Full Month Prepaid	Penalty per Month or Part of Month Overdue	Total Tax Bill
1	28	$2.45	$13 100		43	none	April 3	April 3	none	1%	
2	37	3.71	15 600		53	none	May 26	May 20	none	1%	
3	19	3.43	17 103		57.2	none	June 12	June 10	none	1%	
4	33	2.25	12 180		61.7	none	April 15	Jan. 15	0.25%	1%	
5	20.5	1.27	9 700		42.3	none	July 15	July 31	none	1%	
6	50	0.91	6 300		32	$0.56/m	Sept. 15	Sept. 15	none	1%	
7	37	0.38	2 900		35	$0.26/m	Aug. 30	Aug. 30	none	1%	
8	33	0.42	1 000		21.7	$0.21/m	Oct. 10	Oct. 10	none	1%	
9	24	3.85	10 950		46.5	$1.03/m	May 1	May 4	none	1%	
10	29	2.92	11 310		48.9	$0.45/m	June 10	May 9	0.25%	1%	
11	42.5	1.25	4 009		51.4	none	July 15	Jan. 1	0.25%	1%	
12	67	2.66	18 004		61.3	none	July 15	July 16	0.25%	1%	
13	21.5	2.25	12 107		39.8	$0.38/m	May 15	Oct. 30	none	1%	
14	105	1.83	8 079		36.7	$0.32/m	May 15	Jan. 1	0.50%	1%	
15	71	1.84	10 651		36.7	$0.66/m	May 15	Nov. 11	0.50%	1%	

13·3 PROPERTY INSURANCE

Property insurance protects the owner of private property (buildings or contents) from loss caused by fire, theft, hail, etc. Each policy states what losses are covered and what losses are *not* covered.

Insurance rates covering loss due to fire damage are established according to locality, the type of building construction, the occupancy of the building, the type of fire department protection available, the water supply available, and the frequency of loss for all buildings. Rates covering loss due to theft are established according to locality, the type of contents insured, the type of protection provided (alarm system, etc.), and the frequency of break-ins.

Payment made by the insurance company will not exceed the face value of the insurance policy. An insurance policy is a contract to replace that which is lost; therefore, in almost all cases, the actual cash value at the time of loss is the amount that the insurance company will pay to settle the claim as long as it does not exceed the face value of the policy. An exception is in "valued" policies, where the value of the insured property is agreed upon before the policy is written (for example, specific insurance on jewellery).

FIRE INSURANCE

Policies covering fire insurance protect the homeowner only against losses due to fire and smoke damage; against losses due to wind, hail, and lightning; and against losses due to explosions, vandalism, rioting, and flooding.

HOMEOWNER'S INSURANCE OR EXTENDED COVERAGE

Further protection against losses can be obtained by extending the policy to cover loss of household contents and outbuildings due to the hazards covered by fire insurance. Contents and outbuildings are insured against theft and the homeowner is insured against claims by persons injured on her or his property. Recently, due to inflation, insurance companies have offered homeowner's policies which automatically increase the value of the house and its contents each year since replacement costs tend to increase each year.

Ordinarily, contents of a home are considered to depreciate each year (for example, a TV set has a lower resale value each year). Therefore, if there is a loss due to fire or burglary, only the depreciated value is paid by the insurance company. Insurance can now be purchased which insures a house and contents at their current replacement value. These policies are, of course, more expensive.

EXAMPLE 1 Calculate the premium payable for fire insurance on a home valued at $65 000 in a low risk district if the rate is $4.10 per thousand dollars of insurance.

SOLUTION Annual premium $= \dfrac{65\ 000}{1000} \times 4.10$

$= 266.50$

The premium is $266.50.

EXAMPLE 2   Calculate the premium payable for homeowner's insurance on a home valued at $72 000 if the rate is $5.05 per thousand dollars of insurance.

SOLUTION   Annual premium $= \dfrac{72\ 000}{1000} \times 5.05$

$= 363.60$

The premium is $363.60.

EXAMPLE 3   Calculate the premium payable on a home valued at $101 700 and insured for current replacement value if the rate is $6.79 per thousand dollars of insurance.

SOLUTION   Annual premium $= \dfrac{101\ 700}{1000} \times 6.79$

$= 690.54$

The premium is $690.54.

EXERCISE • SET 1

Calculate the annual premiums for the following fire insurance or homeowner's policies.

	Value of Property	Premium Rate (per thousand dollars)	Annual Premium
1.	$ 56 000	$4.96	
2.	97 000	5.27	
3.	61 500	4.98	
4.	72 250	5.11	
5.	38 700	4.56	
6.	86 300	6.05	
7.	91 850	6.30	
8.	42 650	4.57	
9.	120 000	7.01	
10.	92 500	6.76	

EXERCISE • SET 2

The basic homeowner's policy covers the house and attached buildings (such as a garage), outbuilding (such as a garden shed), household contents and personal belongings, and living expenses the insured would have to pay if a fire or natural disaster forced the family to move to temporary living quarters.

If a home is rented, a tenant's policy is available which covers personal belongings such as furniture, clothing, appliances, TV's and stereos, etc.

Very often insurance purchased to cover the value of a home automatically covers property other than the home, at fixed rates, for example:

Property Coverage	Insured Value
Dwellings	100% of policy value
Outbuildings	10% of policy value
Personal property	40% of policy value
Additional living expenses	20% of policy value

EXAMPLE 4   George Enslen has a homeowner's insurance policy which covers the resale value of his home at $92 500. How much coverage does he have for other risk property?

SOLUTION   Dwellings – coverage = $92 500
Outbuildings – coverage = 92 500 × 0.10
= $9250
Personal property – coverage = 92 500 × 0.40
= $37 000
Additional living expenses – coverage = 92 500 × 0.20
= $18 500

Calculate the amount of insurance coverage on the following properties.

	Face Value of Policy	Dwellings	Out-buildings	Personal Property	Additional Living Expenses
1.	$ 52 000				
2.	79 000				
3.	121 000				
4.	48 000				
5.	155 000				

EXERCISE • SET 3

Since the value of a home and its contents tends to increase with inflation, insurance claims are usually not paid at the current value of the home or at the replacement value of the contents. Most insurance companies take this into account when paying claims.

EXAMPLE 5   George Sebo carries fire insurance on his home which is insured for $50 000. A fire causes $13 500 damage at a time when the resale value of the home has increased to $72 000. How much will George's insurance company pay on his claim?

SOLUTION   Coverage = $50 000
Current value = $72 000

$$\text{Ratio} = \frac{50\ 000}{72\ 000} = \frac{25}{36}$$

$$\text{Payment} = \frac{25}{36} \times 13\ 500$$
$$= 9375.00$$

The insurance company will pay $9375.00.

EXAMPLE 6   A 3-year-old television set, which cost $895 when purchased, was stolen. If the insurance company estimates that a television set has a useful life of ten years, what amount will the owner of the set receive from the insurance claim?

SOLUTION
$$\frac{\text{Remaining life}}{\text{Total life}} = \frac{10 - 3}{10} = \frac{7}{10}$$

$$\text{Claim paid} = \frac{7}{10} \times 895$$
$$= 626.50$$

The insurance company will pay $626.50.

EXAMPLE 7   A 3-year-old camera, which will cost $304 to replace, is stolen. If the insurance company, to which the claim is made, pays this type of claim by depreciating the replacement cost by 10% per year, how much will the company pay on the claim?

SOLUTION
Replacement cost	= $304.00
Depreciation:	
Year 1: 304 × 0.10	= 30.40
Value, end of year 1	273.60
Year 2: 273.60 × 0.10	= 27.36
Value, end of year 2	246.24
Year 3: $246.24 × 0.10	= 24.62
Value, end of year 3	221.62

Claim paid: $221.62

1. Bill Van Den carries fire insurance on his home for a face value of $48 000, but the resale value is $67 000. If a fire causes $20 000 damage to part of the building, how much will Bill's insurance company pay? _____

2. Joyce Irvine insured her home for $60 000 several years ago and she has not changed the policy although her house could now be sold for $85 000. If a fire causes damage of $15 000 to part of the building, how much will Joyce's insurance company pay?

   _____

3. Mary Peroski had her stereo stolen. She purchased it four years ago for $1500. Mary's insurance company estimates the life of the stereo to be seven years. How much will the company pay? _____

4. John MacGregor purchased a stove and refrigerator for a total of $1400 four years ago. A kitchen fire destroyed the two appliances. If John's insurance company estimates the life of the appliances to be twelve years, how much should be paid on his claim?

   _____

5. Kim Stanton had a dining room suite, purchased two years ago, destroyed by water damage. Replacement value is $2950. If Kim's insurance claim payment is made by depreciating the suite at 6% per year, what payment should be made on the claim?

   _____

6. Jane Van Delf had her lawn mower stolen. It will cost $395 to replace. Jane's insurance company depreciates lawn mowers at 8% per year. If Jane purchased the lawn mower five years ago, what should the insurance company pay on her claim? _____

13·4 REVIEW

EXERCISE • SET 1 _____

1. Carol Legogianes purchased a house for $72 700. She made a down payment of $30 000 and assumed a mortgage of $42 700 on which payments are $450 per month (principal and interest). The fixed costs of maintenance are estimated to be: taxes, $1500 per year; utilities, $95 per month; insurance, $290 semi-annually; heating, $1200 per year. Calculate the total fixed costs per month of owning the house if the down payment could have been invested at 10.25% per annum. _____

2. Amortize Carol's mortgage for the first six months if the interest rate on the mortgage is 11.5% per annum.

Calculate the tax rate in mills correct to two places after the decimal.

	Assessment	Property Tax	Rate
3.	$ 55 600 000	$ 2 900 000	
4.	2 870 000	195 000	
5.	75 000	5 600	
6.	25 800 000	1 800 000	
7.	360 000 000	20 900 000	

Calculate the property tax on the following assessments correct to the nearest cent.

	Assessment	Rate (in mills)	Property Tax
8.	$ 92 376	65.0	
9.	87 961	59.8	
10.	42 306	55.2	
11.	105 860	71.6	
12.	20 900	69.5	

Calculate the annual premium for the following fire insurance or homeowner's policies.

	Value of Property	Premium Rate (per thousand dollars)	Annual Premium
13.	$ 55 300	$3.67	
14.	102 700	4.91	
15.	48 500	3.97	
16.	95 300	5.65	
17.	67 600	6.03	

EXERCISE • SET 2

1. A mortgage of $52 000 requires monthly payments of $530 at an interest rate of 10.75% per annum. The down payment was $20 000. Amortize the mortgage and set up a schedule of increase in capital investment for the first 6 months.
2. Gladys Woudstra purchased a house with a down payment of $10 500. She assumed a mortgage of $44 800 with monthly payments of $510 at an interest rate of 12.25% per annum. Amortize the mortgage and set up a schedule of increase in capital investment for the first six months.
3. The village of Grandon has a total assessment of $876 000 and it must collect $49 932 in property taxes. Calculate the mill rate correct to one place after the decimal.

4. A house and lot are assessed at $32 625. The tax rate for the current year is 59.7 mills on the dollar. How much is the tax bill? _____

5. Kerry MacKee receives a property tax bill which requires him to pay his taxes in three instalments of $492.15, $375.50, and $375.00.

  a) What is his total tax bill? _____

  b) If Kerry's property is assessed at $22 500, what tax rate in mills, correct to one place after the decimal, did he pay? _____

Find the amount of insurance coverage on the following properties.

	Face Value of Policy	Dwelling (100%)	Out-buildings (10%)	Personal Property (40%)	Additional Living Expenses (20%)
6.	$100 000				
7.	39 800				
8.	152 000				
9.	67 500				

EXERCISE • SET 3 _____

1. Jane Scherzer assumed a mortgage on her house of $47 500 to be paid back in semi-annual payments of $1200 plus interest at 13.25% per annum. Draw up an amortization schedule for the first three years of Jane's mortgage.

2. Jane's down payment on the house was $15 500. Draw up an increase in capital investment schedule for Jane's mortgage in Question 1.

3. Jasper Deboer owns a house and lot. The lot has a frontage of 38 m. A local improvement charge of $3.75 per metre of lot frontage is added to his tax bill. What charge does Mr. Deboer pay? _____

4. Isabel Jensen owns property with a 53 m frontage. She is required to pay a local improvement tax of $6.30 per metre for a water main. Ms. Jensen has the option of paying the total amount now or of having $88.80 added to her tax bill for the next five years. If she chooses to make the instalment payments, how much interest does Isabel pay? _____

5. A residential property of 40 m frontage is assessed as follows: lot, $19.10 per metre; buildings, $20 890. The property tax is 65 mills per dollar and a further tax of $5.75 per metre for local improvements is added. What is the total property tax bill?

_____

6. Ralph Wright receives a property tax bill for $869.59 due June 15. He is unable to pay the bill until November 30 of the same year. If Ralph is charged 1.5% for each month or part month that the taxes are overdue, what amount will he pay on November 30?

_____

7. Tanya Huber carries fire insurance on her home for a face value of $40 000. A fire cause $5200 damage to one wing of the house at a time when the resale value of the house is $72 500. How much of the damage claim will Tanya's insurance company pay? _____

8. A five and one half year old stove is damaged by fire. Its original purchase price was $395.99. If the insurance company estimates that the stove had a useful life of thirteen years, what amount of the insurance claim will be paid? _____

9. A three year old television, which would cost $875.79 to replace, is stolen. If the insurance company, to which the claim is made, pays by depreciating the replacement cost by 15% per year, what amount will the company pay on the claim? _____

CHAPTER 14

LIFE AND AUTOMOBILE INSURANCE

14·1 LIFE INSURANCE

The purpose of **life insurance** is to protect a family from loss of income in case of the death of the principal wage earner.

An insurance policy may be considered as a form of saving since, for most types of policies, a cash value is attached to the policy after a certain period (usually three years). This amount may be obtained in cash by surrendering the policy. The policy may be used as collateral in obtaining a loan.

The amount paid for the insurance is called the **premium** and is usually a certain amount per year per $1000 of insurance. The amount of the premium varies with the age of the insured at the time the policy commences and with the type of policy purchased.

	Premium Rates (per $1000 of insurance per year)			
Age	20-Year Term	Whole Life	20-Pay Life	Endowment at 65
20	$5.13	$14.58	$25.58	$19.05
22	5.25	15.44	26.64	20.33
24	5.44	16.36	27.76	21.78
26	5.71	17.41	29.00	23.42
28	6.10	18.55	30.32	25.30
30	6.62	19.83	31.77	27.46
32	7.32	21.27	33.35	29.94

Double Indemnity may be purchased on any type of policy at $0.98 per $1000 of insurance.
A **Double Indemnity Clause** written into an insurance policy means that twice the face value of the policy is paid if the insured dies as a result of an accident.

TYPES OF INSURANCE
TERM
Term insurance can be purchased for a specified period of time, or **term** (usually a number of years), as protection against loss of income due to the death of the wage earner during that time. Equal premiums are paid throughout the period that the policy is in force. At the end of the specified term, the policy automatically cancels itself.

This type of insurance is cheap and valuable as income protection while the children of the family are dependants.

WHOLE LIFE

Whole life insurance, also called **straight life** or **ordinary life**, is insurance on which equal premiums are paid throughout the life of the insured. The face value of the policy is paid to the beneficiary when the insured person dies.

This type of insurance may be used as collateral in obtaining loans. It also has a cash value after the first few years the policy is in effect.

Cash Surrender Values – Whole Life (per $1000 of insurance)					
Age When Policy was Purchased	**Cash Value after Policy in Effect for**				
	3 Years	**5 Years**	**10 Years**	**20 Years**	**at 65 Years of Age**
20	$ 9.00	$28.00	$ 96.00	$279.00	$780.00
26	11.00	36.00	123.00	343.00	770.00
32	15.00	46.00	155.00	415.00	729.00

LIMITED PAYMENT LIFE

This is insurance on which equal premiums are paid for a specified period of years, usually 15, 20, 25 or 30 years. At the end of this period no further premiums are paid but the insurance remains in effect for the rest of the life of the insured person. The face value is paid to the beneficiary at the time of the death of the person insured. The *20-Pay Life* referred to in the *Premium Rates* schedule (page 242), is an example of limited payment life insurance.

This insurance carries a cash value and may be used as collateral in the same way as Whole Life policies.

Premiums are higher because they are paid over a shorter period of time. Many people prefer this insurance since it can be completely paid for during the years that their incomes are highest.

ENDOWMENT

For **Endowment** policies, equal premiums are paid for a certain period of time. At the end of the period or at the death of the insured (whichever occurs first), the face value of the policy is paid to the insured or to the beneficiary.

Since the face value of an endowment policy is always paid within or at the end of the specified term, this is the most expensive kind of insurance to buy. It is often used to build up a retirement income. For an *Endowment at 65* policy (see the *Premium Rates* schedule page 242), the insured person pays premiums from the time that the policy is purchased until age 65. At that time, the policy holder receives the face value of the policy.

Many companies offer the insured the opportunity of using the principal from an endowment policy to set up an annuity. The principal is reinvested in the insurance company which makes equal monthly or yearly payments to the insured for a specified period or for the remainder of the insured's life.

EXAMPLE 1   Calculate the annual premium that Jim Essel pays for $50 000 of whole life insurance if Jim purchased the policy when he was 26 years old.

SOLUTION   From the schedule of *Premium Rates*, page 242, in the column headed *Whole Life* and in the row opposite *Age 26*, the premium per $1000 of insurance per year is $17.41.

Jim's annual premium is 50 × $17.41 = $870.50.

EXAMPLE 2   Jim decides to add a Double Indemnity clause to his policy. How much more does he pay for this?

SOLUTION   The premium for double indemnity is $0.98 per $1000 of insurance per year.
Jim pays: 50 × $0.98 = $49.00.

EXAMPLE 3   After he has held the policy in Example 1 for ten years, Jim decides to cancel the policy and take the cash value. How much does he receive?

SOLUTION   In the *Cash Surrender Values* schedule on page 243, the cash value for insurance purchased at age 26 and having been in effect for 10 years is $123.00 per $1000 of insurance.
Jim receives: 50 × $123.00 = $6150.00.

EXERCISE • SET 1

Calculate the annual premiums for the following policies. Refer to the *Premium Rates* schedule on page 242.

	Amount of Insurance Purchased	Age at Time of Purchase	Type of Insurance Purchased	Premium
1.	$15 000.00	26	20-year term	
2.	40 000.00	22	Whole life with double indemnity	
3.	55 000.00	32	20-pay life	
4.	45 000.00	32	20-pay life with double indemnity	
5.	50 000.00	26	Endowment at 65	
6.	10 000.00	22	20-year term with double indemnity	
7.	60 000.00	20	Whole life	
8.	60 000.00	20	Endowment at 65	
9.	25 000.00	30	20-pay life with double indemnity	
10.	25 000.00	30	Endowment at 65	

EXERCISE • SET 2

Calculate the cash values for the following policies. Refer to the *Cash Surrender Values – Whole Life* schedule on page 243.

	Amount of Insurance Purchased	Age of Insured at Time of Purchase	Length of Time Policy was in Effect	Cash Surrender Value
1.	$100 000	20	5 a	
2.	100 000	26	5 a	
3.	100 000	32	5 a	
4.	250 000	20	10 a	
5.	250 000	32	3 a	
6.	500 000	20	until 65 years of age	
7.	700 000	26	20 a	
8.	150 000	26	until 65 years of age	
9.	75 000	20	20 a	
10.	50 000	26	10 a	

EXERCISE • SET 3

1. At age 20, John Caruso purchased a $10 000 Whole Life policy. At age 26, he purchased a $30 000, 20-Year Term policy with a double indemnity clause.

   a) What is John's total premium per year? _____

   b) What is the cost per month for insurance? _____

   c) If John earns $300 a week, what percent (correct to two places after the decimal) of his income is spent on insurance? _____

2. a) At age 20, Betty Lou White purchased a $15 000 Whole Life insurance policy.

   i) What premium does she pay per year? _____

   ii) If Betty Lou pays the premium in monthly payments, what is the amount of each payment? _____

   b) At age 30, on the date that the original policy was purchased, Betty Lou takes the cash value for all but $1000 of the insurance.

   i) What amount did she receive? _____

   ii) How much did Betty Lou actually pay for $14 000 life insurance protection for the 10 year period? _____

3. Calculate the total cost per year of a 20-Pay Life policy for $10 000 if it is purchased:

    a) on the insured's twentieth birthday, _____

    b) on the insured's thirtieth birthday. _____

4. Calculate the total cost per year of a $25 000 Endowment at 65 policy if it is purchased:

    a) on the insured's twentieth birthday, _____

    b) on the insured's twenty-sixth birthday, _____

    c) on the insured's thirty-second birthday. _____

5. On your twentieth birthday, you purchase a $30 000 Whole Life policy.

    a) What will be the cash value at age 65? _____

    b) How much will you pay in premiums for the policy from age 20 to age 65? (Payment on your sixty-fifth birthday is not used in the calculation.) _____

6. On his twentieth birthday, David Cadwell purchased a $30 000 Endowment at 65 policy.

    a) How much does he receive at age 65? _____

    b) How much did David pay in premiums over the term of the policy? _____

    c) What is the monetary gain? _____

14·2 AUTOMOBILE INSURANCE – THIRD PARTY LIABILITY

The main purpose of automobile insurance is to protect the car owner against financial losses which may occur as the result of an accident. Such losses may include the cost of repairs for automobiles or property damage, the cost of medical expenses for passengers in either car, and the loss of income of anyone injured in an accident.

The payments for third party liability and collision insurance are called **premiums**. Rates for premiums depend on many factors, such as:
- Age, sex, and marital status of the driver,
- Where the driver lives,
- Past convictions and claims,
- Whether the car is used for pleasure or business, or both,
- The age and model of the car.

THIRD PARTY LIABILITY

This type of insurance protects the insured owner of a car against legal claims that the insured's car caused injury, sickness, or death to other persons, the **third parties**. These claims are paid by the insurance company of the driver at fault in the accident.

It is generally compulsory to carry insurance against liability for loss caused to other people.

DRIVING RATING

Insurance companies rate drivers according to their driving records. In the schedule below, a driving code rating of 3 means very good; 2, good; 1, fair; and 0, poor. The premiums in this table are for drivers with a rating of 3. Most insurance companies use a rating factor to calculate the premium payable by a driver whose rating is less than 3. We will use a rating factor of 1.4, that is, if a driver with a very good rating (3), moved to a good driving rating (2), multiply the base premium given in the schedule by 1.4 and if a driver moves from good to fair, multiply by the 1.4 factor a second time and so on from one rating to the next lower.

For business *and* pleasure use, add 30% to the premiums given for pleasure use. Most insurance companies allow you to drive your car to work within a certain number of kilometres and still classify you as a pleasure driver only. However, in this section we will assume that the driver travels beyond the allowable kilometre limit if the automobile is classified for Business and Pleasure use.

SURCHARGES

If a driver has a record of 0 and further accidents during the premium year then additional premiums called **surcharges** must be paid. Surcharges are also paid when a driver is convicted of driving illegally.

For Accidents: Add 25% of the regular premium for 2 accidents within the last 3 years. Add 15% for each additional accident within the last 3 years.

For Convictions: Add 20% of the regular premium for each of these convictions under the Highway Traffic Act.
- Exceeding the speed limit
- Any moving traffic offence
- Driving an unstable mechanical vehicle

For Criminal Offences: Add 80% of the regular premium for each of these offences under the Criminal Code of Canada.
- Criminal negligence
- Failing to stop at an accident scene
- Driving while intoxicated
- Dangerous driving

Premium Rates per Year — Third Party Liability				
Class code		Pleasure Use Coverage		
Principal Driver	Driving Rating	$300 000	$500 000	$1 000 000
Female Age 16-20	3	$184	$189	$326
Female Age 21-24	3	177	184	239
Female Age 25-29	3	150	154	177
Male Single Age 16-20	3	474	595	899
Male Single Age 21-24	3	324	329	371
Male Married Age 21-24	3	250	254	287
Male Married Age 25-30	3	226	231	265

- Consider that the rates are the same for both single and married females.
- For both pleasure *and* business use, add 30% to the base premium for pleasure use.

EXAMPLE 1 Calculate the yearly third party liability premium for Don Jackson, single, age 18 with a driving rating of 2, for $300 000 coverage. Don's car will be used mainly for pleasure driving.

SOLUTION Regular premium for a rating of 3 : $474.00
Premium for a rating of 2 : $474.00 × 1.4 = $663.60

EXAMPLE 2 Ruth Bowman, age 26, carries third party liability insurance for $1 000 000 protection. Because of past accident claims, her driving rating has been changed to 0. She was also convicted of dangerous driving within the past year. How much will Ruth pay for her new premium if she uses her car for pleasure?

SOLUTION Regular premium for a rating of 3 : $177.00
Premium for a rating of 0 : 177 × 1.4 × 1.4 × 1.4 = 485.69
Add 80% premium for conviction : $485.69 × 1.8 = $874.24

EXERCISE • SET 1

Calculate the yearly premiums for third party liability for the following drivers.

	Name of Insured	Marital Status	Age	Driving Rating	Use	Coverage	Premium
1.	John Andrews	Single	17	3	Pleasure	$ 300 000	
2.	Dave DeBour	Married	22	2	Pleasure	$1 000 000	
3.	Francine Moore	Single	29	1	Pleasure	$ 500 000	
4.	Bill Harper	Married	23	0	Pleasure	$1 000 000	
5.	Anne Zehr	Single	16	3	Pleasure and business	$ 500 000	
6.	Jim Weber	Married	26	2	Pleasure and business	$1 000 000	
7.	Judith VanCamp	Single	19	0	Pleasure and business	$ 500 000	
8.	Julius Samis	Single	18	0	Pleasure and business	$ 500 000	

EXERCISE • SET 2

Calculate the yearly premiums for third party liability for the following drivers.

	Name of Insured	Marital Status	Age	D*R	Use	Add Surcharges for	Coverage	Premium
1.	Ron Walsh	Single	16	3	Pleasure	Exceeding the speed limit	$ 500 000	
2.	Sam Shaefer	Single	17	3	Pleasure and business	Criminal negligence	500 000	
3.	Roger Stokes	Married	23	2	Pleasure and business	Dangerous driving	1 000 000	
4.	Betty DeWitt	Single	18	2	Pleasure and business	2 accidents within the last 3 a	500 000	
5.	Hilda Stacey	Married	26	1	Pleasure	A moving traffic offence	1 000 000	
6.	Noel LaFrance	Single	18	0	Pleasure and business	Criminal negligence and dangerous driving	300 000	
7.	Betty Star	Single	20	1	Pleasure	3 accidents within the last 3 a	1 000 000	
8.	Paul Schmidt	Single	24	0	Pleasure and business	Driving while intoxicated	300 000	

*DR means driving rating.

EXERCISE • SET 3

1. Find the yearly third party liability premium for James Anderson, single, age 16, with a driving rating of 3, for $500 000 coverage for pleasure driving only. _____

2. Samuel Wilson is single, age 17, a driver with a rating of 0 who was convicted of failing to stop at an accident scene. He applied for a new third party liability policy. What would Samuel's premium be for $300 000 coverage for business and pleasure use?

   _____

3. Elizabeth Bancroft, age 18, has a driving rating of 3 and carries a third party liability insurance policy for $500 000. Elizabeth passed a drivers' education test which entitles her to a 15% deduction in premium payments. What is the premium to give her protection for pleasure use only? _____

4. Marilyn Syme is renewing a $1 000 000 third party liability coverage for pleasure and business use. However, she has been at fault in 3 accidents in the past three years. Marilyn is 20 years old and has a driving rating of 0. What is her premium for the following year? _____

14·3 AUTOMOBILE INSURANCE – COLLISION

Collision insurance pays for repairs to the owner's car that is damaged in a collision or by overturning. The maximum amount of this coverage is limited to the resale value of the car.

This is the most expensive insurance coverage. Therefore, most collision insurance is **deductible**; that is, to reduce the cost of the insurance, the owner agrees to pay the first $25, $50, $100 or $250 of repairs and the insurance company pays the rest. The lower the amount deductible, the higher the premium for collision insurance.

As with third party liability, the premiums depend on such factors as: age, sex, marital status, driving rating, convictions, and two or more accidents within the last three years. However, two new factors are added in collision insurance premiums: the value of the car – the greater the value, the higher the collision insurance; and the amount deductible – the lower the amount deductible, the higher the premium for collision insurance.

When a car is used for pleasure and business, as with third party liability, add 30% to the premiums in the table.

Premium Rates per Year — Collision							
Class Code			***Rating Group of Car**				
		A Deductible		**B** Deductible		**C** Deductible	
Principal Driver	**Driving Rating**	$100	$250	$100	$250	$100	$250
Female Age 16-20	3	282	231	226	183	170	135
Female Age 21-24	3	275	224	219	176	163	128
Female Age 25-29	3	159	124	127	99	96	75
Male Single Age 16-20	3	791	698	634	552	476	406
Male Single Age 21-24	3	527	446	422	356	317	266
Male Married Age 21-24	3	273	222	218	175	163	128
Male Married Age 25-30	3	196	149	156	123	117	96

*In the above rating group of cars, A has a high value; B, a medium value; and C, a low value.

EXAMPLE 1   Jane Kooper, age 18, owns an A rating car. She carries collision insurance with a $100 deductible clause. During the past two years her driving rating has changed to 1 and she has also been responsible for 3 accidents. Jane uses her car for pleasure only. What is her new yearly premium?

SOLUTION   Regular premium for a rating of 3: $282.00
Premium for a driving rating of 1: $282 \times 1.4 \times 1.4 =$ 552.72
Surcharge for accidents: $552.72 (0.25 + 0.15)$ =   221.09
Total premium: $552.72 + 221.09$ = $773.81

EXAMPLE 2   David Hayet carries both third party liability and collision insurance. Dave is single, age 19. He uses his car for pleasure and business and has a very good driving rating of 3. David wants $300 000 coverage for third party liability insurance. He drives a C rating car with a $100 deductible clause for collision. How much total insurance premium would David pay per annum?

SOLUTION   Third party liability
Regular premium for a rating of 3: $474.00
Add 30% for business use: $1.3 \times 474 =$ 616.20
Collision
Regular premium: 476.00
Add 30% for business use: $1.3 \times 476 =$ 618.80
Total premium: $616.20 + 618.80$ = $1235.00

EXERCISE • SET 1

Calculate the yearly premiums for collision insurance for the following drivers, for pleasure use only.

	Name of Insured	Marital Status	Age	Driving Rating	Rating of Car	Amount Deductible	Premium
1.	Bruce Clancy	Single	16	3	A	$100	$
2.	Joseph Zacker	Single	17	3	C	250	
3.	Beth Ross	Married	28	3	B	100	
4.	Doris Yeoman	Single	18	2	A	100	
5.	Tim Chen	Single	21	2	A	250	
6.	Peter Dawson	Single	17	1	B	250	
7.	Nancy Morris	Married	26	1	A	100	
8.	Ann Montague	Single	23	0	C	100	

EXERCISE • SET 2

Calculate the total premiums for the following drivers and automobiles.

	Sex	Marital Status	Age	D R	Use	Surcharges	Liability Coverage	Rating of Car	Collision Deductible	Total Premium
1.	F	Single	17	0	Pleasure	Exceeding speed limit	$ 300 000	C	$250	
2.	M	Single	17	0	Pleasure	Exceeding speed limit	300 000	C	250	
3.	F	Single	22	1	Business and pleasure	2 accidents within last 3 years	500 000	B	100	
4.	M	Married	23	2	Business and pleasure	Dangerous driving	500 000	B	250	
5.	F	Married	26	3	Business and pleasure	3 accidents within last 3 years	1 000 000	A	100	
6.	M	Married	26	3	Business and pleasure	Criminal negligence	1 000 000	A	100	

EXERCISE • SET 3

1. Steven Gardner drives an A rating car for business and pleasure use. He is 18 years old and has a driving rating of 3. If Steven applies for insurance with $250 deductible, find his annual collision premium. _____

2. David Fortier, age 18, wants collision insurance for pleasure driving with $250 deductible on a C rating car. David has been reclassified to a driver rating of 0 and he has also been convicted of failing to stop at an accident scene.

   a) What is his total yearly collision insurance? _____

   b) How much money would David have saved if he had a very good driving rating of 3 with no criminal convictions? _____

3. Find the total annual premium for third party liability and collision for Jane Metcalfe. Jane is 19 years old with a driving rating of 2, and uses her C rating car chiefly for pleasure. She wants $1 000 000 protection for third party liability and $100 deductible for collision. _____

4. May DeRuter passed her driver education at Sussex High School. She was informed by her insurance company that she would be eligible for a 15% deduction in the premium payments. May is 18 with a driving rating of 3. She uses her C rated car for pleasure and business. May has applied for $300 000 coverage for third party liability and $250 deductible for collision. How much total insurance premium would she pay? _____

14·4 POLICY CHANGES AND PREMIUM ALTERATIONS

Most provincial governments require that an insurance policy be purchased for no less than one year. During this policy year, changes may occur in the car owner's insurance needs, for example, the car may be replaced, an additional one purchased, or a 16-year-old may start to drive. The policy must then be re-endorsed and the premium changed to suit the new situation.

Premium alterations are calculated as follows.

● Determine the annual premium for the new requirements.

● Subtract the previous annual premium.

● Multiply the difference by the ratio: $\dfrac{\text{Number of days to expiry}}{365}$

EXAMPLE On September 1, George Barnes paid an annual premium of $160 for his insurance. Three months later, his 16-year-old son started to drive the car occasionally. The new annual premium that covers a teenage driver is $310. How much additional premium must Mr. Barnes pay?

SOLUTION

New annual premium (including his son)	$310
Original premium	160
Difference	$150

Number of days the original policy was in effect: $29 + 31 + 30 + 1 = 91$ days

Amount due: $\$150 \times \dfrac{365\text{-}91}{365} = \$112.60$

Mr. Barnes must pay an additional premium of $112.60.

EXERCISE • SET 1

Calculate any additional amounts owing or refund payments when the following changes are made in insurance coverage.

	Original Premium	Date of Payment of Original Premium	Total Premium after Policy Change	Date of Payment of New Premium	Amount Owing or Refund
1.	$126	July 1	$180	October 1	
2.	325	June 1	165	November 1	
3.	176	August 15	263	November 1	
4.	123	January 1*	362	May 11	
5.	379	March 3	155	July 15	
6.	407	February 6*	306	April 16	
7.	221	May 4	352	December 11	

*Not a leap year

EXERCISE • SET 2

1. On March 1, Harold Watson paid an annual premium of $127 for automobile insurance. Five months later, his classification was changed. The new premium was $269 per annum. How much extra must Harold pay to keep his insurance in effect for the rest of the year? _____

2. Jackie Crossland pays an annual premium of $207 for automobile insurance. After 212 days her classification was changed. The new premium is $265 per annum. What amount must Jackie pay to keep her insurance in effect for the rest of the year?

_____

3. John Ross paid a premium of $406 per annum for his automobile insurance, which allowed his son to drive the family car. Sixty-two days later his son bought his own car and insured it. John Ross's classification was changed and his new premium is $216 per year. To what refund of premium is he entitled? _____

EXERCISE • SET 3

1. Joan Brissard, age 23, has a driver rating of 3 and uses her car for business and pleasure. She carries third party liability of $500 000 and collision insurance at $100 deductible on her type C car.

   a) If there are no surcharges against Joan, what is her total premium for the year?

   _____

   b) If Joan purchased the policy on June 23 and cancelled it on November 10 of the same year, what refund of payment should she receive? _____

2. Jim Georgis, age 18, has a driver rating of 2 and uses his car for pleasure only. He carries third party liability of $300 000 and carries collision insurance at $250 deductible on his type A car.

   a) If since Jim's previous year's payment, he has had 2 accidents and 1 charge of speeding, what will next year's total premium be? _____

   b) If, after next year's policy had been in effect for 136 days, he is convicted of dangerous driving, what additional premium will Jim have to pay for the rest of the year?

   _____

3. Katherine Dupuis, age 27, has a driver rating of 1 and uses her car for pleasure only. She carries third party liability of $500 000, and carries collision insurance of $250 deductible on her type A car. Katherine's insurance company allows her to pay half her yearly insurance premium every 6 months on December 9 and June 9.

   a) How much should she pay on December 9? _____

   b) If Katherine has 2 accidents by January 28, what additional premium should she pay? _____

c) What is her premium on June 9? _____

d) If Katherine is convicted of driving while intoxicated on August 31, what additional premium will she pay? _____

14·5 REVIEW

EXERCISE • SET 1

Calculate the annual premium for each of the following life insurance policies. Refer to the *Premium Rates* schedule on page 242.

	Amount of Insurance Purchased	Age at Time of Purchase	Type of Insurance Purchased	Premium
1.	$100 000	24	Whole Life	
2.	$200 000	22	Whole Life with Double Indemnity	
3.	$200 000	28	20-Year Term	
4.	$150 000	30	20-Pay Life	
5.	$150 000	32	Endowment at 65	

Calculate the annual premium for third party liability for each of the following drivers. Refer to the schedule on page 247.

	Sex	Marital Status	Age	D R	Use	Coverage	Premium
6.	M	Single	16	0	Pleasure	$ 300 000	
7.	F	Single	22	3	Pleasure	$500 000	
8.	F	Married	26	2	Business and pleasure	$1 000 000	
9.	M	Single	23	1	Business and pleasure	$500 000	
10.	M	Married	23	2	Business and pleasure	$300 000	

Calculate the annual premium for collision insurance for pleasure use only for each of the following drivers. Refer to the schedule on page 250.

	Sex	Age	Marital Status	D R	Rating of Car	Collision Deductible	Premium
11.	F	16	Single	0	C	$100	
12.	M	17	Single	1	A	$250	
13.	M	22	Single	2	B	$250	
14.	F	26	Married	3	A	$100	
15.	M	24	Married	3	B	$250	

Calculate any additional amounts owing or refund payments when the following changes are made in insurance coverage.

	Original Premium	Date of Payment of Original Premium	Total Premium After Policy Change	Date of Policy Change	Amount Owing or Refund
16.	$315	Mar. 26	$470	July 1	
17.	$760	June 25	$600	Sept. 4	
18.	$242	May 26	$325	July 9	
19.	$513	Sept. 14	$486	Nov. 30	

EXERCISE • SET 2

Calculate the cash values for the following policies. Refer to the *Cash Surrender Values – Whole Life* schedule on page 243.

	Amount of Insurance Purchased	Age of Insured at Time of Purchase	Length of Time Policy was in Effect	Cash Surrender Value
1.	$100 000	20	20 a	
2.	$50 000	26	10 a	
3.	$150 000	32	5 a	
4.	$75 000	26	20 a	
5.	$100 000	20	3 a	

Calculate the annual premiums for third party liability for the following drivers. Refer to the *Premium Rates* schedule on page 247.

	Sex	Marital Status	Age	D R	Use	Added Surcharges for:	Coverage	Premium
6.	F	Single	17	0	Pleasure	Exceeding the speed limit	$300 000	
7.	M	Single	18	2	Pleasure	Dangerous driving	$300 000	
8.	M	Single	22	2	Business and pleasure	2 accidents within the last 3 years	$500 000	
9.	F	Married	28	3	Business and pleasure	A moving traffic offence	$500 000	
10.	M	Married	29	3	Business and pleasure	Driving while intoxicated	$1 000 000	

11. Jane Leteur is 16 and has a driver rating of 0. She has no charges against her driving record and drives a type C car for pleasure only. What total premium will Jane pay for $300 000 liability coverage and $100 deductible collision insurance? _____

12. Karen Levine is 22 and has a driver rating of 3. She had 1 moving traffic offence and 2 accidents within the last three years. Karen drives a type A car for business and pleasure. What total premium will she pay for $500 000 third party liability and $250 deductible collision insurance? _____

13. John Ricco paid an annual premium of $630 for automobile insurance. After 231 days, his classification was changed. The new premium is $756. How much extra must John pay to keep his insurance in effect for the rest of the year? _____

14. Mary Sparnay paid an annual premium of $720 for automobile insurance which allowed her daughter to drive the family car; 153 days later, her daughter purchased her own car. Mary's premium was reduced to $650 per year. To what return of premium is she entitled? _____

EXERCISE • SET 3

1. At age 20 Harold Ross purchased a $50 000 Whole Life insurance policy. At age 30 he purchased a 20-Year Term policy for $150 000 with a double indemnity clause. What is Harold's total insurance premium per annum? _____

2. Jane Heard purchased a Whole Life policy at age 26 for $100 000 of insurance. At age 65 she took the cash value of the policy.

   a) How much did Jane receive? _____

   b) How much did she pay in premiums over the 39 years? _____

3. On his twenty-sixth birthday, Ken McKee purchased a $100 000 Endowment at 65 policy.

   a) How much does he receive at age 65? _____

   b) What total amount did Ken pay in premiums over the life of the policy? _____

4. Helen Elford, age 18, has a driving rating of 3. She carries third party liability insurance of $300 000 and drives her car for pleasure only. During the year Helen is fined for speeding and has 2 accidents. When she renews her policy, what will her yearly premium be? _____

5. Shirley DeWitt, age 22, has a driving rating of 3 and drives her A car for business and pleasure. She carries $500 000 third party liability and $100 deductible collision insurance. If Shirley's driving rating is changed to 0, how much more will her total insurance premium be? _____

6. Warren Lezur, age 23, has a driving rating of 1 and uses his B car for business and pleasure. He carries third party liability of $300 000 and collision insurance at $250 deductible. Warren pays his yearly premium on August 15.

   a) How much does he pay on August 15? _____

   b) If Warren is convicted of exceeding the speed limit on November 12, what is the increase in his total premium for the rest of the insurance year? _____

   c) If he is married on January 20, to what return of premium is he entitled? _____

CHAPTER 15

STOCKS

Businesses borrow money from the general public by selling issues of **stocks**, which are actually shares in the business. People buy these shares hoping that the business will be successful and therefore that their shares in the business will increase in value. The shares are bought and sold on the stock exchange by **stockbrokers**; the general public must buy and sell stocks using the stockbroker as their agent. Since stocks are purchased on the expectation that the business they represent will increase in value and since the number of stocks bought and sold affects their prices, the value of a stock is continually changing. In this chapter we will study how stocks are bought and sold and the different types of stocks that are available for different investment purposes.

15·1 GENERAL DESCRIPTION

STOCKS

A stock or a share represents ownership of a small portion of a company. The purchaser of a stock certificate pays money for the stock. The company uses this money to further its business operations. In return, the purchaser of the stock becomes a part-owner of the company.

LIMITED COMPANIES

A person in business may run the business, own the land and buildings on which the business operates, provide the money necessary for tools, equipment, and employees' salaries and keep all the profits earned. This type of enterprise is called a **sole proprietorship** and exists today in the form of very small businesses (e.g., local stores, service shops, etc.). The owner decides how the business will be operated and whether or not it should expand, and is responsible for success or failure, profit or loss.

As commercial activities expand and a business grows, a sole proprietor may take in one or more partners to help finance business expansion. These partners share in the profits of the business in proportion to the amount of capital they invest. They share decisions as to how the business should be run; but, if the business fails, they as well as the original owner are personally liable for all debts of the business.

A partner in a business could be financially ruined by failure of another partner to run the business properly. **Partnerships** exist as a current form of business enterprise where only a limited amount of capital is necessary for business operations. A silent partner, who wishes only to invest in this type of business and to see returns from that investment, may choose to become a limited partner, having no active part in the operation of the business and also having liability for losses of the partnership limited to the amount invested.

Where large amounts of capital investment are necessary to operate or expand a business, a third type of business enterprise is necessary. The promoters of the business join together to form a **corporation** or **limited company**. To do this they apply to the government of the province in which they wish to operate the business (or in some cases to the Federal Government) stating the name of the company, the type of business enterprise, the names of the directors, and the amount of capital they want to raise by selling shares in the company. The government may grant a charter and authorize the sale of shares. The company may then sell shares. One of the advantages of a limited company is that although the persons buying shares are part-owners of the company, their liability in case of business failure is limited to the amount of capital they have invested in the shares.

STOCK BUYERS

Insurance companies, trust companies, pension funds, mutual investment funds, and individual investors are purchasers of capital stock. The purpose is to invest money so that it will produce current income, capital gain or a combination of both.

INCOME FROM STOCKS

A corporation's net profits belong to the shareholders since shareholders are part-owners of the company. However, the board of directors of a company decides how much of these earnings will be "ploughed" back into the business and how much will be distributed among the shareholders (in most Canadian corporations about 50% of the earnings is distributed). The amount of earnings to be distributed among the shareholders is called **dividends**. The total dividend divided by the number of shares gives the dividend per share.

Stocks in older, well-established firms tend to declare dividends regularly and at fairly fixed rates and can therefore be counted on to form part of an investment income. Stocks in younger, growing firms may not be as secure financially and cannot always be counted on to produce a stable income from capital investment.

GROWTH OF CAPITAL INVESTED

When a company is incorporated, it issues shares or stocks each worth a certain amount (usually $10, $20, $25, $50 or $100). The original purchaser receives a statement, called a **stock certificate**, stating how many shares he or she holds. The purchaser may keep this stock or sell it. The amount at which a share is issued is its **par value**.

As the company prospers the chance of a stockholder sharing in large profits may appear more likely. The market value of the stock (the price that a buyer is willing to pay for a share in the company) may go up. Shares can then be sold for more than the owner paid for them and the owner has increased her or his capital investment.

A company which operates a business which is expanding and earning higher than average profits and which tends, as well, to reinvest its profits back into the business may not pay large, regular dividends. However its shares may increase in market value more rapidly, providing good capital growth for the investor.

TYPES OF STOCKS

PREFERRED STOCK

A **preferred stock** pays a fixed dividend expressed either as a percent of the par value or in dollars and cents. By law, it is sold originally at a par value which is printed on the stock certificate. Dividends on preferred stock must be paid before any profit is paid to other shareholders. Unless the company is unable to pay the fixed dividends on preferred stock, owners of this stock cannot vote at the company's annual meetings. Preferred shares are classified according to two methods of paying dividends.

Cumulative Preferred Shares – If the company is unable to pay dividends, accumulated unpaid dividends must be paid in future years from profits before common shareholders are paid any dividends.

Participating Preferred Shares – After the fixed dividend is paid, holders of participating preferred shares have certain rights to receive a further share in the earnings of the company along with the common stockholders.

If the preferred shares are issued by a company with a good business record, they provide a fairly secure income from the original investment. Their value, however, does not fluctuate very far from par value; they therefore present little chance to make any appreciable gain in market value.

COMMON STOCK

Common stocks are generally issued at par value or face value. Mining stocks are usually issued at a par value of $1, and industrial stocks at par values of $5, $10, $25, $50, and $100. Because the original sale does not have to be at par value, in recent years more and more stocks have been issued at **no par value** (**n.p.v.**) and are sold at whatever price they bring on the market. Each no par value share is equal to every other no par value share no matter what market price it reaches.

Some of the investment features of common stocks are:

- Common shares are easily bought and sold.
- The shareholder has the right to vote in the election of company directors and to attend company meetings.
- Common shares tend to grow in value as the company's assets increase.
- The common shareholder has the right to share in the earnings of the company.

15·2 BUYING AND SELLING SHARES

A stockbroker buys and sells stocks and other securities for clients. The stocks are bought and sold on the stock market which, in Canada, consists of Stock Exchanges in major cities. Exchanges are linked together and to stockbrokers across the country by teletype, telephone, closed-circuit television, and computers.

A person wishing to buy or sell stock informs a broker who is able to obtain a **quotation** (the current price that sellers are asking for the stock as well as the current price that buyers are offering for the stock – the **ask** and **bid** prices) straight from the floor of the Stock Exchange. The actual buying and selling is done by floor traders. They receive orders by telephone or computer from their clients – the brokers. Floor traders must try to buy or sell for their clients at the best possible prices. The stockbroker charges her or his client a fee which is called **commission** or **brokerage**.

Fixed minimum commission rates charged by brokers were set by the Canadian Securities Institute until April, 1983. At that time, commission fees became negotiable between stockbrokers and their clients. Exceptions were the Alberta and Vancouver Stock Exchanges which still set minimum rates on locally-listed stocks.

Brokerage houses have established their own minimum fees since 1983. These fees are usually based on the price of the stocks or the size of the order. Several firms have cut fees by 25% to 50% below the average fees usually charged and are being called "discount" brokerage firms. These firms buy and sell stocks for their clients but offer few other services. The more traditional brokerage firms offer market analysis, research into a corporation's financial status and prospects, and professional advice to the client. Typical brokerage commissions will be demonstrated in the following examples and exercises.

For transactions of rights, warrants, or fractional shares, the commission fee is the same as it is for corresponding stocks selling at equivalent prices. Minimum commissions range from $2 to $5 on small orders, $45 on medium orders, and much larger commissions, often with discounts, for very large orders.

Brokers buy shares in "lots" of 10, 25, 100, 500, and 1000 shares. Extra fees are charged if the person buying the stocks purchases only part of a "lot".

Newspapers print quotations from the Stock Exchange daily, quoting the number of shares of each stock sold; the high, low, and closing prices of stocks; and the average increase or decrease in price from the day before.

EXAMPLE 1 Find the brokerage commission on the purchase of 3000 shares of Dynet A stock quoted at $0.31 if the brokerage commission is 3.5%.

SOLUTION Selling price: 3000 × 0.31 = $930.00
Commission: 930 × 0.035 = <u>$32.55</u>

EXAMPLE 2 Find the total cost of the purchase of 200 shares of Bomarc B stock quoted at $11.76 if the brokerage commission is 2.5%.

SOLUTION Selling price: 200 × 11.76   = $2 352.00
Commission: 2352 × 0.025   = <u>   58.80</u>
Total cost $2 410.80

EXAMPLE 3 Find the net proceeds from the sale of 40 shares of Carlfield stock quoted at $32.95 if the brokerage commission is 1.67%.

SOLUTION Selling price: 40 × 32.95   = $1 318.00
Commission: 1318 × 0.0167 = <u>   22.01</u>
Net proceeds $1 295.99

EXERCISE • SET 1 _____

Find the brokerage commission on the purchase or sale of each of the following stocks.

	Number of Shares	Price per Share	Commission Rate	Brokerage Commission
1.	1 000	$ 0.675	3.5%	
2.	100	13.57	2.5%	
3.	10	25.75	1.67%	
4.	2 000	0.425	3.5%	
5.	300	11.25	2.5%	
6.	50	33.333	1.67%	

Find the total cost on the purchase of each of the following stocks.

	Number of Shares	Price per Share	Commission Rate	Total Cost
7.	3 000	$ 1.572 5	3.5%	
8.	400	7.677 5	2.5%	
9.	60	38.47	1.67%	
10.	500	0.977 25	3.5%	

Find the net proceeds from the sale of each of the following stocks.

	Number of Shares	Price per Share	Commission Rate	Net Proceeds
11.	2 000	$ 0.556 7	3.5%	
12.	500	2.752 5	3.5%	
13.	300	10.506 7	2.5%	
14.	70	55.25	1.67%	

EXERCISE • SET 2

For sales under $5000, commission rates are often broken down to a percent of the sale plus a flat charge per share.

EXAMPLE 4   Mary Ossini purchased 50 shares of stock quoted at $22.35 per share, from her stockbroker who charged her a commission of 1% of the sale plus $0.25 per share. What was Mary's total cost?

SOLUTION
Selling price: 50 × 22.35 = $1 117.50
Commission: 1 117.50 × 0.01 = 11.18
50 × 0.25 = 12.50   23.68
Total cost $1 141.18

1. Peter Zevenberg purchased 300 shares of stock quoted at $13.40 per share. His stockbroker charged him a commission of 2% of the sale plus $0.08 per share. What was Peter's total cost? _____

2. Katherine McKay purchased 70 shares of stock quoted at $42.65 from her stockbroker who charged her a commission of 1.5% of the sale plus $0.20 per share. What was Katherine's total cost? _____

3. George Jenson sold 700 shares of stock quoted at $5.15 per share. His stockbroker charged him 2.5% of the sale plus $0.05 per share. What were George's net proceeds? _____

4. Georgina Dehahn sold 30 shares of stock quoted at $19.75 per share. If her stockbroker charged a commission of 1.25% of the sale plus $0.22 per share, what were Georgina's net proceeds? _____

EXERCISE • SET 3 _____

Different methods of charging brokerage commission are demonstrated in this exercise. Read the questions carefully.

1. Joyce Seldon bought 500 shares of stock quoted at $50.75 per share. Her broker charged a basic fee of $50.00 per hundred shares. Because Joyce's order was over $5000 she was able to negotiate a 10% reduction in fees with the broker. What was her total cost for the purchase? _____

2. To discourage small investors, a brokerage house has a minimum fee of $45.00 for any stock transaction. The basic fee for stock selling at $10 to $20 is $25.00 per hundred shares. What is the commission on:

a) 100 shares at $11.50? _____

b) 200 shares at $11.50? _____

3. Jim Burra sold 300 shares of stock at $30.55 per share through a stockbroker who charges a basic commission of 5% of the total cost of any sale or purchase. Jim was able to negotiate a reduction of the fee to 100% of the basic fee for the first $5000 of the sale and 90% of the basic fee for the remainder of the selling price. How much did Jim receive in net proceeds? _____

4. Karen Kahn sold 1000 shares of stock at $27.65 per share through her stockbroker who charged a basic fee of 1.5% of the total price of the sale plus $0.20 per share. Karen received a reduction of the fee to 100% of the basic fee for the first $5500 of the price and 90% of the basic fee for the remainder of the selling price. What were her net proceeds? _____

15·3 YIELD

The **yield** of a stock is the rate of return the stockholder receives on the money invested in the stock.

Formula

$$\text{Yield} = \frac{\textbf{Annual dividend per share}}{\textbf{Current market price per share}} \times \textbf{100\%}$$

For examples and exercises in this section, yields are to be calculated correct to two places after the decimal.

EXAMPLE 1   Calculate the yield on common stock declaring an annual dividend of $1.50 per share if the current market price is $25.50.

SOLUTION   Yield $= \dfrac{1.50}{25.50} \times 100\%$

$\qquad\qquad\quad = 5.882\%$

$\qquad\qquad\quad = 5.88\%$

The yield is 5.88%.

EXAMPLE 2   Calculate the yield on an 8% preferred stock, par value $100, if the current market price is $102.

SOLUTION   Annual dividend $= 8\%$ of $100

$\qquad\qquad\qquad\qquad = \$8$

$\qquad\quad$ Yield $= \dfrac{8}{102} \times 100\%$

$\qquad\qquad\qquad = 7.843\%$

$\qquad\qquad\qquad = 7.84\%$

The yield is 7.84%.

EXERCISE • SET 1

Calculate the yield on each stock correct to two places after the decimal.

	Market Value	Dividend	Yield
1.	$ 0.61	$0.025	
2.	10.25	0.50	
3.	8.50	0.27	
4.	0.95	0.01	
5.	15.45	1.16	

Find the dividend and yield on each stock correct to two places after the decimal.

	Market Value Per Share	Par Value Per Share	Dividend Rate	Dividend	Yield
6.	$ 22.25	$ 20.00	5%		
7.	95.00	100.00	4.25%		
8.	102.00	100.00	4.25%		
9.	55.25	50.00	5.5%		
10.	55.25	50.00	5%		

EXERCISE • SET 2

A more accurate method of determining yield is to consider that the percent yield is taken on the *total cost* of the stock to the investor.

EXAMPLE 3   A stock, selling at $1.95, is purchased through a stockbroker who charges a 3.5% commission. If the stock pays a dividend of $0.125 per share, what is its yield?

SOLUTION   Selling price: $1.95
                  Commission: 1.95×0.035 0.068 25
                  Total cost: $2.018 25

$$\text{Yield} = \frac{0.125}{2.018\ 25} \times 100\%$$
$$= 6.193\%$$
$$= 6.19\%$$

The yield is 6.19%.

Find the yield on total cost of each stock correct to two places after the decimal.

	Purchase Price	Rate of Commission	Dividend	Yield
1.	$ 3.76	3.5%	$0.24	
2.	12.54	2.5%	0.755	
3.	21.67	1.67%	1.50	
4.	56.97	1.67%	3.25	
5.	0.95	3.5%	0.055	

EXERCISE • SET 3

Find yields correct to two places after the decimal.
1. If the stock purchased in Question 1, page 264, paid a dividend of $3.75 per share, what was the yield on the total cost per share? _____

2. If the stock selling at $11.50 in Question 2, page 264, paid a dividend of $0.75 per share, what would be the yield on the total cost per share:

   a) if 100 shares are purchased? _____

   b) if 200 shares are purchased? _____

15·4 REVIEW

EXERCISE • SET 1 _____

Find the total cost or the net proceeds on each stock transaction.

	Number of Shares	Price per Share	Commission Rate	Transaction	Total Cost or Net Proceeds
1.	2 000	$ 1.525	3.5%	buy	
2.	300	5.666 7	2.5%	buy	
3.	50	22.37	1.67%	buy	
4.	3 000	0.997 8	3.5%	sell	
5.	400	8.685	2.5%	sell	
6.	20	52.79	1.67%	sell	

Calculate the yield on each stock correct to two places after the decimal.

	Market Value	Dividend	Yield
7.	$ 0.79	$0.055	
8.	32.68	2.45	
9.	7.69	0.50	

Find the dividend and yield on each stock correct to two places after the decimal.

	Market Value Per Share	Par Value Per Share	Dividend Percent	Dividend	Yield
10.	$ 32.75	$ 30	6%		
11.	125.30	100	6.5%		
12.	79.68	75	5.5%		

EXERCISE • SET 2 _____

1. John Klowak purchased 400 shares of stock quoted at $15.60 from his broker who charged him a commission of 1.5% of the sale plus $0.10 per share. What was the total cost? _____

2. Mary Le Clare sold 55 shares of stock quoted at $61.57 through her broker who charged her 1.5% plus $0.25 per share. What were her net proceeds? _____

Find the yield on total cost of each stock correct to two places after the decimal.

	Purchase Price	Rate of Commission	Dividend	Yield
3.	$ 4.76	3.5%	$0.381	
4.	10.45	2.5%	0.836	
5.	72.36	1.67%	4.20	

EXERCISE • SET 3

1. Kate McLean purchased 300 shares of stock quoted at $41.64 per share from her broker who charged her a basic fee of $50.00 per hundred shares. Because of the size of her order Kate was able to negotiate a 10% reduction in fees with her broker. What was the total cost of her purchase? _____

2. Roger Leflar sold 400 shares of stock at $29.35 per share through a broker who charged 1.25% of the total amount of the sale plus $0.20 per share. Roger received a reduction of the fee to 100% of the basic fee for the first $5500 of the sale and 90% of the basic fee for the remainder of the selling price. What were Roger's net proceeds?

_____

3. If the stock in Question 2 paid an annual dividend of $2.65, what was the yield on total cost per share? _____

UNIT
5

Business
Applications

CHAPTER 16

PAYROLL

Gross pay is the total amount earned while **net pay** is the amount paid after deductions for income tax, unemployment insurance, hospitalization, pension plan, union dues, etc., are made.

The gross pay for employees of a firm is calculated according to the number of hours worked, by the amount of work produced (piecework), or by the amount of goods sold (commission).

In general, employees are paid weekly, biweekly (every 2 weeks) or monthly.

Accurate records of all payroll transactions must be kept in company records to be reported to Revenue Canada and other government and private offices.

16·1 GROSS PAY BY THE HOUR

Many employees are paid according to the number of hours that they have worked. Regular hours are usually 7 or 8 hours a day or 35 to 40 hours a week. Any time worked beyond these hours is called **overtime** when the rate of pay per hour is usually 1.5 times the regular pay per hour (time and one half for overtime). Employees working on statutory holidays are usually paid more than time and one half.

EXERCISE • SET 1

For the following payrolls:
- Calculate the total hours worked.
- Multiply total hours by hourly rate to obtain gross pay.

NOTE   No overtime is considered in these payrolls.

1.

Employee	Mon.	Tues.	Wed.	Thurs.	Fri.	Total Hours	Hourly Rate	Gross Pay
M. Ard	8	7	4	8	8		$7.65	
G. Botz	8	8	6	7	7		6.60	
K. Doucette	8	6	7	8	7.5		8.30	
S. Gould	7	7	4	7	7		6.20	
A. Hill	8	8	4	8	4		8.80	
R. Juras	4	4	4	4.5	4.5		7.65	
C. McGregor	8	8	8	8	8		9.50	
B. Moyse	8	7	3	7	6.5		7.65	
J. Potci	6.5	6	0	6	6.5		6.50	
R. Simon	8	8	5	6	5.5		7.25	

2.

Employee	Mon.	Tues.	Wed.	Thurs.	Fri.	Total Hours	Hourly Rate	Gross Pay
N. Abbott	8	8	8	8	7		$6.25	
P. Benschop	7	7.5	7.5	7.5	8		7.25	
R. Carter	7.5	8.5	7	8	8		5.35	
A. Faber	8	7	8	8	8		8.25	
D. Irha	8	8	4	8	8		6.75	
E. Kozak	8	6	8	6.5	8		5.75	
M. Nesbitt	7.5	7.5	7	7	8		7.25	
A. Olsen	8	8	4.5	8	8		6.85	
P. Reall	8	8	8	7	5.5		5.50	
M. Upton	7.5	7.5	7.5	7.5	8		8.25	

For the following statements of pay:
- Calculate the regular earnings by multiplying regular hours by the hourly rate.
- Calculate the overtime earnings by multiplying the overtime hours by the hourly rate then by 1.5.
- Calculate the gross earnings by totalling regular earnings and overtime earnings.

3.

Total Hours		Hour Rate	Earnings		Gross Earnings
Regular	Overtime		Regular	Overtime	
40	6	$8.50			

4.

Total Hours		Hour Rate	Earnings		Gross Earnings
Regular	Overtime		Regular	Overtime	
40	8	$10.25			

5.

Total Hours		Hour Rate	Earnings		Gross Earnings
Regular	Overtime		Regular	Overtime	
40	5.5	$9.65			

6.

Total Hours		Hour Rate	Earnings		Gross Earnings
Regular	Overtime		Regular	Overtime	
35	2.5	$7.40			

7.

Total Hours		Hour Rate	Earnings		Gross Earnings
Regular	Overtime		Regular	Overtime	
35	7.25	$11.25			

8.

Total Hours		Hour Rate	Earnings		Gross Earnings
Regular	Overtime		Regular	Overtime	
35	4.75	$8.75			

EXERCISE • SET 2

1. Calculate the gross pay for the following employees.
   a) If a regular week is 35 hours and any hours accumulated over 35 are overtime hours worked which receive a pay rate of "time and one half" for overtime.
   b) If a regular day is 8 hours and any hours accumulated in any given day over 8 hours are regarded as overtime hours in spite of the number of hours worked in any other given day and receive a pay rate of "time and one half" for overtime.

Employee	Mon.	Tues.	Wed.	Thurs.	Fri.	Rate/h	a)	b)
J. Hyer	5	6	7	9	10	$6.50		
K. LeFage	8	6	4	11	11	7.50		
M. McLean	9	9	7	4	9	8.00		
R. Rossi	10	10	5	8	8	7.75		
L. Schmidt	4	5	5	11	11	6.90		
E. Selig	10	3	6	6	10	7.80		

EXERCISE • SET 3

1. Mary Eisen worked 7 hours a day from Monday to Thursday at regular pay rate of $9.25 per hour. Friday was a statutory holiday and she worked 10 hours at double her regular hourly pay. What was Mary's gross pay for the week? _____

2. Henry Khool worked a regular 35 hour week, Monday to Friday, at $10.35 per hour. On Monday and Tuesday, however, he worked 3 hours extra each day and was paid time and one half for this overtime. Henry also worked 8 hours at double pay on Saturday which was a statutory holiday. Calculate his gross pay for the week. _____

3. John Seda is paid $8.75 per hour for a 7 hour working day. He is paid time and one half for daily overtime and double pay for evenings and weekends. Calculate John's gross pay for a week in which his hours were: Monday, 8 hours daytime; Tuesday, 4 hours evening; Wednesday, 4 hours daytime and 3 hours evening; Thursday, 4 hours evening; Friday, 4 hours evening; Saturday, 6 hours; Sunday, 4 hours. _____

4. Elizabeth MacGregor worked shift work for which the pay was $7.25 per hour for an 8 hour daytime shift. Evening shifts are 6 hours and the wages are adjusted so that total pay for a 6 hour evening shift is the same as total pay for an 8 hour daytime shift. Calculate Elizabeth's gross pay for a week in which she worked the following hours: Monday, a 6 hour evening shift; Tuesday, an 8 hour daytime shift; Wednesday, a 4 hour daytime shift; Thursday, a 6 hour evening shift; Friday, a 3 hour evening shift; Saturday, a 4 hour daytime shift. _____

16·2 GROSS PAY BY THE UNIT

Some factory and farm employees are paid by the units produced. For example, a stamping machine operator could be paid by the number of items the machine stamps in a day and a strawberry picker by the number of boxes of berries picked. Quotas are sometimes set and employees are paid extra for units produced over a given quota.

EXERCISE • SET 1

For the following payrolls:
- Calculate the total number of parts produced by each employee.
- Multiply total parts by piece rate to obtain gross pay.
- Total the column headed Gross Pay to obtain the total gross pay.

1.

	No. Parts Daily					Total Parts	Piece Rate	Gross Pay
Payroll Record Week Ending Nov. 18/-- **SELDON MANUFACTURING COMPANY**								
Employee	**Mon.**	**Tues.**	**Wed.**	**Thurs.**	**Fri.**	**Total Parts**	**Piece Rate**	**Gross Pay**
Bleich, John	158	162	165	171	176		$0.240	
Catto, Henry	83	85	87	83	87		0.490	
Gibbons, Carol	252	238	257	251	254		0.210	
Hahn, Jim	30	31	40	36	36		1.190	
Louks, Hal	257	260	260	267	269		0.175	
Plourde, Jean	36	39	42	41	41		1.110	
Skine, Tim	163	167	161	166	165		0.235	
Tesck, John	121	126	130	120	124		0.455	
							Total Pay	

2.

			Payroll Record					
			Week Ending Nov. 25/--					

SELDON MANUFACTURING COMPANY

Employee	No. Parts Daily					Total Parts	Piece Rate	Gross Pay
	Mon.	Tues.	Wed.	Thurs.	Fri.			
Bleich, John	166	174	162	170	172		$0.245	
Catto, Henry	83	86	83	85	85		0.495	
Gibbons, Carol	253	251	249	253	255		0.215	
Hahn, Jim	32	36	34	38	41		1.195	
Louks, Hal	256	259	261	270	271		0.175	
Plourde, Jean	35	40	41	40	41		1.115	
Skine, Tim	160	159	160	155	165		0.235	
Tesck, John	124	126	130	134	130		0.475	
							Total Pay	

EXERCISE • SET 2

1. In the Seldon Manufacturing Company, stamping machine operators are paid by the number of articles stamped. To encourage productivity, a quota of 500 articles stamped per week is set. Operators are paid $0.42 per stamped piece up to the quota and for any number over 500, they are paid $0.52 per stamped piece. On the following pay sheet, calculate the total stamped per week and the gross earnings for each worker.

Name	Number of Articles					Total Articles	Gross Earnings
	Mon.	Tues.	Wed.	Thurs.	Fri.		
Abraham, J.	101	98	103	105	99		
Cassio, M.	95	97	100	105	101		
Groet, K.	102	102	103	102	102		
McLean, R.	98	99	100	106	100		
Newell, T.	104	105	105	106	105		
Zevenberg, A.	98	98	97	96	96		

EXERCISE • SET 3

Wallace Manufacturing Ltd. pays its employees by the number of articles they produce per day. Pay is determined on a scale which increases as the number of articles produced increases.

Number of Articles Completed per Day	Rate per Article
12 or less	$2.50
13 to 15	2.55
16 to 18	2.65
19 to 21	2.80
22 to 24	3.00
25 to 27	3.25
28 or more	3.55

For example, an employee producing 23 articles in one day is paid (23 × $3.00) or $69.00 for that day's work.

1. Calculate the pay for each day and the gross pay for the week for each employee in the following pay schedule.

Employee	Mon.	Wages	Tues.	Wages	Wed.	Wages	Thurs.	Wages	Fri.	Wages	Gross Weekly Wages
Chada, M.	20		19		18		20		22		
Dehahn, H.	21		22		25		23		21		
Eslen, Y.	14		15		15		16		14		
Haak, C.	19		18		19		18		19		
MacKay, K.	21		22		25		23		21		
Selazi, L.	20		25		25		25		19		

16·3 PAY BY COMMISSION

Manufacturers, producers, and wholesalers employ sales representatives to contact clients and to arrange purchases of the goods they offer for sale. These sales representatives are usually paid a percentage of the selling price of the goods they sell. This percentage is called a **commission**.

EXAMPLE 1   In one year, Henry O'Connell sold a total of $220 000 in goods for Beattie Sporting Goods, Wholesaler. He is paid a commission of 8%. What are Henry's total earnings for the year?

SOLUTION   Commission = Sales × Rate
= 220 000 × 8%
= 220 000 × 0.08
= 17 600

Henry's total earnings are $17 600.

EXAMPLE 2   Catherine Gates represents MacDougall's Auto Parts Co., Ltd. She is paid $460 per month plus a 5% commission on all sales over a $10 000 basic quota. In July, Catherine's sales for the month totalled $30 000. What were her total earnings?

SOLUTION   Basic salary: $ 460
   Total sales   = $30 000
   Less basic quota   =   10 000
   Sales subject to commission   = $20 000
   Commission = 20 000 × 5%
              = 20 000 × 0.05 =   1 000
   Total earnings   = $1 460

   Catherine's total earnings were $1460.

EXAMPLE 3   Jim Verra is a salesman for the Sutton Manufacturing Company. He is paid a commission of 5% on the first $25 000 sales, 8% on the next $75 000 sales, and 12% on all additional sales. What are Jim's earnings for the year if his total sales are $220 000?

SOLUTION   Earnings subject to 12% commission = 220 000 − (25 000 + 75 000)
                                          = 220 000 − 100 000
                                          = 120 000

   Commission:
   5% on $25 000:   25 000 × 0.05 = $ 1 250
   8% on $75 000:   75 000 × 0.08 =   6 000
   12% on $120 000: 120 000 × 0.12 =   14 400
   Total commission   = $21 650

   Jim's earnings for the year are $21 650.

EXERCISE • SET 1

Calculate the commission for each person or district on the following sales reports.

1.

Name	District	Total Sales	Rate of Commission	Commission
G. Abbott	1	$119 575	9%	$
H. Williams	2	90 507	7%	
A. MacRae	3	85 760	8%	
C. Gaetz	4	107 890	11%	
M. Schalon	5 and 6	207 156	6%	
D. McNabb	7	79 115	7%	
R. Holmes	8	150 680	9%	
H. Verrae	9 and 10	189 720	7%	
F. Lee	11	88 360	8%	
G. Donnell	12	101 794	9%	

2.

District	Total Sales	Basic Quota (no commission)	Rate of Commission on Sales over Basic Quota	Commission
1	$575 650	$300 000	5%	$
2	369 730	250 000	6%	
3	797 860	400 000	5%	
4	478 780	200 000	6%	
5	595 600	300 000	6%	
6	789 150	350 000	5%	
7	279 165	110 000	7%	
8	301 569	150 000	7%	
9	898 100	450 000	6%	
10	229 150	90 000	8%	

EXERCISE • SET 2

1. Calculate the total commission paid to each salesperson.

Name	Total Sales	Commission			Total Commission
		5% on First $10 000	8% on Next $50 000	11% on All Additional	
K. Hanford	$ 75 650				
J. Ross	39 810				
M. Dawson	90 870				
C. Vincent	110 690				
L. Redford	92 760				
K. Wilson	56 620				
R. Ingram	81 970				
C. Booth	95 680				

EXERCISE • SET 3

1. In a month, Ms. Elayne Lalonde sold a total of $9160.50 in goods to Moncton Builders Supplies. She is paid a commission of 9% of sales. What were Elayne's earnings for the month? _____

2. Ken Nicks works at National Sports. He is paid a weekly salary of $75 plus 11% commission on net sales. Last week Ken's net sales were $875.20. What were his total earnings for the week? _____

3. Dale Sommers represents Calgary Outfitters. She is paid $450 a month salary plus 6% commission of net sales over $4000. During the month of October Dale had net sales of $8250.88. What were her total earnings for the month of October? _____

4. Glen Galbraith receives a basic monthly salary of $375 plus a commission of 2% on the first $2000 of sales, 4% on the next $2000 of sales, and 6% on all additional sales. If his total sales for the month were $10 289.88, what was Glen's gross income for the month? _____

5. Sandra Tjart sells for Turner Manufacturing. She is paid a monthly commission of 4% on the first $1500 sales, 6% on the next $5000 sales, and 8% on all additional sales. What are Sandra's earnings for the month of October if her total sales were $12 260.25? _____

6. Mark Stein, a sales representative for Cookware, is paid a basic salary of $85 a week plus a commission on his net sales. What rate of commission was he getting if his total earnings for the week were $220.45 and his sales were $3010? _____

16·4 BROKERAGE

Firms manufacturing or producing goods can make sales through a **broker**. A broker is a sales agent for a number of firms who arranges sales, collects the proceeds, and remits the payment to the seller.

Before remitting the payment, the broker deducts the commission, or **brokerage**, and other expenses from the **gross proceeds** (total sales). If the broker can guarantee payment of any sales made on credit, an additional percentage of the gross proceeds is deducted. The balance, forwarded to the seller, is the **net proceeds**.

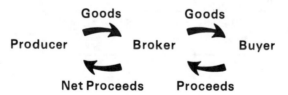

EXAMPLE 1 A broker sells a consignment of 863 kg of pork for Meadowspring Farms. The commission charged is 5% and a guarantee on sales made on credit of 0.75%. The broker was able to sell the pork at $1.41/kg after paying storage charges of $110. What balance should be sent to Meadowspring Farms?

SOLUTION

Gross proceeds:
863 kg at $1.41/kg   = $1 216.83
Charges:
 Commission at 5% of $1216.83   = $ 60.84
 Guarantee at 0.75% of $1216.83 = 9.13
 Storage   = 110.00   179.97
Net proceeds   = $1 036.86

The balance sent to Meadowspring Farms is $1036.86.

EXAMPLE 2   General Groceries Ltd. employs Jane Hancroft as an agent to purchase a consignment of coffee. Jane purchases 40 000 kg of coffee at $2.8215/kg. Transportation costs are $3620 and warehouse storage costs are $0.17/kg. Jane charges a commission fee of 8% of the purchase price. What is the total cost of the coffee to General Groceries Ltd.?

SOLUTION   Purchase price of the coffee: 40 000 × $2.8215 $112 860.00
Charges:

Transportation	3 620.00
Storage: 40 000 × 0.17	6 800.00
Commission at 8% of 112 860	9 028.80
Total cost	$132 308.80

The total cost to General Groceries Ltd. is $132 308.80.

EXERCISE • SET 1

Calculate the net proceeds of each sale made through a broker.

	Gross Proceeds	Brokerage at 6%	Guarantee at 1.25%	Other Expenses	Net Proceeds
1.	$ 3 769.50	$	$	$208.00	$
2.	10 112.75			397.50	
3.	1 756.49			85.75	
4.	5 860.48			156.48	
5.	880.79			37.81	
6.	21 812.00			545.00	
7.	7 681.90			215.00	
8.	4 867.00			311.00	
9.	375.65			29.00	
10.	15 160.45			401.71	

Calculate the total cost of each purchase made through a broker.

	Purchase Price	Brokerage at 5%	Storage at 2%	Other Expenses	Total Cost
11.	$ 1 217.17			$ 89.99	
12.	586.46			55.65	
13.	6 472.21			167.95	
14.	17 927.27			764.91	
15.	3 450.70			136.40	

EXERCISE • SET 2

1. United Brokers sold 350 t of soybean meal for Klintox Farms at $186/t. Broker's charges were: brokerage, $2604; storage and other expenses, $3965. What balance should be sent to Klintox Farms? _____

2. Atlantic Brokers sold 25 200 m² of plywood at $211.50/m². Atlantic charged a brokerage of 6% on the sale, and a guarantee of 1.5%. What were the net proceeds? _____

3. A consignment of Number 2 winter wheat was sold by Western Brokers. The consignment consisted of 275 t at $125.29/t. The brokers charged their customer a commission of 5%; a guarantee on sales, 1%; storage, $13/t. What is the balance due to the customer? _____

EXERCISE • SET 3

1. Co-op Brokers acted as purchasing agent for Duncan Importers. They agreed to purchase P.E.I. potatoes in 50 kg bags at $6.25 per bag for Duncan Importers. Co-op purchased 1250 bags of potatoes. The additional charges were: 5% commission; shipping expenses, 75¢ per bag. What was the total cost to Duncan Importers? _____

2. Columbia Brokers sold for their principal, Victoria Farms, 875 bags of Canadian type Spanish onions at $7.25 per bag. The following deductions were made: brokerage, 4.5%; guarantee on sales, 1.5%; shipping charges, 20¢ a bag; storage, 15¢ a bag. What was the amount on the cheque that Columbia Brokers sent to Victoria Farms? _____

3. Geldart and Blakney Brokers acted for Diaz Grain Company for the purchase of 875 t of oats at $105.30/t. The brokers' charges were: commission, 5.5%; shipping charges, $19.78/t; insurance expenses, 2% of the sale; other expenses, $9652.50. Including the purchase and the expenses, what was the total cost to Diaz Grain Company? _____

16·5 PAYROLL DEDUCTIONS

Employers are responsible for deducting weekly, biweekly, or monthly payments to Revenue Canada for an employee's income tax contributions. Also employers are responsible for deducting unemployment insurance premiums and contributions to the Canada Pension Plan from the employee's gross pay. Tables, which list the deductions according to the employee's gross wages and the length of the pay period, are available from government offices. Standard premiums for provincial health insurance plans are also deducted according to provincial fees and regulations.

Other deductions, agreed upon by employer and employee, may also be deducted from gross pay. These deductions may include union dues, premiums for private group insurance, premiums to dental insurance plans, payments toward purchase of Canada Savings Bonds, etc.

EXERCISE • SET 1

For the following payrolls:
- Total the deductions.
- Subtract the total deductions from the gross wages to obtain the net pay.
- Crosstotal to check your work.

1.

Employee	Gross Wages	Deductions				Total Deducted	Net Pay
		Income Tax	Unemp. Ins.	Pension	Hosp.		
Bawman, T.	$212.00	$21.80	$4.88	$3.12	$ 8.00		
Cuneo, C.	271.50	38.15	6.23	4.19	15.00		
Descoches, P.	243.00	28.05	5.59	3.68	15.00		
Garcia, A.	286.00	35.55	6.58	4.46	15.00		
Kastner, B.	315.00	43.95	7.25	4.99	15.00		
Shank, M.	236.00	28.30	5.43	3.57	8.00		
Totals							

2.

Employee	Gross Wages	Deductions				Total Deducted	Net Pay
		Income Tax	Unemp. Ins.	Pension	Hosp.		
Anco, R.	$312.00	$48.15	$7.18	$4.92	$ 8.00		
Frey, J.	371.50	59.80	8.53	5.99	15.00		
Hueston, W.	343.00	56.75	7.89	5.48	15.00		
LaHaye, G.	386.00	64.35	8.87	6.26	15.00		
Pitre, E.	415.00	71.85	9.56	6.74	15.00		
Trull, L.	336.00	55.30	7.73	5.36	8.00		
Totals							

EXERCISE • SET 2

Calculate the net pay for each employee.
- Regular earnings are calculated by multiplying the regular hours worked by the hourly rate.
- Overtime is calculated at 1.5 times the hourly rate.
- Subtract the total deductions from the gross earnings to obtain the net pay.

| Emp. No. | Hours | | Hourly Rate | Earnings | | | Deductions | | | | | Net Pay |
	Reg.	O.T.		Reg.	O.T.	Gross	Inc. Tax	Ins.	Hosp.	Pen-sion	Total	
1	40	5	$10.80				55.04	9.57	15.00	5.60		
2	40	2	12.40				62.25	9.78	15.00	4.70		
3	36		4.50				28.20	3.69	8.00	6.10		
4	32		5.40				22.80	4.80	8.00	4.90		
5	40	8	8.60				32.63	9.51	15.00	6.10		
6	40	1	4.50				36.49	4.21	8.00	7.80		
7	26		4.50				21.84	2.24	8.00	2.70		
8	40	7	4.50				27.93	4.88	8.00	9.60		

EXERCISE • SET 3

Karl Reiner works at Dale Manufacturing and is paid weekly. Complete the following pay statements for him for the 6 weeks from March 2 to April 6. Then record the information from the pay statements onto the Employee's Earnings Record and calculate the six-weeks totals.

1.

DALE MANUFACTURING

5	122	86	03	02	40	2	9	50	
Dept. #	Employee #	Year	Mo.	Day	Regular	O/T	Rate/h		Gross
		Pay Period End			Hours Worked				

STATEMENT OF EARNINGS AND DEDUCTIONS

CREDIT TO THE ACCOUNT OF

Karl Reiner
86 North Drive
Edmonstone

WE HAVE CREDITED THIS AMOUNT TO YOUR BANK ACCOUNT

NOT NEGOTIABLE – ADVICE ONLY

AMOUNT

DEDUCTIONS								
70 35	6 65	9 39	18 00	4 50				
FEDERAL TAX	C.P.P.	UNEMPL. INS.	HOSP. INS.	UNION DUES	GROUP INS.	MISC.	NET PAY	

2.

DALE MANUFACTURING

5	122	86	03	09	40	5	9	50	
Dept. #	Employee #	Year	Mo.	Day	Regular	O/T	Rate/h		Gross
			Pay Period End		Hours Worked				

STATEMENT OF EARNINGS AND DEDUCTIONS

CREDIT TO THE ACCOUNT OF	Karl Reiner 86 North Drive Edmonstone	WE HAVE CREDITED THIS AMOUNT TO YOUR BANK ACCOUNT NOT NEGOTIABLE – ADVICE ONLY	AMOUNT

DEDUCTIONS										
82	40	7	46	9	78	18	00	4	50	
FEDERAL TAX		C.P.P.		UNEMPL. INS.		HOSP. INS.		UNION DUES		GROUP INS.	MISC.	NET PAY

3.

DALE MANUFACTURING

5	122	86	03	16	36	nil	9	50	
Dept. #	Employee #	Year	Mo.	Day	Regular	O/T	Rate/h		Gross
			Pay Period End		Hours Worked				

STATEMENT OF EARNINGS AND DEDUCTIONS

CREDIT TO THE ACCOUNT OF	Karl Reiner 86 North Drive Edmonstone	WE HAVE CREDITED THIS AMOUNT TO YOUR BANK ACCOUNT NOT NEGOTIABLE – ADVICE ONLY	AMOUNT

DEDUCTIONS										
51	05	5	46	7	87	18	00	4	50	
FEDERAL TAX		C.P.P.		UNEMPL. INS.		HOSP. INS.		UNION DUES		GROUP INS.	MISC.	NET PAY

4.

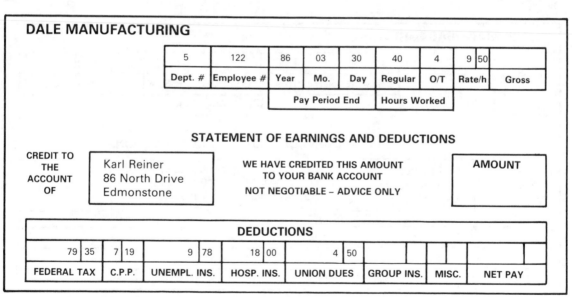

DALE MANUFACTURING

5	122	86	03	23	40	8	9	50	
Dept. #	Employee #	Year	Mo.	Day	Regular	O/T	Rate/h		Gross
			Pay Period End			Hours Worked			

STATEMENT OF EARNINGS AND DEDUCTIONS

CREDIT TO THE ACCOUNT OF	Karl Reiner 86 North Drive Edmonstone	WE HAVE CREDITED THIS AMOUNT TO YOUR BANK ACCOUNT NOT NEGOTIABLE – ADVICE ONLY	AMOUNT

DEDUCTIONS

97	60	8	18	9	78	18	00	4	50						
FEDERAL TAX		C.P.P.		UNEMPL. INS.		HOSP. INS.		UNION DUES		GROUP INS.		MISC.		NET PAY	

5.

DALE MANUFACTURING

5	122	86	03	30	40	4	9	50	
Dept. #	Employee #	Year	Mo.	Day	Regular	O/T	Rate/h		Gross
			Pay Period End			Hours Worked			

STATEMENT OF EARNINGS AND DEDUCTIONS

CREDIT TO THE ACCOUNT OF	Karl Reiner 86 North Drive Edmonstone	WE HAVE CREDITED THIS AMOUNT TO YOUR BANK ACCOUNT NOT NEGOTIABLE – ADVICE ONLY	AMOUNT

DEDUCTIONS

79	35	7	19	9	78	18	00	4	50						
FEDERAL TAX		C.P.P.		UNEMPL. INS.		HOSP. INS.		UNION DUES		GROUP INS.		MISC.		NET PAY	

6.

DALE MANUFACTURING

5	122	86	04	06	40	3	9	50	
Dept. #	Employee #	Year	Mo.	Day	Regular	O/T	Rate/h		Gross
			Pay Period End		Hours Worked				

STATEMENT OF EARNINGS AND DEDUCTIONS

CREDIT TO THE ACCOUNT OF

Karl Reiner
86 North Drive
Edmonstone

WE HAVE CREDITED THIS AMOUNT
TO YOUR BANK ACCOUNT

NOT NEGOTIABLE – ADVICE ONLY

AMOUNT

DEDUCTIONS

74	85	6	92		9	73	18	00		4	50								
FEDERAL TAX		C.P.P.		UNEMPL. INS.		HOSP. INS.		UNION DUES		GROUP INS.			MISC.		NET PAY				

7. Complete the Employee's Earnings Record for Karl Reiner.

EMPLOYEE'S EARNINGS RECORD

No.: 122   Personal Exemption: 3
Name: Karl Reiner
Address: 86 North Drive
Social Insurance No.: 00-000-000
Rate: 9.50 per hour   Hosp.: 18.00

Week	Date	Earnings			Deductions					Total Deduc-tions	Net Pay
		Reg.	O.T.	Total	Inc. Tax	C.P.P.	Un. Ins.	Union Dues	Hosp.		
	Total										

EXERCISE • SET 1

1. For the following payroll:
  • Calculate the total hours worked.
  • Multiply total hours by hourly rate to obtain gross pay.

Employee	Hours					Total Hours	Hourly Rate	Gross Pay
	Mon.	Tues.	Wed.	Thurs.	Fri.			
B. Carey	8	8	8	8	8		$7.35	
A. Felix	8	8	4	8	8		6.30	
J. Ing	8	8	4	9	7.5		8.50	
P. Luther	7	7	7	6	6.5		7.05	
V. Oleka	6.5	6.5	7	7	6.5		5.80	
M. Ridi	7.5	6	6.5	7.5	6.5		8.60	
D. Row	8	8	4	8	6		7.35	
J. Ulrich	4	8	4.5	8	4.5		5.50	
G. Wilde	5	5	5	7.5	7.5		8.90	
M. Zerbes	8	8	8	6	6		6.90	

For the following statements of pay:
  • Calculate the regular earnings by multiplying regular hours by hourly rate.
  • Calculate the overtime earnings by multiplying overtime hours by hourly rate then by 1.5.
  • Calculate the gross earnings by totalling regular earnings and overtime earnings.

2.

Total Hours		Hour Rate	Earnings		Gross Earnings
Regular	Overtime		Regular	Overtime	
40	5.5	$7.60			

3.

Total Hours		Hour Rate	Earnings		Gross Earnings
Regular	Overtime		Regular	Overtime	
40	6.5	$9.65			

4.

Total Hours		Hour Rate	Earnings		Gross Earnings
Regular	Overtime		Regular	Overtime	
35	5.25	$10.50			

5. For the following payroll:
   - Calculate the total number of parts produced by each employee.
   - Multiply total parts by piece rate to obtain gross pay.
   - Total the column headed Gross Pay to obtain the total gross pay.

Payroll Record

Week Ending Nov. 11/--

SELDON MANUFACTURING COMPANY

Employee	No. Parts Daily					Total Parts	Piece Rate	Gross Pay
	Mon.	Tues.	Wed.	Thurs.	Fri.			
Aceti, Susan	71	75	74	73	71		$0.550	
Daigle, John	123	125	126	126	125		0.460	
Hall, Theresa	25	24	26	26	24		1.240	
Lakey, Fiona	92	95	97	94	96		0.515	
Penny, Bob	146	149	142	150	149		0.235	
						Total Pay		

6. For each salesperson:
   - Multiply sales by rate of commission (the decimal equivalent of the percent) to obtain commission.
   - Total the commission column to obtain total commission paid.

Roche

Sales Report For The Month Ending: Jan 31, 19--

Salesperson	Total Sales for Month	Rate of Commission	Commission
Adolph, G.	$18 430.50	5.75%	
Ashley, V.	11 765.95	7.5%	
Beckler, T.	8 214.66	11.5%	
Brisco, P.	19 677.40	12%	
Harper, Y.	7 311.48	10.75%	
Inglis, K.	15 230.11	8%	
Lazar, D.	6 875.89	4.5%	
McKay, O.	12 764.33	5.5%	
Total Commission Paid			

7. Calculate the net proceeds of the following sales made through a broker.

Gross Proceeds	Brokerage at 5.5%	Guarantee at 1.5%	Other Expenses	Net Proceeds
$15 678.50			$1 345.00	
21 986.75			2 120.35	

8. Calculate the total costs of the following purchases made through a broker.

Purchase Price	Brokerage at 4.5%	Storage at 1.5%	Other Expenses	Total Cost
$ 7 569.70			$567.80	
23 752.89			885.50	

9. Complete the following weekly Payroll Sheet.
- Total the deductions.
- Subtract total deductions from gross wages to find the take-home pay.
- Verify your work.

Employee	Gross Wages	Deductions					Total Deducted	Take-Home Pay
		Income Tax	Unemp. Ins.	Pension	Hosp.			
Atton, W.	$200.20	$17.80	$3.66	$3.66	$ 8.70			
Brinkman, G.	234.00	25.65	4.22	4.14	8.70			
Bruce, K.	260.50	31.50	4.65	4.61	12.85			
Bunner, C.	277.25	34.60	4.92	4.91	13.70			
Burrows, J.	258.85	29.65	4.62	4.58	11.85			
Chekker, S.	270.65	32.95	4.81	4.79	12.85			
Fries, A.	230.60	25.80	4.15	4.07	8.85			
Herman, B.	200.55	15.75	3.30	3.33	8.70			
Kivell, R.	255.45	28.55	4.56	4.52	12.70			
Mandeno, T.	184.00	13.85	3.39	3.24	7.85			
Totals								

EXERCISE • SET 2

1. Calculate the gross pay for the following employees.
   a) If a regular week is 40 hours and any hours accumulated over 40 are overtime hours worked and receive a pay rate of time and one half for overtime.
   b) If a regular day is 7 hours and any hours accumulated in any given day over 7 hours are regarded as overtime hours despite the number of hours worked in any other given day and receive a pay rate of time and one half for overtime.

Employee	Mon.	Tues.	Wed.	Thurs.	Fri.	Rate/h	a)	b)
J. Hyer	7	7	7	8	8	$7.80		
K. LeFage	7	6	8	10	10	6.60		
L. Schmidt	9	9	10	11	10	8.90		
E. Selig	8	8	9	10	10	8.50		

2. The following workers are paid $1.22 for a lathe-turned spindle. A quota of 200 spindles per week is set. In any given week any spindles turned in excess of 200 are paid at the rate of $1.48 per spindle. Calculate the number of spindles turned and the gross pay for each worker.

Name	Number of Pieces					Total Pieces	Gross Pay
	Mon.	Tues.	Wed.	Thurs.	Fri.		
Atkins, J.	42	43	43	42	40		
Degrande, M.	35	36	37	40	40		
Neystrom, K.	40	40	45	45	46		
Ziegler, N.	38	38	43	43	44		

3. Calculate the total commission paid to each salesperson.

Name	Total Sales	Commission			Total Commission
		5% on First $5000	7.5% on Next $25 000	13% on all Additional	
Ross, J.	$ 95 650				
Vilia, K.	137 500				
Urkhart, F.	101 759				

4. West Coast Wholesalers sold 10 500 m² of plywood for Vancouver Mills. West Coast charged a brokerage fee of 5.5%, a guarantee of 0.75%, and other expenses of $1976.50. What amount did Vancouver Mills receive if West Coast sold the plywood at $198/100 m²? _____

5. Calculate the net pay for each employee.
- Regular earnings are calculated by multiplying regular hours worked by hourly rate.
- Overtime is calculated at the rate of 1.5 times hourly rate.
- Subtract total deductions from total earnings to obtain the net pay.

Emp. No.	Hours Reg.	Hours O.T.	Hourly Rate	Earnings Reg.	Earnings O.T.	Earnings Gross	Inc. Tax	Ins.	Hosp.	Pension	Total	Net Pay
13	40	2	12.45				62.25	7.60	12.00	4.70		
14	36		4.50				28.20	4.80	8.00	6.10		
15	32		5.40				22.80	3.80	10.00	4.90		
16	40	8	8.60				32.63	4.80	10.00	6.10		
17	40	1	4.50				36.49	6.10	8.00	7.80		
18	26		4.50				21.84	2.30	10.00	2.70		
19	40	7	4.50				27.93	7.40	8.00	9.60		
20	16		4.50				19.68	2.20	8.00	2.20		

EXERCISE • SET 3

1. Hans Vanalpen worked 8 hours a day from Monday to Friday at a regular rate of $8.75 per hour. He worked 3 hours on Friday night at time and one half for overtime and all day Saturday (8 hours), which was a statutory holiday, for double pay. What was his gross pay for the week? _____

2. Mary Hahn is paid $7.65 per hour for a regular 8 hour working day. She is paid time and one half for overtime on weekdays and double her regular pay for any hours worked on weekends. Calculate Mary's gross pay for a week in which she worked the following hours: Monday, 9 hours; Tuesday, 8 hours; Wednesday, 4 hours; Thursday, 10 hours; Friday, 6 hours; Saturday, 4 hours; Sunday, 4 hours. _____

3. Jules Lesabe works at Wallace Manufacturing Ltd. on piecework. He is paid according to the piecework scale for Wallace Manufacturing given on page 275. Calculate Jules's gross weekly earnings for a week in which his production was: Monday, 17 articles; Tuesday, 20; Wednesday, 22; Thursday, 22; Friday, 20. _____

4. Jenny Harper is a sales representative. She is paid a basic salary of $125 per week plus a commission of 5% on her first $2000 of sales, and 8% on any further sales. What was Jenny's gross pay in a week in which her sales were $2756.65? _____

5. Heather Chan is a saleswoman for Canada Masonry Ltd. She is paid a monthly commission of 5% on her first $2000 of sales, 7% on her next $3000, and 9% on all additional sales. What are Heather's earnings for the month of April if her total sales were $14 869.98? _____

6. Honsberger Brokers acted for Thames Foods Ltd. for the purchase of 10 000 kg of soybean oil at $0.6677/kg. The broker charged: 4.5% commission; shipping charges, $0.09/kg; insurance expenses, 1.5% of the purchase price; other expenses, $976.54. What was the total cost to Thames Foods? _____

7. Jane Haradah is employed at Canadian Plastics Limited as an hourly paid worker. Her hourly pay is $7.65. In the first four weeks of January, Jane's records show the following information.

Week ending January 6: regular hours, 40; overtime hours, 4; income tax, $53.85; C.P.P., $5.64; unemployment insurance, $8.09; hospitalization, $8.00

Week ending January 13: regular hours, 40; overtime hours, 8; income tax, $73.25; C.P.P, $6.47; unemployment insurance, $9.15; hospitalization, $8.00

Week ending January 20: regular hours, 36; no overtime; income tax, $38.15; C.P.P., $4.26; unemployment insurance, $6.33; hospitalization, $8.00

Week ending January 27: regular hours, 40; overtime hours, 10; income tax, $80.80; C.P.P., $6.92; unemployment insurance, $9.68; union dues, $15.00; hospitalization, $8.00

Enter the above amounts on the employee's earnings record. Calculate the net pay for each week and totals for the 4-week period. Check by cross totalling.

EMPLOYEE'S EARNINGS RECORD

No.: 14   **Personal Exemption: 1**

Name: Jane Haradah

Address: 744 Union Road

Social Insurance No.: 00-000-000

Rate: Hosp.:

Week	Date	Earnings			Deductions					Total Deductions	Net Pay
		Reg.	O.T.	Total	Inc. Tax	C.P.P.	Un. Ins.	Union Dues	Hosp.		
Total											

CHAPTER 17

DISCOUNTS

A **discount** is a reduction in price given by one business to another, by a retailer to a preferred customer, or by any business to encourage either large orders or prompt payment of accounts. Discounts are usually expressed as a percent of the price placed on each article or as a percent of the total amount of an invoice.

17·1 RETAIL DISCOUNTS

Many retail firms encourage customers to return to make further purchases by allowing a discount on the goods the customer buys.

EXAMPLE 1   Jim McKee is a painter. He contracts with individual householders to do interior or exterior painting. Jim guarantees his work for five years and therefore uses top quality paint. He has found that the brand of paint carried by Thom's Hardware gives him the best results, and he buys all his paint from this store, paying cash at the time of purchase. After Jim had been purchasing paint at Thom's Hardware for several months, he received this invoice.

THOM'S HARDWARE

Vendu à / Sold to J. McKee

Livré à / Shipped to Ottawa, Ont. K2S 0N4

Adresse / Address 21 Toronto Street

Via Truck   **Date** July 5, 19--

Comm. du Client / Customer's Order 1765	Vendeur / Salesman JM	Condition / Terms n/30	F.A.B. / F.O.B.

Quantity	Description	Price	Amount
5 cans	Exterior gloss #3912	$21.49	$107.45
5 cans	Exterior flat #3913	16.95	84.75
			$192.20
	Less 20%		38.44
	Total		153.76
	Provincial Sales Tax 7%		10.76
	Grand Total		**$164.52**

By deducting 20% from Jim's bill, Thom's was indicating that it appreciated Jim's business and was encouraging Jim to continue purchasing his paint at Thom's Hardware. From that date, Jim has continued to buy his paint from Thom's and is always given a 20% discount. How was the discount on the invoice calculated?

SOLUTION   *First Method*

Retail price = $192.20

Discount of 20% = 192.20 × 0.20

= $38.44

Discounted price = Retail price − Discount

= 192.20 − 38.44

= $153.76

If it is not necessary to show the amount of the discount, the calculation will be much easier to perform on a calculator if the following method is used.

Second Method

Discounted price = Retail price − Discount

= 192.20 − 192.20 × 0.20

= 192.20 (1 − 0.20)

= 192.20 × 0.80

= $153.76

The second method can be expressed as a formula.

Formula

Discounted Price = Retail Price (100% − Discount)

where the discount is expressed as a percent.

EXAMPLE 2   Armstrong Construction Wholesale sells construction supplies to local building firms. Any firm dealing continuously with Armstrong is given a 15% discount on purchases. Invoices are sent out once a month, and only the retail price and discounted price are shown. Calculate the discounted price on an invoice that shows a retail price of $1596.80.

SOLUTION   Discounted price = 1596.80 (100% − 15%)

= 1596.80 × 85%

= 1596.80 × 0.85

= 1357.28

The discounted price is $1357.28.

EXERCISE • SET 1

1. Calculate the amount of each discount and the discounted price.

Retail Price	Rate of Discount	Amount of Discount	Discounted Price
$ 39.60	20%		
59.20	15%		
147.80	25%		
1 369.00	30%		
588.20	35%		
28.30	7%		
88.40	12%		
195.50	18%		
1 864.20	21%		
798.40	17%		
21.95	8.5%		
137.55	12.5%		
19.95	20.5%		
1 464.75	22.5%		
988.52	10.5%		

2. Calculate each discounted price.

Retail Price	Rate of Discount	Discounted Price
$ 565.00	15%	
89.50	20%	
1 690.50	30%	
22.70	10%	
295.80	25%	
33.35	8%	
125.82	12%	
637.55	18%	
69.95	22%	
1 876.57	21%	
29.75	22.5%	
148.50	20.5%	
576.90	28.2%	
54.56	32.3%	
1 585.75	10.5%	

EXERCISE • SET 2

For each invoice:
- Calculate the total retail price.
- Calculate the discount to the nearest cent.
- Subtract the discount from the retail price.
- Calculate the provincial sales tax, where indicated.
- Calculate the total amount of the invoice.

1.

Kent Hardware

Sold to: Schwartz Construction   Date: March 20, 19--   Terms: n/30

Qty.	Description	Price	Amount
1	Cement mixer	$179.95	$179.95
2	18.2 L cans driveway sealer	9.95	19.90
2	Caulking guns	11.99	23.98
5	Tubes concrete patch	1.85	9.25
	Amount		
	Less 20%		
	Sub-Total		
	Provincial Sales Tax 5%		
	Total		$

2.

✦(shadedale nurseries)✦

Sold to: *Nelson College*   Date: March 21, 19--

Qty.	Description	Price	Amount
150	Boxes Green Gem	$ 4.00	$600.00
12	Japanese Yews	16.40	196.80
12	Dwarf Scot's Pine	19.50	234.00
8	Ponderosa Pine	17.30	138.40
	Amount		
	Less 20%		
	Total		

3.

macdonald tire

Sold to: J. Stromm   Date: March 30, 19--

Qty.	Description	Price	Amount
8	9.00/20 Lug tires	$103.98	$ 831.84
8	10.00/20 Safety lug tires	132.98	1063.84
8	7.50/20 Lug tires	83.23	665.84
	Amount		
	Less 22.5%		
	Subtotal		
	Provincial Sales Tax 7%		
	Total		

4.

Baker Meats

Sold to: City Restaurant   March 30, 19--

Qty.	Description	Price	Amount
5 kg	pork chops	$4.54	$22.70
10 kg	sirloin steak	4.75	47.50
9.5 kg	T-bone	5.05	47.98
8.7 kg	ham steaks	5.25	45.68
	Amount		
	Less 18%		
	Total		

For each invoice:
- Extend each item.
- Calculate the total retail price.
- Calculate the discounted price to the nearest cent.

5.

O_E_'S OFFICE EQUIP_E_T LTD

Sales and Service   57 Pitt St., St. John, N.B.   E2L 2W8   Tel. 391-7647

Sold to: *Office Sevices Ltd.*   Date: *March 15*
       St. John, N.B.   Date Delivered: *March 18, 19_*

Qty.	Description	Price	Amount
3	# 314-045 files	$100.45	$
5	# 307-130 Roll Away files	229.50	
5	# 305-120 Computer Printout file	178.50	
			————
	Less 20%		

Invoice No. *17121*

6.

Ree's Jewellers Victoria, B.C.

Sold to: *Students' Council Hillview S.S.*   Date: *March 30, 19_*
       Victoria, B.C.   V8N 2N4   Invoice No. *39165*

Qty.	Description	Price	Amount
9	Scholarship pins (gold)	$ 26.75	$
23	Scholarship pins (silver)	7.50	
1	Trophy	119.37	
			————
	Less 33%		

7.

PRO SPORTS

9 High Street Calgary, Alberta   T2K 3N5

Sold to: Badminton Club
c/o J. Snider, Calgary

Invoice No. 6672   **Your Order No.** 78196
Date: March 29, 19--

Qty.	Description	Price	Amount
10	Badminton rackets	$59.95	
15	Pkgs. Birds	4.95	
10	Racket Presses	9.95	
10	Racket Head Covers	10.95	

Less 22.5%

8.

city centre (H) hardware

Sold to: Hal's Carpentry Shop
Charlottetown, P.E.I.

Invoice No. 37615
Date: March 29, 19_

Qty.		Price	Amount
1	Radial arm saw	$399.98	$
1	Shop Vacuum	39.99	
1	Sawdust pick-up attachment	29.98	
2	Tool Cabinets	64.98	
2	Screwdriver sets	9.99	
2	Bench vices	24.98	

Less 15.5%

EXERCISE • SET 3

1. J.W. White Limited ordered lumber worth $895.95 from Armstrong Construction Limited. The lumber was delivered and a 23.5% discount was allowed. How much did J.W. White Limited pay for the lumber? _____

2. Tony wants to earn money cutting lawns this summer. His father has told him that he must buy his own lawn-mower. Tony went to his friend, George Lee, who owns a hardware store to find out what one would cost. Mr. Lee offers to sell Tony a lawn-mower, priced at $129.30, and tells Tony that he will allow a 15.5% discount off the regular price. He will also allow Tony to pay for the mower in 8 equal weekly payments over the summer. If Tony buys the mower, how much will each weekly payment be? _____

3. John Leclerq bought a snowmobile from a local dealer for $1895. The dealer also sold him a snowmobile suit at $65.95, one for his wife at $59.95, two suits for his children at $36.95 each, two pairs of boots at $16.95 each, two pairs of boots at $10.49 each, and four pairs of leather mitts at $17.98 each. John was allowed a discount of 45% on the clothing. How much did he owe the snowmobile dealer? _____

4. Blue Water Electric bought a television set for $389.50. It was marked up at 35% of the cost price and then sold to a friend of the owner at a 20% discount on the selling price. What was the rate of profit on the cost price? _____

5. Joan Allan bought a car in 1985 for $7250. In 1986 she decided to sell it for the price she paid minus 30% of that price. A friend was interested in buying the car and Joan offered to sell it to her friend at a 15% discount on the price she had intended to ask. What did Joan ask her friend to pay for the car? _____

17·2 CASH DISCOUNTS

Retail merchants buy the articles they sell from wholesale businesses or from manufacturing firms. The merchant sends in an order for the items required, these items are shipped by the wholesaler or the manufacturer and an invoice is mailed. The invoice lists the items shipped, the price of each item, and the total amount to be paid for the shipment.

Generally, the invoice is checked against the items in the shipment and then approved for payment. Because it is expensive to hold unpaid accounts, the wholesaler or manufacturer encourages the retailer to pay promptly. This is done by offering the retailer a **cash discount** if the invoice is paid within a stated period of time. The amount of the cash discount and the period during which it applies are noted in an abbreviated form in the invoice item **terms**.

Beattie Sporting Goods Co. Ltd.

Sold to: Ted's Sport Shop
Seagrave, Ontario L0C 1G0

Invoice No. 76660
Date: March 15, 19--
Terms: 3/30, n/60

Qty.	Description	Price	Net
30	Baseball bats: #2-87630	List $19.95 less 20%	$487.80
10	Fish nets: #3-76951	List $5.95 less 30% and 10%	37.49
			$516.29

Abbreviations used to state the terms under which cash discounts are given are listed below.

Abbreviation	Meaning
3/20	A 3% cash discount is allowed if the invoice is paid within 20 days after the invoice date.
n/30	The total amount due, which is stated on the invoice, must be paid within 30 days. After 30 days, interest on the amount due will be charged.
2% 10th prox. *or* 2/10 prox.	A 2% cash discount is allowed if the invoice is paid by the 10th of the month following the month in which the invoice is dated.
net E.O.M. prox. *or* n/E.O.M. prox.	The net amount of the invoice is due on or before the end of the month following the month in which the invoice is dated.

Terms of payment may include two or more of these conditions. For example, 5/10, 2/30, n/60 means that a discount of 5% of the net amount will be deducted if the invoice is paid within 10 days. If the invoice is *not* paid in 10 days, a discount of 2% of the net amount will be deducted if the invoice is paid on or before 30 days after the date of the invoice. The net amount of the invoice is due in 60 days if neither of the previous conditions is met. After 60 days interest will be charged.

> *Formula*
>
> Amount after discount = Amount of invoice (100% − Discount) where the discount is expressed as a percent.

EXAMPLE   An invoice for $1295.55, dated March 3, 1985, has terms 2/10, n/30. How much should be paid:
a) on March 11, 1985?
b) on March 15, 1985?

SOLUTION   **a)** March 11 is 8 days after the date of the invoice. Therefore, a discount of 2% of the net amount may be taken.

$$\text{Amount after discount} = 1295.55\ (100\% - 2\%)$$
$$= 1295.55 \times 98\%$$
$$= 1295.55 \times 0.98$$
$$= 1269.639$$

The amount to be paid on March 11 is $1269.64.

b) March 15 is more than 10 days after the invoice date. Therefore, the net amount of the invoice is due.

The amount to be paid on March 15 is $1295.55.

EXERCISE • SET 1

For each invoice:
• Extend and total each line.
• Find the date on which the invoice should be paid to obtain the best terms.
• Calculate what amount should be paid on that date.

1.

fairview sports wholesale

Sold to: J. Hock Ltd.
Hamilton, Ontario
L9C 5E5

Date: March 15, 19--
Terms: 3/10, n/30 **Via:** Our Van

Qty.	Description	Unit Price	Amount
96	Baseball Gloves #B37	$35.40	
65	Softballs #T17	15.25	
110	Pkgs. Golf Balls #K19	5.29	
72	Baseball Bats #S14	19.95	
		Total $	

a) Date to obtain best terms _____

b) Amount _____

2.

morton industries

Sold to: Bell Products Ltd.
Calgary, Alberta

Via: Intercity Transport
Invoice No. 18961

Terms: 2/10, n/30
March 21, 19--

Qty.	Description	Unit Price	Extension
36	Catalogue #19-875	$3.79	
72	Catalogue #20-317	2.25	
15	Catalogue #25-418	3.92	
25	Catalogue #37-525	2.86	
70	Catalogue #21-618	3.08	
55	Catalogue #27-346	2.11	
Interest of 1% per month is payable on overdue accounts.		**Total**	

a) Date to obtain best terms _____

b) Amount _____

3.

Milton Furniture 147 Avon Rd. Kitchener, Ontario

Sold to: Oxford Furniture   Date: **March 20, 19_** Terms: 1/20, n/30

Qty.	Description	Unit Price	Amount
12	Pole Lamp #76	$20.95	
20	Pole Lamp #H12	25.36	
8	Ceiling Fixture #A-3	89.37	
6	Ceiling Fixture #A-7	79.58	
5	Bracket Lamp #BL-10	18.87	
10	Table Lamp #TL-9	14.56	
10	Table Lamp #TL-12	23.45	
1% per month charged on all overdue accounts		**Total**	

a) Date to obtain best terms _____

b) Amount _____

EXERCISE • SET 2

Calculate the amount to be paid on each invoice. Use the method shown in the example.

	Date of Invoice	Amount of Invoice	Terms	Date Invoice Paid	Amount Paid
1.	Mar. 5, 1985	$1 236.50	2/10, n/30	Mar. 13, 1985	
2.	July 7, 1985	563.76	2/10, n/30	July 15, 1985	
3.	Apr. 2, 1985	339.57	3/10, n/30	Apr. 11, 1985	
4.	Sept. 10, 1986	1 547.68	3/10, n/30	Sept. 18, 1986	
5.	1986 08 21	424.36	2/10, n/30	1986 08 30	
6.	Feb. 6, 1986	2 567.48	1/10, n/30	Feb. 15, 1986	
7.	July 10, 1986	976.57	3/10, 1/30, n/60	July 15, 1986	
8.	July 10, 1986	976.57	3/10, 1/30, n/60	July 25, 1986	
9.	July 10, 1986	976.57	3/10, 1/30, n/60	Aug. 25, 1986	
10.	May 3, 1985	1 857.89	3/10, 2/30, n/60	May 10, 1985	
11.	Sept. 5, 1985	675.75	2% 10th prox., n 30th prox.	Oct. 15, 1985	
12.	Oct. 15, 1985	675.75	2% 10th prox., n 30th prox.	Oct. 20, 1985	
13.	July 15, 1986	1 358.67	3% 10th prox., 1% E.O.M. prox.	Aug. 31, 1986	

EXERCISE • SET 3

1. On the ledger page below, accounts due to be paid are shown. The date, terms, and amount of each invoice are given. Each day the bookkeeper checks the page and pays whichever invoices are due on the day on which the best possible terms are obtained. Assume that you are the bookkeeper for a month. Calculate when the invoice should be paid and for how much a cheque for payment of the invoice should be made out.

Accounts Payable					page 6
Date	Account	Date of Invoice	Amount of Invoice	Terms	Amount Paid
	Standard Mfg. Co. Ltd.	Feb. 23	$ 835.90	2/10, n/30	
	Chips Wholesale Ltd.	Feb. 25	1 397.60	3/10, 2/30, n/60	
	Welbrook Mills Ltd.	Feb. 28	537.77	1/10, n/30	
	Adams Stationery	Mar. 2	89.36	2/10, n/30	
	Fisher's Supplies Ltd.	Mar. 8	696.85	2/20, n/30	
	Haliburton Wholesale Ltd.	Mar. 10	237.57	3/10, n/30	
	Hilton Mfg. Ltd.	Mar. 15	1 569.98	5/10, 2/30, n/60	
	Bayfield Sales & Services	Mar. 18	396.20	3% 10th prox., n/60	

17·3 TRADE DISCOUNTS

Many manufacturers and wholesalers publish catalogues listing the products that they have for sale. These catalogues are issued to the retailers who are buyers or potential buyers of the products. Each item in the catalogue is given a **list price**. This price is not usually what retailers pay for the item; they are allowed a discount or discounts on the quoted list price. The amount of the list price minus the discount is called the **net price**.

With the catalogue is a sheet of **trade discounts** available to the retailer. Catalogues are expensive to publish, but the sheets of trade discounts may be changed readily and cheaply.

Discounts may be a regular discount to all retailers, a second discount available for orders over a certain number of units, and special discounts reducing the price of certain items because costs have been reduced or rapid turnover of these items is being encouraged.

Formula

$$\text{Net Price} = \text{List Price} (100\% - \text{Trade Discount})$$

where Trade Discount is expressed as a percent.

EXAMPLE 1   A portable electric heater is listed in a manufacturer's catalogue at $42.95 with a trade discount of 30%. What is the net price?

SOLUTION   Net Price = 42.95 (100% − 30%)
= 42.95 × 70%
= 42.95 × 0.70
= 30.065

The net price is $30.07.

CHAIN DISCOUNTS

If more than one discount is given on the list price, the formula for calculating net price is:

Formula

Net Price = List Price × (100% − Discount #1) × (100% − Discount #2)
where Discounts are expressed as percents.

If more than two discounts are allowed, continue the multiplication process.
Net Price = List Price × (100% − Discount #1) × (100% − Discount #2) × (100% − Discount #3) × (100% − Discount #4) and so on, as required

EXAMPLE 2 Kali's Auto Shop orders 25 sets of booster cables listed at $16.95 each with a regular trade discount of 28% plus a further discount of 12% for orders of 20 sets or more. How much does the auto shop pay for the booster cables?

SOLUTION

$$\text{List Price} = 25 \times 16.95$$
$$= \$423.75$$
$$\text{Net Price} = 423.75 \times (100\% - 28\%) \times (100\% - 12\%)$$
$$= 423.75 \times 72\% \times 88\%$$
$$= 423.75 \times 0.72 \times 0.88$$
$$= 268.488$$

The net price for the booster cables is $268.49.

EXERCISE • SET 1

For each invoice:
- Multiply the number of items by the list price.
- Multiply this product by (100% − Discount), expressed as a decimal quantity, to obtain the amount.
- Total the extensions to find the total amount.

1.

BONDI Bottling Company Limited

Sold to: Fairview Golf Club
Fergus, Ontario
N1M 1Z8   **Date:** March 19, 19--

Qty.	Description	Unit Price	Amount
15	Cases regular cola	$12.95 less 20%	$
30	Cases orange drink	$13.50 less 30%	
40	Cases ginger ale	$12.70 less 33%	
		Total Amount	$

2.

dunley sports limited

Sold to: Ali's Sport Shop
Mount Pearl, Newfoundland
A1N 2A2

Date: September 13, 19--

Qty.	Description	Amount
15	Heart Skis #596A List Price $170.00 less 30%	$
18	Hexel Skis #316C List Price $175.00 less 25%	
24	Regnol Skis #22-37 List Price $235.50 less 35%	
36	Pairs Ski Boots, Langen #319-736 List Price $215.76 less 22.5%	

Total Amount $

3.

Canada Biscuit Company

Mo. Day Yr. 03 15	837 Whse Code	91763 Customer Order No.	301976 Original Invoice
Quantity	**Product Description**		**Amount**
5 cases	Oatmeal cereal @ 23.75 per case Less 33.3%		$
8 cases	Sugar oatmeal @ 24.85 per case Less 28.5%		
12 cases	100% bran cereal @ 23.95 per case Less 32.5%		
9 cases	Rice sweet cereal @ 24.55 per case Less 27.75%		
1% per month charged on overdue accounts		**Invoice Amount**	$

For each invoice:
- Multiply the number of items by the unit price.
- Then multiply the result by (100% − Discount #1) expressed as a decimal quantity.
- Then multiply the result by (100% − Discount #2) expressed as a decimal quantity, to obtain the amount.
- Total the extensions to obtain the total amount of the invoice.

4.

Modern Plumbing Supply Company

Wholesale Distribution

376 Maple Street   Ottawa, Ontario K1M 0N7   Phone: 397-4174

Qty. Ordered	Make	Description	Amount
24	Gales	Gaskets #3175 @ $0.78 less 35% and 10%	$
125	ATSM	Screws #461-3-5 @ $0.09 less 15% and 5%	
197	Kerr	Connectors #276-53 @ $0.37 less 22% and 8%	
21	Wesley	Control Cups #33A @ $0.98 less 40% and 15%	
1% per month charged on overdue accounts		**Total Amount Due**	$

5.

eastern electric supply

Sold to: Blue Water Electric   March 21, 19--

Qty.	Description	Unit Price	Trade Discount	Amount
50	Fuse Boxes #189A	$3.25	15% and 5%	
144	Utility cords #20A	2.15	20% and 10%	
305	Conduits	2.10	5% and 2%	
207 m	#10 wire per metre	1.42	8% and 5%	

1.5% per month is charged on all unpaid accounts.   **Amount Due**

6.

OWENVAR PAINT CORP

Sold to: Tikala Paint & Varnish   47 Main Street
Chatham, Ontario N7L 1A5

May 21, 19--
Shipped Via: Interprovincial Van

Qty.	Description	Unit Price	Amount
96	1 L B-31 white exterior gloss, less 10% and 2%	$5.85	
85	1 L B-33 white exterior semi-gloss, less 15% and 3%	5.85	
138	1 L A-21 white interior gloss, less 18% and 5%	5.65	
155	1 L A-24 white interior semi-gloss, less 20% and 8%	5.65	
350	0.5 L A-21 white interior gloss, less 10% and 2.5%	3.55	
375	0.5 L A-24 white interior semi-gloss, less 15% and 3.5%	3.00	
		Total Amount Due	

For each invoice:
- Extend each item to find the amount after discounts.
- Total to find the amount due.
- Check the terms and calculate the net amount payable if the invoice is paid on the date which will allow the best terms to be obtained.

7.

Invoice No. 17835

hardware supplies limited

Ship Via: Provincial Trucking   Terms: 3/10, n/30   March 30, 19—

Qty.	Description	Unit Price	Amount
56	Hacksaws - less 20%	$3.75	$
136	Bandsaw Blades - less 15%	6.85	
90	Claw Hammers - less 30.5 %	4.75	
124	Wrenches-less 25% and 5%	4.85	
86	Cutting Pliers - less 12.5% and 2%	6.79	
1.5% is charged on all overdue accounts		**Total Amount Due**	$

a) Date to obtain best terms _____

b) Amount _____

8.

A-1 Leather Goods Limited

Sold to: Mall Gift Shop
Saskatoon, Saskatchewan
S7M 1W4

Date: May 5, 19--
Terms: 2/15, n/30

Invoice No. 3591
Via: Interprovincial Trucking

Qty.	Description	Unit Price	Amount
36	Ladies' Flight Bags, less 20%, 5%	$ 73.95	
55	Overniter Cases, less 25%, 2%	31.95	
38	Men's Two-Suiter, less 20%, 5%	85.89	
25	Ladies' Three-Piece Luggage Sets less 25%, 12.5%	127.99	
85	Ladies' Tote Bags #312A, less 15%, 2%	30.99	
		Amount due	

a) Date to obtain best terms _____

b) Amount _____

9.

Rika Importers

To: Chelli's Jewellers Edmonton, Alberta T5E 4C3
Via: Truck   **Invoice No:** 3912

Date: April 17, 19--
Terms: 2% 10th prox., net E.O.M. prox.

Qty.	Description	Trade Discount	Unit Price	Amount
8	96-piece dinner sets #A135	40%, 5%	$167.96	
5	52-piece dinner sets #A137	35%, 2%	123.98	
10	32-piece dinner sets #B199	30%, 2%	52.58	
65	5-piece place settings #M11	37.5%, 5%	28.57	
30	Coffee Pots #N12	25%, 1%	9.98	
1% per month on all over due accounts			**Total Amount Due**	

a) Date to obtain best terms _____
b) Amount _____

EXERCISE • SET 2

Calculate each net price using the method shown in Example 2. Remember to round off each answer correct to the nearest cent.

	List Price	Rate of Trade Discounts	Net Price
1.	$ 125.00	20%, 10%	
2.	38.00	30%, 20%	
3.	276.00	40%, 10%	
4.	595.50	40%, 20%	
5.	19.50	20%, 5%	
6.	48.70	20%, 5%	
7.	137.95	25%, 15%	
8.	15.87	33%, 12%	
9.	1 869.48	27%, 14%	
10.	22.95	22%, 6%	
11.	157.63	28%, 10%, and 5%	
12.	55.75	32%, 11%, and 8%	
13.	3 579.64	22.5%, 10%, and 6%	
14.	747.86	23.5%, 11.5%, and 9.5%	
15.	11.89	33.3%, 15.25%, and 6.5%	

EXERCISE • SET 3

Express each rate of profit correct to two places after the decimal.

1. Schulz Stereophonics Limited purchased 15 stereo consoles listed at $1065 each. Schulz received an invoice for $15 975 less 25% and 15%, and paid it in time to obtain a cash discount of 2%. If Schulz sold the sets at the list price of $1065, what rate of profit on actual cost price was made? _____

2. Marie's Gift Shoppe purchased 20 sets of kitchen storage jars listed at $13.50. Marie's received an invoice for $270 less 30% and 5% with no cash discount. The store sold 14 of the sets at the list price of $13.50, and the rest were sold at a special discount of 20%. What rate of profit on the actual cost price was made? _____

3. Jacques' Drapes Limited bought 15 m of material for a list price of $8.95/m. Jacques' received an invoice for $134.25 less trade discounts of 20% and 10%. The material was made into 3 pairs of drapes that were sold at $69.96 a pair. The labour cost of making a pair of drapes is $10.50. What rate of profit did Jacques' Drapes make on the cost price of a pair of drapes? _____

17·4 SINGLE DISCOUNT EQUIVALENT TO A SERIES OF TRADE DISCOUNTS

If a series of discounts is taken on a list price, a retailer would need to know exactly what discount is being given in order to price the goods for sale. That is, it is necessary to know what single rate of discount is equivalent to a series of discounts given on the goods.

Formula

Single equivalent discount = $1.00 - [(1.00 - \text{Discount \#1}) \times (1.00 - \text{Discount \#2})]$ where rate of discount is expressed as a decimal quantity.

EXAMPLE 1   Calculate the single discount equivalent to discounts of 20% and 10%.

SOLUTION   Single equivalent discount $= 1.00 - [(1.00 - 0.20) \times (1.00 - 0.10)]$
$$= 1.00 - (0.80 \times 0.90)$$
$$= 1.00 - 0.72$$
$$= 0.28$$
$$= 28\%$$

The single equivalent discount of 20% and 10% is 28%.

EXAMPLE 2   Calculate the single discount equivalent to discounts of 15%, 10%, and 5% correct to two places after the decimal.

SOLUTION   Single equivalent discount
$$= 1.00 - [(1.00 - 0.15) \times (1.00 - 0.10) \times (1.00 - 0.05)]$$
$$= 1.00 - (0.85 \times 0.90 \times 0.95)$$
$$= 1.00 - 0.726\ 75$$
$$= 0.273\ 25$$
$$= 27.325\%$$

The single equivalent discount of 15%, 10%, and 5% is 27.33%.

EXAMPLE 3   The list price of a bicycle is $129.95. Discounts of 20%, 10%, and 5% apply. Calculate:
a) the single equivalent discount,
b) the net price.

SOLUTION   **a)** Single equivalent discount
$$= 1.00 - [(1.00 - 0.20) \times (1.00 - 0.10) \times (1.00 - 0.05)]$$
$$= 1.00 - (0.80 \times 0.90 \times 0.95)$$
$$= 1.00 - 0.684$$
$$= 0.316\ 000$$
$$= 31.60\%$$
The single equivalent discount of 20%, 10%, and 5% is 31.60%.

b) Net price = 129.95 (1.00 − 0.316)

= 129.95 × 0.684

= 88.8858

= 88.89

The net price of the bicycle is $88.89.

EXERCISE • SET 1

Calculate each single equivalent discount and the net price. Calculate the rate of discounts correct to two places after the decimal where necessary.

	List Price	Discounts	Single Equivalent Discount	Net Price
1.	$ 69.95	20% and 5%		
2.	105.40	10% and 5%		
3.	395.60	15% and 10%		
4.	725.50	30% and 25%		
5.	8.95	10% and 8%		
6.	11.45	30%, 10%, and 5%		
7.	276.50	25%, 15%, and 5%		
8.	899.95	25%, 15%, and 10%		
9.	1 250.50	35%, 15%, and 5%		
10.	2.95	40%, 5%, and 2%		
11.	360.00	10%, 8%, and 2%		
12.	5.95	12%, 10%, and 2%		
13.	515.25	20%, 16%, and 6%		
14.	2 340.00	20%, 12%, and 2%		
15.	995.95	11%, 10%, and 5%		

EXERCISE • SET 2

EXAMPLE 4 The net price of a boat was $1215 after trade discounts of 10% and 10% were allowed. What was the list price?

SOLUTION Single equivalent discount

$$= 1.00 - [(1.00 - 0.10) \times (1.00 - 0.10)]$$
$$= 1.00 - (0.90 \times 0.90)$$
$$= 1.00 - 0.81$$
$$= 0.19$$
$$= 19\%$$

Net price = List price − Discount
List price = 100% of List price
Discount = 19% of List price
Net price = 81% of List price
  $1215 = 81% of List price
    $= 0.81 \times$ List price
List price $= \dfrac{1215}{0.81}$
    $= 1500$

The list price was $1500.

Calculate each list price.

	Net Price	Discounts	List Price
1.	$ 26.50	20% and 10%	$
2.	88.95	30% and 5%	
3.	6.75	20% and 15%	
4.	125.00	10%, 10%, and 5%	
5.	1 356.00	20%, 10%, and 5%	
6.	90.45	10%, 5%, and 5%	
7.	734.25	10%, 6%, and 2%	
8.	57.40	6%, 4%, and 2%	
9.	111.24	10%, 7%, and 3%	

EXERCISE • SET 3

1. Two wholesalers offer a pool table at the same list price of $978.50. The first wholesaler gives one cash discount of 33%, while the second lists it at discounts of 25% and 10%. By calculating the single discount equivalent to the two discounts offered by the second wholesaler, determine which is the better offer. ———

2. Two catalogues list the same coffee maker at $42.88. One gives discounts of 20% and 9%, while the other gives discounts of 25% and 5%. Calculate the single equivalent discount of each set of discounts to determine which is the better offer.

———, ———, ———

3. Consumer's Drug Mart can purchase generic drugs of the same quality from two drug manufacturers. Parker Drugs Inc. offers a list price less 30% and 12% and promises a 3% cash discount for prompt payment. Grady Pharmaceuticals offers a list price less 20%, 15%, and 2% but bills all customers at net within 20 days. If Consumer's Drug Mart pays all invoices on the day that they are received, which firm should they choose to deal with? _____

17·5 REVIEW

EXERCISE • SET 1

1. For this invoice
- Extend each item.
- Calculate the discounted amount.
- Add the provincial sales tax.
- Total the invoice.

Owen's Office Equipment Limited

— Sales & Service —
57 Pitt St., St. John, N.B.
Telephone 391-7647

Sold to: Invoice No.   37129
Office Services Limited   Date: April 12
St. John   Date Delivered: April 15, 19--

Qty.	Description	Price	Amount
5	Typewriters A-55	$559.79	$
3	Desks #137-569	227.50	
3	Files #314-045	100.45	
		Less 22.5%	
		Add Sales Tax: 5%	
		Total	$

2. Calculate the amount to be paid on each invoice.

Date of Invoice	Amount of Invoice	Terms	Date Invoice Paid	Amount Paid
May 4, 1985	$1 376.50	3/30, n/60	June 2, 1985	
Mar. 6, 1985	865.75	2/10, n/30	Mar. 15, 1985	
July 15, 1986	2 567.85	2/10, 1/30, n/60	July 31, 1986	
Jan. 21, 1986	648.56	3/10, 2/30, n/60	Jan. 25, 1986	
Apr. 25, 1986	3 976.48	2/10, 1/30, n/60	Apr. 30, 1986	
1985 03 21	586.98	2/10, n/30	1985 03 31	
1986 05 31	1 650.50	2/10, n/30	1986 06 12	
June 7, 1986	375.80	2% 10th prox., n 30th prox.	July 5, 1986	
Sept. 18, 1986	2 465.85	3% 10th prox., n 30th prox.	Oct. 9, 1986	
1986 10 06	792.50	1% 10th prox., n E.O.M. prox.	1986 11 09	

3. Make the extensions in this invoice and calculate the total amount due.

Modern Plumbing Supply Company

376 Maple Street   Ottawa, Ontario   Phone: 379-4174

Wholesale Distribution

Qty. Ordered	Make	Description	Amount
72	Gales	Gaskets #3175 @ $0.78 less 35% and 15%	
175	ATSM	Screws #461-3-5 @ $0.09 less 15%	
207	Kerr	Connectors #276-53 @ $0.37 less 22% and 5%	
38	Wesley	Control Cups #33A @ $0.98 less 35% and 10%	
		Total Amount Due	

4. Calculate each single equivalent discount, correct to two places after the decimal. Then calculate the net price.

List Price	Discounts	Single Equivalent Discount	Net Price
$ 129.95	30%		
79.80	25%		
8.95	15%		
16.49	16%		
289.50	33%		
565.49	25% and 15%		
29.95	30% and 5%		
890.50	30% and 15%		
2 395.50	30% and 10%		
6.95	20% and 5%		
345.60	20%, 10%, and 5%		
56.75	15%, 10%, and 5%		
1 250.25	25%, 15%, and 10%		
666.50	20%, 15%, and 10%		
395.00	30%, 25%, and 15%		

EXERCISE • SET 2

1. Calculate each discounted price.

Retail Price	Rate of Discount	Discounted Price
$595.00	20%	$
99.50	15%	
227.30	18%	
33.95	22%	
156.85	17.5%	
267.95	22.5%	

2. For this ledger, calculate the date on which payment of each invoice should be made to obtain the best terms and the amount to be paid under those terms.

	Accounts Payable				**Page 8**
Date	**Account**	**Date of Invoice**	**Amount of Invoice**	**Terms**	**Amount Paid**
	Standard Mfg. Co.	April 12	$1 395.75	2/10, n/30	
	Haliburton Wholesale	April 15	976.30	3/10, 1/20, n/30	
	Wellbrook Mills Ltd.	April 18	2 765.45	1/10, n/30	
	Adams Stationery	April 20	76.50	2/10, n/30	
	Chips Wholesale Ltd.	April 21	1 976.40	3/10, 2/30, n/60	
	Bayfield Sales & Services	April 25	475.65	3% 10th prox., n/E.O.M. prox.	

3. Calculate each net price.

List Price	Rate of Trade Discount(s)	Net Price
$ 395.75	20%	
1 850.85	33%	
2 675.80	35%	
595.75	22%	
476.50	18%	
3 879.95	39%	
250.00	20% and 10%	
1 876.50	15% and 5%	
915.40	18% and 7%	
396.37	22% and 8%	
42.65	23% and 4%	
279.00	20%, 10%, and 5%	
1 565.45	22%, 8%, and 5%	
58.67	22.5%, 10%, and 5%	
747.50	20.5%, 11.5%, and 2%	
33.95	15.5%, 10.5%, and 1%	

4. Calculate each single equivalent discount and the list price. Express the discount correct to two places after the decimal, where necessary.

Net Price	Discounts	Single Equivalent Discount	List Price
$ 583.40	15% and 10%		
73.50	20%, 15%, and 5%		
2 587.95	30%, 10%, and 2.5%		

EXERCISE • SET 3

1. You are a clerk at Vince's Supermarket. The manager gives you a 5% discount on all food items that you purchase in the store and a discount of 10% on all other items. Just as you leave work, you pick out a roast of beef priced at $10.98, oranges at $1.99, apples at $1.89, two cans of peas at $0.72 each, a package of cherry turnovers for $1.49, a bottle of shampoo at $3.29, and two magazines at $1.45 each. You make up your own bill and leave your payment in the cash register. How much will you leave? _____

2. You have worked for two weeks in the accounts department of Shopper's Department Store under the supervision of the previous bookkeeper, who left yesterday. You are on your own today, March 20, and are in charge of paying invoices due at the best possible terms. Enter invoices you pay today in the following journal with amounts paid.

Accounts Payable		Date of Invoice	Amount of Invoice	Terms	*page 10*
Date	**Account**				
March 19--		19--			
	Jones Warehouse Ltd. *paid $389.68*	Feb. 25	$ 397.63	2/15, n/30	
	Caroll's Fabrics	Feb. 28	1576.96	2/20, n/30	
	Drug Wholesaler's *paid $881.00*	Mar. 5	898.98	2/10, n/30	
	City Chocolates	Mar. 5	387.47	2/15, n/30	
	Canadian Dry Goods	Mar. 9	1876.46	3/20, n/30	
	Adams Stationery	Mar. 10	137.55	3/10, n/30	
	Holton Mfg. Ltd.	Mar. 10	525.64	2/15 1/20, n/30	
	Bayfield Wholesale	Mar. 10	1564.87	2/10, n/30	
	Standard Mfg. Co. Ltd.	Mar. 15	739.48	2/10, n/30	
	Logan's Wholesale	Mar. 17	1257.38	3/10, 2/20, n/30	

3. Brown's Auto Repairs has two prices quoted to them on radial tires: $89.75 less 35% per tire and $89.75 less 25% and 8% per tire.

   a) Which is the better offer? _____

   b) How much will Brown's save per tire by taking the better offer? _____

4. The list price of a toaster broiler oven in two different catalogues is the same. However, one catalogue lists discounts of 32% and 11%, while the other catalogue lists discounts of 28%, 15%, and 3.5%. Which is the better offer? _____

CHAPTER 18

FOREIGN EXCHANGE

Historically, each of the many nations in the world has developed its own form of money. Since money is the agent by which goods are traded and since goods are imported and exported between nations, the value of the money system of one nation must be compared with that of another.

This chapter presents questions and examples that illustrate how the money of one country compares with that of another and the means by which the money of one country can be exchanged for that of another.

18·1 EXCHANGE RATES

If you have taken a trip across the border to the United States you know that it saves a lot of trouble if you take American money with you. When Canadian money is used to make purchases or payments in the U.S.A., calculations must be made for every purchase to determine how many Canadian dollars are equivalent to the American price. These calculations are necessary because a Canadian dollar does not have exactly the same "buying power" as a U.S. dollar.

A traveller planning to go to the United States purchases U.S. currency at a Canadian bank. Suppose that for $1000 in U.S. money the traveller is charged $1200 in Canadian currency. The amount that the bank charges is calculated from the current **rate of exchange** of Canadian dollars for U.S. dollars, fixed by the foreign exchange market. In this particular case, the rate of exchange was one U.S. dollar for 1.20 Canadian dollars. On another occasion the traveller might find the rate of exchange to be one U.S. dollar for 1.2479 Canadian dollars as shown in the accompanying table.

On the foreign exchange market, currencies of different countries are bought and sold in the same way that livestock or metals are traded in their markets. A foreign exchange rate quoted by the Canadian Foreign Exchange Market is the current price of a unit of that foreign money in Canadian dollars.

Here is a table of foreign exchange rates; the current rates may be found in the business section of a newspaper and may change daily.

Foreign Country	Currency Unit	Value of Unit in Canadian Dollars	Value of $1 Canadian in Foreign Units*
United States	dollar	$1.247 9	0.801 35
Britain (U.K.)	pound	1.760 8	0.567 92
Australia	dollar	1.126 9	0.887 39
Austria	schilling	0.063 0	15.873
Bahamas	dollar	1.247 9	0.801 35
Belgium	franc	0.021 80	45.872
Bermuda	dollar	1.247 9	0.801 35
Denmark	krone (pl. kroner)	0.122 9	8.136 7
France	franc	0.145 3	6.882 3
Greece	drachma	0.012 29	81.367
Hong Kong	dollar	0.160 10	6.246 1
Italy	lira (pl. lire)	0.000 733	1 364.3
Jamaica	dollar	0.402 4	2.485 1
Japan	yen	0.005 327	187.72
Lebanon	pound	0.249 6	4.006 4
Mexico	peso	0.008 0	125.00
Netherlands	guilder	0.395 2	2.530 4
Norway	krone	0.159 4	6.273 5
South Africa	rand	0.995 8	1.004 2
Spain	peseta	0.007 83	127.71
Sweden	krona (pl. kronor)	0.152 6	6.553 1
Switzerland	franc	0.558 2	1.791 5
West Germany	mark	0.444 4	2.250 2

Table title: **Foreign Exchange Rates**

*The values in this column are found by dividing the values of the third column into 1.

EXAMPLE 1   Change $50 U.S. to Canadian dollars. Use the rate from the table of *Foreign Exchange Rates*.

SOLUTION $1.00(U.S.)   = $1.2479(Can)
$50.00(U.S.) = 50.00 × 1.2479
= 62.395
= $62.40(Can)

EXAMPLE 2 Change 2000 French francs to Canadian dollars. Use the rate from the table of *Foreign Exchange Rates*.

SOLUTION
$$1 \text{ franc} = \$0.1453(\text{Can})$$
$$2000 \text{ francs} = 2000 \times 0.1453$$
$$= 290.60$$
$$= \$290.60(\text{Can})$$

EXAMPLE 3 Change $25.00 Canadian to French francs.

SOLUTION
$$\$1.00(\text{Can}) = 6.8823 \text{ French francs}$$
$$\$25.00(\text{Can}) = 25.00 \times 6.8823$$
$$= 172.0575$$
$$= 172.06 \text{ French francs}$$

EXAMPLE 4 Change $75.00 Canadian to British currency.

SOLUTION
$$\$1.00(\text{Can}) = £0.567 \ 92(\text{U.K.})$$
$$\$75.00(\text{Can}) = 75.00 \times 0.567 \ 92$$
$$= 42.594$$
$$= £42.59(\text{U.K.})$$

EXERCISE • SET 1

Change the following amounts to Canadian dollars. Obtain the current exchange rates from a newspaper or use the table of *Foreign Exchange Rates* on page 320.

	Foreign Country	Foreign Currency	Amount of Foreign Currency	Amount in Canadian Dollars
1.	West Germany	marks	1 000	
2.	Japan	yen	1 500	
3.	U.S.A.	dollars	50	
4.	Bermuda	dollars	180	
5.	Hong Kong	dollars	250	
6.	Switzerland	francs	1 250	
7.	Sweden	kronor	75	
8.	Mexico	pesos	1 212	
9.	Norway	kroner	1 525	
10.	Greece	drachmas	10 375	

Change the following amounts in Canadian dollars to the currency of the given foreign country. Obtain the exchange rates from a newspaper or use the table of *Foreign Exchange Rates*. Calculate each amount correct to two places after the decimal.

	Amount in Canadian Dollars	Foreign Country	Foreign Currency	Amount of Foreign Currency
11.	$ 100.00	West Germany	marks	
12.	125.00	Italy	lire	
13.	750.00	South Africa	rand	
14.	125.00	Belgium	francs	
15.	250.00	Denmark	kroner	
16.	15.00	Spain	pesetas	
17.	21.50	Japan	yen	
18.	1 250.00	Australia	dollars	
19.	575.50	Lebanon	pounds	
20.	72.55	France	francs	

EXERCISE • SET 2

Obtain the exchange rates from a newspaper or use the table of *Foreign Exchange Rates* to answer the following questions.

1. The Photography Club ordered a manual, not available in Canada, from the American Photographic Association in Rochester, New York. The manual is priced at $20.95 U.S.   What should the manual cost in Canadian dollars? _____

2. Jim McLeod ordered a piece of equipment needed to complete a project for the Science Fair from a British scientific equipment manufacturer. The price, in the British catalogue, was £7.90. What should Jim pay in Canadian dollars for a money order for this amount? _____

3. Anne Coroni has a pen pal in Japan. She wrote and asked her friend to purchase and send her 6 pairs of chopsticks. If the chopsticks cost 220 yen a pair and parcel post will cost 300 yen,

a) how many yen should Anne send her friend? _____

b) How much should a money order for this amount be in Canadian dollars? _____

4. Mary Koehler sent a cheque for $125 Canadian to her mother in West Germany. Her mother cashed the cheque at her West German bank. How many marks did Mary's mother receive? (Round off to the nearest mark.) _____

5. On a trip to Greece, Paul James charged a sweater priced at 800 drachmas to his credit card account. What amount in Canadian dollars would be charged to his account? _____

6. Sheri Holmes stayed at a hotel in Mexico for 9 nights at $37.50 a night paid in Canadian dollars to her travel agent. What amount in Mexican pesos should the hotel management receive from Sheri's travel agent? (Round off to the nearest peso.) _____

EXERCISE • SET 3

1. If 1 Spanish peseta is worth $0.007 92 Canadian, how much, in Canadian dollars, are 795 pesetas worth? _____

2. Change $195.78 Canadian to West German marks if the exchange rate is 1 mark to $0.4455 Canadian. (Round off to the nearest mark.) _____

3. Change $1547.50 Canadian to Danish kroner if the exchange rate is 1 krone to $0.1227 Canadian. (Round off to the nearest krone.) _____

4. Arthur Johannsen sent a money order for $1000 Canadian to Japan. If the exchange rate is 1 yen to $0.007 217 Canadian, how much was the money order worth in Japanese yen? (Round off to the nearest yen.) _____

18·2 CARRYING FUNDS TO A FOREIGN COUNTRY

Before he or she leaves on a trip, a traveller can purchase **travellers' cheques**, **letters of credit**, or **bank drafts** from the bank. All of these banking forms are really promises by a bank to transfer the stated amount of foreign money to the foreign bank which gives the traveller currency in exchange for a banking form.

To issue travellers' cheques and similar forms, the head office of each chartered bank must be able to buy and hold large sums of foreign money. In the Montreal and Toronto foreign exchange markets, the chartered banks and the Bank of Canada buy and sell foreign currency. If a bank has more of a certain foreign currency than it needs, it notifies a broker and tells how much it wants to sell and what price it is asking. The broker then contacts other banks until a buyer offering an acceptable buying price is found. The day-to-day buying prices set the current exchange rate within limits imposed by the International Monetary Fund and the governments of the different countries.

TRAVELLERS' CHEQUES

Travellers' cheques are a convenient and safe method of transporting money. They may be issued in denominations of $10, $20, $50, $100 or $500. When a traveller purchases a travellers' cheque, he or she signs it. It must be signed again when the cheque is cashed. Consequently the purchaser is the only person who can cash the cheque.

Travellers' cheques may be issued in the currency of a specific country. For example, a Canadian travelling to the United States will buy cheques which may be cashed in U.S. currency. Almost every bank sells American Express Travellers' Cheques.

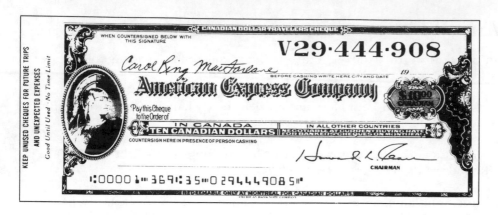

The travellers' cheque illustrated here is cashable in Canadian dollars in Canada without charge. Like all travellers' cheques it can be cashed in banks, restaurants, gas stations, motels, etc. The purchaser of this cheque signs her or his name in the upper left hand corner when the cheque is purchased and again in the presence of the person cashing the cheque.

LETTERS OF CREDIT

For larger sums of money, a bank may issue a letter of credit to a traveller or a business. This document authorises the purchaser to obtain any sum of foreign currency up to an amount specified in the letter from a foreign bank or other agency. The purchaser may make several withdrawals until the total amount stated has been withdrawn.

As the traveller moves from one country to another, a letter of credit may be used to obtain funds in the currency of any of the countries visited. For this reason the form is usually called a **circular letter of credit**.

BANK DRAFTS

A bank draft is a cheque instructing a foreign bank or agency to pay the traveller a stated amount of foreign currency. The traveller, upon arriving in the specified country, receives this amount. The bank which issues the draft pays the foreign bank or agency the amount of the draft from its stores of foreign currency.

The draft illustrated here is in U.S. currency and can be cashed at the New York address shown.

| The First Canadian Bank | No. **0000-0000** |
| **Bank of Montreal** | March 28   19-- |

Pay to the order of _____ $500.00 U.S.

Five hundred -------------------------------- xx/100

To
Bank of Montreal
45 South Street
New York, N.Y.

for Bank of Montreal

Page No.

EXAMPLE 1 George Miller purchased $2000 of U.S. travellers' cheques from his bank. How much did he have to pay for them in Canadian funds?

SOLUTION From the table of *Foreign Exchange Rates*
$1.00(U.S.) = $1.2479(Can)
$2000.00(U.S.) = 2000 × 1.2479
     = 2495.80
     = $2495.80(Can)

EXAMPLE 2 Leigh Vincetti is given a circular letter of credit for $3000 Canadian for expenses on a business trip to Australia. She draws $390 Australian on the second day of her trip. What amount is charged to Leigh's letter of credit?

SOLUTION From the table of *Foreign Exchange Rates*
$1.00(Aus) = $1.1269(Can)
$390.00(Aus) = 390 × 1.1269
     = 439.491
     = $439.49(Can)

EXAMPLE 3 A draft of $1275 Canadian is drawn by a Canadian bank on a branch in Paris, France. What is the draft worth in French francs?

SOLUTION $1.00(Can) = 6.8823 French francs
$1275.00(Can) = 1275 × 6.8823
     = 8774.9325
     = 8774.93 French francs

EXERCISE • SET 1

Obtain current exchange rates from a newspaper and use them to answer the following questions or use the table of *Foreign Exchange Rates*.

1. What will it cost in Canadian currency to purchase travellers' cheques for the following amounts in U.S. dollars?

   a) $100 _____   **b)** $10 _____   **c)** $20 _____   **d)** $50 _____

   e) $450 _____   **f)** $750 _____   **g)** $1500 _____   **h)** $2500 _____

2. How much would $750 Canadian in travellers' cheques (correct to the nearest currency unit) be worth in:

   a) United States dollars, _____   **b)** British pounds, _____

   c) French francs, _____   **d)** Italian lire, _____

   e) Spanish pesetas, _____   **f)** Swiss francs, _____

   g) Mexican pesos, _____   **h)** Jamaican dollars? _____

EXERCISE • SET 2

Use the table of *Foreign Exchange Rates* or exchange rates from a newspaper to answer the following questions.

1. A Canadian tourist travelling in Europe carries travellers' cheques payable in Canadian dollars. What amount of foreign funds will the traveller receive if the cheques are cashed as follows (correct to the nearest currency unit)?

   a) a $100 cheque in England _____

   b) a $50 cheque in France _____

   c) a $100 cheque in Denmark _____

   d) a $50 cheque in the Netherlands _____

   e) a $50 cheque in Belgium _____

   f) a $20 cheque in Switzerland _____

   g) a $100 cheque in West Germany _____

   h) a $100 cheque in Italy _____

2. John Sinclair plans an extended selling trip and carries a circular letter of credit for $2000 Canadian with him. He draws the following amounts of foreign currency against his letter of credit: $300 U.S. in Hawaii; 60 000 yen in Osaka, Japan; $1500 in Hong Kong; $500 Australian in Sydney, Australia. Show the total charges against his letter of credit in Canadian dollars. _____

3. A traveller carries bank drafts for: $150 Canadian on a London, England bank; $200 Canadian on a bank in Paris, France; $250 Canadian on a bank in West Berlin. What amount did the traveller receive for each draft, in the currency of the country in which the draft was cashed, correct to the nearest currency unit? _____, _____, _____

4. Clare went to Britain for 6 months. She paid her return air fare to her travel agent in Canada and purchased travellers' cheques at her bank in British pounds. Clare purchased 45 travellers' cheques worth £50 each. What did she pay for them in Canadian funds? _____

EXERCISE • SET 3

Use the table of *Foreign Exchange Rates* or exchange rates from a newspaper to answer these questions.

1. Tom Price's credit card statement showed a charge of $50.92 Canadian for a suit he purchased in Hong Kong on a recent trip. What did the suit cost in Hong Kong dollars correct to two places after the decimal? _____

2. A Canadian purchased $500 U.S. in travellers' cheques from a bank in Canada.

   a) How much did they cost in Canadian dollars? _____

b) If the cheques were cashed in Mexico for Mexican pesos, how much did the traveller receive correct to the nearest peso? _____

3. A Canadian travelling to Jamaica took travellers' cheques totalling $400 U.S.

    a) If seven $50 cheques are cashed in Jamaica, how many Jamaican dollars will be received? _____

    b) The traveller cashes the remaining $50 cheque upon returning home. How many Canadian dollars will be received? _____

4. A Canadian travelling in Lebanon takes travellers' cheques for 500 British pounds.

    a) How much did she pay in Canadian dollars? _____

    b) How much are the British pounds worth in Lebanese pounds, correct to two places after the decimal? _____

    c) If the traveller spent 2800 Lebanese pounds in Lebanon and then cashed the amount she had left on her return to Canada, how much did she receive in Canadian dollars? _____

18·3 EXPORT AND IMPORT TRANSACTIONS

Goods labelled *Imported from Hong Kong*, *Product of U.S.A.*, *Made in Japan*, *Grown in Mexico*, *Made in England*, etc., are available in stores all over Canada. These imports must be paid for by the Canadian companies that import them, in the currency of the country from which they were shipped. Similarly, foreign companies importing Canadian goods must pay for them in Canadian dollars. Such payments may be made through the bank by either of the following methods.

COMMERCIAL LETTER OF CREDIT

When ordering goods from a foreign company, the buyer obtains a commercial letter of credit from her or his bank guaranteeing payment for the goods ordered. This letter is sent to the seller's bank. As soon as the seller can show documents proving that the goods have been shipped and cleared through the proper inspection authorities, the seller's bank can make this deposit since payment by the buyer's bank is guaranteed by the letter of credit.

DOCUMENTARY DRAFT

When an order is received from a foreign buyer, the seller ships the goods and has her or his bank draw a documentary draft on the foreign company for the payment. This draft, or written order, may require payment "at sight" or within a specified period of time (30, 60 or 90 days). The seller's bank sends this written order to its branch or agent in the buyer's country. The foreign branch presents the draft to the buyer for acceptance. Once the buyer has accepted the terms of the draft, the buyer may collect the goods. Then the seller's bank holds the draft until its due date. When the draft has been paid, the payment is deposited in the seller's bank account.

EXAMPLE 1   A Canadian importer receives a documentary draft from Australia for $376 Australian. What amount of Canadian currency is necessary to pay for the draft?

SOLUTION   From the table of *Foreign Exchange Rates*

$1.00(Aus)   = $1.1269(Can)
$376.00(Aus) = 376.00 × 1.1269
             = 423.714
             = 423.71

$423.71 in Canadian funds will pay the draft.

EXAMPLE 2   A Canadian exporter receives a commercial letter of credit for $213 in Canadian funds from a Hong Kong firm. How much did the letter of credit cost the firm in Hong Kong dollars?

SOLUTION   From the table of *Foreign Exchange Rates*

$1.00(Can)   = $6.2461(Hong Kong)
$213.00(Can) = 213.00 × 6.2461
             = 1330.419
             = 1330.42

The letter of credit cost $1330.42 in Hong Kong funds.

EXERCISE • SET 1

Obtain the exchange rates from a newspaper or use the table of *Foreign Exchange Rates* to answer the following questions.

1. What amount of Canadian funds will pay for each of the following documentary drafts?

   a) 1000 marks from a bank in West Germany _____

   b) 107 525 lire from a bank in Italy _____

   c) 1 536 700 yen from a bank in Japan _____

   d) 7695 francs from a bank in France _____

   e) $19 766 from a bank in Hong Kong _____

   f) 10 970 drachmas from a bank in Greece _____

   g) 1432 rand from a bank in South Africa _____

   h) 12 593 guilders from a bank in the Netherlands _____

2. A Canadian firm receives the following documentary drafts and commercial letters of credit. What did they cost in the currency of the country from which they were sent? (Give answers correct to two places after the decimal.)

   a) A commercial letter of credit from Italy for $167(Can) _____

   b) A documentary draft from Sweden for $1250(Can) _____

   c) A draft from Australia for $769(Can) _____

   d) A letter of credit from Bermuda for $5975(Can) _____

e) A draft from Switzerland for $1200(Can) _____

f) A letter of credit from Belgium for $4379(Can) _____

g) A draft from France for $1725(Can) _____

EXERCISE • SET 2

Obtain the exchange rates from a newspaper or use the table of *Foreign Exchange Rates* to answer the following questions.

1. Fine Leathers, Importers orders 20 leather coats from Italy at 57 471 lire each. What amount of Canadian funds will be necessary to pay a commercial letter of credit for the coats? _____

2. Jane's Novelties Limited sends the following order to Mexicraft Limited.
   10 hats, #3197 @ 60 pesos each
   15 straw handbags, #5173B @ 85 pesos each
   30 pairs of sandals, #5H671C @ 92 pesos per pair
   a) How much is the total order in pesos? _____

   b) What amount in Canadian dollars will pay the commercial letter of credit for the order? _____

3. Hilroy Tractors, Owen Sound, receives an order for tractor parts totalling $10 575 Canadian from a firm in Lebanon. For what amount in Lebanese pounds will the Lebanese firm pay to have its bank settle a documentary draft drawn on the company for the order? (Give your answer correct to two places after the decimal.) _____

4. Woodcrafts Limited, Victoria, received the following order from Golden Gate Furniture Limited, San Francisco. Prices are taken from Woodcrafts' catalogue which gives list prices in Canadian dollars.
   5, #3193 dry sinks @ $107.35 each
   20, #1156 side chairs @ $20.75 each
   5, #1156A tables @ $159.50 each

   a) What is the total amount of the order in Canadian dollars? _____

   b) For what amount in U.S. dollars should the company's bank draw from Golden Gate Furniture's bank account to settle a documentary draft for the order? _____

EXERCISE • SET 3

Sometimes a firm selling to a foreign buyer cannot wait the 30, 60 or 90 days necessary to have payment made to its bank account. The following example shows how payment can be obtained earlier.

Hilroy Tractors received an order for tractor parts totalling $10 575 from a Lebanese firm in Question 3, of the previous exercise. Hilroy had their bank draw a documentary draft on the bank of the Lebanese firm. Here is the draft.

$10 575   **Owen Sound, Ontario, Canada**
December 5, 19 – –

60 **d** after **sight** pay to the order of

CANBANK the sum of

Ten thousand five hundred and seventy-five · $\frac{\text{xx}}{100}$ Dollars

Value received and charge to the account of

L.B. Company   **Hilroy Tractors Limited**
Beirut, Lebanon

Accept and return

    Hilroy Tractors' bank (Canbank) sends this draft to its branch in Beirut, who forward it to L.B. Company on December 9. L.B. Company accepts it and signs it on December 10; then returns it to the Beirut branch of Canbank. The branch sends the accepted draft to Canbank in Owen Sound, and notifies Hilroy Tractors who ship the tractor parts to Lebanon.

    Hilroy Tractors, however, do not want to wait 60 days after December 10 to receive payment for tractor parts already shipped. They may have the draft **discounted** at their bank. Suppose that Hilroy ask the bank to discount the draft on December 15.

Current interest rates are 8.75% per annum.

Due date of the draft is December 10 + 60 d + 3 d grace* which will take the payment date to February 11.

*The days of grace are the extra days allowed for payment after a bill or note falls due.

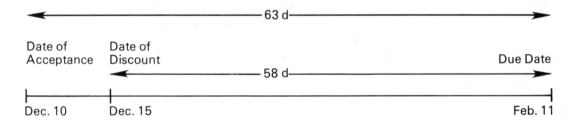

The period for which the draft is discounted is from December 15 to February 11.

Number of days: Dec. 31 − 15   16 d   (days remaining in December)
                     Jan.   31 d
                     Feb. $\underline{11\ d}$
                                   58 d

Discount = Amount of draft × Rate × Time

$$= 10\ 575 \times 0.0875 \times \frac{58}{365}$$

$$= 147.035\ 958\ 9$$

$$= 147.04$$

Canbank pays Hilroy Tractors: $10 575.00 − $147.04 = $10 427.96 (the proceeds)

Find the due date, length of discount period, discount and proceeds on each of the following documentary drafts if the current interest rate is 9.25% per annum.

1. A draft for $1860, payable 30 days after sight, accepted in New York on November 3 and discounted in Halifax on November 10

   _____, _____, _____, _____

2. A draft for $10 000, payable 60 days after sight, accepted in London, England on December 2 and discounted in Toronto on December 30

   _____, _____, _____, _____

3. A draft for $5267, payable 90 days after sight, accepted in Tokyo, Japan on March 10 and discounted in Vancouver on April 5

   _____, _____, _____, _____

4. A draft for $30 500, payable 60 days after sight, accepted in Seattle on May 25 and discounted in Winnipeg on June 15

   _____, _____, _____, _____

18·4 REVIEW

EXERCISE • SET 1

Change the following amounts to Canadian dollars. Obtain current exchange rates from a newspaper or use the table of *Foreign Exchange Rates*.

	Foreign Country	Foreign Currency	Amount of Foreign Currency	Amount in Canadian Dollars
1.	Bahamas	dollars	1 000	
2.	South Africa	rand	1 500	
3.	Greece	drachmas	5 190	
4.	Austria	schillings	9 800	

Change the following amounts in Canadian dollars to the currency of the given foreign country. Obtain the exchange rates from a newspaper or use the table of *Foreign Exchange Rates*. Calculate each amount correct to two places after the decimal where necessary.

	Amount in Canadian Dollars	Foreign Country	Foreign Currency	Amount of Foreign Currency
5.	$ 500	Japan	yen	
6.	1 400	Denmark	kroner	
7.	750	Spain	pesetas	
8.	2 300	Britain	pounds	

9. What will it cost in Canadian currency to purchase travellers' cheques for the following amounts in U.S. dollars?

a) $250 _____   b) $550 _____

c) $1250 _____   d) $5000 _____

10. How much would $1200 Canadian travellers' cheques (correct to the nearest currency unit) be worth in:

a) Australian dollars, _____   b) Norwegian kroner, _____

c) Jamaican dollars, _____   d) South African rand? _____

11. What amount of Canadian funds will pay for each of the following documentary drafts?

a) 986 000 yen from a bank in Japan _____

b) 20 000 guilders from a bank in the Netherlands _____

c) 260 000 pesos from a bank in Mexico _____

d) 2350 dollars from a bank in U.S. _____

12. A Canadian firm receives the following documents. What will they cost in the funds of the country from which they were sent (correct to the nearest currency unit)?

a) A commercial letter of credit from U.S. for $1295 Canadian _____

b) A documentary draft from Mexico for $950 Canadian _____

EXERCISE • SET 2 _____

Use the table of *Foreign Exchange Rates* or exchange rates from a newspaper to answer the following questions.

1. Riverview College arranged a ski trip to Stowe, Vermont. The college Students' Council obtained a package deal at $300 in U.S. funds per student. What did it cost each skier in Canadian dollars? _____

2. George Cancila ordered a Mathematics of Finance text from a publisher in New York listed in an American catalogue at $29.95 in U.S. funds. What will George pay in Canadian dollars? _____

3. A tourist travelling in the Bahamas carried $1000 Canadian in travellers' cheques. How much Bahamian currency did she receive if she cashed all the cheques? _____

4. A business woman carried a letter of credit for $2500 in Canadian funds. She drew 10 000 pesos in Mexico City, $300 U.S. in Tampa, Florida, and £500 in London, England. What are the total charges against her letter of credit in Canadian funds? _____

5. Gerrard's Antiques purchased 3 pieces of antique furniture in England. The furniture was shipped with a commercial letter of credit to cover the total invoice in British pounds. If the items purchased were an antique chair worth £500, a reception table worth £950, and an antique desk worth £1570,

  a) what is the total invoice in British pounds? _____

  b) What is the commercial letter of credit in Canadian dollars? _____

EXERCISE • SET 3

Use the table of *Foreign Exchange Rates* or exchange rates from a newspaper where necessary to answer the following questions.

1. If 1 Danish krone is worth 0.1234 Canadian dollars, how much is $1455 Canadian worth in Danish kroner (correct to the nearest krone)? _____

2. Change $978 Canadian to U.S. dollars if $1 U.S. is worth $1.2080 Canadian. _____

3. A Canadian travelling to Bermuda took travellers' cheques totalling $750 U.S.

  a) If three $100 cheques and eight $50 cheques were cashed in Bermuda, how many Bermudan dollars were received? _____

  b) If the remaining $50 was cashed on returning home, how many Canadian dollars did the traveller receive? _____

4. A Canadian travelling to Hong Kong takes travellers' cheques for 450 British pounds.

  a) How much did he pay in Canadian dollars? _____

  b) If he spent 4400 Hong Kong dollars in Hong Kong and cashed the remainder on returning home to Canada, how much Canadian currency did he receive? _____

5. Find the due date, length of discount period, discount, and proceeds for a draft for $8550 payable 60 days after sight, accepted in Berne, Switzerland on June 9 and discounted in Saint John on June 30, if the current interest rate is 8.75% per annum.

  _____ , _____ , _____ , _____

CHAPTER 19

TAXES

In Canada there are three main levels of government: municipal governments (city, town, village, and township councils), provincial governments, and the Federal Government. All three levels of government provide services for the people under their jurisdictions. To do this, the governments must have money; funds to pay the people in government and to finance the physical and social services they provide.

In this chapter the examples and exercises explain the methods by which governments collect the money they need to provide the services required by the people who elect them.

19·1 RESIDENTIAL AND COMMERCIAL PROPERTY TAXES AND BUSINESS TAX

The tax on residential property is called a **residential property tax**, and the tax on business property is called a **commercial property tax**. Real estate used for operating a business is sometimes taxed at a different rate from property that is used only for residential purposes. The tax rates differ because municipalities may receive provincial grants to help reduce residential property taxes.

The owner of a property used for business pays the commercial property tax, but the operator of the business (who may or may not own the property) must pay an additional tax which is levied on the business operation. The tax is called a **business tax** and may be based on the rental value of the property, the capital value of the property (land, buildings, equipment), the floor area in use, the annual value of the merchant's stock in trade, the annual retail or wholesale turnover, or licence fees. Business taxes vary widely from province to province.

EXAMPLE 1   Lakeland Electronics Co. Ltd. owns and operates a business on property assessed at \$15 100. The commercial property tax rate is 62.3 mills. A business tax of 31% of the commercial property tax is added to the tax bill. What is the total tax bill?

SOLUTION

Commercial Property Tax

Assessment = \$15 100
Rate = 62.3 mills per dollar
      = \$0.0623 per dollar

Commercial property tax is \$940.73.

Commercial property tax
= Assessment × Rate
= 15 100 × 0.0623
= 940.730

Business Tax

Commercial property tax = \$940.73
Rate = 31%
     = 0.31

Business tax is \$291.63.

Business tax
= Commercial property tax × Rate
= 940.73 × 0.31
= 291.626

Total tax bill = Commercial property tax + Business tax
               = \$940.73 + \$291.63
               = \$1232.36

EXAMPLE 2 James Lee rents the building in which he operates a grocery store. The property is assessed at \$21 300. The commercial property tax rate is 52.6 mills per dollar and the business tax is 35% of the commercial property tax.
a) How much does the owner of the property pay in commercial property tax?
b) How much does Mr. Lee pay in business tax?

SOLUTION
Commercial Property Tax

a) Assessment = \$21 300   Commercial property tax = Assessment × Rate
        Rate = 52.6 mills   = 21 300 × 0.0526
            = \$0.0526   = \$1120.380

The commercial property tax is \$1120.38.

Business Tax

b) Property tax = \$1120.38   Business tax = Property tax × Rate
         Rate = 35%   = 1120.38 × 0.35
             = 0.35   = 392.133

Mr. Lee pays a business tax of \$392.13.

EXERCISE • SET 1

Complete the following table.

	Assessment		Commercial Property Taxes		Business Taxes		Total Tax Bill
	Land	Buildings	Tax Rate (mills/ dollars)	Tax	Rate as a Percent of C.P.T.*	Tax	
1.	\$15 000	\$40 000	65.7		22%		
2.	9 000	27 000	66.2		20%		
3.	20 000	45 000	61.5		25%		
4.	11 000	35 000	58.9		30%		
5.	7 000	21 000	60.5		15%		
6.	12 500	32 500	59.5		21%		
7.	8 500	29 250	67.8		30%		
8.	19 500	37 250	62.6		31%		

*C.P.T. is Commercial Property Tax.

A municipality issues its property tax bills to tax payers with the following conditions for payment.

First instalment, 35%, due April 15
Second instalment, 32.5%, due June 25
Third instalment, 32.5%, due August 31

Calculate the amount of each instalment for each of the property tax bills listed below.

	Tax Bill	Instalment #1	Instalment #2	Instalment #3
9.	$ 407.85			
10.	397.60			
11.	813.40			
12.	197.25			
13.	516.31			
14.	970.45			
15.	1 375.41			
16.	205.37			
17.	571.14			
18.	720.83			

EXERCISE • SET 2

EXAMPLE 3   Hope Ingram owns property assessed as follows: land, $2000; building, $11 000. She rents the first floor of the building as a retail store and the second floor as an apartment. For tax purposes the assessment is divided as follows.

	Land	Buildings	Tax Rate (mills)
Commercial	80%	65%	54.8
Residential	20%	35%	47.3

What is Hope's total tax bill?

SOLUTION   Residential Property Tax

Assessment on land	= 20% of $2000	$ 400
Assessment on buildings	= 35% of $11 000	3 850
		$4 250

Residential property tax = Assessment × Rate
= 4250 × 0.0473
= 201.025

The residential property tax is $201.03.

Commercial Property Tax

Assessment on land   = 80% of $2000 $1 600
Assessment on buildings = 65% of $11 000   7 150
                                                  $8 750

Commercial property tax = Assessment × Rate
                        = 8750 × 0.0548
                        = 479.500

The commercial property tax is $479.50.

Total tax bill = Residential tax + Commercial tax
             = $201.03 + $479.50
             = $680.53

The following are assessment records taken from municipal tax rolls. Find the total tax bill in each case.

1. Property: 516 Regent Street   Lot No. 2167

Assessment	Land	Buildings
Commercial	$10 000	$21 000
Residential	nil	22 000

Tax Rate: Commercial: 54.9 mills
          Residential: 50.5 mills

Total tax bill _____

2. Property: 7915 Beacon St.

Assessment:	Commercial		Residential	
	Land	Buildings	Land	Buildings
	$9 000	$29 000	$11 000	$51 000

Tax Rate: Commercial: 48.7 mills

          Residential: 44.5 mills

Total tax bill _____

3. Property: 371 Seventh St. W.   **Zone:** R3

Tax Rate: Commercial, 37.5 mills

             Residential, 32.6 mills

Assessment: $45 000

Commercial = 30%

Residential = 70%

Total tax bill _____

4. Property: 3539 Waterloo St.

    Assessed Value: $65 000

    Use: Commercial − 35%

           Residential − 65%

Tax Rate: Commercial, 32 mills

         Residential, 27.9 mills

Total tax bill _____

EXERCISE • SET 3

EXAMPLE 4 Property at 139 Main Street is listed on the municipal assessment rolls as follows.

Owner: George Barry

first floor rented to Martha Milne to operate a shoe store

second floor rented to Joseph Orr as an apartment

	Land	**Buildings**	**Rate**
Assessment	$3 500	$18 000	
Commercial	85%	60%	51.8 mills
Residential	15%	40%	46.2 mills

Business tax: 40% of commercial property tax

Find:

a) total of tax bill sent to George Barry,   **b)** business tax paid by Martha Milne.

SOLUTION   **a)** Residential Property Tax

           Assessment on land   = 15% of $3500 $ 525

           Assessment on buildings = 40% of $18 000   <u> 7 200</u>

                                                          $7 725

           Residential property tax = 7725 × 0.0462

                              = 356.895

        The residential property tax is $356.90.

        Commercial Property Tax

        Assessment on land   = 85% of $3500 $ 2 975

        Assessment on buildings = 60% of $18 000   <u> 10 800</u>

                                                       $13 775

        Commercial property tax = 13 775 × 0.0518

                              = 713.545

        Commercial property tax is $713.55.

        The total tax bill sent to George Barry is:

        356.90 + 713.55 = $1070.45.

    b) Business Tax

        Business tax = 40% of commercial property tax

                  = 0.40 × 713.55

                  = 285.420

        The business tax paid by Martha Milne is $285.42.

Complete the following table.

| | Assessment | | Property Taxes | | | | | | Business Tax | | |
| | | | Commercial | | | Residential | | | | | |
	Land	Buildings	% of Assessment*1	Tax Rate (mills/dollars)	Tax	% of Assessment	Rate (mills/dollar)	Tax	Total Property Tax	Rate as a % of C.P.T.*2	Tax
1.	11 500	18 000	L 80% B 65%	61.8		L 20% B 35%	59.3			22%	
2.	11 300	21 500	L 85% B 70%	61.8		L 15% B 30%	59.3			22%	
3.	22 130	33 400	L 75% B 62%	61.8		L 25% B 38%	59.3			22%	
4.	21 830	48 700	L 55% B 61%	58.6		L 45% B 39%	56.7			31%	
5.	32 310	56 400	L 61% B 72%	58.6		L 39% B 28%	56.7			31%	
6.	13 140	34 700	L 60% B 50%	58.6		L 40% B 50%	56.7			34%	
7.	11 230	36 970	L 73% B 62%	49.7		L 27% B 38%	42.3			26%	
8.	12 710	20 860	L 50% B 41%	49.7		L 50% B 59%	42.3			26%	

*1 L represents land and B represents buildings.
*2 C.P.T. is commercial property tax.

9. A building in which the first floor is rented as a store and the second as an apartment is assessed as follows.

	Land	Buildings	Rate
Total assessment	$3 200	$20 100	
Residential	10%	40%	41.7 mills
Commercial	90%	60%	48.6 mills

What is the total tax bill? _____

10. The property at 279 Blake Street is listed on the municipal assessment rolls as follows.
Owner: Howard C. Levitt
first floor rented to G.S. Goetz for purpose of operating a men's clothing store
second floor rented to E.C. Moore as an apartment

	Land	Buildings	Rate
Total assessment	$1650	$16 370	
Commercial	82%	75%	62.3 mills
Residential	18%	25%	58.1 mills

Business tax is 35% of commercial property tax. Find:

a) total tax bill sent to Howard C. Levitt. _____

b) business tax paid by G.S. Goetz. _____

19·2 DIRECT FEDERAL TAXES: INCOME TAX

Federal income tax regulations change from year to year. To gain up-to-date information the student should obtain the current income tax forms and tax guide. The information needed to solve the problems in this section can be obtained from these forms.

EXERCISE • SET 1

PERSONAL EXEMPTIONS

All employers are required to make regular income tax deductions from their employees' incomes at regular intervals such as weekly or monthly. The amount of the deduction varies from person to person.

When a person accepts employment, he or she must fill out a TD1 form stating the tax exemptions which he or she is claiming. The TD1 form reproduced here is for Jack Kwapis who has taken a position as assistant accountant at Blake, Puccini, and Associates. Jack is claiming personal exemptions for himself, his wife (who does not work), and his two children aged 3 and 5.

- A duly completed copy of this return must be filed by an individual with an employer on commencement of employment, and

  (a) you are in receipt of salary, wages, commissions or other remuneration

  or filed with the payor, if

  (b) you are in receipt of a superannuation or pension benefit (including an annuity payment) made pursuant to or under a superannuation or pension fund or plan, or

  (c) you are in receipt of a benefit under the Unemployment Insurance Act, 1971, or

  (d) you are in receipt of an adult training allowance paid under the National Training Act except to the extent that it was paid as or on account of an allowance for personal or living expenses while living away from home.

  and in any case,

  (e) within **seven** days of any change in your exemptions.

- **This return need not be filed by employees claiming the "Basic Personal Exemption" only.**

- If you do not file this return, as required, income tax will be deducted as though you were a single person without dependants.

- If you believe there are other exemptions that you could claim on your income tax return you may ask your District Taxation Office whether they may be taken into account in arriving at your tax deduction.

- Do not claim a child or other dependant whose net income for the year will exceed $3,870.

- Net income of your spouse or dependants includes any pension or supplement under the Old Age Security Act or any similar Act of a province, benefits under the Canada or Quebec Pension Plan and the Unemployment Insurance Act, 1971.

- Vous êtes tenu de remettre un exemplaire dûment rempli de la présente déclaration à votre employeur au début de votre emploi

  a) si vous avez reçu un traitement, un salaire, des commissions ou une autre forme de rémunération;

  au payeur

  b) si vous avez reçu des prestations de retraite ou de pension (y compris des arrérages de rente) en vertu d'un fonds ou d'un régime de pension ou de retraite,

  c) si vous avez reçu des prestations en vertu de la Loi de 1971 sur l'assurance-chômage,

  d) si vous avez reçu une allocation de formation professionnelle des adultes versée en vertu de la Loi nationale sur la formation, sauf dans la mesure où ces sommes vous ont été versées à titre ou au titre d'indemnité pour frais personnels lorsque vous viviez hors de chez vous;

  et, quoi qu'il en soit,

  e) dans les **sept** jours suivant tout changement dans vos déductions.

- Les employés qui demandent uniquement «l'Exemption personnelle de base» n'ont pas besoin de produire cette déclaration.

- Faute de produire la présente déclaration, tel qu'exigé, l'impôt sur le revenu sera retenu comme si vous étiez célibataire sans personnes à charge.

- Si vous croyez avoir droit à d'autres exemptions dans votre déclaration d'impôt sur le revenu, demandez à votre bureau de district d'impôt si vous pouvez en tenir compte en calculant votre retenue de l'impôt.

- Vous ne pouvez compter un enfant ou une autre personne à charge dont le revenu net pour l'année dépassera $3,870.

- Le revenu net de votre conjoint ou des personnes à votre charge comprend toute pension ou tout supplément en vertu de la Loi sur la sécurité de la vieillesse ou en vertu de toute loi provinciale semblable, ainsi que les prestations du Régime de pensions du Canada, du Régime de rentes du Québec ou de la Loi de 1971 sur l'assurance-chômage.

FAMILY OR LAST NAME (Print) – NOM DE FAMILLE (en caractères d'imprimerie)	USUAL FIRST NAME AND INITIALS – PRÉNOM USUEL ET INITIALES	EMPLOYEE NO. – NUMÉRO DE L'EMPLOYÉ
KWAPIS	JACK W.	

ADDRESS – ADRESSE
89 NORTH ST.
KINGSTON, ONTARIO

SOCIAL INSURANCE NUMBER
NUMÉRO D'ASSURANCE SOCIALE
474 401 974

DATE OF BIRTH – DATE DE NAISSANCE
Day-Jour 03 | Month-Mois 07 | Year-Année 53

Complete the "Claim for Exemptions" area on the reverse side and enter your "Net Claim". ▶ $ 7771.20 ◀ Remplissez la section «Exemptions réclamées», au verso, et inscrivez la «Réclamation nette».

Refer to the "Table" below and enter the applicable "Net Claim Code" ▶ 9 ◀ Consultez la «Table» ci-dessous et inscrivez le «Code de réclamation nette» approprié.

Table of Net Claim Codes 1983 *Table des codes de réclamation nette*

Net Claim – Réclamation nette Exceeding – Not exceeding Excédant – N'excédant pas	Net Claim Code Code de réclamation nette	Net Claim – Réclamation nette Exceeding – Not exceeding Excédant – N'excédant pas	Net Claim Code Code de réclamation nette
$3,769 — $3,820	1	$ 7,060 — $ 7,740	8
3,820 — 4,420	2	7,740 — 8,470	9
4,420 — 5,070	3	8,470 — 9,260	10
5,070 — 5,640	4	9,260 — 10,040	11
5,640 — 6,370	5	10,040 — 10,780	12
6,370 — 6,710	6	10,780 — 11,380	13
6,710 — 7,060	7	11,380 and up – et plus	X
Exemption from Tax Deduction as claimed below – Exonération de la retenue de l'impôt réclamée ci-dessous			O

- Your "Net Claim Code" is used by the employer or the payor to determine the tax deduction required from payments received as listed in (a) to (d) above.

- Votre employeur ou le payeur utilise votre «Code de réclamation nette» pour déterminer l'impôt à déduire des paiements décrits en a) à d) ci-dessus.

Claim for Exemption from Tax Deduction—*Valid for current calendar year only.*

This area is to be completed by an individual who is receiving remuneration that is subject to tax deduction but who wishes to claim exemption because "Total estimated income from all sources for the year" including taxable benefits but excluding Family Allowance payments, will be less than the "Net Claim" above. No claim may be made here by a person not resident in Canada for the whole year unless your earnings in Canada will be less than your exemptions apportioned to the period of residence in Canada. If you qualify for this exemption, your "Net Claim Code" is "O".

Demande d'exonération de la retenue de l'impôt — *Valable pour l'année civile en cours seulement.*

La présente section doit être remplie par un particulier dont la rémunération est assujettie à la retenue de l'impôt et qui désire en être exonéré parce que le «Total des revenus estimatifs de toutes provenances pour l'année», y compris les avantages imposables mais excluant les allocations familiales, sera inférieur à la «Réclamation nette» susmentionnée. Si vous ne résidiez pas au Canada pendant toute l'année, vous ne pouvez demander cette exonération, à moins que vous n'estimiez que vos gains au Canada seront inférieurs à vos exemptions proportionnelles à votre période de résidence au Canada. Si vous avez droit à la présente exonération, votre «Code de réclamation nette» est «O».

Income to date this year from all sources—*Revenu de toutes provenances jusqu'ici cette année* – – – – – – – – ▶ $ _____

Estimated income for remainder of year from all sources—*Revenu estimatif de toutes provenances d'ici la fin de l'année* – – ▶ $ _____

Total estimated income from all sources for the year—*Total des revenus estimatifs de toutes provenances pour l'année* – – ▶ $ _____

Claim for Exemptions—*Exemptions réclamées*
Basic Personal Exemption—*Exemption personnelle de base*
Married or Equivalent Exemption—*Exemption de marié(e) ou l'équivalent*

▶ $ 3,770

If applicable, claim only one of these 4 items—*S'il y a lieu, ne réclamer qu'un seul des 4 articles*

Married and supporting spouse—*Marié(e) et soutien d'un conjoint*

☐ 1. whose net income while married, will not exceed
dont le revenu net pendant le mariage, ne dépassera pas } $570   Claim—*Réclamez* $3,300

☐ 2. whose net income while married, will exceed
dont le revenu net pendant le mariage, dépassera } $570 but not
sans dépasser $3,870

Less: spouse's net income—*Moins le revenu net du conjoint* $ _____
Claim—*Réclamez* $ _____   ▶ $ 3300

Single, divorced, separated or widow(er)—*Célibataire, divorcé(e), séparé(e) ou veuf(veuve)*

(See information in item A below) *(Voir les indications de l'alinéa A ci-après)*
If the dependant's net income for the year—*Si le revenu net de la personne à charge, pour l'année,*

☐ * 3. Supporting dependant whose net income will not exceed
Soutien d'un parent dont le revenu ne dépassera pas } $570   Claim—*Réclamez* $3,300

☐ * 4. Supporting dependant whose net income will exceed
Soutient d'un parent dont le revenu net dépassera } $570 but not
sans dépasser $3,870

Less: dependant's *net income—Moins le revenu net de la personne à charge* * $ _____
Claim—*Réclamez* $ _____

*Name and relationship to you:
Nom et lien de parenté avec vous:

Exemption for Wholly Dependent Children—*Exemption pour enfants entièrement à charge*

See information in item B below. Provide details below.   *Voir les indications de l'alinéa B ci-après. Fournissez des précisions.*
Under age 18 at December 31st—If net income will not exceed $2,450, claim $710. If net income will exceed $2,450 claim $710 minus one-half the amount in excess of $2,450.
Age 18 or over at December 31st—If net income will not exceed $2,570, claim $1,300. If net income will exceed $2,570 but not $3,870, claim $1,300 minus the amount in excess of $2,570.
Moins de 18 ans au 31 décembre—Si le revenu net ne doit pas excéder $2,450, réclamez $710. Si le revenu net doit excéder $2,450 sans excéder $3,870, réclamez $710 moins la moitié du montant en sus de $2,450.
Âgé de 18 ans ou plus au 31 décembre—Si le revenu net ne doit pas excéder $2,570, réclamez $1,300. Si le revenu net doit excéder $2,570 sans excéder $3,870, réclamez $1,300 moins le montant excédant $2,570.

Name of child (Attach list if space is insufficient)—*Nom de l'enfant (Annexez une liste si l'espace est insuffisant)*	Estimated annual net income—*Revenu annuel net estimatif*	Date of birth *Date de naissance* Day *Jour*	Month *Mois*	Year *Année*	If over 21, state school attended or whether infirm—*S'il a plus de 21 ans, indiquez l'école fréquentée ou dites s'il est infirme.*	
GEORGE W.	NIL	01	08	79		▶ $ 710
ANNE E.	NIL	19	11	81		▶ $ 710
						▶ $ 8490

Exemption for Other Dependants—*Exemption pour autres personnes à charge*

Parents, Grandparents, Brothers, Sisters, Aunts or Uncles Resident in Canada (including in-laws).
Père, mère, grands-parents, frères, soeurs, tantes et oncles résidant au Canada (et ceux du conjoint).
See information in item C and provide details below.
Voir les indications de l'alinéa C et fournissez des précisions ci-après.

Name and address of dependant *Nom et adresse de la personne à charge* (Attach list if space is insufficient) *(Annexez une liste si l'espace est insuffisant)*	Dependant's—*Personne à charge* Net income *Revenu net*	Year of birth *Année de naissance*	Estimated cost to you of support of dependant—*Montant estimatif que vous dépenserez pour l'entretien de la personne à charge*	If over 21, state school attended or whether infirm—*Si elle ou plus de 21 ans, indiquez l'école fréquentée ou dites si elle est infirme.*	
					▶ $ _____
					▶ $ _____

Age Exemptions—*Exemptions en raison d'âge*

If you are 65 years of age or over—*Si vous êtes âgé de 65 ans ou plus*
If your spouse is 65 years of age or over you may claim any unused balance of the exemption amount (maximum $2,360)—*Si votre conjoint a 65 ans ou plus, vous pouvez déduire la fraction inutilisée de l'exemption jusqu'à concurrence de $2,360.*   Claim—*Réclamez* $2,360 ▶ $ _____

Unused Balance *Fraction inutilisée* ▶ $ _____

Pension Income or Qualified Pension Income Exemption—*Déduction au titre du revenu de pensions ou du revenu de pensions admissible*

If you are 60 years of age or over and have qualified pension income or are 65 years of age or over and have pension income, claim the lesser of $1,000 or the amount received.
Si vous êtes âgé de 60 ans ou plus et vous avez un revenu de pensions admissible ou vous êtes âgé de 65 ans ou plus et vous avez un revenu de pensions, réclamez le moins élevé des montants suivants: $1,000 ou le montant reçu. ▶ $ _____

Disability Exemptions—*Exemptions pour invalidité*

For persons blind at any time in the year, or confined to a bed or wheelchair for a substantial period each day throughout any 12 month period ending in the year.—*Pour les personnes aveugles à une date quelconque de l'année et pour celles qui doivent garder le lit ou demeurer dans un fauteuil roulant pendant de longues périodes chaque jour au cours de toute période de 12 mois se terminant dans l'année.*

For yourself—*Pour vous-même*   Claim—*Réclamez* $2,360 ▶ $ _____
You may claim any unused balance of the disability exemption (maximum $2,360) to which your spouse, child, grandchild or supported individual (see item A below) is entitled.—*Vous pouvez réclamer toute fraction inutilisée de l'exemption pour invalidité (jusqu'à concurrence de $2 360) à laquelle votre conjoint, enfant, petit-enfant ou personne à votre charge a droit (voir A ci-après).*

Unused Balance *Fraction inutilisée* ▶ $ _____

Student Exemptions—*Exemptions pour les étudiants*

1. Claim $50 for each month in the year you will be a student in full-time attendance at only the following: a university or college or an institution offering job retraining courses.
Réclamez $50 pour chaque mois de l'année où vous fréquenterez à plein temps une université, un collège ou un établissement dispensant des cours de formation professionnelle. ▶ $ _____

2. Claim your tuition fees less the total amount of all scholarships, fellowships or bursaries exceeding $500 which you will receive during the calendar year.—*Réclamez vos frais de scolarité moins le montant global (excédant $500) de toutes les bourses d'études, de perfectionnement (fellowships) ou d'entretien que vous recevrez au cours de l'année civile.* ▶ $ _____

Total—*Total* ▶ $ 8490.00

Deduct: Taxable Family Allowance Payments (To be received in year for children claimed above.)
Déduire: le montant des versements imposables d'allocations familiales *(À recevoir au cours de l'année pour les enfants nommés ci-dessus.)* ▶ $ 718.80

Net Claim— (Will not be less than $3,770. Enter this amount on reverse side.)
***Réclamation nette*—** *(Ne doit pas être inférieure à $3,770. Inscrire le montant au verso.)* ▶ $ 7771.20

According to the deductions claimed and the amount of salary for the pay period, the employer obtains the amount of tax from tables of taxation provided by the Federal Government. The employer then deducts this amount of income tax from the employee's salary and remits it to Revenue Canada.

Obtain a TD1 form for this year and calculate the total personal exemptions (basic personal exemption, married exemption, and exemption for wholly dependent children) for each of the following taxpayers.

1. Age 17, single, no dependents _____

2. Age 19, single, no dependents _____

3. Age 24, married, wife has no income, no other dependents _____

4. Age 72, married, wife's age is 61, no other dependents _____

5. Age 25, married, wife's income is $3500, no other dependents _____

6. Age 23, married, wife's income is $920, no other dependents _____

7. Age 23, married, husband has no income, one child age one year _____

8. Age 26, married, wife has no income, one child born during current taxation year, one child 3 years old _____

9. Age 32, married, wife has no income, one child 2 years old, one child 5 years old, one child 8 years old _____

10. Age 46, married, husband's income is $1000, one child 17 years old, one child 14 years old; neither of the children earned any income and both attended school

_____

Obtain a current Federal General Tax Guide and read the sections in the Guide under the heading "Claim for Personal Exemptions" headed "Basic Personal Exemption", "Married Exemption", "Exemption for Wholly Dependent Children", and "Additional Personal Exemptions". Also read the schedules included with current income tax forms that are referred to in the above sections.

At present (1983 tax year), a summary of these sections provides the following information.

TAXPAYER OR DEPENDENT	EXEMPTION CLAIM
1. Basic Personal Exemption	$3770
2. Married Exemption and supporting spouse who has no income or income under $570	3300
3. Married Exemption and supporting spouse who has income between $570 and $3870	3870 minus spouse's income
4. Married Exemption and supporting spouse who has income over $3870	NIL Spouse files separate income tax return.

5. Exemption for Wholly Dependent Children under 18   710
   (income less than $2450)

   Exemption for Wholly Dependent Children under 18   710 minus half
   (income between $2450 and $3870)   (child's income − $2450)

6. Exemption for Wholly Dependent Children 18 and over   1300
   (income less than $2570)

   Exemption for Wholly Dependent Children 18 and over   1300 minus (child's income − $2570)
   (income between $2570 and $3870)

7. Nieces and nephews who have no other support   same as wholly dependent children

8. Equivalent to Married Exemption (widow, widower, divorced, separated, single parent); exemption to be claimed under the heading "Single, divorced, separated or widow(er)"   Claim exemption as in 2 or 3; generally using oldest child as dependent in place of spouse and *not* claiming that child under the exemption for wholly dependent children.

9. Equivalent to Married Exemption when a person other than a child is used in place of spouse; exemption to be claimed under the heading "Single, divorced, separated, or widow(er)"; using parent, grandparents, brothers, sisters, aunts, and uncles in place of spouse   Claim exemption as in 2 or 3, only *one* person may be claimed and that person may *not* be claimed elsewhere.

10. Exemption for Other Dependents Living in Canada (parents, grandparents, brothers, sisters, aunts, and uncles); claim under the heading "Exemption for Other Dependents"   Claim exemption as in 5 or 6, that person may *not* be claimed elsewhere.

Using current Federal Income Tax forms and Tax Guide, match the current exemptions with those in the above summary and calculate total personal exemptions for the following taxpayers.

11. Age 50, married, wife's income is $975, one child age 22 who earned $900 for summer work, attended university for the rest of the year _____

12. Age 22, single, mother (widow) lives with her and has no income _____

13. Age 36, married, wife's income is $3766, mother-in-law (widow) lives with them and has an income of $575 but is otherwise dependent, two children ages 7 and 10 _____

14. Age 40, married, wife's income is $1137, father (widower) lives with them and is totally dependent except for Old Age Security Pension, one child age 14 attends school, one child age 18 attends school and earned $725 _____

15. Age 43, widow, mother lives with her and is wholly dependent, son age 22 attends university and earned $695 _____

Revenue Canada
Taxation

Revenu Canada
Impôt

1983
T1 GENERAL

Federal and Ontario
Individual Income Tax Return

**Working Copy
Retain for
your records**

Identification

Note: 1. For your records, please enter the information preprinted on your mailing copy or the corrections made to that information.

2. Detailed information can be found in the Guide under the corresponding line number.

Social Insurance Number
4 7 4 4 0 1 9 7 4

Name   JACK W. KWAPIS

Address   89 NORTH STREET

KINGSTON

ONTARIO

Spouse's Social Insurance Number
4 7 4 1 0 1 3 6 7

Date of Birth	Day 0 3	Month 0 7	Year 1 9 5 3

On December 31, 1983, I was: Married 1 ☒ Widow(er) 2 ☐ Divorced 3 ☐ Separated 4 ☐ Single 5 ☐

Name of Spouse   Wanda E. Kwapis

Address of Spouse: same as mine ☒ or

If the name or address shown above is incorrect, print the necessary corrections below:

Name
Usual First Name and Initial   Surname, Family or Last Name

Address
Number, Street, Apt. No., P.O. Box No. or R.R. No.

City
Province   Postal Code

Type of work or occupation in 1983

Name of present employer

Your Province or Territory of Residence on December 31, 1983, was: ONTARIO

If self-employed in 1983, please state province of self-employment:

If you became or ceased to be a resident of Canada in 1983, give:

	Day	Month		Day	Month
Date of Entry			or Departure		

If taxpayer is deceased, please give date of death: Day   Month   Year

Please do not use this area

Calculation of Total Income

Income from Employment

Total Earnings Before Deductions from Box (C) on all T4 slips (attach copy 2 of T4 slips)	**01**	26 000 00	⊙
Commissions from Box (L) on all T4 slips, included in above total	**02**		
Other employment income including training allowances, tips and gratuities, etc. (please specify)	**03**	NIL	⊙
Total employment earnings (add lines 01 and 03) 04		26 000 00	
Subtract: Employment expense deduction - If line 04 above is $2,500.00 or more, claim $500.00. If less, claim 20% of line 04. **05**		500 00	⊙
Other allowable expenses (please specify) **06**			⊙
Total employment expenses (add lines 05 and 06) 07			▷
Net employment earnings (subtract line 07 from line 04) 08		25 500 00	

Pension Income

Old Age Security Pension (attach copy of T4A(OAS) slip)	**09**		⊙
Canada or Quebec Pension Plan benefits (attach copy 2 of T4A(P) slip)	**10**		⊙
Other pensions or superannuation (attach copy 3 of T4A slips)	**11**		⊙

Income from Other Sources

Taxable Family Allowance payments (attach copy of TFA1 slip)	**12**	718 90	⊙
Unemployment Insurance benefits (attach copy 2 of T4U slip)	**13**		⊙
Taxable amount of dividends from taxable Canadian corporations (attach completed Schedule 4)	**14**		⊙
Interest and other investment income (attach completed Schedule 4)	**15**	298 72	⊙
Rental income (Schedule 7) Gross **83** Net **16**			⊙
Taxable capital gains (Allowable capital losses) - complete and attach Schedule 2	17		
Indexed Security Investment Plan taxable capital gains (allowable capital losses) (attach copy of form T5-ISIP)	**915**		⊙
Other income (please specify)	**18**		⊙

Self-Employed Income

Business income	Gross **84**	Net **19**		⊙
Professional income	Gross **85**	Net **20**		⊙
Commission income	Gross **86**	Net **21**		⊙
Farming income	Gross **87**	Net **22**		⊙
Fishing income	Gross **88**	Net **23**		⊙

Total Income (add lines 08 to 23 inclusive - please enter this amount on line 24 on page 2)   24   26 517 52   ▷ 26 517 52

12

Please do not use this area	**82**	
Please do not use this area	**900**	

2 Calculation of Taxable Income

Total Income (from line 24 on page 1) 24 | 26 517 52

Deductions from Total Income

Canada or Quebec Pension Plan contributions		
Contributions through employment from Box (D) on all T4 slips (maximum $300.60)	25	300 60
Contribution payable on self-employed earnings (from page 3)	26	
Unemployment Insurance premiums from Box (E) on all T4 slips (maximum $460.72)	29	460 72
Registered pension plan contributions	32	1040 00
Registered retirement savings plan premiums (attach receipts)	33	
Registered home ownership savings plan contributions (attach receipts)	34	
Annual union, professional or like dues (attach receipts)	35	500 00
Tuition fees - claimable by student only (attach receipts)	36	
Child care expenses (complete and attach Schedule 5)	37	
Allowable business investment losses	38	
Other deductions (please specify)	39	

Add lines 25 to 39 inclusive 40 | 2101 32 ▷ 2101 32

Net Income (subtract line 40 from line 24) 41 | 24 416 20

Add: Accumulated Forward Averaging Amount Withdrawal (from form T581) 917 | 41(a)

Claim for Personal Exemptions

Basic Personal Exemption	Claim $3,770.00	3770 00
Age Exemption - If you were born in 1918 or earlier	Claim $2,360.00	

If you did not receive the Old Age Security Pension, attach a letter giving reasons.

Married Exemption - If applicable, please check ✓ box 1. or 2.

Married on or before December 31, 1983, and supported spouse in 1983

1. whose net income in that year, while married, was not over $570.00 1. ☐ Claim $3,300.00

2. whose net income in that year, while married, was over $570.00 2. ☐ 3,870 00

but not over $3,870.00

Subtract: spouse's net income while married

42 | 3300 00

If your marital status changed Claim

in 1983, please give date of change

Exemption for Wholly Dependent Children - Provide details below and claim according to child's age and net income. See Guide if child's net income exceeds limit.
Children born in 1966 or later - Claim $710.00 for each child whose net income was not over $2,450.00
Children born in 1965 or earlier - Claim $1,300.00 for each child whose net income was not over $2,570.00
and who, if born in 1961 or earlier, was in full-time attendance at a school or university or was infirm.

Name of child (attach list if space insufficient)	Relationship to you	Date of birth of child Day	Month	Year	If born in 1961 or earlier state whether infirm or school attended	Net income in 1983 $	Claim
GEORGE W.	SON	01	08	79		NIL	710 00
ANNE E.	DAUGHTER	19	11	81		NIL	710 00

Total claim for wholly dependent children 43 | 1420 00 ▷ 1420 00

Additional Personal Exemptions from Schedule 6 attached 44

Total Personal Exemptions (add above items) 45 | 8490 00 ▷ 8 490 00

Subtract line 45 from line 41(a) 46 | 15 926 20

Other deductions from Net Income

Standard deduction - Claim $100.00 (no receipts required) or total at line 50 below, but not both	47	100 00
Medical expenses - (attach receipts and complete Schedule 9)	48	
Subtract: 3% of 'Net Income' (line 41 above)		
Allowable portion of medical expenses		
Add: Charitable donations (attach all receipts)	49	
Total (If this amount is greater than $100.00, enter on line 47 above)	50	
Interest, dividends and capital gains deduction (attach completed Schedule 4)	51	
Pension income deduction	52	298 72
Deduction for blind persons or persons confined to a bed or wheelchair		
Claim relates to: Self ☐ or dependant other than spouse (specify)	53	
Education deduction (attach completed form T2202 or T2202A)	54	
Deductions transferred from spouse (attach completed Schedule 3)	55	
Gifts to Canada or a province (attach receipts)	56	
Unemployment Insurance benefit repayment payable from page 3	58	
Non-capital losses of other years	59	
Capital losses of other years (1972 to 1982)	60	

Add lines 47, 51 to 60 inclusive 61 | 398 72 ▷ 398 72

Subtract line 61 from line 46 61(a)

Subtract: Forward Averaging Elective Income Deduction from form T540 911

Taxable Income (enter this amount on page 4) 62 | 15 527 48

4 Summary of Tax and Credits
There are two methods of tax calculation (see Guide).

Taxable Income from line 62 on page 2 **15 527 48**

Calculation of Federal Tax Payable:

Federal Tax from Tax Table	(A)	**2528 00** *(column 2)*
Subtract: Unused portion of Spouse's Federal Tax Reduction	913	**200 00** •*(column 4)*
	(B)	**2328 00**
Federal Tax Payable - from line (B) or from line 63 on Schedule 1		63

Subtract: **Federal Political Contribution Tax Credit** from calculation on page 3 — 64

Share-Purchase Tax Credit from form T2111 — 922 •

Business Investment Tax Credit from form T2038(IND.) — 65 •

Employment Tax Credit Claimed from form T2208 — 66

Total of above credits **2328 00** ◊ **2328 00**

Federal Tax Payable Before Federal Forward Averaging Tax

Add: **Federal Forward Averaging Tax on Elective Income** from form T540 — 66(a)

Net Federal Tax Payable

Add: **Ontario Tax Payable** from Tax Table in Guide or from line 67 on Schedule 1 — 67 **1339 40** *(column 3)*

Add: Ontario Forward Averaging Tax on Elective Income from form T540 — 67(a)

Net Ontario Tax Payable **1339 40** ◊ **1339 40**

Canada Pension Plan Contribution Payable on Self-Employed Earnings from page 3 — 68

Unemployment Insurance Benefit Repayment Payable from page 3 — 69

Total Payable 70 **3667 40** •

Total Federal Political Contributions		
960 _____		
⊙	**Total tax deducted per information slips** 71 **3542 60** • ⊙	
Tax Adjusments	**Ontario Tax Credits** 74 •	
961 _____ •		
	Canada Pension Plan Overpayment 75 •	
Foreign Taxes Paid	**Unemployment Insurance Overpayment** 76 •	
962 _____ •		
⊙	**Amounts paid by instalments** 77 •	
Net Foreign Income	**Child Tax Credit** (from Schedule 10) 78 •	
963 _____		
⊙	Forward Averaging Tax Credit (from form T581) 923 • ⊙	
	Refund of Business Investment Tax Credit (from form T2038-IND.) 924 • ⊙	
975 _____	**Total Credits** **3542 60** ◊ **3542 60**	

Please enter this difference in applicable space below. **124 80**

A difference of less than $1.00 is neither charged nor refunded.

IMPORTANT: The inside front cover of your guide tells you when to expect your refund.

Refund 79 _____ •   Balance Due 80 **124 80** •

Amount Enclosed **124 80** •

Please attach cheque or money order **payable to the Receiver General. Do not mail cash.**
Payment is due not later than April 30, 1984.

Name and address of any individual or firm, other than the taxpayer, who has prepared this return for compensation.

Name _____

Address _____

Telephone

I hereby certify that the information given in this return and in any documents attached is true, correct and complete in every respect and fully discloses my income from all sources.

Please sign here _____

Date **April 30/84**   Telephone

It is a serious offence to make a false return.

Privacy Act Personal Information Bank number RC-T-P20

Form authorized and prescribed by order of the Minister of National Revenue for purposes of Part I of the Income Tax Act, Part I of the Canada Pension Plan and Part VIII of the Unemployment Insurance Act, 1971.

EXERCISE • SET 2

Many taxpayers who are paid wages or salaries and have no other source of income fill out a "special" or short income tax form which indicates where information received from the employer (in the form of standardized government T4 slips which are received before the end of February for income, etc., from the previous year) is to be recorded as well as personal exemptions and deductions.

Reproduced on pages 345 to 347 is a T1 Special Tax Form filled out by Jack Kwapis who earns $26 000 as an assistant accountant and whose personal exemptions you have already seen calculated in Exercise • Set 1. The sources of the information you see filled in are:

Income	T4 form from employer
Family Allowance Income	TFA1 slip issued by Health and Welfare Canada to Jack's wife
Interest Income	T5 form issued by the bank which paid him the indicated interest on his savings account
Canada or Quebec Pension Plan Contributions	T4 form from his employer
Unemployment Insurance Premiums	T4 form from his employer
Registered Pension Plan Contributions	T4 form from his employer
Annual Union or Professional Dues	T4 form from his employer or an official receipt
Total Tax Deducted	T4 form from his employer

For each of the following taxpayers, first calculate total income, total deductions, net income, total personal exemptions, medical expenses, and charitable donations. Then calculate the taxable income. Using current income tax tables, find the federal and provincial taxes and the total amount of tax owed.

1. Age 19; single; annual salary $16 530; Canada Pension Plan contributions, $215.14; Unemployment Insurance Premiums, $405.70

   Total tax: _____

2. Age 23; single; annual salary $17 200; Canada Pension Plan contributions, $277.20; Unemployment Insurance Premiums, $460; registered pension plan contributions, 4% of salary; union dues, $144; tuition fees for a night school course, $240

   Total tax: _____

3. Age 30; married; annual salary, $21 600; wife's income, $2000; one child 3 years old; Canada Pension Plan contributions, $300.60; Unemployment Insurance Premiums, $460.72; registered pension plan contributions, $480; Registered Retirement Savings Plan premiums, $2000; union dues, $226

   Total tax: _____

4. Age 20; unmarried; total earnings from 3 months work, $4797.60; tuition fees, $1265; attended a post-secondary institution for 8 months of the fiscal year; Unemployment Insurance Premiums, $42.75; Canada Pension Plan contributions, $47.25

Total tax: _____

5. Age 44; married; annual salary, $28 300; wife has no income; two children ages 14 and 18 attend secondary school and earned $325 and $2050 respectively; Canada Pension Plan contributions, $300.60; Unemployment Insurance Premiums, $460.72; registered pension plan contributions, 4% of salary; professional dues, $435

Total tax: _____

EXERCISE • SET 3

Before starting this exercise, read the information in the Federal Tax forms that you have obtained previously under the following headings: Employment Expense deduction, Taxable Family Allowance Payments, Interest and Investment Income, Rental Income, and Capital Cost Allowance.

A summary of the information you should obtain from reading the tax return and the tax guide follows. This information is obtained from the 1983 income tax forms. Since tax rules change frequently, you may find some differences.

EMPLOYMENT EXPENSE DEDUCTION

Most employees or part-time workers may claim $500 or 20% of 'total employment earnings', but it *must be the smaller* of the two amounts. However, in the case of a commission salesman, claims for employment expenses are claimed later under the heading "Other Allowable Expenses" and the regular "Employment Expense Deduction" is *not* claimed. If expenses *are* claimed under "Other Allowable Expenses" a separate form must be completed.

TAXABLE FAMILY ALLOWANCE PAYMENTS

The total amount of family allowance payments received by the mother *must* be entered as income by the parent receiving the higher income. The mother, however, is usually the person claiming "Child Tax Credits" whether she needs to declare any income or not and she does so on a separate tax return.

INTEREST AND INVESTMENT INCOME

Interest paid to the taxpayer on bank savings and on investments such as bonds, dividends from stock, mortgages, and annuities must be declared on a special form called a schedule and then entered on the Tax Return proper. At present, $1000 of this interest, if it is paid by a Canadian bank, corporation, or government, may be deducted later on the income tax return on the line reading "Interest, dividends and capital gains deduction".

RENTAL INCOME

All rents received by the taxpayer must be declared by the taxpayer on a special schedule headed "Statement of Real Estate Rentals". This schedule provides the taxpayer with spaces to enter the gross rent received and the expenses incurred to obtain the rental income such as property taxes, maintenance and repairs, mortgage interest, insurance, utilities, etc. Expenses are deducted from rents and the gross income and the net income are re-entered in the main body of the Tax Return.

CAPITAL COST ALLOWANCE (DEPRECIATION)

Certain assets used by a taxpayer to earn income (such as an apartment building) become less valuable over time and use. The government sets rates at which their value can be decreased each year called a capital cost allowance (C.C.A.). This decrease in value must be calculated on a special schedule headed "Capital Cost Allowance" and used as an income tax deduction. This deduction is then entered as an expense on the schedule for real estate rentals or used as an expense in declaration of business income. For example, a person renting boats to fishermen might calculate the depreciation allowance on the boats each year and use this depreciation as an expense in his Statement of Income and Expense which he would file with his tax return.

The depreciation allowance (C.C.A.) is not necessarily always claimed since it increases the capital gain (profit) on an asset when it is sold.

1. Kenneth Murphy is a commission salesman. He is 43 years of age, married, and has three children 18, 14, and 6 years. His wife's income last year was $1200 and that of his children was negligible.

   a) From the following information concerning Mr. Murphy's income and expenses from employment, calculate his net income from commissions. Assume all expenses incurred in earning commission are deductible.
   Commissions earned, $47 675
   Expenses: accounting fees paid, $150; telephone, $582; hotel accommodation, $2575; advertising and promotion, $576.50; bank charges $51.20; office supplies and postage, $287.35; gasoline, insurance, and auto repairs, $1813.68; share of household expenses allotted to one room as an office, $1574 _____

   b) The undepreciated capital cost of the automobile at the beginning of the year is $6400. Calculate the Capital Cost Allowance on the automobile using a depreciation rate of 30%. _____

   c) Using the following additional information and current income tax forms, calculate the balance of tax payable or refundable for Mr. Murphy.
   Registered pension fund contribution, $3500; taxable amount of dividends received from taxable Canadian corporations, $597.20; interest received on Canada Savings Bonds, $300; charitable donations, $550; Registered Retirement Savings Plan contributions, $1500; income tax instalments paid, $2700 _____

2. Rachel Drucker owns an apartment building containing 6 apartments. Rentals received last year total $21 675. Expenses of the apartment building are as follows: insurance, $540; interest paid on the mortgage, $2200; municipal taxes, $1620; repairs and maintenance, $776. Capital cost allowance is to be calculated at the rate of 5% on the undepreciated balance of $39 000 at the beginning of the year.

   a) Calculate Ms. Drucker's net income from real estate rentals. _____

   b) Calculate the balance of income tax payable or refundable using the current year's tax rates and the following information.
   Ms. Drucker is 39 years of age, is married, but her husband files a separate tax form. However she claims the deductions for their 3 children ages 12, 10, and 8. Rachel's T4 slip from employment shows the following information: salary, $20 800; Unemployment Insurance contributions, $300.60; Canada Pension Plan premiums,

$460.72; registered pension plan, 4% of salary; union dues, $120; medical expenses, $187.50; charitable donations, $105; income tax deducted, $3775.65 _____

19·3 INDIRECT FEDERAL TAXES

About 35% of the revenue of the Federal Government comes from taxes on manufactured goods and taxes on imported goods. These taxes are paid to the government before the goods are sold to the consumer and are therefore indirect taxes, "hidden" in the retail price of the goods.

Indirect taxes are applied to goods when they are sold by the manufacturer to the wholesaler or retailer or in the case of imports when they enter Canada.

CUSTOM DUTIES

The **customs duty** is a tax on a product imported into Canada, designed to make the product's final selling price comparable to that of similar Canadian products. This is a protective device that allows more expensive Canadian products to compete on the commercial market. The duty rate is called a **tariff** and depends on the nature of the product and the country from which the product is imported.

AD VALOREM DUTY

The rate is set as a percentage of the price paid by the Canadian importer.

SPECIFIC DUTY

The tax is set per unit of mass or measure (a specified number of cents per kilogram, per metre, per cubic metre, etc.).

British Preferential Tariff

These are special lower rates for imports from Great Britain and members of the British Commonwealth (Australia, Bahamas, Bermuda, India, Nigeria, etc.).

Most Favoured Nation Tariff

The rates are set to encourage trade with certain nations with whom Canada has a trade agreement (United States, Switzerland, Japan, France, Russia, China, Italy, Israel, Egypt, Brazil, Cuba, etc.).

General Tariff

The rates are for imports from all other nations (Afghanistan, Hungary, Libya, Romania, Thailand, etc.).

Tariffs for Calculating Customs Duties

These values are current at the time of publication, but may be changed at any time.

Goods	British Preferred	Most Favoured Nation	General
Automobiles	Free	11.4%	27.5%
Baskets, wire	10%	12.9%	35%
Bottles, glass	14.6%	14.6%	32.5%
Brushes	14.6%	14.6%	40%
Cabinets, wood	15%	16.9%	45%
Combs	10%	14.6%	30%
Drills, hand	10%	14.6%	35%
Fabrics, wholly cotton	22.5%	22.5%	35%
Jewellery, gold	17.6%	17.6%	45%
Jewellery, unfinished (for manufacture)	17.5%	17.5%	45%
Pencils, lead	10%	14.6%	35%
Perfumery (non-alcohol)	14.6%	14.6%	40%
Phonographs and parts thereof	5.6%	5.6%	25%
Plastic	15%	15%	30%
Radio and television apparatus	Free	11.4%	25%
Watches	14.6%	14.6%	35%*

*but not less than 40¢

EXERCISE • SET 1

EXAMPLE 1 What is the ad valorem duty on 250 m of cotton cloth imported from Great Britain and invoiced at $695.73?

SOLUTION Invoice price = $695.73
Ad Valorem Duty = 695.73 × 0.225
= 156.539

The Ad Valorem duty is $156.54.

1. What is the ad valorem duty on a shipment of wire baskets, total value $197.37 Canadian, from U.S.A.? _____

2. What is the ad valorem duty on a shipment of lead pencils from the U.S.A. invoiced at $36.45 Canadian? _____

3. What is the ad valorem duty on a car valued at $8975 Canadian shipped into Canada from the U.S.A.? _____

4. What is the ad valorem duty on a shipment of 100 gold bracelets worth $75.95 Canadian each from Hungary? _____

5. What is the ad valorem duty on a shipment of 50 colour TV sets priced at $495 Canadian each from Japan? _____

6. What is the ad valorem duty on a shipment of 75 watches valued at $69.50 Canadian each from Switzerland? _____

EXERCISE • SET 2

FEDERAL SALES TAX

A general sales tax of 9% is imposed by the Federal Government on the manufacturer's sale price of all goods produced and manufactured in Canada and also on the *duty-paid value* of all imported goods. Special classes of goods which are exempted from this tax or which are taxed at a lower rate include: educational materials and articles used for cultural and religious purposes; food products; electricity and natural gas; some building materials; materials and machinery used by fishermen, miners, farmers, and lumbermen in their trades.

EXAMPLE 2   What is the federal sales tax on a stove priced by a Canadian manufacturer at $376.50?

SOLUTION
Invoice price = $376.50
Federal sales tax = 376.50 × 0.09
= 33.885

The federal sales tax is $33.89.

EXAMPLE 3   What is the total of the ad valorem duty and the federal sales tax on a shipment of plastic wrap (boxed for sale as household wrap) from the U.S.A. invoiced at $215.10 Canadian?

SOLUTION
Invoice price = $215.10
Ad Valorem duty = 215.10 × 0.15
= 32.265
= $32.27
Duty-paid value = 215.10 + 32.27
= $247.37
Federal Sales tax = 247.37 × 0.09
= 22.263
= $22.26
Total duty and tax = $32.27 + $22.26
= $54.53

1. Calculate the federal sales tax on the following manufactured items.

   a) a lawn mower, manufacturer's price, $77.95 _____

   b) a stove, priced by the manufacturer at $307 _____

   c) a bicycle, priced by the manufacturer at $80.25 _____

   d) 20 lawn chairs, manufacturer's price, $5.75 each _____

2. The total cost to manufacture a jigsaw is $20.25. The manufacturer adds on a margin of profit of 10% of cost price.

   a) What is the manufacturer's price for the jigsaw? _____

   b) What is the federal sales tax? _____

   c) What does the jigsaw cost a retailer? _____

3. If a retailer puts a 30% markup on his cost price for the jigsaw in Question 2, what is the retail price to the customer? _____

4. Find the ad valorem duty, the duty-paid value, the federal sales tax (on the duty-paid value), and the total cost of:
   a) a shipment of wire bicycle baskets valued at $395.50 Canadian from Hungary.

   _____ , _____ , _____ , _____

   b) a shipment of 20 boxes of combs priced at $2.00 Canadian a box from Italy.

   _____ , _____ , _____ , _____

   c) a shipment of 150 bottles of perfume (non-alcohol) at $5.75 Canadian a bottle from France.

   _____ , _____ , _____ , _____

   d) a shipment of 350 boxes of lead pencils at $1.25 Canadian a box from England.

   _____ , _____ , _____ , _____

EXERCISE • SET 3 _____

An additional tax is levied on some luxury items whether they are produced in Canada or imported. This **excise tax** is levied on the duty-paid value of imported goods at the port of entry or on the manufacturer's sale price of Canadian products at the time of sale by the manufacturer.

Excise Tax Rates

Goods	Rate
Lighters	10¢ per lighter
Coin, disc or token operated games or amusement devices	10%
Smoker's accessories	10%
Cigars	20.5%
Matches	10%
Clocks and watches	10%*
Jewellery	10%
Cigarettes (for each 5 cigarettes or fraction of 5)	4.76¢
Playing cards (for every 54 or fraction of 54)	20¢
Wine (per litre), less than 7% alcohol	19.30¢
Champagne and sparkling wines (per litre)	40.21¢

* of the amount by which the sales price or duty-paid value of each watch or clock exceeds $50.00

EXAMPLE 4 What is the total of ad valorem duty, federal sales tax, and excise tax on a shipment of gold jewellery from Thailand invoiced at $5222 Canadian?

SOLUTION Invoice price = $5222
Ad Valorem Duty = 5222 × 0.45
    = $2349.90
Duty-paid value = $5222 + $2349.90
    = $7571.90
Federal Sales Tax = 7571.90 × 0.09
    = 681.471
    = $681.47
Excise Tax = 7571.90 × 0.10
    = 757.190
    = $757.19
Total duty and tax = $2349.90 + $681.47 + $757.19
    = $3788.56

EXAMPLE 5 Find the total cost of importing from Switzerland a shipment of 100 watches invoiced at $92.50 Canadian per watch.

SOLUTION

Invoice price = 92.50 × 100

            = 9250.00 $ 9 250.00

Ad valorem duty = 9250.00 × 0.146

               = 1350.500   1 350.50

Duty-paid value = $10 600.50

Federal Sales Tax = 10 600.50 × 0.09

             = 954.045   954.05

Duty-paid value per watch

    = 10 600.50 ÷ 100

    = 106.005

    = 106.01

Excise Tax

    = (106.01 − 50.00) × 0.10

    = 56.01 × 0.10

    = 5.60

Total excise tax: 5.60 × 100

             = 560   560.00

Total value of shipment $12 114.55

1. The Fine Arts Department of Confan College ordered five dozen artist's brushes from England at $11.39 Canadian per dozen.

a) Calculate the ad valorem duty. _____

b) Calculate the duty-paid value. _____

c) Calculate the federal sales tax. _____

d) How much did Confan College pay for the brushes? _____

2. Stelmac Importers ordered a shipment of 20 hand drills from England at $16.13 Canadian a drill.

a) What is the ad valorem duty? _____

b) What is the duty-paid value? _____

c) What is the federal sales tax? _____

d) What is the total cost to Stelmac Importers? _____

3. Rimer's Jewellers ordered 50 watches from Switzerland at $86.21 Canadian per watch.

a) What is the ad valorem duty? _____

b) What is the duty-paid value? _____

c) Calculate the excise tax. _____

d) Calculate the federal sales tax. _____

e) What is the total cost of the watches to Rimer's Jewellers? _____

4. Southern Importers ordered 1000 gold chain necklaces from France at $95.75 Canadian a necklace.

   a) Calculate the ad valorem duty. _____

   b) Calculate the duty-paid value. _____

   c) Calculate the excise tax. _____

   d) Calculate the federal sales tax. _____

   e) What did Southern Importers pay for the order? _____

5. In Question 4, if Southern Importers add on a markup of 35%, what is their wholesale selling price per gold chain necklace? _____

6. Rimer's Jewellers bought some of the necklaces in Question 5 from Southern Importers and added a retail markup of 50%. How much does a customer buying a gold chain necklace from Rimer's Jewellers pay? _____

7. Collins-Sharpe and Company ordered a grandfather clock from England worth $795.75 Canadian.

   a) What is the excise tax? (There is no ad valorem duty.) _____

   b) What is the federal sales tax? _____

   c) If a retail markup of 30% is added by Collins-Sharpe and Company, how much will a customer have to pay to purchase the clock? _____

19·4 REVIEW

EXERCISE • SET 1

1. Calculate the municipal taxes on a commercial property assessed for: land $10 000, buildings $36 000; if the commercial tax rate is 58.6 mills to the dollar and the business tax is 15% of the commercial property tax. _____

2. Jill Szever owns a store which is assessed for: land $8000 and buildings $24 000. If the commercial property tax is 44.7 mills and the business tax is 20% of the commercial property tax, what are the total taxes for the store? _____

3. Using the current income tax forms, calculate the total personal exemptions for Jane Trefold who is 21, single, and has no dependents. _____

4. Using the same forms, calculate the total personal exemption for Hap Nickel who is 35, married, wife's income $2100, has 3 children aged 8, 11, and 13, and has no other dependents. _____

5. Kay Henry is 45 and a widow. Her mother lives with her and is totally dependent. Kay has one son, age 21, attending university who had a net summer income of $1795. Calculate Kay's total personal exemptions. _____

6. What is the ad valorem duty on a shipment of combs from Italy invoiced at $587.98 Canadian? _____

7. What is the ad valorem duty on a shipment of semi-precious stones for manufacturing costume jewellery if the invoice price is $3789 and if the stones are shipped from Romania? _____

EXERCISE • SET 2 _____

1. Property: 1194 Sparks Street   Zone: C2

Assessment	Land	Buildings	Rate
Commercial	$8 000	$10 000	56.7 mills
Residential	2 000	15 000	50.8 mills

Calculate the total tax bill. _____

2. Property: 72 Cliffside Terrace
Assessment: $75 000

	Percent	Rate
Commercial	65%	42.3 mills
Residential	35%	40.5 mills

Calculate the total tax bill. _____

For each taxpayer, calculate total income, total deductions, net income, personal exemptions, and taxable income. Using current income tax forms, calculate the federal and provincial taxes and the total tax due.

3. Age 22; single; total earnings from 4 months work, $5673.92; tuition fees $765; attended a post-secondary institution for 8 months of the year; Unemployment Insurance Premiums, $123.50; Canada Pension Plan contributions, $156.70

Total tax:_____

4. Age 33; married; annual salary, $27 800; wife's income, $1250; two children, 4 and 6 years old; Canada Pension Plan contributions, $359.20; Unemployment Insurance Premiums, $459.34; registered pension plan contributions, $1350; Registered Retirement Savings Plan premiums, $1000; union dues, $275

Total tax: _____

5. a) Calculate the federal sales tax on the manufacturer's price of $247 for a refrigerator. _____

  b) If the retailer puts a 40% markup on his cost price, what is the retail price to the customer? _____

6. Find the ad valorem duty, the duty-paid value, the federal sales tax on the duty-paid value, and the total cost of a shipment of non-alcoholic perfume from France invoiced at $2769.50 Canadian. _____ , _____ , _____ , _____

EXERCISE • SET 3

1. Property at 795 Ridgewood Road is listed on the municipal assessment rolls as follows.
Owner: James E. Kline
first floor rented to Audrey Brown for purposes of operating a hardware store
second floor rented to C.A. Haak as an apartment

	Land	Buildings	Rate
Total assessment	$8 900	$30 500	
Commercial	67%	60%	52.3 mills
Residential	33%	40%	50.7 mills

Business tax = 30% of the commercial property tax

Calculate: **a)** total tax bill sent to James Kline, _____

           b) business tax paid by Audrey Brown. _____

2. Helen Van Tuyl rents the second floor of her home as an apartment. The rent totalled $4740 for the past year. Expenses charged to the apartment during the year were: insurance, $297.50; share of interest paid on the mortgage, $950; share of municipal taxes, $578.30; share of water and sewage, $99.80; repairs and maintenance, $369.50. Helen claims no capital cost allowance.

a) Calculate Helen Van Tuyl's net income from real estate rentals. _____

b) Calculate the balance of the income tax payable or refundable using the current year's tax rates and the following information.
Mrs. Van Tuyl is a widow, 42 years old, with one child, 17 years old, in secondary school, who earned a total of $1397.60 during the past year. She has no other dependents.
Her T4 slip from employment shows the following information: salary, $18 760; Unemployment Insurance contributions, $286.40; Canada Pension Plan premiums, $430.50; registered company pension plan, $750; union dues, $250; income tax deducted, $3276.40 _____

3. Western Imports Limited ordered 500 gold bracelets from Thailand at $75.80 Canadian per bracelet.

a) Calculate the ad valorem duty. _____

b) Calculate the duty-paid value. _____

c) Calculate the federal sales tax. _____

d) Calculate the excise tax. _____

e) How much did Western Imports pay for the order? _____

UNIT
6

Mathematics
of
Investment

CHAPTER 20

DEPRECIATION

When a business purchases assets such as buildings, machinery, and office equipment, the expected life of each asset is determined. The cost of the asset, then, is a cost of doing business continually over the number of years that it is expected to be useful.

Since the asset is part of the total value of the capital goods owned by the business, its value as a capital good must be gradually "written off" over its lifetime. This gradual decrease in value assigned to an asset is called **depreciation**. Depreciation is a cost of doing business and is called **depreciation expense** in income statements. Accounting departments have several methods of depreciating capital assets and the most important ones will be discussed and demonstrated in this chapter.

20·1 STRAIGHT LINE DEPRECIATION

The **straight line** method of depreciation assumes that the expense of an asset, such as a typewriter, is the same for each year that it is useful.

EXAMPLE   Wallace Sales purchased an electronic typewriter for $1200. It is expected that the typewriter will be used for five years and have a trade-in value of $200 on a new typewriter at the end of the five years.
a) What is the straight line depreciation per year?
b) Draw up a straight line depreciation schedule for the 5 year period.

SOLUTION   **a)** Total cost of the typewriter
$$= 1200 - 200$$
$$= \$1000$$

Depreciation expense per year $= \dfrac{1000}{5}$

$$= \$200$$

b) Straight Line Depreciation Schedule

Year	(1) Book Value at Beginning of Year	(2) Depreciation	Accumulated Depreciation	(1)-(2) Book Value at End of Year
1	$1 200	$200	$ 200	$1 000
2	1 000	200	400	800
3	800	200	600	600
4	600	200	800	400
5	400	200	1 000	200

EXERCISE

1. A photocopier is purchased at a price of $10 000 and has an expected life of 5 years. It is estimated that it will have a trade-in value of $2000 at the end of the 5 years.

   a) What is the straight line depreciation per year? _____

   b) Draw up a straight line depreciation schedule for the 5 year period.

2. Del Van Haak purchased a tractor for $22 000 which he expects to use for 8 years at which time he estimates that he can turn it in for $4000 on a new tractor. Draw up a straight line depreciation schedule for the tractor for the 8 year period.

3. Kali's Hardware purchased a delivery van for $12 500. They expect to keep the van for 4 years at which time they estimate that they can turn it in for $4000. During its fourth year of use the van was in an accident and totally demolished. What was its book value at the time of the accident? _____

4. Quality Printers Limited purchased an offset duplicator at a price of $2600 with an expected life of 5 years and no trade-in value. At the end of 4 years the duplicator was sold for $900.

   a) What was the book value at the time of sale? _____

   b) Would you consider that the company made a profit or loss and by how much?

20·2 FIXED RATE DEPRECIATION

Many accountants depreciate capital assets at a **fixed rate**, a constant percent of the original cost.

EXAMPLE Jenning's Hardware has a wooden frame garage at the back of its premises. The original building cost $15 000 and it is depreciated at a rate of 10% per year. Draw up a depreciation schedule for the first six years.

SOLUTION Depreciation Schedule

Year	(1) Book Value at Beginning of Year	(2) Depreciation (1) × 0.10	Accumulated Depreciation	(1)-(2) Book Value at End of Year
1	$15 000.00	$1 500.00	$1 500.00	$13 500.00
2	13 500.00	1 350.00	2 850.00	12 150.00
3	12 150.00	1 215.00	4 065.00	10 935.00
4	10 935.00	1 093.50	5 158.50	9 841.50
5	9 841.50	984.15	6 142.65	8 857.35
6	8 857.35	885.74	7 028.39	7 971.61

EXERCISE

1. Dalt's Groceteria and Meats purchased a freezer vault for $20 000. It is to be depreciated at the rate of 20% per year. Draw up a depreciation schedule for the first six years following the method of the example.

2. Northern Mines Ltd. purchased mine excavating equipment at a cost of $550 000. It is to be depreciated at the rate of 50% per year. Draw up a depreciation schedule for the first four years following the method of the example.

3. Riverview Hospital purchased emergency generating equipment for $179 500. It is to be depreciated at the rate of 25% per year. Calculate the book value of the equipment at the beginning of the fourth year. _____

4. Carter's Travel Association bought an outdoor electric sign for $32 000. The sign depreciates at the rate of 35% per year. Calculate the accumulated depreciation at the end of the fifth year. _____

20·3 DEPRECIATION AS AN INCOME TAX DEDUCTION

The Federal Government allows businesses to use the fixed rate depreciation of their capital assets as part of the cost of doing business. The book value at the beginning of the year is called the **Undepreciated Capital Cost** (U.C.C.) for that year. The depreciation taken when income tax is filed is called the **Capital Cost Allowance** (C.C.A.) for that year. The government sets rates at which the C.C.A. can be taken, for example: ships (15%); frame buildings (10%); cars (30%); outdoor advertising signs (35%); and telephone systems (8%).

EXAMPLE John Gremalski drives a car, owned by his business, for business trips only. The U.C.C. of the car at the beginning of 1984 is $8500. Calculate the C.C.A. and the U.C.C. at the end of each tax year for 1984, 1985, and 1986 if the Income Tax Act allows John a C.C.A. rate of 30%.

SOLUTION Depreciation Schedule

Year	U.C.C. at Beginning of Year	C.C.A. (30%)	U.C.C. at End of Year
1984	$8 500.00	$2 550.00	$5 950.00
1985	5 950.00	1 785.00	4 165.00
1986	4 165.00	1 249.50	2 915.50

EXERCISE

1. Complete the following depreciation schedule.

Year	U.C.C. at Beginning of Year	C.C.A. (25%)	U.C.C. at End of Year
1985	$10 900.00	_____	_____
1986	_____	_____	_____
1987	_____	_____	_____
1988	_____	_____	_____

2. Draw up a depreciation schedule, as in Question 1, for 1985, 1986, 1987, and 1988 for an asset with U.C.C. at the beginning of 1985 of $29 600 and C.C.A. rate 15%.

3. A corporation owns an aircraft used for business purposes. It has a U.C.C. of $375 000 at the beginning of 1985 and its C.C.A. rate is 40%. Calculate its U.C.C. at the beginning of 1990. _____

4. Union Ship Lines owns its own private docks which had a U.C.C. of $750 000 at the end of 1980. C.C.A. rate is 5%. Calculate the U.C.C. for the docks at the end of 1986. _____

20·4 DEPRECIATION BY UNITS OF PRODUCTION

Sometimes an asset, such as a piece of machinery, is depreciated according to the number of units of work it produces in any given year. To depreciate by this method, the total number of units that the machine will produce in its lifetime must be estimated.

EXAMPLE Canacom Ltd. purchases a stamping machine at a cost of $57 000. It is estimated that, during its life, it will stamp 3 000 000 drawer pulls. Calculate the depreciation each year if it stamps the following numbers of drawer pulls.

Year	Number of Units Stamped
1	250 000
2	325 000
3	350 000
4	270 000

SOLUTION Cost per unit produced $= \dfrac{57\ 000}{3\ 000\ 000} = \$0.019$

Year	Number of Units Stamped	Depreciation
1	250 000	250 000 × 0.019 = $4 750.00
2	325 000	325 000 × 0.019 = 6 175.00
3	350 000	350 000 × 0.019 = 6 650.00
4	270 000	270 000 × 0.019 = 5 130.00

EXERCISE

1. Draw up a depreciation schedule showing book value at the beginning of the year, depreciation, accumulated depreciation, and book value at the end of the year for the stamping machine in the preceding example.

2. Frazer Publishing purchased a bookbinding machine at a cost of $360 000. It is estimated that it will bind 2 000 000 books and then be scrapped. Calculate the depreciation each year and draw up a depreciation schedule as in Question 1 if the following numbers of books are bound.

Year	Books Bound
1	300 000
2	250 000
3	500 000
4	420 000
5	350 000

3. Mainline Cleaners Incorporated purchased an industrial dryer at a cost of $72 000. It is estimated that it will dry 900 000 garments and then be scrapped. Calculate the depreciation for the year in which the machine was used to dry 36 500 garments.

4. Lakeview Industries purchased a delivery van for $15 000. It is estimated that it will be driven 200 000 km and then be scrapped. Calculate the depreciation for a year in which it was driven 60 000 km.

20·5 DEPRECIATION BY SERVICE HOURS

Since machinery with moving parts will eventually wear out, depreciation can be taken according to the number of hours per year that a machine is used. An estimate of the total production hours for the machine's lifetime must be made at the time it is purchased.

EXAMPLE 1 The motor for a drive shaft cost $1665 when it was purchased. Its estimated productive life is 18 500 hours. Calculate the depreciation expense each year if the motor is used for the following numbers of hours.

Year	Hours Used
1	3 600
2	4 000
3	3 200
4	3 800

SOLUTION   Cost per hour $= \dfrac{1665}{18\ 500} = \$0.09$

Year	Hours Used	Depreciation
1	3 600	3 600 × 0.09 = \$324.00
2	4 000	4 000 × 0.09 = 360.00
3	3 200	3 200 × 0.09 = 288.00
4	3 800	3 800 × 0.09 = 342.00

EXAMPLE 2   A steam generator is purchased for \$560 000. Its estimated life is 880 000 hours and at that time it will have a scrap value of \$76 000. Calculate the depreciation per year if the generator is used for 80 000 hours per year for 11 years.

SOLUTION   Cost per hour $= \dfrac{560\ 000 - 76\ 000}{880\ 000}$

$$= \dfrac{484\ 000}{880\ 000} = \$0.55$$

Depreciation per year $= 80\ 000 \times 0.55 = \$44\ 000$

EXERCISE

1. Draw up a depreciation schedule showing book value at the beginning of the year, depreciation, accumulated depreciation, and book value at the end of the year for the motor in Example 1.
2. Sheo Auditing Incorporated installed an air cooling system for their offices. The system cost \$18 000 and its estimated life is 30 000 hours. Calculate the depreciation for each year and complete the following depreciation schedule.

Depreciation Schedule

Book Value at Beginning of Year	Number of Hours Used	Depreciation	Accumulated Depreciation	Book Value at End of Year
\$18 000	2 700	_____	_____	_____
_____	3 100	_____	_____	_____
_____	3 300	_____	_____	_____
_____	2 600	_____	_____	_____
_____	3 550	_____	_____	_____

3. Bayfield Motel purchased a motor for the filtering system of their swimming pool at a cost of $765 with an estimated life of 15 000 hours and a scrap value of $60. If the motor runs for 3000 hours a year, find the annual depreciation. _____

20·6 REVIEW

EXERCISE

1. Hillcrest Printers purchased a photocopier for $11 900 which they expect to use for 9 years and which should have a trade-in value of $2000 at that time. Draw up a straight line depreciation schedule for the photocopier for the 9 year period.

2. Sterling Business College purchased an emergency electrical generating system, at a cost of $27 500, to turn on spotlights in the halls in case of a power failure. It is to be depreciated at the rate of 25% per year. Calculate the book value at the end of 6 years. _____

3. Jim's Dairy Bar owns a fluorescent sign outside the building which has a U.C.C. of $7600 at the end of 1986. If it is depreciated at the rate of 35% per year, what is its U.C.C. at the end of 1992? _____

4. Halifax Hardware purchased a key cutting machine which cost $1980. It is estimated that, during its life, it will cut 100 000 keys. Complete the following depreciation schedule for the machine.

Depreciation Schedule

Book Value at Beginning of Year	Number of Units Cut	Depreciation	Accumulated Depreciation	Book Value at End of Year
$1 980	5 000	_____	_____	_____
_____	6 000	_____	_____	_____
_____	4 500	_____	_____	_____

5. A steam generator was purchased for $15 000. Its estimated life is 40 000 hours; after this it will have a scrap value of $3000. Complete the following depreciation schedule for the generator.

Depreciation Schedule

Book Value at Beginning of Year	Number of Hours Used	Depreciation	Accumulated Depreciation	Book Value at End of Year
$15 000	7 000	_____	_____	_____
_____	8 500	_____	_____	_____
_____	9 000	_____	_____	_____
_____	8 000	_____	_____	_____

CHAPTER 21
COMPOUND INTEREST

We have considered many examples in which interest is paid on money borrowed or lent. Banks offer special types of savings accounts that pay higher rates of interest if money is left in them for longer periods of time than in regular chequing accounts. If that money is left untouched, interest will be paid into the account and becomes part of the principal when the next interest period ends. The bank then pays interest on the interest that has been added to the original principal. This is called **compound interest**.

In this chapter we will study how this type of interest accumulates and discuss applications to special situations in the business world.

21·1 ACCUMULATED INTEREST

Suppose that James Williams borrows $100 and agrees to pay 8% per annum simple interest on the loan. At the end of the five years, he is to pay back the $100. James's payments for the five years are shown in the following table.

Year	Amount of the Loan at the Beginning of the Year	Simple Interest at 8% per annum	Payment at the End of the Year
1	$100.00	100 x 0.08 = 8.00	$ 8.00
2	100.00	100 x 0.08 = 8.00	8.00
3	100.00	100 x 0.08 = 8.00	8.00
4	100.00	100 x 0.08 = 8.00	8.00
5	100.00	100 x 0.08 = 8.00	108.00
		Total amount repaid	$140.00

Suppose, however, that when he made the loan, Mr. Williams agreed to make no payment until the end of the five years. At this time he is to pay back the $100 plus the accumulated or **compound interest**. His debt from year to year, and his final payment of the loan plus interest are shown in the following table.

Year	Amount owing at the beginning of the year	Interest at 8% per annum	Amount owing at the end of the year
1	$100.00	100.00 x 0.08 = 8.00	$108.00
2	108.00	108.00 x 0.08 = 8.64	116.64
3	116.64	116.64 x 0.08 = 9.33	125.97
4	125.97	125.97 x 0.08 = 10.08	136.05
5	136.05	136.05 x 0.08 = 10.88	146.93
		Total amount repaid	$146.93

In this case the $46.93 in interest paid on the loan is called compound interest.

Tables have been constructed to help us make calculations of the amounts accumulated when the interest is compounded over a period of time. These tables show the amounts to which $1 will accumulate at different interest rates over given periods of time.

We can calculate the amount James Williams owed on the loan on which interest accumulated by formula.

principal borrowed   number of interest periods

$$A = 100(1 + 0.08)^5$$

interest rate as a decimal quantity

To find the value of $(1 + 0.08)^5$ or $(1.08)^5$, turn to the tables headed *Amount of 1* in the Appendix. Look down the column headed 8% to the number listed in the row opposite $n = 5$.

n	6%	6.5%	7%	8%	9%	10%
1	1.060 000	1.065 000	1.070 000	1.080 000	1.090 000	1.100 000
2	1.123 600	1.134 225	1.144 900	1.166 400	1.188 100	1.210 000
3	1.191 016	1.207 950	1.225 043	1.259 712	1.295 029	1.331 000
4	1.262 477	1.286 466	1.310 796	1.360 489	1.411 582	1.464 100
5	1.338 226	1.370 087	1.402 552	1.469 328	1.538 624	1.610 510
6	1.418 519	1.459 142	1.500 730	1.586 874	1.677 100	1.771 561
7	1.503 630	1.553 987	1.605 781	1.713 824	1.828 039	1.948 717
8	1.593 848	1.654 996	1.718 186	1.850 930	1.992 563	2.143 589
9	1.689 479	1.762 570	1.838 459	1.999 005	2.171 893	2.357 948
10	1.790 848	1.877 137	1.967 151	2.158 925	2.367 364	2.593 742

$(1.08)^5 = 1.469\ 328$

$A = 100(1.08)^5 = 146.9328$

$= \$146.93$

EXAMPLE 1   What is the amount (accumulated value) of $200 invested at 9% per annum, compounded annually for 3 years?

SOLUTION

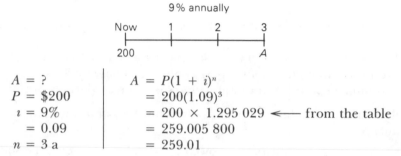

$A = ?$

$P = \$200$

$i = 9\%$

$\quad = 0.09$

$n = 3$ a

$A = P(1 + i)^n$

$\quad = 200(1.09)^3$

$\quad = 200 \times 1.295\ 029 \longleftarrow$ from the table

$\quad = 259.005\ 800$

$\quad = 259.01$

The amount of $200 at 9% per annum compounded annually for three years is $259.01.

EXAMPLE 2   What is the amount (accumulated value) of $1325 invested at 7% per annum compounded annually for 8 years?

SOLUTION

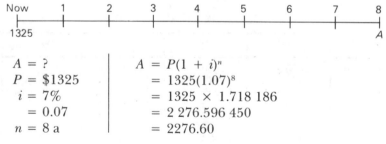

$A = ?$

$P = \$1325$

$i = 7\%$

$\quad = 0.07$

$n = 8$ a

$A = P(1 + i)^n$

$\quad = 1325(1.07)^8$

$\quad = 1325 \times 1.718\ 186$

$\quad = 2\ 276.596\ 450$

$\quad = 2276.60$

The amount of $1325 for 8 years at 7% per annum compounded annually is $2276.60.

EXAMPLE 3   What is the amount of $1325 invested for 8 years at 7% per annum compounded semi-annually?

SOLUTION

NOTE   There are two interest periods per year; therefore there are $8 \times 2 = 16$ interest periods and $n = 16$.
The interest rate for one year is 7%; therefore the interest rate for one interest period (half a year) is $7\% \div 2 = 3.5\%$ and $i = 3.5\%$.

$$
\begin{aligned}
A &= ? \\
P &= \$1325 \\
i &= \frac{7\%}{2} = 3.5\% \\
&= 0.035 \\
n &= 2 \times 8 = 16
\end{aligned}
\qquad
\begin{aligned}
A &= P(1 + i)^n \\
&= 1325(1.035)^{16} \\
&= 1325(1.733\ 986) \\
&= 2\ 297.531\ 450 \\
&= 2297.53
\end{aligned}
$$

The amount is $2297.53.

EXERCISE

Complete the following table.

	Principal	Time	Annual Rate	Compounded	Accumulated Value		
1.	$ 350	15 a	6%	annually	$350(1.06)^{15}$	=	$350 \times 2.396\ 558$
						=	_____
2.	$1 475	5 a	7%	semi-annually	$1\ 475(1.035)^{10}$	=	$1\ 475 \times 1.410\ 599$
						=	_____
3.	$ 545	7 a	8%	quarterly	$545(1.02)^{28}$	=	$545 \times 1.741\ 024$
						=	_____
4.	$3 436	5 a	5.5%	annually	$3\ 436(1.055)^{5}$	=	$3\ 436 \times$ _____
						=	_____
5.	$1 225	3 a	6%	semi-annually	$1\ 225(1.03)^{6}$	=	$1\ 225 \times$ _____
						=	_____
6.	$5 500	6 a	6%	quarterly	$5\ 500(1.015)^{24}$	=	$5\ 550 \times$ _____
						=	_____
7.	$4 250	10 a	5%	semi-annually	$4\ 250(1.025)^{20}$	=	$4\ 250 \times$ _____
						=	_____
8.	$1 235	3 months	12%	monthly	$1\ 235(1.01)^{3}$	=	$1\ 235 \times$ _____
						=	_____

9. Calculate A. _____

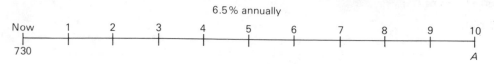

6.5% annually

10. Calculate A. _____

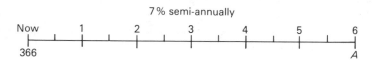

7% semi-annually

11. Calculate A. _____

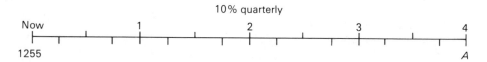

10% quarterly

Calculate each accumulated value.

	Principal	Time	Annual Rate	Compounded	Accumulated Value
12.	$ 324	12 a	5.5%	annually	
13.	775	4 a	7%	semi-annually	
14.	1 407	9 a	6%	quarterly	
15.	3 275	8 a	6%	semi-annually	
16.	490	6 a	8%	quarterly	
17.	1 950	15 a	7%	annually	
18.	520	14 a	4%	semi-annually	
19.	835	25 a	8%	annually	
20.	2 325	10 months	12%	monthly	
21.	5 765	1.5 a	18%	quarterly	

22. Ms. Scott sold her cottage and received $26 750 cash. She deposited the money in a savings account at 8% per annum compounded quarterly. After four years how much money did Ms. Scott have to purchase another cottage if she made no withdrawals from her account? _____

23. What is the accumulated value or amount of $3450 for nine years if interest is calculated at 8% per annum compounded quarterly? _____

24. Bill Barnes deposited $55 in a special savings account. He moved and forgot about the account. The bank managed to locate Bill ten years later. If the bank pays interest at the rate of 10% per annum compounded quarterly, how much money did Bill have in the account? _____

25. A loan of $25 000 bears interest at a rate of 8% per annum, compounded semi-annually. What is the amount of the debt at the end of five years? _____

21·2 DAILY INTEREST ACCOUNTS

Because most banks and savings institutions hold individual accounts in computer data files, it is possible for them to offer interest which is **compounded daily**. These accounts do not offer interest rates as high as those for prime savings accounts, but in accounts which are active (i.e., money is deposited and withdrawn frequently) the interest which accumulates is more than in an active account for which the interest is paid only on the minimum balance for the month.

EXAMPLE Mary Carnahan has a daily interest savings account on which interest is compounded daily at 8% per annum if a minimum balance of $2000 is kept in the account. If she has a balance of $3567 in the account for 30 days with no deposits or withdrawals, how much is in the account at the end of the 30 days?

SOLUTION

$A = ?$
$P = \$3567$
$i = 8\% \div 365$
$\quad = 0.08 \div 365$
$\quad = 0.000\ 219\ 2$
$n = 30\ \text{d}$

$A = P(1 + i)^n$
$\quad = 3567 \times (1.000\ 219\ 2)^{30}$
$\quad = 3590.53$

Mary has $3590.53 in the account at the end of the 30 days.

NOTE Tables of the *Amount of 1* at current interest rates divided by 365 are too lengthy to publish in this book. If you have a calculator with a key marked $\boxed{y^x}$ or $\boxed{x^y}$ you can solve the example by entering 1.000 219 2, then press the $\boxed{y^x}$ or $\boxed{x^y}$ key, then entering 30, then press the $\boxed{=}$ key followed by the $\boxed{\times}$ key, then entering 3567, press the $\boxed{=}$ key to obtain the answer.

If you try this and are successful, answer the questions in the following exercise. If not, continue with Section 21.3.

EXERCISE

1. Calculate the amount in a daily interest account at the end of 15 days if the principal is $1500 and the interest rate is 4% per annum compounded daily, if no deposits or withdrawals are made. _____

2. Calculate the amount in a daily interest account at the end of 20 days if the principal at the beginning of the period is $4600, no deposits or withdrawals are made, and interest is compounded daily at the rate of 7.5% per annum. _____

3. Calculate the amount in a daily interest account at the end of 90 days if the principal at the beginning of the period is $5900, no deposits or withdrawals are made, and interest is compounded daily at the rate of 6.25% per annum. _____

4. Joan Sachs has a daily interest savings account which pays daily interest at the rate of 4% per annum if the balance is under $1000 and daily interest at the rate of 6.5% per annum if the balance is $1000 or more. If she had a balance of $3275 at the beginning of a 30 day period, but withdrew $2500 15 days after the beginning of the period,

   a) what balance did Joan have in the account at the end of the period if she made no further deposits or withdrawals? _____

   b) How much interest did her account accumulate? _____

5. Calculate the real annual rate of interest earned in the account in Question 4. _____

21·3 FURTHER CALCULATIONS OF AMOUNTS

If George McCance deposits $725 in the bank and leaves it to collect accumulated interest for 5.5 years, the interest for the last half year cannot be calculated by the methods of Section 21·1 since the table does not show half yearly periods.

The following examples show how the calculations of amounts can be made in situations where interest accumulates for a specified number of interest periods followed by only part of an interest period.

EXAMPLE 1   What is the amount or accumulated value of $725 invested at 7% per annum compounded annually for 5.5 years?

SOLUTION

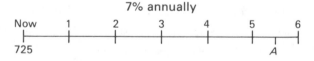

Step 1:
At the end of five years

$A = ?$ $A = P(1 + i)^n$
$P = \$725$ $= 725(1.07)^5$
$i = 7\%$ $= 725 \times 1.402\ 552$
$\quad = 0.07$ $= 1\ 016.850\ 200$
$n = 5\ a$

The amount at the end of 5 years is $1016.85.

Step 2:
This amount $1016.85 is left invested for another half year.
For the half year

A = ?
P = \$1016.85
i = 7% per annum
    = 3.5% for a half year
    = 0.035
n = 1 (one period of half
      a year at 3.5%)

$A = P (1 + i)^n$
    = $1016.85(1.035)^1$
    = 1016.85×1.035
    = 1 052.439 750

The amount of $725 for 5.5 years at 7% per annum compounded annually is $1052.44.

The two steps in the above solution can be done in one calculation.
A = (Amount for 5 years)(1.035)
   = $725(1.07)^5(1.035)^1$
   = Amount for 5.5 years
The amount of work involved in doing Example 1 may be decreased as is demonstrated in Example 2 and Example 3.

EXAMPLE 2 What is the amount of $342 invested at 6% per annum compounded semi-annually for 7.75 years?

SOLUTION

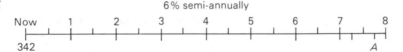

The rate for a half year = $\dfrac{6\%}{2}$ = 3% = 0.03

The rate for a quarter year = $\dfrac{6\%}{4}$ = 1.5% = 0.015

$A = 342 \times (1.03)^{15} \times (1.015)$

             ↑   ↑
     3% for fifteen   1.5% for one
  half year periods quarter year period

    = $342 \times 1.557\ 967 \times 1.015$
    = 540.817 084 7

The accumulated value of $342 at 6% per annum compounded semi-annually for 7.75 years is $540.82.

EXAMPLE 3 What is the amount of $342 invested at 5% per annum compounded annually for 7 years and 2 months?

SOLUTION

The rate per year is 5%.

The rate for 2 months is $0.05 \times \dfrac{2}{12} = 0.008\ 333\ 333$

$$A = 342 \times (1.05)^7 \times (1 + 0.05 \times \tfrac{2}{12})$$

$$\underset{\substack{\text{5\% for} \\ \text{seven years} \\ \text{compounded} \\ \text{annually}}}{\uparrow} \qquad \underset{\substack{\text{5\% for two} \\ \text{months out} \\ \text{of twelve} \\ \text{months}}}{\uparrow}$$

$$A = 342 \times 1.407\ 100 \times (1 + 0.05 \times \tfrac{1}{6})$$

$$A = 342 \times 1.407\ 100 \times 1.008\ 333\ 333$$
$$= 485.238\ 434\ 8$$
$$= 485.24$$

The amount of \$342 invested at 5% per annum compounded annually for 7 years and 2 months is \$485.24.

EXERCISE

Complete the following table.

	Principal	Time	Annual Rate	Compounded	Accumulated Value
1.	\$ 453	4.5 a	6%	annually	$A = \$\ 453(1.06)^4(1.03)$ $= 453 \times \underline{\hspace{2cm}} \times \underline{\hspace{1cm}}$ $= \underline{\hspace{4cm}}$
2.	453	4.25 a	6%	annually	$A = 453(1.06)^4(1.015)$ $= 453 \times \underline{\hspace{2cm}} \times \underline{\hspace{1cm}}$ $= \underline{\hspace{4cm}}$
3.	453	4.25 a	6%	semi-annually	$A = 453(1.03)^8(1.015)$ $= 453 \times \underline{\hspace{2cm}} \times \underline{\hspace{1cm}}$ $= \underline{\hspace{4cm}}$
4.	453	4.75 a	6%	semi-annually	$A = 453(1.03)^9(1.015)$ $= 453 \times \underline{\hspace{2cm}} \times \underline{\hspace{1cm}}$ $= \underline{\hspace{4cm}}$
5.	453	4 a 1 mo	12%	quarterly	$A = 453(1.03)^{16}(1.01)$ $= 453 \times \underline{\hspace{2cm}} \times \underline{\hspace{1cm}}$ $= \underline{\hspace{4cm}}$
6.	1 375	3 a 1 mo	12%	semi-annually	$A = 1\ 375(1.06)^6(1.01)$ $= 1\ 375 \times \underline{\hspace{2cm}} \times \underline{\hspace{1cm}}$ $= \underline{\hspace{4cm}}$
7.	985	3 a 2 mo	12%	semi-annually	$A = 985(1.06)^6(1.02)$ $= 985 \times \underline{\hspace{2cm}} \times \underline{\hspace{1cm}}$ $= \underline{\hspace{4cm}}$
8.	832	8.5 mo	12%	monthly	$A = 832(1.01)^8(1.005)$ $= 832 \times \underline{\hspace{2cm}} \times \underline{\hspace{1cm}}$ $= \underline{\hspace{4cm}}$

Complete the following table.

	Principal	Time	Annual Rate	Compounded	Accumulated Value
9.	$ 595	8.5 a	7%	annually	
10	1 255	3.25 a	8%	annually	
11.	733	7.25 a	6%	semi-annually	
12.	3 000	10.75 a	4%	semi-annually	
13.	1 205	3 a 1 mo	6%	quarterly	
14.	1 100	10 a 1 mo	12%	semi-annually	
15.	955	5 a 2 mo	12%	semi-annually	
16.	432	3.5 mo	6%	monthly	

Complete the following table.
Compound interest = Accumulated value − Principal

	Principal	Time	Annual Rate	Compounded	Compound Interest
17.	$ 300	10 a	5%	annually	
18.	1 260	5 a	7%	semi-annually	
19.	725	4 a	8%	quarterly	
20.	3 590	15.5 a	5%	semi-annually	
21.	4 698	10 a 3 mo	6%	quarterly	
22.	10 670	3 a 9 mo	8%	quarterly	
23.	1 355	26 a	5%	annually	
24.	987	18 a	8%	semi-annually	

25. What is the amount of $569 invested at 5.5% per annum compounded annually for 3 years and 2 months? _____

26. To what amount will $1392 accumulate if it is invested at 7% per annum compounded annually for 10 years and 1 month? _____

27. To what amount will $2561 accumulate if it is invested at 7% per annum compounded semi-annually for 8 years and 2 months? _____

28. To what amount will $5840 accumulate if it is invested at 8% per annum compounded quarterly for 2 years and 1 month? _____

29. What is the accumulated value of $786 if it accumulates interest at the rate of 6% per annum compounded semi-annually for 9 years and 7 months? _____

30. What is the amount at the end of 10 years and 4 months of $3796 drawing interest at the rate of 8% per annum compounded quarterly? _____

31. How much interest accumulates in 3 years on a bank deposit of $500 at 6% per annum compounded quarterly? _____

32. Henry Ross owes a credit company $300. The company charges interest at the rate of 1.5% per month on the unpaid balance (principal and interest). If Henry pays nothing to the company for 1.5 years, how much interest has accumulated on his debt? _____

33. A university is given $1 250 000 for a building project. If work on the project is not started for 5 years, how much extra money is available if the gift is invested at 6% per annum compounded quarterly? _____

34. If the university had been able to invest the money in Question 33 at 7% per annum compounded semi-annually, how much extra money would have been available?

    _____

35. a) Which is the better way of investing $1000 for 10 years: in a savings account at 8% per annum compounded quarterly, or in a trust account at 9% per annum compounded annually? _____

    b) How much more interest is accumulated by the better investment? _____

36. Roger's grandfather left him $3000 in a trust account paying interest at 9% per annum compounded annually. The terms of the trust state that Roger can withdraw the accumulated interest on or after his twenty-first birthday, but he cannot receive any of the principal until his thirty-fifth birthday.
    a) If Roger received the trust account on his fifth birthday, how much can he withdraw when he is 21? _____

    b) If he withdrew the accumulated interest on his twenty-first birthday and then made no more withdrawals, how much is in the account on his thirty-fifth birthday?

    _____

21·4 PRESENT VALUE

Sometimes an investor needs to know how much money must be invested now in order to have a certain amount of money available at a future date.

EXAMPLE 1 How much money must be deposited in a trust account now so that the account will amount to $5500 in 10 years at 6% per annum compounded annually?

SOLUTION $P = ?$ $\qquad$ $A = P(1 + i)^n$
$\qquad$ $A = \$5500$ $\qquad$ $5500 = P(1.06)^{10}$
$\qquad$ $i = 6\%$ $\qquad\qquad$ $P = \dfrac{5500}{(1.06)^{10}}$
$\qquad\quad\ = 0.06$
$\qquad$ $n = 10$ a $\qquad\qquad\quad = 5500 \times \dfrac{1}{(1.06)^{10}}$
$\qquad\qquad\qquad\qquad\qquad\ = 5500 \times 0.558\ 395$
$\qquad\qquad\qquad\qquad\qquad\ = 3\ 071.172\ 500$
$\qquad\qquad\qquad\qquad\qquad\ = 3071.17$

$\left.\begin{array}{l}\text{The value of } \dfrac{1}{(1.06)^{10}} \\[4pt] \text{is given in the tables} \\ \text{headed } \textit{Present Value of 1} \\ \text{in the Appendix.}\end{array}\right\}$

The principal of \$3071.17 is the present value of \$5500 due in ten years at 6% per annum compounded annually.

Formula

$$P.V. = A\,\frac{1}{(1 + i)^n}$$

Where: $P.V.$ is the present value.
$\qquad$ A is the amount.
$\qquad$ i is the rate at which interest is calculated
$\qquad$ expressed as a decimal quantity.
$\qquad$ n is the number of interest periods.

EXAMPLE 2 Find the principal that will amount to \$435 in 5 years at 7% per annum compounded annually.

SOLUTION

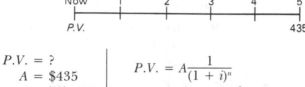

$P.V. = ?$ $\qquad$ $P.V. = A\dfrac{1}{(1 + i)^n}$
$\quad A = \$435$
$\quad\ i = 7\%$ $\qquad\qquad\quad = 435 \times \dfrac{1}{(1.07)^5}$
$\qquad = 0.07$
$\quad\ n = 5$ a $\qquad\qquad\quad = 435 \times 0.712\ 986$
$\qquad\qquad\qquad\qquad\quad = 310.148\ 910\ 0$
$\qquad\qquad\qquad\qquad\quad = 310.15$

The principal that will amount to \$435 in five years at 7% per annum is \$310.15.

EXAMPLE 3   What is the present value of a loan of $2500 due in 2 years, if the rate of interest is 8% per annum compounded quarterly?

SOLUTION

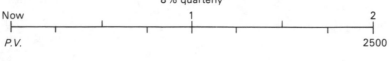

8% quarterly

Now   1   2

P.V.   2500

$P.V. = ?$
$\quad A = \$2500$
$\quad i = \dfrac{8\%}{4}$
$\quad\quad = 2\%$
$\quad\quad = 0.02$
$\quad n = 4 \times 2$
$\quad\quad = 8$

$P.V. = A\dfrac{1}{(1 + i)^n}$

$\quad = 2500 \times \dfrac{1}{(1.02)^8}$

$\quad = 2500 \times 0.853\ 490$

$\quad = 2\ 133.725\ 000$

$\quad = 2133.73$

The present value is $2133.73.

EXAMPLE 4   How much money should be invested now at 8% per annum compounded annually to amount to $3260 in 5.5 years?

SOLUTION

8% annually

Now   1   2   3   4   5   6

P.V.

3260

Step 1
Take the amount back 6 months to find the present value after five years.

$P.V. \text{ at end of year 5} = 3260 \times \dfrac{1}{1.04}$

$\quad\quad\quad = 3260 \times 0.961\ 538$

$\quad\quad\quad = 3\ 134.613\ 880$

Step 2
Take the new amount back five years to find the present value now.

$P.V. \text{ now} = 3\ 134.613\ 880 \times \dfrac{1}{(1.08)^5}$

$\quad\quad\quad = 3\ 134.613\ 880 \times 0.680\ 583$

$\quad\quad\quad = 2\ 133.364\ 918$

The present value is $2133.36.

The problem may be solved in one step.

$P.V. = 3260 \times \dfrac{1}{1.04} \times \dfrac{1}{(1.08)^5}$

$\quad\quad = 3260 \times 0.961\ 538 \times 0.680\ 583$

$\quad\quad = 2\ 133.364\ 918$

The present value is $2133.36.

EXERCISE

Complete the following table.

	Amount	Time	Annual Rate	Compounded	Present Value
1.	$5 775	15 a	5%	annually	$P.V. = 5775 \times \dfrac{1}{(1.05)^{15}}$ = _____
2.	1 356	2 a	7%	semi-annually	$P.V. = 1356 \times \dfrac{1}{(1.035)^{4}}$ = _____
3.	795	7 a	6%	quarterly	$P.V. = 795 \times \dfrac{1}{(1.015)^{28}}$ = _____
4.	8 973	3.5 a	10%	semi-annually	$P.V. = 8973 \times \dfrac{1}{(1.05)^{7}}$ = _____
5.	2 525	2.25 a	12%	quarterly	$P.V. = 2525 \times \dfrac{1}{(1.03)^{9}}$ = _____
6.	3 250	7 mo	12%	monthly	$P.V. = 3250 \times \dfrac{1}{(1.01)^{7}}$ = _____
7.	355	2.5 a	6%	annually	$P.V. = 355 \times \dfrac{1}{(1.06)^{2}} \times \dfrac{1}{(1.03)}$ = _____
8.	1 575	4.25 a	8%	semi-annually	$P.V. = 1575 \times \dfrac{1}{(1.04)^{8}} \times \dfrac{1}{(1.02)}$ = _____

9. Calculate the *P.V.* _____

10. Calculate the *P.V.* _____

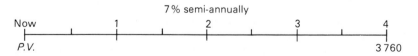

11. Calculate the *P.V.* _____

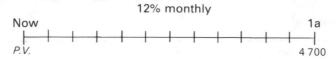

12. Calculate the *P.V.* _____

Find each present value.

	Amount	Time	Annual Rate	Compounded	Present Value
13.	$ 1 754	17 a	5.5%	annually	
14.	2 360	6 a	5%	semi-annually	
15.	987	3 a	8%	quarterly	
16.	8 795	8.5 a	7%	semi-annually	
17.	365	1.5 a	10%	semi-annually	
18.	550	14 mo	12%	monthly	
19.	11 500	1.25 a	12%	quarterly	
20.	3 755	10 a 1 mo	6%	semi-annually	
21.	5 675	7 a 1 mo	6%	semi-annually	

22. What sum put in a savings account now will amount to $8000 in 10 years time if the savings account draws interest at the rate of 8% per annum compounded quarterly? _____

23. George Watt promises to pay $10 000 in 3 years time; however, he finds that he can pay the debt immediately. What cash settlement should he make if money is worth 6.5% compounded annually? _____

24. How much should Henry Upton invest now to pay for a round-the-world cruise for himself and his wife when he retires in 5 years? The cruise will cost $7900 per person and Henry can get 8% per annum compounded semi-annually on his investment. _____

25. Two offers are received by Henry Simmons for his house. One is a cash offer of $46 000. The other is an offer of $20 000 cash and $29 500 to be paid in three years. If money is worth 9% per annum compounded annually, which is the better offer? _____

26. Joan Howard is selling her business. She owes $5000 payable in 4 years and $7000 payable in 1.5 years. If the current interest rate is 10% per annum compounded quarterly, what would be a reasonable cash settlement of Ms. Howard's debts?

    _____

27. Two construction firms submit bids on the construction of a library. One firm promises to finish the building in 2 years for $260 000 to be paid when the building is completed. The other firm also promises to finish the building in 2 years but wants payments of $60 000 on the completion of every 6 months' work. Financially, which is the better bid if money is worth 8% per annum compounded quarterly? _____

21·5 REVIEW

EXERCISE

1. Larry Solomon invested $1750 for 7 years at 11% per annum compounded semi-annually. What is the accumulated value of his investment at the end of the 7 years?

   _____

2. Connie Weisfield moved from Victoria and left $15 in a trust company account which she forgot about. If the account was a premium savings account paying interest at the rate of 6% per annum compounded quarterly, how much was in the account 5 years later? _____

3. How much interest accumulates in 4 years on an investment of $5500 at 12% per annum compounded monthly? _____

4. Gerry Kivell deposited $795 in a trust account at 8% per annum compounded semi-annually. How much is in the account at the end of 2 years and 3 months? _____

5. Mary Hahn deposited $1795 in an account which pays interest at the rate of 8% per annum compounded quarterly. How much is in the account at the end of 10 months? _____

6. How much money must Douglas Chambers deposit in a trust account now to have an accumulated value of $10 000 for his granddaughter's college education at the end of 5 years? Interest is accumulated at the rate of 9% per annum compounded semi-annually. _____

7. How much money must Georgina Hind deposit in a trust account paying compound interest at the rate of 10% per annum compounded quarterly to have saved $6000 for her child's education at the end of 6 years? _____

8. What principal must be deposited now to amount to $20 000 in 1 year and 7 months at 10% per annum compounded quarterly? _____

CHAPTER 22
ANNUITIES

An **annuity** is a sequence of equal payments made at regular intervals. An **ordinary annuity** is one in which the payments are made at the end of each interval. Some examples of annuities are mortgage payments, pension payments, insurance premiums, and instalment payments for furniture, cars, etc.

In this chapter we will study ordinary annuities to determine how compound interest affects the value of the payments.

22·1 AMOUNT OF AN ORDINARY ANNUITY

Examples of ordinary annuities are:
a) A depositor deposits $100 in a savings account at the end of each year for five years.
b) The winner of a scholarship is paid $1000 at the end of each year for four years.
c) A pensioner receives Canada Pension Plan payments at the end of each month.
d) A car is purchased by making equal payments at the end of each month for two years.
Each payment is called the **rent** (R). The time between payments is called the **payment period** or rent interval. The time from the beginning of the first payment period to the end of the last one is called the **term** of the annuity.

A depositor puts $500 in a savings account at the end of each year for four years at 6% interest compounded annually. What is the accumulated value (amount) of her savings?

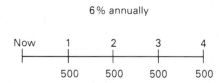

The $500 she deposited at the end of the first year is worth $500(1.06)^3$ at the end of the fourth year.
The $500 she deposited at the end of the second year is worth $500(1.06)^2$ at the end of the fourth year.
The $500 she deposited at the end of the third year is worth $500(1.06)^1$ at the end of the fourth year.
The $500 she deposited at the end of the fourth year is worth $500 at the end of the fourth year.

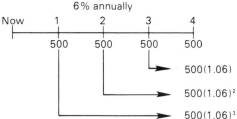

The accumulated value (amount) is:

$500 + 500(1.06) + 500(1.06)^2 + 500(1.06)^3$
$= 500[1 + (1.06) + (1.06)^2 + (1.06)^3]$
$= 500[1 + 1.06 + 1.123\ 600 + 1.191\ 016]$
$= 500[4.374\ 616]$
$= 2\ 187.308\ 000$

The amount of $500 deposited at the end of each year for four years at 6% per annum compounded annually is $2187.31.

The amount is usually represented by A or by A_n where n is the number of rent intervals.

Formula

$$A_n = Rs_{\overline{n}|\ i}$$

Where: A_n is the amount of the annuity.

R is the rent or the amount of each payment.

$s_{\overline{n}|\ i}$ is the amount of an annuity of $1 at a rate i for n intervals.

The value of $s_{\overline{n}|\ i}$ can be found from the *Amount of an Annuity of 1* table in the Appendix.

EXAMPLE 1 The sum of $100 is deposited at the end of each year for 4 years. If interest is 6% per annum compounded annually, what is the amount at the end of 4 years?

SOLUTION

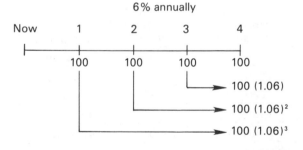

$A_n = ?$

$R = \$100$

$n = 4\ a$

$i = 6\%$

$\quad = 0.06$

$s_{\overline{n}|\ i} = s_{\overline{4}|\ 0.06}$

$A_n = Rs_{\overline{n}|\ i}$

$\quad = 100 s_{\overline{4}|\ 0.06}$

The value of $s_{\overline{4}|\ 0.06}$ can be found in the table.
Look under 6% for $n = 4$.

$A_n = 100 \times 4.374\ 616$

$\quad = 437.461\ 600$

$\quad = \$437.46$

The amount of $100 paid at the end of each year for 4 years at 6% compounded annually is $437.46.

EXAMPLE 2   Suppose that a depositor deposited $250 at the end of every 6 months for 4 years at 6% per annum compounded semi-annually. What is the accumulated value of the savings?

SOLUTION

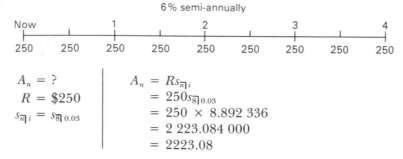

$A_n = ?$

$R = \$250$

$s_{\overline{n}|i} = s_{\overline{8}|\,0.03}$

$A_n = Rs_{\overline{n}|i}$

$= 250s_{\overline{8}|\,0.03}$

$= 250 \times 8.892\ 336$

$= 2\ 223.084\ 000$

$= 2223.08$

The amount of $250 paid at the end of every six months for four years at 6% per annum compounded semi-annually is $2223.08.

EXERCISE

Calculate the amount of each annuity.

	Annuity Payment (R)	Terms in Years	Frequency of Payment	Annual Interest Rate	Compounded	Amount (A_n) of the Annuity
1.	$ 365	4	yearly	7%	annually	
2.	1 940	10	yearly	9%	annually	
3.	3 972	3	yearly	8%	annually	
4.	869	7	yearly	6.5%	annually	
5.	185	4	half-yearly	9%	semi-annually	
6.	392	5	half-yearly	12%	semi-annually	
7.	1 535	2	half-yearly	10%	semi-annually	
8.	8 765	3.5	half-yearly	9%	semi-annually	
9.	60	2	every 3 months	8%	quarterly	
10.	250	2.5	every 3 months	12%	quarterly	
11.	875	5	every 3 months	10%	quarterly	
12.	45	1	monthly	12%	monthly	

13. Henry Black smoked an average of one pack of cigarettes a day for 5 years. The cigarettes cost $2.25 a package. How much could Mr. Black have saved if at the end of each year he had deposited the money he spent on smoking in a savings account paying interest at the rate of 8% per annum? _____

14. When John Hames was born, his father agreed to deposit $240 a year, on John's birthday, in a university savings fund. If the fund pays interest at the rate of 10% per annum, what will be the accumulated value of the money when John is 18 years old?

——————

15. Mary Smiley saves $50 a month. At the end of every half year she deposits her savings in an annuity fund paying interest at the rate of 9% per annum compounded semi-annually. What amount does Mary collect if the annuity fund repays her the principal and accumulated interest at the end of 15 years? ——————

16. On Andrea's first birthday, her grandfather gave her a 9% $1000 bond which had 20 years to run, and on which interest was paid semi-annually. The bond was held in trust by Andrea's mother, who invested the interest as it came due in a trust company account which paid interest at the rate of 10% per annum, compounded semi-annually. What was the total value of the gift when Andrea reached the age of 21?

——————

22·2 FINDING THE ANNUITY PAYMENTS WHICH ACCUMULATE TO A GIVEN AMOUNT

I wish to purchase a new car in three years. I estimate that I will need $2000 to pay the balance necessary for the new car after I have turned in my present car. How much money must I deposit in my savings account at the end of every 3 months in order to have the $2000 in 3 years, if the bank pays interest at the rate of 6% per annum compounded quarterly?

Let the amount deposited at the end of each three-month period be R.

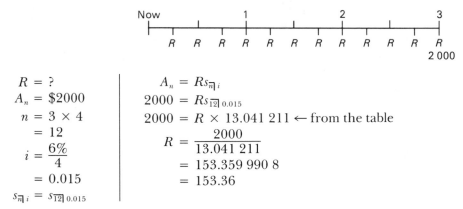

6% quarterly

$$R = ?$$
$$A_n = \$2000$$
$$n = 3 \times 4$$
$$\quad = 12$$
$$i = \frac{6\%}{4}$$
$$\quad = 0.015$$
$$s_{\overline{n}|\,i} = s_{\overline{12}|\,0.015}$$

$$A_n = Rs_{\overline{n}|\,i}$$
$$2000 = Rs_{\overline{12}|\,0.015}$$
$$2000 = R \times 13.041\ 211 \leftarrow \text{from the table}$$
$$R = \frac{2000}{13.041\ 211}$$
$$\quad = 153.359\ 990\ 8$$
$$\quad = 153.36$$

The amount deposited at the end of each three-month period is $153.36.

Formula

$$R = \frac{A_n}{s_{\overline{n}|i}}$$

Where: R is the amount of each payment (the rent).

A_n is the amount of the annuity after n payments.

$s_{\overline{n}|i}$ is the amount of an annuity of \$1 at a rate i for n intervals.

EXAMPLE Blaine worked every weekend during his last year in secondary school. How much would he have to put in a credit company savings account at the end of each month to save enough to have \$2000 for his first year of post-secondary education, if the credit company pays interest at the rate of 12% per annum compounded monthly? (Blaine makes 12 equal monthly payments.)

SOLUTION

12% monthly

$R = ?$

$A_n = \$2000$

$n = 12$ mo

$i = \dfrac{12\%}{12}$

$\quad = 0.01$

$s_{\overline{n}|i} = s_{\overline{12}|\,0.01}$

$R = \dfrac{A_n}{s_{\overline{n}|i}}$

$\quad = \dfrac{2000}{s_{\overline{12}|\,0.01}}$

$\quad = \dfrac{2000}{12.682\ 503}$

$\quad = 157.697\ 577\ 5$

$\quad = 157.70$

Blaine would have to deposit \$157.70 each month to have \$2000 saved.

EXERCISE

Calculate the payment for each payment period for each annuity.

	Amount (A_n)	Term in Years	Frequency of Payment	Annual Interest Rate	Compounded	Annuity Payment (R)
1.	$ 1 000	5	yearly	8%	annually	
2.	5 500	10	yearly	7%	annually	
3.	2 500	4	yearly	10%	annually	
4.	3 950	11	yearly	9%	annually	
5.	1 000	5	semi-annually	8%	semi-annually	
6.	4 650	10	semi-annually	7%	semi-annually	
7.	2 600	3.5	semi-annually	10%	semi-annually	
8.	12 525	11	semi-annually	9%	semi-annually	
9.	1 000	2	quarterly	12%	quarterly	
10.	4 950	5	quarterly	10%	quarterly	
11.	390	0.75	monthly	18%	monthly	
12.	1 500	1	monthly	12%	monthly	

13. How much must be deposited each year in a fund which earns 8% per annum compounded annually so that $9500 will be accumulated at the end of 10 years?

_____

14. The mortgage on J. Fund's house is to be renewed in three years, at which time the principal due will be $12 000. Miss Fund is earning more money now than she expected and hopes to pay off the mortgage when it comes due. If she can invest her savings at 9% per annum compounded semi-annually, how much would she have to invest at the end of each half year to have the amount she needs to pay off the mortgage? _____

15. George Gamble plans to remodel the front of his business office a year from now. He estimates that it will cost $5900. How much must George deposit at the end of each month in a special account paying interest at 12% per annum compounded monthly so that he will have enough money accumulated in the account to pay cash for the remodelling? _____

22·3 PRESENT VALUE OF AN ANNUITY

A man wishes to deposit enough money in a trust account now so that his daughter can withdraw $1500 at the end of each year for the next four years. If money is worth 6% compounded annually, how much must he deposit? The solution of this problem is in two steps.
● Find the amount A_n of the annuity.
● Find the present value of A_n.

Step 1

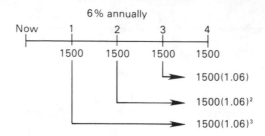

$A_n = 1500 + 1500(1.06) + 1500(1.06)^2 + 1500(1.06)^3$

Use the shorter method given in Section 22·1 to find A_n.

$A_n = ?$	$A_n = Rs_{\overline{n}|i}$
$R = \$1500$	$\quad = 1500\, s_{\overline{4}|\,0.06}$
$s_{\overline{n}|i} = s_{\overline{4}|\,0.06}$	$\quad = 1500 \times 4.374\,616$
	$\quad = 6\,561.924\,000$

Step 2

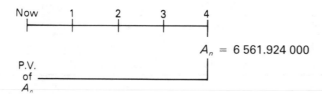

The present value of $6 561.924 000 at 6% compounded annually for four years is:

$$P.V.\ of\ A_n = 6\,561.924\,000 \times \frac{1}{(1.06)^4}$$
$$= 6\,561.924\,000 \times 0.792\,094$$
$$= 5\,197.660\,628$$
$$= 5197.66$$

The amount that must be deposited now to provide $1500 at the end of each year for four years at 6% per annum compounded annually is $5197.66.

Formula

$$P.V. = Ra_{\overline{n}|i}$$

Where: $P.V.$ is the present value of the annuity.

R is the amount of each payment.

$a_{\overline{n}|i}$ is the $P.V.$ of an annuity of $1 at a rate i for n intervals.

The value of $a_{\overline{n}|i}$ can be found from the *Present Value of an Annuity of 1* table in the Appendix.

EXAMPLE 1 The sum of $100 is paid at the end of each year for 4 years. What is the present value if interest is calculated at 6% per annum annually?

SOLUTION

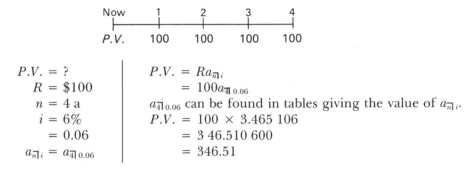

$P.V. = ?$	$P.V. = Ra_{\overline{n}\,i}$
$R = \$100$	$\quad = 100a_{\overline{4}\,0.06}$
$n = 4\text{ a}$	$a_{\overline{4}\,0.06}$ can be found in tables giving the value of $a_{\overline{n}\,i}$.
$i = 6\%$	$P.V. = 100 \times 3.465\ 106$
$\quad = 0.06$	$\quad = 3\ 46.510\ 600$
$a_{\overline{n}\,i} = a_{\overline{4}\,0.06}$	$\quad = 346.51$

n	3.5%	4%	4.5%	5%	5.5%	6%
1	0.966 184	0.961 538	0.956 938	0.952 381	0.947 867	0.943 396
2	1.899 694	1.886 095	1.872 668	1.859 410	1.846 320	1.833 393
3	2.801 637	2.775 091	2.748 964	2.723 248	2.697 933	2.673 012
4	3.673 079	3.629 895	3.587 526	3.545 951	3.505 150	3.465 106
5	4.515 052	4.451 822	4.389 977	4.329 477	4.270 284	4.212 364

The present value of payments of $100 a year for four years at 6% per annum is $346.51.

EXAMPLE 2 A debt is to be paid in instalments of $375 at the end of each year for 7 years. If money is worth 5% per annum compounded annually, what sum paid now would discharge the debt?

SOLUTION

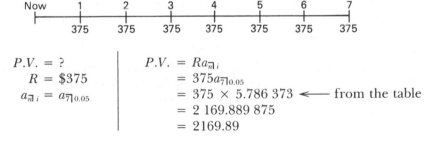

$P.V. = ?$	$P.V. = Ra_{\overline{n}\,i}$
$R = \$375$	$\quad = 375a_{\overline{7}\,0.05}$
$a_{\overline{n}\,i} = a_{\overline{7}\,0.05}$	$\quad = 375 \times 5.786\ 373 \longleftarrow$ from the table
	$\quad = 2\ 169.889\ 875$
	$\quad = 2169.89$

The present value of an annuity of $375 at the end of each year for 7 years at 5% per annum compounded annually is $2169.89.

EXERCISE

Find the present value of each annuity.

	Annuity Payment	Term in Years	Frequency of Payment	Annual Interest Rate	Compounded	Present Value
1.	$ 250	2	yearly	8%	annually	
2.	1 000	10	yearly	7%	annually	
3.	500	20	yearly	8%	annually	
4.	2 950	4	yearly	9%	annually	
5.	250	2	semi-annually	8%	semi-annually	
6.	500	10	semi-annually	11%	semi-annually	
7.	1 000	10	semi-annually	9%	semi-annually	
8.	725	11	semi-annually	7%	semi-annually	
9.	175	5	quarterly	8%	quarterly	
10.	500	10	quarterly	10%	quarterly	
11.	50	2	monthly	12%	monthly	
12.	50	2	monthly	18%	monthly	

13. An endowment policy comes due and the policy holder has the choice of taking a cash value immediately or an equivalent annuity of $1325 a year payable at the end of each year for 20 years. If money is worth 9% per annum compounded annually, what would be the immediate cash value? _____

14. Bert Hunter owes money to a loan company. He promises to pay $47.50 at the end of each month for 7 months. Interest was calculated at the rate of 2% per month and is included in his payments of $47.50. What cash settlement should Bert be able to make now to cancel the debt? _____

15. A legacy provides that the beneficiary may either take payments of $150 at the end of every 6 months period for fifteen years or an immediate cash payment. If money is valued at 9% per annum compounded semi-annually, how much would the immediate cash payment be? _____

22·4 FINDING THE ANNUITY PAYMENTS GIVEN THE PRESENT VALUE

Recall that the amount of each payment of an annuity is represented by R in the formula
$$P.V. = Ra_{\overline{n}|\,i}$$
Dividing both sides of this formula by $a_{\overline{n}|\,i}$ gives
$$R = \frac{P.V.}{a_{\overline{n}|\,i}}$$

Formula

$$R = \frac{P.V.}{a_{\overline{n}|\,i}}$$

Where: R is the amount of each payment.
$P.V.$ is the present value of the annuity.
$a_{\overline{n}|\,i}$ is the present value of an annuity of $1 at a rate i for n intervals.

EXAMPLE 1 The sum of $7000 is placed in a trust fund earning interest at the rate of 5.5% per annum compounded annually. The trust fund is to repay the principal and interest in equal annual payments at the end of each year for 5 years. What is the amount of each payment?

SOLUTION

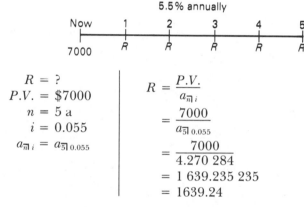

$R = ?$
$P.V. = \$7000$
$n = 5\text{ a}$
$i = 0.055$
$a_{\overline{n}|\,i} = a_{\overline{5}|\,0.055}$

$$R = \frac{P.V.}{a_{\overline{n}|\,i}}$$

$$= \frac{7000}{a_{\overline{5}|\,0.055}}$$

$$= \frac{7000}{4.270\ 284}$$

$$= 1\ 639.235\ 235$$

$$= 1639.24$$

The amount of each payment is $1639.24.

EXAMPLE 2 Ms. Howie's insurance policy comes due. She has the choice of taking $13 500 cash now or an annuity to be paid in equal instalments (principal and interest) at the end of each six months period for 10 years. If money is worth 8% per annum compounded semi-annually, what is the amount of each semi-annual payment?

SOLUTION

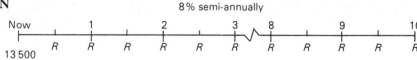

$$R = ?$$
$$P.V. = \$13\,500$$
$$n = 20$$
$$i = \frac{0.08}{2}$$
$$= 0.04$$
$$a_{\overline{n}|i} = a_{\overline{20}|\,0.04}$$

$$R = \frac{P.V.}{a_{\overline{n}|i}}$$
$$= \frac{13\,500}{a_{\overline{20}|\,0.04}}$$
$$= \frac{13\,500}{13.590\,326}$$
$$= 993.353\,654\,6$$
$$= 993.35$$

The amount of each payment is $993.35.

EXERCISE

Calculate the payment for each annuity.

	Present Value	Term in Years	Frequency of Payment	Annual Interest Rate	Compounded	Annuity Payment
1.	$ 5 000	5	yearly	7%	annually	
2.	13 000	15	yearly	8%	annually	
3.	4 500	4	yearly	9%	annually	
4.	16 500	20	yearly	7%	annually	
5.	1 500	5	semi-annually	8%	semi-annually	
6.	1 500	2	semi-annually	9%	semi-annually	
7.	10 500	15	semi-annually	8%	semi-annually	
8.	20 000	20	semi-annually	10%	semi-annually	
9.	350	1	quarterly	10%	quarterly	
10.	2 000	3	quarterly	8%	quarterly	
11.	1 250	1.5	monthly	12%	monthly	
12.	525	1	monthly	18%	monthly	

13. Stephanie Taylor bought a new washing machine for $499.98 with no down payment. She will pay for it in ten equal monthly payments with interest charged at 1% per month compounded monthly. If the first payment is to be made one month from the date of purchase, how much will each payment be? _____

14. Jim Armstrong deposited the $8000 his grandfather gave him for his college expenses in a savings account at 9% per annum compounded annually. He wants to withdraw the same amount each year for 4 years. How much should Jim withdraw each year if his first withdrawal is made one year from now? _____

15. Joanne Miller buys a new house and obtains a mortgage of $16 500 at 10% per annum compounded semi-annually. The mortgage is to run for 15 years and equal payments of principal and interest are to be made every half year. How much will each payment be? _____

22·5 AMORTIZATION

In repaying a debt it is often an advantage to be able to make equal payments over regular periods of time. These payments must include principal and interest. The calculation of the amount of each payment and of a table or schedule showing how much of each payment goes toward paying the principal and how much is used to pay the interest due is called the **amortization** of the debt. The example that follows shows how these calculations are made.

EXAMPLE A mortgage of $5000 bearing interest at 6% per annum is to be repaid in five years by equal payments of principal and interest at the end of each year. Calculate the amount of each payment and set up an amortization schedule.

SOLUTION First find the annuity payment for which the P.V. is $5000. (This is the amount of each equal payment.)

$$R = ?$$
$$P.V. = \$5000$$
$$n = 5\,a$$
$$i = 6\% = 0.06$$
$$a_{\overline{n}|i} = a_{\overline{5}|0.06}$$

$$R = \frac{P.V.}{a_{\overline{n}|i}}$$
$$= \frac{5000}{a_{\overline{5}|0.06}}$$
$$= \frac{5000}{4.212\,364}$$
$$= 1\,186.981\,942$$
$$= 1186.98$$

The equal payments are $1186.98 each.

Amortization Schedule

Year	(1) Unpaid Principal at Beginning of Year	(2) Interest for Year at 6% (1) x 0.06	(3) Annual Payment of Debt	(4) Payment on Principal at End of Year (3) − (2)
1	$5 000.00	$300.00	$1 186.98	$ 886.98
2	4 113.02	246.78	1 186.98	940.20
3	3 172.82	190.37	1 186.98	996.61
4	2 176.21	130.57	1 186.98	1 056.41
5	1 119.80	67.19	1 186.99*	1 119.80
Summary:	0	$934.91	$5 934.91	$5 000.00

*Since annual payments are estimated to be $1186.98 by dropping $0.001 942 from each calculated payment of $1 186.981 942 it is necessary to make the final payment $1186.99 to adjust the total repayment of principal to $5000. Final payments are usually adjusted to compensate for overpayment or underpayment of principal due to this type of estimation.

EXERCISE

1. Calculate the payments and draw up an amortization schedule for a debt of $1000, bearing interest at 8% per annum, to be paid off in 3 years by equal instalments, including principal and interest.

2. A purchase amounting to $300 is to be repaid in 6 equal monthly instalments, including principal and interest. Interest is charged at the rate of 1.5% per month. Calculate the monthly payments and draw up an amortization schedule.

3. A mortgage of $9000 is to be repaid in 10 equal yearly payments, including principal and interest. Interest is charged at the rate of 10% per annum compounded annually. Calculate the yearly payments and draw up an amortization schedule for the mortgage.

4. A car costing $5500 is to be paid for by making equal payments, including principal and interest, every 3 months for 2 years. Interest is charged at the rate of 18% per annum compounded quarterly. Calculate the amount of the equal payments and draw up an amortization schedule of the debt.

22·6 REVIEW

EXERCISE

Calculate the amount of each annuity.

	Annuity Payment (R)	Term in Years	Frequency of Payment	Annual Interest Rate	Compounded	Amount (A_n) of the Annuity
1.	$ 549	5	yearly	6.5%	annually	
2.	3 737	8	half-yearly	9%	semi-annually	
3.	990	7	quarterly	10%	quarterly	
4.	75	2	monthly	18%	monthly	

5. Jean Harper saves $100 per month. Every 3 months she deposits her savings in an annuity fund paying interest at the rate of 8% per annum compounded quarterly. How much is in the fund at the end of 6 years? _____

Calculate the payment for each payment period for each annuity.

	Amount of the Annuity (A_n)	Term in Years	Frequency of Payment	Annual Interest Rate	Compounded	Annuity Payment (R)
6.	$5 000	3	yearly	6.5%	annually	
7.	2 500	6	semi-annually	7%	semi-annually	
8.	6 700	4	quarterly	10%	quarterly	
9.	4 000	3	monthly	12%	monthly	

10. Helen Gagnon plans to redecorate the interior of her bookstore in 3 years. How much must she deposit in a savings account every 3 months if the account accumulates interest at the rate of 8% per annum compounded quarterly and if she plans to have $10 000 in the account at the end of the 3 year period? _____

Find the present value for each annuity.

	Annuity Payment	Term in Years	Frequency of Payment	Annual Interest Rate	Compounded	Present Value
11.	$ 500	8	yearly	6.5%	annually	
12.	1 500	7	semi-annually	9%	semi-annually	
13.	2 000	5	quarterly	6%	quarterly	
14.	1 200	4	monthly	12%	monthly	

15. Margaret Nuestrom makes a loan with a trust company. She promises to pay $76.50 at the end of every month for 3 years. If interest is calculated at the rate of 1.5% per month and is included in her payment of $76.50, what cash settlement should cancel the debt now? _____

Calculate the payment each payment period for each annuity.

	Present Value	Term in Years	Frequency of Payment	Annual Interest Rate	Compounded	Annuity Payment
16.	$ 4 500	5	yearly	7%	annually	
17.	21 000	6	semi-annually	7%	semi-annually	
18.	10 000	8	quarterly	8%	quarterly	
19.	2 500	1.5	monthly	18%	monthly	

20. Jan Homenick purchased a new television set for $1297.50 with no down payment. She is to make 24 equal monthly payments which include interest charges at 1.5% per month compounded monthly. If the first payment is to be made one month from the date of purchase, how much will each payment be? _____

21. A mortgage of $10 000 is to be repaid in 3 years with equal quarterly payments of principal and interest. If interest is charged at the rate of 14% per annum compounded quarterly, calculate the amount of each equal payment and amortize the mortgage for the 3 year period.

CHAPTER 23

BONDS

In Chapter 15 we considered how stocks are bought and sold on the stock market and you looked in the daily newspapers for quotations on their prices. You may have seen quotations for bond prices on the same newspaper pages. **Bond** issues are another way by which businesses and governments borrow money from the general public. Bonds are bought and sold in much the same way as stocks although there is no bond exchange. Bonds are generally purchased as longer term investments and are not passed from one purchaser to another as frequently as stocks. For this and other reasons, prices of bonds fluctuate more slowly than those of stocks.

This chapter considers the investment features of bonds, how prices are set, yields, and how municipalities finance large projects through a type of bond issue called a **debenture**.

23·1 GENERAL DESCRIPTION OF A BOND

Bonds are issued by a government or a large corporation when it needs to borrow money. Bonds are bought by people who have money to invest and who wish to earn a fixed rate of interest on their money.

Bonds are "safer" investments than stocks. The buyer of a bond is a **creditor** of the company and is paid the interest due on her or his money before the **shareholders** or stockholders receive dividends. (See Section 15·1.)

Bonds are secure because they are a type of mortgage. If the money borrowed by the corporation is not repaid at the end of the term of the loan, the investor may lay a claim to the total assets of the corporation. Governments, provincial and public corporations (such as Ontario Hydro) do not issue bonds with a mortgage as security. The weight of a government's promise to pay is as strong a form of security as a mortgage.

In the sample bond the "borrower" is Ontario Hydro, which promises to pay the purchaser of the bond $1000 when the bond becomes due. This amount is the **face value** or denomination of the bond. It is also the amount that the original purchaser lends the company. The date of issue of the bond and the date of maturity are both printed on the bond. Notice that the bond contains a promise to the purchaser that the face value will be paid. The length of time between the date of issue of the bond and the date of maturity is called the **term** of the bond.

The fixed rate of interest for this bond is 9.25% compounded annually. Thus the purchaser receives $1000 \times 0.0925 = $92.50 every year as interest on the money paid for the bond.

Ontario Hydro

GUARANTEED BY
THE
PROVINCE OF ONTARIO

$1,000

CUSIP 683078 AV 1

9-1/4%
COUPON BOND

DUE
6th JANUARY 2004
(Subject to prior redemption)

INTEREST PAYABLE
6th January and 6th July

TYPES OF BONDS

BEARER BONDS

Principal and interest are paid to the person who holds the bond.

REGISTERED BONDS

The holder of the bond is registered with the "borrower" and is the only one who may claim the principal. If the bond is sold, the registration must be changed to the new owner.

METHODS OF PAYING INTEREST

BEARER BONDS

Attached to the bond are coupons. Each coupon states the date on which the interest is due and the amount of the interest. On the interest date, the holder of the bond cuts off or "clips" the coupon. The holder then presents the coupon to the bank which pays the holder cash for the coupon.

FULLY REGISTERED BONDS

The name of the holder of the bond is registered with the "borrower" and the holder is paid interest on the stated interest date by cheque. When the bond matures the holder is also paid the face value of the bond by cheque.

COUPON REGISTERED BONDS

The name of the holder is registered with the "borrower", but interest coupons are attached to the bond. The holder of the bond "clips" the coupons and cashes them.

23·2 PURCHASE AND SALE OF BONDS

Bonds sold on the date of issue or shortly thereafter are sold at face value. The bank or broker who sells the bond does not receive a commission. Usually bonds are issued in multiples of $100.

In Canada there is no Bond Market similar to a Stock Exchange. However, bonds are bought and sold continually by brokers, since the owner of a bond may not wish to hold it for the full term. Brokers receive their fees from the difference between the price at which they buy the bonds and the price at which they sell them.

The price that a purchaser pays for the bond depends on:
- the face value,
- the number of interest payments still to be made,
- the financial stability of the issuer of the bond,
- the current rate of interest.

The current market values of bonds are listed each day in the newspapers. If the quoted price of the bond is less than $100 it is selling at a **discount**. If the quoted price of the bond is more than $100 it is selling at a **premium**.

EXAMPLE 1   John Connell owns a $500 Ontario Hydro Bond bearing interest at 9% on February 1 of each year. He sells it on February 17 at 101.5. What are the proceeds?

SOLUTION   Selling price of the bond = 5 × 101.5
$$= \$507.50$$

Since the last interest payment was on February 1, John should collect interest for the 16 days from February 1 to February 17 during which time he still had his $500 invested in the bond. Since the buyer did not have her money invested for this amount of time, she must pay John interest for the 16 days in February as part of the cost of the bond. The buyer will collect interest for the whole period from February 1 to the next February 1 when the interest becomes due on February 1 of the next year.

Time from Feb. 1 to Feb. 17 = 16 d

Accrued Interest for 16 d = Principal × Rate × Time
$$= 500 \times 0.09 \times \frac{16}{365}$$
$$= 1.972\ 602\ 739$$
$$= \$1.97$$

Total Proceeds = 507.50 + 1.97
$$= \$509.47$$

EXAMPLE 2   On February 17, Wilma Johnson bought a 7% Government of Canada Bond, face value $1000 and bearing interest coupons payable semi-annually, on October 1 and April 1, at 99.45. What was the cost including accrued interest?

SOLUTION   Cost of the bond = 10×99.45
$$= \$994.50$$

Since the seller last collected interest on October 1, part of the interest payment to be made on April 1 (from October 1 to February 17) belongs to the seller. The buyer must pay this interest as part of the price of the bond.

Time (Oct. 1 to Feb. 17) = $(31-1) + 30 + 31 + 31 + 17$
$$= 139 \text{ d}$$

Accrued Interest = Principal $\times$ Rate $\times$ Time
$$= 1000 \times 0.07 \times \frac{139}{365}$$
$$= \$26.66$$

Total cost = $994.50 + 26.66$
$$= \$1021.16$$

The bond cost $1021.16.

EXERCISE

Calculate the total proceeds on the sale of each bond.

	Face Value	Quoted Price (per $100)	Date Purchased	Annual Interest Payable on	Annual Rate of Interest	Total Proceeds
1.	$ 100	100.40	July 31	Jan. 1	8%	
2.	100	96.25	Dec. 31	Sept. 15	7.25%	
3.	500	102.00	June 4	Feb. 1	9%	
4.	500	99.25	Dec. 15	April 1	7.75%	
5.	300	74	June 30	Jan. 1	6.5%	
6.	1 000	77	April 1	March 1	9.25%	
7.	1 500	90.50	Sept. 2	Jan. 1	7.5%	
8.	2 000	58	Nov. 15	Jan. 1	7.5%	
9.	600	101.50	Jan. 18	March 2	9.5%	
10.	1 500	101.00	June 30	June 2	9.5%	
11.	3 000	96	July 15	Sept. 15	8%	
12.	10 000	99.9	May 12	Oct. 1	7.75%	

13. George Martin owns a $500 Consumers' Gas Bond, bearing interest at 8.75% on January 1 of each year. He sells it on April 30 at 83. What are the proceeds?

14. James Brown buys a 7.5% Ontario Government Bond, face value $1000 and interest payable February 15. He purchased the bond on June 30 at 82. What is the total cost of the bond?

15. Martha Holmes buys a $1000 Province of Alberta Bond, at 8.25% payable March 15 each year. If the purchase is made on October 15 at 80.50, what is the total cost of the bond?

16. A Quebec Hydro Bond, face value $1500, is sold at 101.50 on January 1. If the bond bears interest at 9.5% payable February 1 of each year, what are the total proceeds?

_____

23·3 'BID' PRICE

How is the market price of a bond determined? Although the bond has a certain "face value" on which a fixed rate of interest is paid, brokers buying and selling bonds must set the prices of the bonds so that they yield a fair interest rate to the investor. The yield rate is determined by the security behind the bond, the ability of the issuer to meet coupon payments, the current rates of interest, etc. After the broker decides on the yield rate for a certain bond, he or she then determines **'bid'** on the bond – the price that should be paid for the bond in order that it will yield the desired rate of interest as an investment.

EXAMPLE 1   What is the 'bid' price for a $100, 7% bond bearing yearly coupons and having 5 years to run, if it is to yield 9%? Calculate the discount and set up an Accumulation of Discount schedule.

SOLUTION

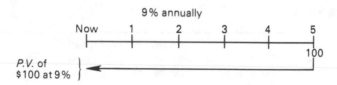

Step 1
P.V. of face value of the bond
How much money *now* will amount to $100 in 5 years at 9%?

$$P.V. = 100 \times \frac{1}{(1.09)^5}$$
$$= 100 \times 0.649\,931$$
$$= \$64.99$$

Step 2
The value of each coupon
The bond bears interest coupons at 7% yearly, therefore each coupon is worth $100 × 0.07 = $7.00

Step 3
P.V. of coupon payments

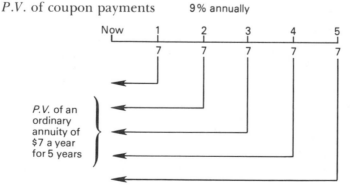

How much money must be invested *now* at 9% per annum to pay $7 a year for 5 years?

This amount is the P.V. of an ordinary annuity of $7 a year for 5 years at 9% per annum compounded annually.

$$P.V. = 7.00 \times a_{\overline{5}|\,0.09}$$
$$= 7.00 \times 3.889\,651$$
$$= \$27.23$$

Step 4
Bid Price $= 64.99 + 27.23$
$ = \$92.22$

Step 5
Discount $= 100 - 92.22$
$ = \$7.78$

Step 6

	(1)	(2)	(3)	(4) = (2) − (3)	(5) = (1) + (4)
	Book Value at	9% Yield on		Increase in	Book Value at
Year	First of Year	Book Value	Coupon	Book Value	End of Year
1	$92.22	$8.30	$7.00	$1.30	$93.52
2	93.52	8.42	7.00	1.42	94.94
3	94.94	8.54	7.00	1.54	96.48
4	96.48	8.68	7.00	1.68	98.16
5	98.16	8.83	7.00	1.83	99.99* 100.00

Accumulation of Discount Schedule

*There may be a cent more or less in the final book value due to the rounding off of decimals.

EXAMPLE 2 Determine the 'bid' price for a $500, 10% bond bearing yearly coupons and having 5 years to run, if it is to yield 8%. Calculate the premium and set up an Amortization of Premium schedule.

SOLUTION Step 1
P.V. of face value of the bond

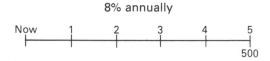

8% annually

$$P.V. = 500 \times \frac{1}{(1.08)^5}$$
$$= 500 \times 0.680\,583$$
$$= \$340.29$$

Step 2
The value of each coupon $= 500 \times 0.10$
$ = \$50.00$

Step 3
P.V. of coupon payments

8% annually

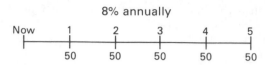

$$P.V. = 50 \times a_{\overline{5}|0.08}$$
$$= 50 \times 3.992\,710$$
$$= \$199.64$$

Step 4
Bid Price = 340.29 + 199.64
= $539.93

Step 5
Premium = 539.93 − 500.00
= $39.93

Step 6

	Amortization of Premium Schedule				
Year	(1) Book Value at First of Year	(2) 8% Yield on Book Value	(3) Coupon	(4) = (3) − (2) Decrease in Book Value	(5) = (1) − (4) Book Value at End of Year
1	$539.93	$43.19	$50.00	$6.81	$533.12
2	533.12	42.65	50.00	7.35	525.77
3	525.77	42.06	50.00	7.94	517.83
4	517.83	41.43	50.00	8.57	509.26
5	509.26	40.74	50.00	9.26	500.00

EXERCISE

1. What is the 'bid' price for a $100, 6% bond bearing yearly coupons and having 5 years to run, if it is to yield 7%? Set up an Accumulation of Discount schedule. _____

2. Find the 'bid' price and set up an Amortization of Premium schedule for a $500, 6% bond bearing yearly coupons and having 7 years to run, if it is to yield 5%. _____

3. A $1000, 9% bond bearing yearly coupons and having 5 years to run is to yield 7%. Find the bid price and set up an Accumulation of Discount or Amortization of Premium schedule. _____

4. A $1000, 7% bond bearing yearly coupons and having 5 years to run is to yield 9%. Find the bid price and set up an Accumulation of Discount or Amortization of Premium Schedule. _____

5. A $10 000, 7.75% bond bearing yearly coupons has 6 years to run and is to yield 8%. Find the bid price and set up an Accumulation of Discount schedule. _____

6. A $25 000, 9.25% bond bearing yearly coupons is issued to run for 8 years and is to yield 8%. Find the bid price and set up an Amortization of Premium schedule. _____

7. A $500, 9% bond bearing half yearly coupons has 3 years to run and is to yield 7%. Find the bid price and set up an Amortization of Premium schedule. _____

23·4 CIVIC FINANCING: DEBENTURES

When a municipality or a corporation wishes to borrow money, it can offer no security to the lender except the ability to collect taxes or profits. To raise money needed for large projects, it issues a special type of bond called a **debenture**.

A debenture must be paid back at the end of its term and the government or corporation issuing the debenture must plan to set aside enough money to do this. Repayment of the interest and face value of a debenture is illustrated most easily by considering a method used by a municipality to set aside funds to repay its debenture issues.

REPAYMENT OF DEBENTURES BY THE SINKING FUND METHOD

In repaying debentures by the annuity method, lenders receive a repayment of principal and interest each year. Most persons interested in buying debentures prefer to receive interest payments each year and the face value of the debenture at the end of the term. To provide this type of repayment to the debenture purchaser, the municipality issuing the debentures must arrange to finance interest payments each year and put away enough money in a **sinking fund** to repay the total face value of the debentures when they come due.

EXAMPLE 1 A municipality sells a $500 000 issue of 20 year, 8% sinking fund debentures. It pays the interest annually and sets aside sufficient money each year in a sinking fund, earning 6% per annum, to accumulate to $500 000 in 20 years. How much must the city budget each year for interest and sinking fund payments?

SOLUTION Step 1.
Find the annual interest payment.
Annual interest on the debentures $= 500\,000 \times 0.08$
$$= \$40\,000$$

Step 2
Find the rent of the annuity payments which will accumulate to $500 000 in 20 years at 6% per annum. (See Section 22·2.)

$R = ?$
$A_n = \$500\,000$
$n = 20$ a
$i = 0.06$
$s_{\overline{n}|i} = s_{\overline{20}|\,0.06}$

$R = \dfrac{A_n}{s_{\overline{n}|i}}$

$= \dfrac{500\,000}{s_{\overline{20}|\,0.06}}$

$= \dfrac{500\,000}{36.785\,591}$

$= 13\,592.278\,56$

$= 13\,592.28$

The annual payment to the sinking fund is $13 592.28.
Total annual payment = 40 000 + 13 592.28
$$= \$53\ 592.28$$

The municipality must budget $53 592.28 of its tax money each year towards repayment (principal and interest) of its debenture debt.

EXAMPLE 2   The town of Hillcrest sells a $75 000 issue of 8 year, 7.75% sinking fund debentures. Interest is to be paid annually and the sinking fund can be invested at 6% interest per annum. Calculate the amount of the town's budget that must be set aside each year towards payment of the debenture issue and set up a Sinking Fund Schedule.

SOLUTION   Annual interest = 75 000 × 0.0775
$$= \$5812.50$$

Amount set aside in the sinking fund each year = Payment on an annuity of $75 000 for 8 years at 6% per annum

$$R = ?$$
$$A_n = \$75\ 000$$
$$n = 8\ \text{a}$$
$$i = 0.06$$
$$S_{\overline{n}|\,i} = S_{\overline{8}|\,0.06}$$

$$R = \frac{A_n}{S_{\overline{n}|\,i}}$$
$$= \frac{75\ 000}{S_{\overline{8}|\,0.06}}$$
$$= \frac{75\ 000}{9.897\ 468}$$
$$= 7\ 577.695\ 629$$
$$= 7577.70$$

The amount set aside in the sinking fund each year is $7577.70.

	Sinking Fund Schedule			
Year	**(1)** Amount in S.F. at First of Year	**(2) = (1) × 0.06** Interest Accumulated in S.F. at 6% per Annum	**(3)** Annual Payment to S.F. at End of Year	**(4) = (1) + (2) + (3)** Amount in S.F. at End of Year
1	$ 0	$ 0	$7 577.70	$ 7 577.70
2	7 577.70	454.66	7 577.70	15 610.06
3	15 610.06	936.60	7 577.70	24 124.36
4	24 124.36	1 447.46	7 577.70	33 149.52
5	33 149.52	1 988.97	7 577.70	42 716.19
6	42 716.19	2 562.97	7 577.70	52 856.86
7	52 856.86	3 171.41	7 577.70	63 605.97
8	63 605.97	3 816.36	7 577.70	75 000.03

EXERCISE

1. York County finances the purchase and construction of a county park by an issue of $60 000, 10 year, 7% sinking fund debentures. Interest is paid annually; a sinking fund is established at 6% per annum to repay the principal at the end of the 10 year period. How much must the county budget each year to finance its debenture debt?

   _____

2. Set up a Sinking Fund schedule to show accumulation of sinking fund payments for the 10 year period of the debenture issue of Question 1.

3. South City finances a $2.5 million city hall by issuing 15 year debentures at 7%. The city makes interest payments each year and sets up a sinking fund invested at 7% for repayment of principal at the end of 15 years. Calculate the total payment South City must make each year and set up a Sinking Fund schedule to show accumulation of principal.

   _____

4. The town of St. Stephen sells a $75 000 issue of 10 year, 8% sinking fund debentures, bearing half-yearly coupons. If a sinking fund accumulates interest at 7%, compounded semi-annually, and if payments are made to the fund at the end of every six month period, what payment must the town budget for each half year? Set up a Sinking Fund schedule for the debenture issue. _____

23·5 REVIEW

EXERCISE

1. Calculate the total proceeds from the sale of a $1000 bond with yearly coupons of 6.25% payable on October 1 of each year if it is sold on December 15 at 102.75.

   _____

2. Calculate the cost of a $500 bond with yearly coupons of 7% payable on March 1 of each year if it is purchased on November 20 at a quoted price of 92.25. _____

3. Connie Liefson owns a $1500 B.C. Hydro bond bearing interest at 8.75% per annum on July 1 each year. She sells it on October 15 at 97.5. What are the proceeds? _____

4. Hal Meir purchased a $5000 N.B. Electric bond bearing interest at 11.75% per annum on September 15 each year. If he sells it on December 29 at 98.6, what are the proceeds? _____

5. Calculate the 'bid' price for a $500 bond bearing yearly coupons at 9% and having 4 years to run, if it is to yield 10%. Set up an Accumulation of Discount schedule.

   _____ , _____

6. Calculate the 'bid' price for a $1000 bond bearing yearly coupons at 9% and having 5 years to run if it is to yield 8%. Set up an Amortization of Premium schedule.

_____ , _____

7. The municipality of Silver Valley financed improvements to its water system through an issue of $150 000, 5 year, 9% sinking fund debentures. Interest is paid annually and a sinking fund is established at 7% per annum to repay the principal at the end of the 5 year period. How much must the municipality budget each year to finance its debenture debt? _____

8. Set up a Sinking Fund schedule to show accumulation of sinking fund payments for the 5 year period of the debenture issue in Question 7.

APPENDIX

AMOUNT OF 1 $(1 + i)^n$

n	0.5%	1%	1.5%	2%	2.5%
1	1.005 000	1.010 000	1.015 000	1.020 000	1.025 000
2	1.010 025	1.020 100	1.030 225	1.040 400	1.050 625
3	1.015 075	1.030 301	1.045 678	1.061 208	1.076 891
4	1.020 150	1.040 604	1.061 364	1.082 432	1.103 813
5	1.025 251	1.051 010	1.077 284	1.104 081	1.131 408
6	1.030 378	1.061 520	1.093 443	1.126 162	1.159 693
7	1.035 529	1.072 135	1.109 845	1.148 686	1.188 686
8	1.040 707	1.082 857	1.126 493	1.171 659	1.218 403
9	1.045 911	1.093 685	1.143 390	1.195 093	1.248 863
10	1.051 140	1.104 622	1.160 541	1.218 994	1.280 085
11	1.056 396	1.115 668	1.177 949	1.243 374	1.312 087
12	1.061 678	1.126 825	1.195 618	1.268 242	1.344 889
13	1.066 986	1.138 093	1.213 552	1.293 607	1.378 511
14	1.072 321	1.149 474	1.231 756	1.319 479	1.412 974
15	1.077 683	1.160 969	1.250 232	1.345 868	1.448 298
16	1.083 071	1.172 579	1.268 986	1.372 786	1.484 506
17	1.088 487	1.184 304	1.288 020	1.400 241	1.521 618
18	1.093 929	1.196 147	1.307 341	1.428 246	1.559 659
19	1.099 399	1.208 109	1.326 951	1.456 811	1.598 650
20	1.104 896	1.220 190	1.346 855	1.485 947	1.638 616
21	1.110 420	1.232 392	1.367 058	1.515 666	1.679 582
22	1.115 972	1.244 716	1.387 564	1.545 980	1.721 571
23	1.121 552	1.257 163	1.408 377	1.576 899	1.764 611
24	1.127 160	1.269 735	1.429 503	1.608 437	1.808 726
25	1.132 796	1.282 432	1.450 945	1.640 606	1.853 944
26	1.138 460	1.295 256	1.472 710	1.673 418	1.900 293
27	1.144 152	1.308 209	1.494 800	1.706 886	1.947 800
28	1.149 873	1.321 291	1.517 222	1.741 024	1.996 495
29	1.155 622	1.334 504	1.539 981	1.775 845	2.046 407
30	1.161 400	1.347 849	1.563 080	1.811 362	2.097 568
31	1.167 207	1.361 327	1.586 526	1.847 589	2.150 007
32	1.173 043	1.374 941	1.610 324	1.884 541	2.203 757
33	1.178 908	1.388 690	1.634 479	1.922 231	2.258 851
34	1.184 803	1.402 577	1.658 996	1.960 676	2.315 322
35	1.190 727	1.416 603	1.683 881	1.999 890	2.373 205
36	1.196 681	1.430 769	1.709 140	2.039 887	2.432 535
37	1.202 664	1.445 076	1.734 777	2.080 685	2.493 349
38	1.208 677	1.459 527	1.760 798	2.122 299	2.555 682
39	1.214 721	1.474 123	1.787 210	2.164 745	2.619 574
40	1.220 794	1.488 864	1.814 018	2.208 040	2.685 064
41	1.226 898	1.503 752	1.841 229	2.252 200	2.752 190
42	1.233 033	1.518 790	1.868 847	2.297 244	2.820 995
43	1.239 198	1.533 978	1.896 880	2.343 189	2.891 520
44	1.245 394	1.549 318	1.925 333	2.390 053	2.963 808
45	1.251 621	1.564 811	1.954 213	2.437 854	3.037 903
46	1.257 879	1.580 459	1.983 526	2.486 611	3.113 851
47	1.264 168	1.596 263	2.013 279	2.536 344	3.191 697
48	1.270 489	1.612 226	2.043 478	2.587 070	3.271 490
49	1.276 842	1.628 348	2.074 130	2.638 812	3.353 277
50	1.283 226	1.644 632	2.105 242	2.691 588	3.437 109

AMOUNT OF 1 $(1 + i)^n$

n	3%	3.5%	4%	4.5%	5%	5.5%
1	1.030 000	1.035 000	1.040 000	1.045 000	1.050 000	1.055 000
2	1.060 900	1.071 225	1.081 600	1.092 025	1.102 500	1.113 025
3	1.092 727	1.108 718	1.124 864	1.141 166	1.157 625	1.174 241
4	1.125 509	1.147 523	1.169 859	1.192 519	1.215 506	1.238 825
5	1.159 274	1.187 686	1.216 653	1.246 182	1.276 282	1.306 960
6	1.194 052	1.229 255	1.265 319	1.302 260	1.340 096	1.378 843
7	1.229 874	1.272 279	1.315 932	1.360 862	1.407 100	1.454 679
8	1.266 770	1.316 809	1.368 569	1.422 101	1.477 455	1.534 687
9	1.304 773	1.362 897	1.423 312	1.486 095	1.551 328	1.619 094
10	1.343 916	1.410 599	1.480 244	1.552 969	1.628 895	1.708 144
11	1.384 234	1.459 970	1.539 454	1.622 853	1.710 339	1.802 092
12	1.425 761	1.511 069	1.601 032	1.695 881	1.795 856	1.901 207
13	1.468 534	1.563 956	1.665 074	1.772 196	1.885 649	2.005 774
14	1.512 590	1.618 695	1.731 676	1.851 945	1.979 932	2.116 091
15	1.557 967	1.675 349	1.800 944	1.935 282	2.078 928	2.232 476
16	1.604 706	1.733 986	1.872 981	2.022 370	2.182 875	2.355 263
17	1.652 848	1.794 676	1.947 901	2.113 377	2.292 018	2.484 802
18	1.702 433	1.857 489	2.025 817	2.208 479	2.406 619	2.621 466
19	1.753 506	1.922 501	2.106 849	2.307 860	2.526 950	2.765 647
20	1.806 111	1.989 789	2.191 123	2.411 714	2.653 298	2.917 757
21	1.860 295	2.059 431	2.278 768	2.520 241	2.785 963	3.078 234
22	1.916 103	2.131 512	2.369 919	2.633 652	2.925 261	3.247 537
23	1.973 587	2.206 114	2.464 716	2.752 166	3.071 524	3.426 152
24	2.032 794	2.283 328	2.563 304	2.876 014	3.225 100	3.614 590
25	2.093 778	2.363 245	2.665 836	3.005 434	3.386 355	3.813 392
26	2.156 591	2.445 959	2.772 470	3.140 679	3.555 673	4.023 129
27	2.221 289	2.531 567	2.883 369	3.282 010	3.733 456	4.244 401
28	2.287 928	2.620 172	2.998 703	3.429 700	3.920 129	4.477 843
29	2.356 566	2.711 878	3.118 651	3.584 036	4.116 136	4.724 124
30	2.427 262	2.806 794	3.243 398	3.745 318	4.321 942	4.983 951
31	2.500 080	2.905 031	3.373 133	3.913 857	4.538 039	5.258 069
32	2.575 083	3.006 708	3.508 059	4.089 981	4.764 941	5.547 262
33	2.652 335	3.111 942	3.648 381	4.274 030	5.003 189	5.852 362
34	2.731 905	3.220 860	3.794 316	4.466 362	5.253 348	6.174 242
35	2.813 862	3.333 590	3.946 089	4.667 348	5.516 015	6.513 825
36	2.898 278	3.450 266	4.103 933	4.877 378	5.791 816	6.872 085
37	2.985 227	3.571 025	4.268 090	5.096 860	6.081 407	7.250 050
38	3.074 783	3.696 011	4.438 813	5.326 219	6.385 477	7.648 803
39	3.167 027	3.825 372	4.616 366	5.565 899	6.704 751	8.069 487
40	3.262 038	3.959 260	4.801 021	5.816 365	7.039 989	8.513 309
41	3.359 899	4.097 834	4.993 061	6.078 101	7.391 988	8.981 541
42	3.460 696	4.241 258	5.192 784	6.351 615	7.761 588	9.475 526
43	3.564 517	4.389 702	5.400 495	6.637 438	8.149 667	9.996 679
44	3.671 452	4.543 342	5.616 515	6.936 123	8.557 150	10.546 497
45	3.781 596	4.702 359	5.841 176	7.248 248	8.985 008	11.126 554
46	3.895 044	4.886 941	6.074 823	7.574 420	9.434 258	11.738 515
47	4.011 895	5.037 284	6.317 816	7.915 268	9.905 971	12.384 133
48	4.132 252	5.213 589	6.570 528	8.271 456	10.401 270	13.065 260
49	4.256 219	5.396 065	6.833 349	8.643 671	10.921 333	13.783 849
50	4.383 906	5.584 927	7.106 683	9.032 636	11.467 400	14.541 961

AMOUNT OF 1 $(1 + i)^n$

n	6%	6.5%	7%	8%	9%	10%
1	1.060 000	1.065 000	1.070 000	1.080 000	1.090 000	1.100 000
2	1.123 600	1.134 225	1.144 900	1.166 400	1.188 100	1.210 000
3	1.191 016	1.207 950	1.225 043	1.259 712	1.295 029	1.331 000
4	1.262 477	1.286 466	1.310 796	1.360 489	1.411 582	1.464 100
5	1.338 226	1.370 087	1.402 552	1.469 328	1.538 624	1.610 510
6	1.418 519	1.459 142	1.500 730	1.586 874	1.677 100	1.771 561
7	1.503 630	1.553 987	1.605 781	1.713 824	1.828 039	1.948 717
8	1.593 848	1.654 996	1.718 186	1.850 930	1.992 563	2.143 589
9	1.689 479	1.762 570	1.838 459	1.999 005	2.171 893	2.357 948
10	1.790 848	1.877 137	1.967 151	2.158 925	2.367 364	2.593 742
11	1.898 299	1.999 151	2.104 852	2.331 639	2.580 426	2.853 117
12	2.012 196	2.129 096	2.252 192	2.518 170	2.812 665	3.138 428
13	2.132 928	2.267 488	2.409 845	2.719 624	3.065 805	3.452 271
14	2.260 904	2.414 874	2.578 534	2.937 194	3.341 727	3.797 498
15	2.396 558	2.571 841	2.759 032	3.172 169	3.642 482	4.177 248
16	2.540 352	2.739 011	2.952 164	3.425 943	3.970 306	4.594 973
17	2.692 773	2.917 046	3.158 815	3.700 018	4.327 633	5.054 470
18	2.854 339	3.106 654	3.379 932	3.996 020	4.717 120	5.559 917
19	3.025 600	3.308 587	3.616 528	4.315 701	5.141 661	6.115 909
20	3.207 135	3.523 645	3.869 684	4.660 957	5.604 411	6.727 500
21	3.399 564	3.752 682	4.140 562	5.033 834	6.108 808	7.400 250
22	3.603 537	3.996 606	4.430 402	5.436 540	6.658 600	8.140 275
23	3.819 750	4.256 386	4.740 530	5.871 464	7.257 874	8.954 302
24	4.048 935	4.533 051	5.072 367	6.341 181	7.911 083	9.849 733
25	4.291 871	4.827 699	5.427 433	6.848 475	8.623 081	10.834 706
26	4.549 383	5.141 500	5.807 353	7.396 353	9.399 158	11.918 177
27	4.822 346	5.475 697	6.213 868	7.988 061	10.245 082	13.109 994
28	5.111 687	5.831 617	6.648 838	8.627 106	11.167 140	14.420 994
29	5.418 388	6.210 672	7.114 257	9.317 275	12.172 182	15.863 093
30	5.743 491	6.614 366	7.612 255	10.062 657	13.267 678	17.449 402
31	6.088 101	7.044 300	8.145 113	10.867 669	14.461 770	19.194 342
32	6.453 387	7.502 179	8.715 271	11.737 083	15.763 329	21.113 777
33	6.840 590	7.989 821	9.325 340	12.676 050	17.182 028	23.225 154
34	7.251 025	8.509 160	9.978 114	13.690 134	18.728 411	25.547 670
35	7.686 087	9.062 255	10.676 581	14.785 344	20.413 968	28.102 437
36	8.147 252	9.651 301	11.423 942	15.968 172	22.251 225	30.912 681
37	8.636 087	10.278 636	12.223 618	17.245 626	24.253 835	34.003 949
38	9.154 252	10.946 747	13.079 271	18.625 276	26.436 680	37.404 343
39	9.703 507	11.658 286	13.994 820	20.115 298	28.815 982	41.144 778
40	10.285 718	12.416 075	14.974 458	21.724 522	31.409 420	45.259 256
41	10.902 861	13.223 119	16.022 670	23.462 483	34.236 268	49.785 181
42	11.557 033	14.082 622	17.144 257	25.339 482	37.317 532	54.763 699
43	12.250 455	14.997 993	18.344 355	27.366 640	40.676 110	60.240 069
44	12.985 482	15.972 862	19.628 460	29.555 972	44.336 960	66.264 076
45	13.764 611	17.011 098	21.002 452	31.920 449	48.327 286	72.890 484
46	14.590 487	18.116 820	22.472 623	34.474 085	52.676 742	80.179 532
47	15.465 917	19.294 413	24.045 707	37.232 012	57.417 649	88.197 485
48	16.393 872	20.548 550	25.728 907	40.210 573	62.585 237	97.017 234
49	17.377 504	21.884 205	27.529 930	43.427 419	68.217 908	106.718 957
50	18.420 154	23.306 679	29.457 025	46.901 613	74.357 520	117.390 853

PRESENT VALUE OF 1 $\dfrac{1}{(1 + i)^n}$

n	0.5%	1%	1.5%	2%	2.5%	3%
1	0.995 025	0.990 099	0.985 222	0.980 392	0.975 610	0.970 874
2	0.990 075	0.980 296	0.970 662	0.961 169	0.951 814	0.942 596
3	0.985 149	0.970 590	0.956 317	0.942 322	0.928 599	0.915 142
4	0.980 248	0.960 980	0.942 184	0.923 845	0.905 951	0.888 487
5	0.975 371	0.951 466	0.928 260	0.905 731	0.883 854	0.862 609
6	0.970 518	0.942 045	0.914 542	0.887 971	0.862 297	0.837 484
7	0.965 690	0.932 718	0.901 027	0.870 560	0.841 265	0.813 092
8	0.960 885	0.923 483	0.887 711	0.853 490	0.820 747	0.789 409
9	0.956 105	0.914 340	0.874 592	0.836 755	0.800 728	0.766 417
10	0.951 348	0.905 287	0.861 667	0.820 348	0.781 198	0.744 094
11	0.946 615	0.896 324	0.848 933	0.804 263	0.762 145	0.722 421
12	0.941 905	0.887 449	0.836 387	0.788 493	0.743 556	0.701 380
13	0.937 219	0.878 663	0.824 027	0.773 033	0.725 420	0.680 951
14	0.932 556	0.869 963	0.811 849	0.757 875	0.707 727	0.661 118
15	0.927 917	0.861 349	0.799 852	0.743 015	0.690 466	0.641 862
16	0.923 300	0.852 821	0.788 031	0.728 446	0.673 625	0.623 167
17	0.918 707	0.844 377	0.776 385	0.714 163	0.657 195	0.605 016
18	0.914 136	0.836 017	0.764 912	0.700 159	0.641 166	0.587 395
19	0.909 588	0.827 740	0.753 607	0.686 431	0.625 528	0.570 286
20	0.905 063	0.819 544	0.742 470	0.672 971	0.610 271	0.553 676
21	0.900 560	0.811 430	0.731 498	0.659 776	0.595 386	0.537 549
22	0.896 080	0.803 396	0.720 688	0.646 839	0.580 865	0.521 893
23	0.891 622	0.795 442	0.710 037	0.634 156	0.566 697	0.506 692
24	0.887 186	0.787 566	0.699 544	0.621 721	0.552 875	0.491 934
25	0.882 772	0.779 768	0.689 206	0.609 531	0.539 391	0.477 606
26	0.878 380	0.772 048	0.679 021	0.597 579	0.526 235	0.463 695
27	0.874 010	0.764 404	0.668 986	0.585 862	0.513 400	0.450 189
28	0.869 662	0.756 836	0.659 099	0.574 375	0.500 878	0.437 077
29	0.865 335	0.749 342	0.649 359	0.563 112	0.488 661	0.424 346
30	0.861 030	0.741 923	0.639 762	0.552 071	0.476 743	0.411 987
31	0.856 746	0.734 577	0.630 308	0.541 246	0.465 115	0.399 987
32	0.852 484	0.727 304	0.620 993	0.530 633	0.453 771	0.388 337
33	0.848 242	0.720 103	0.611 816	0.520 229	0.442 703	0.377 026
34	0.844 022	0.712 973	0.602 774	0.510 028	0.431 905	0.366 045
35	0.839 823	0.705 914	0.593 866	0.500 028	0.421 371	0.355 383
36	0.835 645	0.698 925	0.585 090	0.490 223	0.411 094	0.345 032
37	0.831 487	0.692 005	0.576 443	0.480 611	0.401 067	0.334 983
38	0.827 351	0.685 153	0.567 924	0.471 187	0.391 285	0.325 226
39	0.823 235	0.678 370	0.559 531	0.461 948	0.381 741	0.315 754
40	0.819 139	0.671 653	0.551 262	0.452 890	0.372 431	0.306 557
41	0.815 064	0.665 003	0.543 116	0.444 010	0.363 347	0.297 628
42	0.811 009	0.658 419	0.535 089	0.435 304	0.354 485	0.288 959
43	0.806 974	0.651 900	0.527 182	0.426 769	0.345 839	0.280 543
44	0.802 959	0.645 445	0.519 391	0.418 401	0.337 404	0.272 372
45	0.798 964	0.639 055	0.511 715	0.410 197	0.329 174	0.264 439
46	0.794 989	0.632 728	0.504 153	0.402 154	0.321 146	0.256 737
47	0.791 034	0.626 463	0.496 702	0.394 268	0.313 313	0.249 259
48	0.787 098	0.620 260	0.489 362	0.386 538	0.305 671	0.241 999
49	0.783 183	0.614 119	0.482 130	0.378 958	0.298 216	0.234 950
50	0.779 286	0.608 039	0.475 005	0.371 528	0.290 942	0.228 107

PRESENT VALUE OF 1 $\dfrac{1}{(1+i)^n}$

n	3.5%	4%	4.5%	5%	5.5%	6%
1	0.966 184	0.961 538	0.956 938	0.952 381	0.947 867	0.943 396
2	0.933 511	0.924 556	0.915 730	0.907 029	0.898 452	0.889 996
3	0.901 943	0.888 996	0.876 297	0.863 838	0.851 614	0.839 619
4	0.871 442	0.854 804	0.838 561	0.822 702	0.807 217	0.792 094
5	0.841 973	0.821 927	0.802 451	0.783 526	0.765 134	0.747 258
6	0.813 501	0.790 315	0.767 896	0.746 215	0.725 246	0.704 961
7	0.785 991	0.759 918	0.734 828	0.710 681	0.687 437	0.665 057
8	0.759 412	0.730 690	0.703 185	0.676 839	0.651 599	0.627 412
9	0.733 731	0.702 587	0.672 904	0.644 609	0.617 629	0.591 898
10	0.708 919	0.675 564	0.643 928	0.613 913	0.585 431	0.558 395
11	0.684 946	0.649 581	0.616 199	0.584 679	0.554 911	0.526 788
12	0.661 783	0.624 597	0.589 664	0.556 837	0.525 982	0.496 969
13	0.639 404	0.600 574	0.564 272	0.530 321	0.498 561	0.468 839
14	0.617 782	0.577 475	0.539 973	0.505 068	0.472 569	0.442 301
15	0.596 891	0.555 265	0.516 720	0.481 017	0.447 933	0.417 265
16	0.576 706	0.533 908	0.494 469	0.458 112	0.424 581	0.393 646
17	0.557 204	0.513 373	0.473 176	0.436 297	0.402 447	0.371 364
18	0.538 361	0.493 628	0.452 800	0.415 521	0.381 466	0.350 344
19	0.520 156	0.474 642	0.433 302	0.395 734	0.361 579	0.330 513
20	0.502 566	0.456 387	0.414 643	0.376 889	0.342 729	0.311 805
21	0.485 571	0.438 834	0.396 787	0.358 942	0.324 862	0.294 155
22	0.469 151	0.421 955	0.379 701	0.341 850	0.307 926	0.277 505
23	0.453 286	0.405 726	0.363 350	0.325 571	0.291 873	0.261 797
24	0.437 957	0.390 121	0.347 703	0.310 068	0.276 657	0.246 979
25	0.423 147	0.375 117	0.332 731	0.295 303	0.262 234	0.232 999
26	0.408 838	0.360 689	0.318 402	0.281 241	0.248 563	0.219 810
27	0.395 012	0.346 817	0.304 691	0.267 848	0.235 605	0.207 368
28	0.381 654	0.333 477	0.291 571	0.255 094	0.223 322	0.195 630
29	0.368 748	0.320 651	0.279 015	0.242 946	0.211 679	0.184 557
30	0.356 278	0.308 319	0.267 000	0.231 377	0.200 644	0.174 110
31	0.344 230	0.296 460	0.255 502	0.220 359	0.190 184	0.164 255
32	0.332 590	0.285 058	0.244 500	0.209 866	0.180 269	0.154 957
33	0.321 343	0.274 094	0.233 971	0.199 873	0.170 871	0.146 186
34	0.310 476	0.263 552	0.223 896	0.190 355	0.161 963	0.137 912
35	0.299 977	0.253 415	0.214 254	0.181 290	0.153 520	0.130 105
36	0.289 833	0.243 669	0.205 028	0.172 657	0.145 516	0.122 741
37	0.280 032	0.234 297	0.196 199	0.164 436	0.137 930	0.115 793
38	0.270 562	0.225 285	0.187 750	0.156 605	0.130 739	0.109 239
39	0.261 413	0.216 621	0.179 665	0.149 148	0.123 924	0.103 056
40	0.252 572	0.208 289	0.171 929	0.142 046	0.117 463	0.097 222
41	0.244 031	0.200 278	0.164 525	0.135 282	0.111 339	0.091 719
42	0.235 779	0.192 575	0.157 440	0.128 840	0.105 535	0.086 527
43	0.227 806	0.185 168	0.150 661	0.122 704	0.100 033	0.081 630
44	0.220 102	0.178 046	0.144 173	0.116 861	0.094 818	0.077 009
45	0.212 659	0.171 198	0.137 964	0.111 297	0.089 875	0.072 650
46	0.205 468	0.164 614	0.132 023	0.105 997	0.085 190	0.068 538
47	0.198 520	0.158 283	0.126 338	0.100 949	0.080 748	0.064 658
48	0.191 806	0.152 195	0.120 898	0.096 142	0.076 539	0.060 998
49	0.185 320	0.146 341	0.115 692	0.091 564	0.072 549	0.057 546
50	0.179 053	0.140 713	0.110 710	0.087 204	0.068 767	0.054 288

PRESENT VALUE OF 1 $\dfrac{1}{(1 + i)^n}$

n	6.5%	7%	8%	9%	10%
1	0.938 967	0.934 579	0.925 926	0.917 431	0.909 091
2	0.881 659	0.873 439	0.857 339	0.841 680	0.826 446
3	0.827 849	0.816 298	0.793 832	0.772 183	0.751 315
4	0.777 323	0.762 895	0.735 030	0.708 425	0.683 013
5	0.729 881	0.712 986	0.680 583	0.649 931	0.620 921
6	0.685 334	0.666 342	0.630 170	0.596 267	0.564 474
7	0.643 506	0.622 750	0.583 490	0.574 034	0.513 158
8	0.604 231	0.582 009	0.540 269	0.501 866	0.466 507
9	0.567 353	0.543 934	0.500 249	0.460 428	0.424 098
10	0.532 726	0.508 349	0.463 193	0.422 411	0.385 543
11	0.500 212	0.475 093	0.428 883	0.387 533	0.350 494
12	0.469 683	0.444 012	0.397 114	0.355 535	0.318 631
13	0.441 017	0.414 964	0.367 698	0.326 179	0.289 664
14	0.414 100	0.387 817	0.340 461	0.299 247	0.263 331
15	0.388 827	0.362 446	0.315 242	0.274 538	0.239 392
16	0.365 095	0.338 735	0.291 890	0.251 870	0.217 629
17	0.342 813	0.316 574	0.270 269	0.231 073	0.197 845
18	0.321 890	0.295 864	0.250 249	0.211 994	0.179 859
19	0.302 244	0.276 508	0.231 712	0.194 490	0.163 508
20	0.283 797	0.258 419	0.214 548	0.178 431	0.148 644
21	0.266 476	0.241 513	0.198 656	0.163 698	0.135 131
22	0.250 212	0.225 713	0.183 941	0.150 182	0.122 846
23	0.234 941	0.210 947	0.170 315	0.137 781	0.111 678
24	0.220 602	0.197 147	0.157 699	0.126 405	0.101 526
25	0.207 138	0.184 249	0.146 018	0.115 968	0.092 296
26	0.194 496	0.172 195	0.135 202	0.106 393	0.083 905
27	0.182 625	0.160 930	0.125 187	0.097 608	0.076 278
28	0.171 479	0.150 402	0.115 914	0.089 548	0.069 343
29	0.161 013	0.140 563	0.107 328	0.082 155	0.063 039
30	0.151 186	0.131 367	0.099 377	0.075 371	0.057 309
31	0.141 959	0.122 773	0.092 016	0.069 148	0.052 099
32	0.133 295	0.114 741	0.085 200	0.063 438	0.047 362
33	0.125 159	0.107 235	0.078 889	0.058 200	0.043 057
34	0.117 520	0.100 219	0.073 045	0.053 395	0.039 143
35	0.110 348	0.093 663	0.067 635	0.048 986	0.035 584
36	0.103 613	0.087 535	0.062 625	0.044 941	0.032 349
37	0.097 289	0.081 809	0.057 986	0.041 231	0.029 408
38	0.091 351	0.076 457	0.053 690	0.037 826	0.026 735
39	0.085 776	0.071 455	0.049 713	0.034 703	0.024 304
40	0.080 541	0.066 780	0.046 031	0.031 838	0.022 095
41	0.075 625	0.062 412	0.042 621	0.029 209	0.020 086
42	0.071 010	0.058 329	0.039 464	0.026 798	0.018 260
43	0.066 676	0.054 513	0.036 541	0.024 584	0.016 600
44	0.062 606	0.050 946	0.033 834	0.022 555	0.015 091
45	0.058 785	0.047 613	0.031 328	0.020 692	0.013 719
46	0.055 197	0.044 499	0.029 007	0.018 984	0.012 472
47	0.051 828	0.041 587	0.026 859	0.017 416	0.011 338
48	0.048 665	0.038 867	0.024 869	0.015 978	0.010 307
49	0.045 695	0.036 324	0.023 027	0.014 659	0.009 370
50	0.042 906	0.033 948	0.021 321	0.013 449	0.008 519

AMOUNT OF AN ANNUITY OF 1 $S_{\overline{n}|i}$

n	0.5%	1%	1.5%	2%	2.5%
1	1.000 000	1.000 000	1.000 000	1.000 000	1.000 000
2	2.005 000	2.010 000	2.015 000	2.020 000	2.025 000
3	3.015 025	3.030 100	3.045 225	3.060 400	3.075 625
4	4.030 100	4.060 401	4.090 903	4.121 608	4.152 516
5	5.050 251	5.101 005	5.152 267	5.204 040	5.256 329
6	6.075 502	6.152 015	6.229 551	6.308 121	6.387 737
7	7.105 879	7.213 535	7.322 994	7.434 283	7.547 430
8	8.141 409	8.285 671	8.432 839	8.582 969	8.736 116
9	9.182 116	9.368 527	9.559 332	9.754 628	9.954 519
10	10.228 026	10.462 213	10.702 722	10.949 721	11.203 382
11	11.279 167	11.566 835	11.863 262	12.168 715	12.483 466
12	12.335 562	12.682 503	13.041 211	13.412 090	13.795 553
13	13.397 240	13.809 328	14.236 830	14.680 332	15.140 442
14	14.464 226	14.947 421	15.450 382	15.973 938	16.518 953
15	15.536 548	16.096 896	16.682 138	17.293 417	17.931 927
16	16.614 230	17.257 864	17.932 370	18.639 285	19.380 225
17	17.697 301	18.430 443	19.201 355	20.012 071	20.864 730
18	18.785 788	19.614 748	20.489 376	21.412 312	22.386 349
19	19.879 717	20.810 895	21.796 716	22.840 559	23.946 007
20	20.979 115	22.019 004	23.123 667	24.297 370	25.544 658
21	22.084 011	23.239 194	24.470 522	25.783 317	27.183 274
22	23.194 431	24.471 586	25.837 580	27.298 984	28.862 856
23	24.310 403	25.716 302	27.225 144	28.844 963	30.584 427
24	25.431 955	26.973 465	28.633 521	30.421 862	32.349 038
25	26.559 115	28.243 200	30.063 024	32.030 300	34.157 764
26	27.691 911	29.525 632	31.513 969	33.670 906	36.011 708
27	28.830 370	30.820 888	32.986 679	35.344 324	37.912 001
28	29.974 522	32.129 097	34.481 479	37.051 210	39.859 801
29	31.124 395	33.450 388	35.998 701	38.792 235	41.856 296
30	32.280 017	34.784 892	37.538 681	40.568 079	43.902 703
31	33.441 417	36.132 740	39.101 762	42.379 441	46.000 271
32	34.608 624	37.494 068	40.688 288	44.227 030	48.150 278
33	35.781 667	38.869 009	42.298 612	46.111 570	50.354 034
34	36.960 575	40.257 699	43.933 092	48.033 802	52.612 885
35	38.145 378	41.660 276	45.592 088	49.994 478	54.928 207
36	39.336 105	43.076 878	47.275 969	51.994 367	57.301 413
37	40.532 785	44.507 647	48.985 109	54.034 255	59.733 948
38	41.735 449	45.952 724	50.719 885	56.114 940	62.227 297
39	42.944 127	47.412 251	52.480 684	58.237 238	64.782 979
40	44.158 847	48.886 373	54.267 894	60.401 983	67.402 554
41	45.379 642	50.375 237	56.081 912	62.610 023	70.087 617
42	46.606 540	51.878 989	57.923 141	64.862 223	72.839 808
43	47.839 572	53.397 779	59.791 988	67.159 468	75.660 803
44	49.078 770	54.931 757	61.688 868	69.502 657	78.552 323
45	50.324 164	56.481 075	63.614 201	71.892 710	81.516 131
46	51.575 785	58.045 885	65.568 414	74.330 564	84.554 034
47	52.833 664	59.626 344	67.551 940	76.817 176	87.667 885
48	54.097 832	61.222 608	69.565 219	79.353 519	90.859 582
49	55.368 321	62.834 834	71.608 698	81.940 590	94.131 072
50	56.645 163	64.463 182	73.682 828	84.579 401	97.484 349

AMOUNT OF AN ANNUITY OF 1 $S_{\overline{n}|i}$

n	3%	3.5%	4%	4.5%	5%	5.5%
1	1.000 000	1.000 000	1.000 000	1.000 000	1.000 000	1.000 000
2	2.030 000	2.035 000	2.040 000	2.045 000	2.050 000	2.055 000
3	3.090 000	3.106 225	3.121 600	3.137 025	3.152 500	3.168 025
4	4.183 627	4.214 943	4.246 464	4.278 191	4.301 125	4.342 266
5	5.309 136	5.362 466	5.416 323	5.470 710	5.525 631	5.581 091
6	6.468 410	6.550 152	6.632 975	6.716 892	6.801 913	6.888 051
7	7.662 462	7.779 408	7.898 294	8.019 152	8.142 008	8.266 894
8	8.892 336	9.051 687	9.214 226	9.380 014	9.549 109	9.721 573
9	10.159 106	10.368 496	10.582 795	10.802 114	11.026 564	11.256 260
10	11.463 879	11.731 393	12.006 107	12.288 209	12.577 893	12.875 354
11	12.807 796	13.141 992	13.486 351	13.841 179	14.206 787	14.583 498
12	14.192 030	14.601 962	15.025 805	15.464 032	15.917 127	16.385 591
13	15.617 790	16.113 030	16.626 838	17.159 913	17.712 983	18.286 798
14	17.086 324	17.676 986	18.291 911	18.932 109	19.598 632	20.292 572
15	18.598 914	19.295 681	20.023 588	20.784 054	21.578 564	22.408 664
16	20.156 881	20.971 030	21.824 531	22.719 337	23.657 492	24.641 140
17	21.761 588	22.705 016	23.697 512	24.741 707	25.840 366	26.996 403
18	23.414 435	24.499 691	25.645 413	26.855 084	28.132 385	29.481 205
19	25.116 868	26.357 181	27.671 229	29.063 562	30.539 004	32.102 671
20	26.870 374	28.279 682	29.778 079	31.371 423	33.065 954	34.868 318
21	28.676 486	30.269 471	31.969 202	33.783 137	35.719 252	37.786 076
22	30.536 780	32.328 902	34.247 970	36.303 378	38.505 214	40.864 310
23	32.452 884	34.460 414	36.617 889	38.937 030	41.430 475	44.111 847
24	34.426 470	36.666 528	39.082 604	41.689 196	44.501 999	47.537 998
25	36.459 264	38.949 857	41.645 908	44.565 210	47.727 099	51.152 588
26	38.553 042	41.313 102	44.311 745	47.570 645	51.113 454	54.965 981
27	40.709 634	43.759 060	47.084 214	50.711 324	54.669 126	58.989 109
28	42.030 923	46.290 627	49.967 583	53.993 333	58.402 583	63.233 510
29	45.218 850	48.910 799	52.966 286	57.423 033	62.322 712	67.711 354
30	47.575 416	51.622 677	56.084 938	61.007 070	66.438 848	72.435 478
31	50.002 678	54.429 471	59.328 335	64.752 388	70.760 790	77.419 429
32	52.502 759	57.334 502	62.701 469	68.666 245	75.298 829	82.677 498
33	55.077 841	60.341 210	66.209 527	72.756 226	80.063 771	88.224 760
34	57.730 177	63.453 152	69.857 909	77.030 256	85.066 959	94.077 122
35	60.462 082	66.674 013	73.652 225	81.496 618	90.320 307	100.251 364
36	63.275 944	70.007 603	77.598 314	86.163 966	95.836 323	106.765 189
37	66.174 223	73.457 869	81.702 246	91.041 344	101.628 139	113.637 274
38	69.159 449	77.028 895	85.970 336	96.138 205	107.709 546	120.887 324
39	72.234 233	80.724 906	90.409 150	101.464 424	114.095 023	128.536 127
40	75.401 260	84.550 278	95.025 516	107.030 323	120.799 774	136.605 614
41	78.663 298	88.509 537	99.826 536	112.846 688	127.839 763	145.118 923
42	82.023 196	92.607 371	104.819 598	118.924 789	135.231 751	154.100 464
43	85.483 892	96.848 629	110.012 382	125.276 404	142.993 339	163.575 989
44	89.048 409	101.238 331	115.412 877	131.913 842	151.143 006	173.572 669
45	92.719 861	105.781 673	121.029 392	138.849 965	159.700 156	184.119 165
46	96.501 457	110.484 031	126.870 568	146.098 214	168.685 164	195.245 719
47	100.396 501	115.350 973	132.945 390	153.672 633	178.119 422	206.984 234
48	104.408 396	120.388 257	139.263 206	161.587 902	188.025 393	219.368 367
49	108.540 648	125.601 846	145.833 734	169.859 357	198.426 663	232.433 627
50	112.796 867	130.997 910	152.667 084	178.503 028	209.347 996	246.217 476

AMOUNT OF AN ANNUITY OF 1 $S_{\overline{n}|i}$

n	6%	6.5%	7%	8%	9%	10%
1	1.000 000	1.000 000	1.000 000	1.000 000	1.000 000	1.000 000
2	2.060 000	2.065 000	2.070 000	2.080 000	2.090 000	2.100 000
3	3.183 600	3.199 225	3.214 900	3.246 400	3.278 100	3.310 000
4	4.374 616	4.407 175	4.439 943	4.506 112	4.573 129	4.641 000
5	5.637 093	5.693 641	5.750 739	5.866 601	5.984 711	6.105 100
6	6.975 319	7.063 728	7.153 291	7.335 929	7.523 335	7.715 610
7	8.393 838	8.522 870	8.654 021	8.922 803	9.200 435	9.487 171
8	9.897 468	10.076 856	10.259 803	10.636 628	11.028 474	11.435 888
9	11.491 316	11.731 852	11.977 989	12.487 558	13.021 036	13.579 477
10	13.180 795	13.494 423	13.816 448	14.486 562	15.192 930	15.937 425
11	14.971 643	15.371 560	15.783 599	16.645 487	17.560 293	18.531 167
12	16.869 941	17.370 711	17.888 451	18.977 126	20.140 720	21.384 284
13	18.882 138	19.499 808	20.140 643	21.495 297	22.953 385	24.522 712
14	21.015 066	21.767 295	22.550 488	24.214 920	26.019 190	27.974 983
15	23.275 970	24.182 169	25.129 022	27.152 114	29.360 916	31.772 482
16	25.672 528	26.754 010	27.888 054	30.324 283	33.003 399	35.949 730
17	28.212 880	29.493 021	30.840 217	33.750 226	36.973 705	40.544 703
18	30.905 653	32.410 067	33.999 033	37.450 244	41.301 338	45.599 173
19	33.759 992	35.516 722	37.378 965	41.446 263	46.018 459	51.159 090
20	36.785 591	38.825 309	40.995 492	45.761 964	51.160 120	57.274 999
21	39.992 727	42.348 954	44.865 177	50.422 921	56.764 530	64.002 499
22	43.392 290	46.101 636	49.005 739	55.456 755	62.873 338	71.402 749
23	46.995 828	50.098 242	53.436 141	60.893 296	69.531 939	79.543 024
24	50.815 577	54.354 628	58.176 671	66.764 759	76.789 813	88.497 327
25	54.864 512	58.887 679	63.249 038	73.105 940	84.700 896	98.347 059
26	59.156 383	63.715 378	68.676 470	79.954 415	93.323 977	109.181 765
27	63.705 766	68.856 877	74.483 823	87.350 768	102.723 135	121.099 942
28	68.528 112	74.332 574	80.697 691	95.338 830	112.968 217	134.209 936
29	73.639 798	80.164 192	87.346 529	103.965 933	124.135 356	148.630 930
30	79.058 186	86.374 864	94.460 786	113.283 211	136.307 539	164.494 023
31	84.801 677	92.989 230	102.073 041	123.345 868	149.575 217	181.943 425
32	90.889 778	100.033 530	110.218 154	134.213 537	164.036 987	201.137 767
33	97.343 165	107.535 710	118.933 425	145.950 620	179.800 315	222.251 544
34	104.183 755	115.525 531	128.258 765	158.626 670	196.982 344	245.476 699
35	111.434 780	124.034 690	138.236 878	172.316 804	215.710 755	271.024 368
36	119.120 867	133.096 945	148.913 460	187.102 148	236.124 723	299.126 805
37	127.268 119	142.748 247	160.337 402	203.070 320	258.375 948	330.039 486
38	135.904 206	153.026 883	172.561 020	220.315 945	282.629 783	364.043 434
39	145.058 458	163.973 630	185.640 292	238.941 221	309.066 463	401.447 778
40	154.761 966	175.631 916	199.635 112	259.056 519	337.882 445	442.592 556
41	165.047 684	188.047 990	214.609 570	280.781 040	369.291 865	487.851 811
42	175.950 545	201.271 110	230.632 240	304.243 523	403.528 133	537.636 992
43	187.507 577	215.353 732	247.776 497	329.583 005	440.845 665	592.400 692
44	199.758 032	230.351 725	266.120 851	356.949 646	481.521 775	652.640 761
45	212.743 514	246.324 587	285.749 311	386.505 617	525.858 734	718.904 837
46	226.508 125	263.335 685	306.751 763	418.426 067	574.186 021	791.795 321
47	241.098 612	281.452 504	329.224 386	452.900 152	626.862 762	871.974 853
48	256.564 529	300.746 917	353.270 093	490.132 164	684.280 411	960.172 338
49	272.958 401	321.295 467	378.998 999	530.342 737	746.865 648	1 057.189 572
50	290.335 905	343.179 672	406.528 929	573.770 156	815.083 556	1 163.908 529

PRESENT VALUE OF AN ANNUITY OF 1 $a_{\overline{n}|i}$

n	0.5%	1%	1.5%	2%	2.5%	3%
1	0.995 025	0.990 099	0.985 222	0.980 392	0.975 610	0.970 874
2	1.985 099	1.970 395	1.955 883	1.941 561	1.927 424	1.913 470
3	2.970 248	2.940 985	2.912 200	2.883 883	2.856 024	2.828 611
4	3.950 496	3.901 966	3.854 385	3.807 729	3.761 974	3.717 098
5	4.925 866	4.853 431	4.782 645	4.713 460	4.645 829	4.579 707
6	5.896 384	5.795 476	5.697 187	5.601 431	5.508 125	5.417 191
7	6.862 074	6.728 195	6.598 214	6.471 991	6.349 391	6.230 283
8	7.822 959	7.651 678	7.485 925	7.325 481	7.170 137	7.019 692
9	8.779 064	8.566 018	8.360 517	8.162 237	7.970 866	7.786 109
10	9.730 412	9.471 305	9.222 185	8.982 585	8.752 064	8.530 203
11	10.677 027	10.367 628	10.071 118	9.786 848	9.514 209	9.252 624
12	11.618 932	11.255 077	10.907 505	10.575 341	10.257 765	9.954 004
13	12.556 151	12.133 740	11.731 532	11.348 374	10.983 185	10.634 955
14	13.488 708	13.003 703	12.543 382	12.106 249	11.690 912	11.296 073
15	14.416 625	13.865 053	13.343 233	12.849 264	12.381 378	11.937 935
16	15.339 925	14.717 874	14.131 264	13.577 709	13.055 003	12.561 102
17	16.258 632	15.562 251	14.907 649	14.291 872	13.712 198	13.166 118
18	17.172 768	16.398 269	15.672 561	14.992 031	14.353 364	13.753 513
19	18.082 356	17.226 009	16.426 168	15.678 462	14.978 891	14.323 799
20	18.987 419	18.045 553	17.168 639	16.351 433	15.589 162	14.877 475
21	19.887 979	18.856 983	17.900 137	17.011 209	16.184 549	15.415 024
22	20.784 059	19.660 379	18.620 824	17.658 048	16.765 413	15.936 917
23	21.675 681	20.455 821	19.330 861	18.292 204	17.332 110	16.443 608
24	22.562 866	21.243 387	20.030 405	18.913 926	17.884 986	16.935 542
25	23.445 638	22.023 156	20.719 611	19.523 456	18.424 376	17.413 148
26	24.324 018	22.795 204	21.398 632	20.121 036	18.950 611	17.876 842
27	25.198 028	23.559 608	22.067 617	20.706 898	19.464 011	18.327 031
28	26.067 689	24.316 443	22.726 717	21.281 272	19.964 889	18.764 108
29	26.933 024	25.065 785	23.376 076	21.844 385	20.453 550	19.188 455
30	27.794 054	25.807 708	24.015 838	22.396 456	20.930 293	19.600 441
31	28.650 800	26.542 285	24.646 146	22.937 702	21.395 407	20.000 428
32	29.503 284	27.269 589	25.267 139	23.468 335	21.849 178	20.388 766
33	30.351 526	27.989 693	25.878 954	23.988 563	22.291 881	20.765 792
34	31.195 548	28.702 666	26.481 728	24.498 592	22.723 786	21.131 837
35	32.035 371	29.408 580	27.075 595	24.998 619	23.145 157	21.487 220
36	32.871 016	30.107 505	27.660 684	25.488 842	23.556 251	21.832 253
37	33.702 504	30.799 510	28.237 127	25.969 453	23.957 318	22.167 235
38	34.529 854	31.484 663	28.805 052	26.440 641	24.348 603	22.492 462
39	35.353 089	32.163 033	29.364 583	26.902 589	24.730 344	22.808 215
40	36.172 228	32.834 686	29.915 845	27.355 479	25.102 775	23.114 772
41	36.987 291	33.499 689	30.458 961	27.799 489	25.466 122	23.412 400
42	37.798 300	34.158 108	30.994 050	28.234 794	25.820 607	23.701 359
43	38.605 274	34.810 008	31.521 232	28.661 562	26.166 446	23.981 902
44	39.408 232	35.455 454	32.040 622	29.079 963	26.503 849	24.254 274
45	40.207 196	36.094 508	32.552 337	29.490 160	26.833 024	24.518 713
46	41.002 185	36.727 236	33.056 490	29.892 314	27.154 170	24.775 449
47	41.793 219	37.353 699	33.553 192	30.286 582	27.467 483	25.024 708
48	42.580 318	37.973 959	34.042 554	30.673 120	27.773 154	25.266 707
49	43.363 500	38.588 079	34.524 683	31.052 078	28.071 369	25.501 657
50	44.142 786	39.196 118	34.999 688	31.423 606	28.362 312	25.729 764

PRESENT VALUE OF AN ANNUITY OF 1 $a_{\overline{n}|i}$

n	3.5%	4%	4.5%	5%	5.5%	6%
1	0.966 184	0.961 538	0.956 938	0.952 381	0.947 867	0.943 396
2	1.899 694	1.886 095	1.872 668	1.859 410	1.846 320	1.833 393
3	2.801 637	2.775 091	2.748 964	2.723 248	2.697 933	2.673 012
4	3.673 079	3.629 895	3.587 526	3.545 951	3.505 150	3.465 106
5	4.515 052	4.451 822	4.389 977	4.329 477	4.270 284	4.212 364
6	5.328 553	5.242 137	5.157 872	5.075 692	4.995 530	4.917 324
7	6.114 544	6.002 055	5.892 701	5.786 373	5.682 967	5.582 381
8	6.873 955	6.732 745	6.595 886	6.463 213	6.334 566	6.209 794
9	7.607 687	7.435 332	7.268 791	7.107 822	6.952 195	6.801 692
10	8.316 605	8.110 896	7.912 718	7.721 735	7.537 626	7.360 087
11	9.001 551	8.760 477	8.528 917	8.306 414	8.092 536	7.886 875
12	9.663 334	9.385 074	9.118 581	8.863 252	8.618 518	8.383 844
13	10.302 738	9.985 648	9.682 852	9.393 573	9.117 079	8.852 683
14	10.920 520	10.563 123	10.222 825	9.898 641	9.589 648	9.294 984
15	11.517 411	11.118 387	10.739 546	10.379 658	10.037 581	9.712 249
16	12.094 117	11.652 296	11.234 015	10.837 770	10.462 162	10.105 895
17	12.651 321	12.165 669	11.707 191	11.274 066	10.864 609	10.477 260
18	13.189 682	12.659 297	12.159 992	11.689 587	11.246 074	10.827 603
19	13.709 837	13.133 939	12.593 294	12.085 321	11.607 654	11.158 116
20	14.212 403	13.590 326	13.007 936	12.462 210	11.950 382	11.469 921
21	14.697 974	14.029 160	13.404 724	12.821 153	12.275 244	11.764 077
22	15.167 125	14.451 115	13.784 425	13.163 003	12.583 170	12.041 582
23	15.620 410	14.856 842	14.147 775	13.488 574	12.875 042	12.303 379
24	16.058 368	15.246 963	14.495 478	13.798 642	13.151 699	12.550 358
25	16.481 515	15.622 080	14.828 209	14.093 945	13.413 933	12.783 356
26	16.890 352	15.982 769	15.146 611	14.375 185	13.662 495	13.003 166
27	17.285 365	16.329 586	15.451 303	14.643 034	13.898 100	13.210 534
28	17.667 019	16.663 063	15.742 874	14.898 127	14.121 422	13.406 164
29	18.035 767	16.983 715	16.021 889	15.141 074	14.333 101	13.590 721
30	18.392 045	17.292 033	16.288 889	15.372 451	14.533 745	13.764 831
31	18.736 276	17.588 494	16.544 391	15.592 811	14.723 929	13.929 086
32	19.068 865	17.873 552	16.788 891	15.802 677	14.904 198	14.084 043
33	19.390 208	18.147 646	17.022 862	16.002 549	15.075 069	14.230 230
34	19.700 684	18.411 198	17.246 758	16.192 904	15.237 033	14.368 141
35	20.000 661	18.664 613	17.461 012	16.374 194	15.390 552	14.498 246
36	20.290 494	18.908 282	17.666 041	16.546 852	15.536 068	14.620 987
37	20.570 525	19.142 579	17.862 240	16.711 287	15.673 999	14.736 780
38	20.841 087	19.367 864	18.049 990	16.867 893	15.804 738	14.846 019
39	21.102 500	19.584 485	18.229 656	17.017 041	15.928 662	14.949 075
40	21.355 072	19.792 774	18.401 584	17.159 086	16.046 125	15.046 297
41	21.599 104	19.993 052	18.566 109	17.294 368	16.157 464	15.138 016
42	21.834 883	20.185 627	18.723 550	17.423 208	16.262 999	15.224 543
43	22.062 689	20.370 795	18.874 210	17.545 912	16.363 032	15.306 173
44	22.282 791	20.548 841	19.018 383	17.662 773	16.457 851	15.381 182
45	22.495 450	20.720 040	19.156 347	17.774 070	16.547 725	15.455 832
46	22.700 918	20.884 654	19.288 371	17.880 067	16.632 915	15.524 370
47	22.899 438	21.042 936	19.414 709	17.981 016	16.713 664	15.589 028
48	23.091 244	21.195 131	19.535 607	18.077 158	16.790 203	15.650 027
49	23.276 565	21.341 472	19.651 298	18.168 722	16.862 751	15.707 572
50	23.455 618	21.482 185	19.762 008	18.255 925	16.931 518	15.761 861

PRESENT VALUE OF AN ANNUITY OF 1 $a_{\overline{n}|i}$

n	6.5%	7%	8%	9%	10%
1	0.938 967	0.934 579	0.925 926	0.917 431	0.909 091
2	1.820 626	1.808 018	1.783 265	1.759 111	1.735 537
3	2.648 476	2.624 316	2.577 097	2.531 295	2.486 852
4	3.425 799	3.387 211	3.312 127	3.239 720	3.169 865
5	4.155 679	4.100 197	3.992 710	3.889 651	3.790 787
6	4.841 014	4.766 540	4.622 880	4.485 919	4.355 261
7	5.484 520	5.389 289	5.206 370	5.032 953	4.868 419
8	6.088 751	5.971 299	5.746 639	5.534 819	5.334 926
9	6.656 104	6.515 232	6.246 888	5.995 247	5.759 024
10	7.188 830	7.023 582	6.710 081	6.417 658	6.144 567
11	7.689 042	7.498 674	7.138 964	6.805 191	6.495 061
12	8.158 725	7.942 686	7.536 078	7.160 725	6.813 692
13	8.599 742	8.357 651	7.903 776	7.486 904	7.103 356
14	9.013 842	8.745 468	8.244 237	7.786 150	7.366 687
15	9.402 669	9.107 914	8.559 479	8.060 688	7.606 080
16	9.767 764	9.446 649	8.851 369	8.312 558	7.823 709
17	10.110 577	9.763 223	9.121 638	8.543 631	8.021 553
18	10.432 466	10.059 087	9.371 887	8.755 625	8.201 412
19	10.734 710	10.335 595	9.603 599	8.950 115	8.364 920
20	11.018 507	10.594 014	9.818 147	9.128 546	8.513 564
21	11.284 983	10.835 527	10.016 803	9.292 244	8.648 694
22	11.535 196	11.061 241	10.200 744	9.442 425	8.771 540
23	11.770 137	11.272 187	10.371 059	9.580 207	8.883 218
24	11.990 739	11.469 334	10.528 758	9.706 612	8.984 744
25	12.197 877	11.653 583	10.674 776	9.822 580	9.077 040
26	12.392 373	11.825 779	10.809 978	9.928 972	9.160 945
27	12.574 998	11.986 709	10.935 165	10.026 580	9.237 223
28	12.746 477	12.137 111	11.051 078	10.116 128	9.306 567
29	12.907 490	12.277 674	11.158 406	10.198 283	9.369 606
30	13.058 676	12.409 041	11.257 783	10.273 654	9.426 914
31	13.200 635	12.531 814	11.349 799	10.342 802	9.479 013
32	13.333 929	12.646 555	11.434 999	10.406 240	9.526 376
33	13.459 089	12.753 790	11.513 888	10.464 441	9.569 432
34	13.576 609	12.854 009	11.586 934	10.517 835	9.608 575
35	13.686 957	12.947 672	11.654 568	10.566 821	9.644 159
36	13.790 570	13.035 208	11.717 193	10.611 763	9.676 508
37	13.887 859	13.117 017	11.775 179	10.652 993	9.705 917
38	13.979 210	13.193 473	11.828 869	10.690 820	9.732 651
39	14.064 986	13.264 928	11.878 582	10.725 523	9.756 956
40	14.145 527	13.331 709	11.924 613	10.757 360	9.779 051
41	14.221 152	13.394 120	11.967 235	10.786 569	9.799 137
42	14.292 161	13.452 449	12.006 699	10.813 366	9.817 397
43	14.358 837	13.506 962	12.043 240	10.837 950	9.833 998
44	14.421 443	13.557 908	12.077 074	10.860 505	9.849 089
45	14.480 228	13.605 522	12.108 402	10.881 197	9.862 808
46	14.535 426	13.650 020	12.137 409	10.900 181	9.875 280
47	14.587 254	13.691 608	12.164 267	10.917 597	9.886 618
48	14.635 919	13.730 474	12.189 136	10.933 575	9.896 926
49	14.681 615	13.766 799	12.212 163	10.948 234	9.906 296
50	14.724 521	13.800 746	12.233 485	10.961 683	9.914 814